TUSCANY

TUSCANY

Anne Mueller von der Haegen
Ruth Strasser

KÖNEMANN

Frontispiece: Cypress alley and fields near Chianciano

Highlights:
Villa Guinigi-Museo Nazionale, Lucca, p. 78
Villa Celle, Pistoia, p. 114
Duomo Santo Stefano, Prato, p. 128
Duomo Santa Maria del Fiore, Florence, p. 169
Galleria degli Uffizi, Florence, p. 186
S. Francesco, Arezzo, p. 282
Pinacoteca Nazionale, Siena, p. 386
Museo Diocesano, Pienza, p. 400
Piazza della Cisterne, San Gimignano, p. 433
Campo dei Miracoli, Pisa, p. 502

© 2000 Könemann Verlagsgesellschaft mbH, Bonner Strasse 126, D-50968 Cologne

Publishing and Art Direction: Peter Feierabend
Project Management: Ute Edda Hammer, Kerstin Ludolph, Assistant: Ulla Wöhrle
Editing: Katrin Boskamp-Priever
Layout: Wilhelm Schäfer, typocepta, Cologne
Picture Research: Monika Bergmann
Production: Stefan Bramsiepe
Lithography: Digiprint, Erfurt

Original Title: *Kunst & Architektur Toskana*

© 2001 for this English edition: Könemann Verlagsgesellschaft mbH

Translation from German: Paul Aston, Peter Barton, Susan James, Eithne McCarthy, & Iain Macmillan
in association with Cambridge Publishing Management
Editing: Jane Carroll & Allison McKechnie in association with Cambridge Publishing Management
Typesetting: Cambridge Publishing Management
Project Management: Steven Carruthers for Cambridge Publishing Management
Project Coordination: Tammi Reichel
Production: Stefan Bramsiepe
Printing and Binding: Neue Stalling, Oldenburg
Printed in Germany

ISBN 3-8290-2652-8

10 9 8 7 6 5 4 3 2

Table of Contents

View over the town center

City Walls

Piazza del Duomo

View over the town

Evening over the city

View of the Piazza Grande

Landscape near Siena

Tree-lined avenue

Palaces on the banks of the Arne

View of the sea

Landscape with cypresses

The Cultural and Artistic Landscape of Tuscany –
the Cradle of the Renaissance   Ruth Strasser

A summer evening at any country house in Tuscany: the light of the setting sun floods a landscape that unfolds before your eyes in an unusual palette of color ranging from straw yellow, through dark violet, and silvery green to deepest black. The ridges of the softly undulating hills melt into almost contourless crests. In the background, the Apuan Alps, the Apennines, and Monte Amiata tower like the framework of a stage set. In this entirely natural scenery, a second structure becomes apparent only on closer inspection: a man-made pattern resembling a woven fabric. Pasture and arable land is fringed by endless drystone walling and flecked with rectangular, square, or diamond-shaped patches that mark farmsteads, olive groves, and vineyards as well as small hilltop townships, with slender towers, which are ringed by walls. Human activity has left its traces. This is the cultivated land of Tuscany. *Cultivate* derives ultimately from Latin *colere*, meaning "to till," but also "look after, uphold."

You can discern the beginnings of agricultural activity in the archaeological and architectural accretions of millennia of settlement, but the evidence is just as compelling in the trees typical of Tuscany:

Landscape in the Crete hills

the olive trees, which, with their loose structure and indistinct outlines, seem to break up in the landscape but with their light-colored foliage leave a trail of silvery filigree over the hills, or the cypresses, whose clear silhouettes mark borders, indicate direction, and stake out subdivisions. Both were left behind by the original Etruscan inhabitants and have literally taken root here. Indeed, Tuscany itself takes its name from the Etruscans living here in the first millennium B.C. The term *Tuscia*, the land of the Etruscans, was introduced under the administrative reforms of the Roman emperor Diocletian (A.D. 284–305), becoming Toscana in the Middle Ages. (The Greek name for the same people, *Tyrrhenoi*, provided the name for the sea further south, the Tyrrhenian Sea or Etruscan Sea.) High up on ridges commanding expansive river valleys, the cities founded by the Etruscans – Volterra, Cortona, Arezzo, and Fiesole – are still with us. Archaeological digs have revealed necropolises that bear witness to the former glory of Etruscan settlements close to the sea and along the "Iron Way" – Populonia, Roselle, and Vetulonia. Even in the roads running east–west across modern Tuscany, the infrastructure system between the Etruscan port of Spina on the Adriatic and the Mediterranean in the west is still clearly traceable.

Artists from many centuries have succumbed to the influence of Etruscan sculpture. For example, Arnolfo di Cambio's depictions of the Madonna with Child show a close resemblance to the old Etruscan goddess *mater matuta* (Museo Nazionale Archeologico, Florence), and even the figure of Nicodemus holding the dead Christ in Michelangelo's late *Pietà* (Museo dell'Opera del Duomo, Florence) recalls a death scene on an Etruscan sarcophagus in the possession of the Buonarroti family. Other examples include the elongated Etruscan bronze figure, called by Gabriele D'Annunzio the *Ombra della sera* (Evening Shadow), which is echoed in the statues of Alberto Giacometti, or the sculptures of Marino Marini, which explicitly allude to the ancient Etruscan origins of artistic sculpture.

After the conquest of the Etruscan cities by the superior military might of the Romans, the subjection of Etruria proceeded very rapidly. The Etruscan language had almost completely vanished by the beginning of our era, even though many elements of Etruscan culture were adopted by the Romans and initially some of the Roman senatorial families were of Etruscan origin. But the Romans have also left their mark, notably in some outstanding engineering achievements such as the great Roman consular roads built from Rome towards Gaul, all leading from south to north: the Via Flaminia in eastern Tuscany, the Via Cassia in the center, and the Via Aurelia following the Tyrrhenian coast, which is still today numbered Strada Statale 1. A remarkable feature is the

Landscape near San Quirico d'Orcia

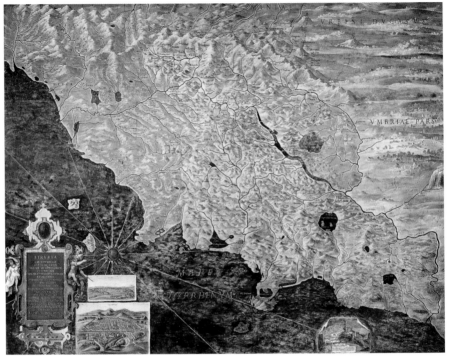

Ignazio Danti (1536–1586), 16th-century fresco map of Etruria, Galleria delle Carte Geografiche, Musei Vaticani, Rome

chessboard layout of the cities of the Tuscan plain. Florence, Pistoia, Lucca, and Pisa were originally set up as colonies for Roman veterans on the Cardo-Decumanus system, with a forum in the middle. Surviving or excavated thermal baths and theaters, villas with subterranean hot water conduits, the foundations of amphitheaters in Lucca and Florence which had medieval houses built on them, columns and capitals reused as spoil in Christian churches, and richly decorated sarcophagi – all these are reminders of ancient Roman art and architecture.

The region was converted to Christianity between the 2nd and 4th centuries. At the time of the Emperor Constantine's edict of 313 which permitted the practicing of

Florence   Arezzo   Grosseto   Livorno   Lucca

Christian religion, Tuscia was already organized into local churches. The term *plebes* for church communities was corrupted into *pievi*, or parish churches. Most Tuscan bishoprics were established during this period: not only provincial capitals but also small towns such as Volterra or Fiesole are centers of dioceses. While the free imperial cities of the north never claimed state sovereignty over large territories, in Tuscany the *contado* or hinterland of a city belonged directly to the city. Thus *civitas* and diocese have been largely one and the same since the 5th century onward.

The numerous small hilltop settlements that grew up in early medieval times under Lombard or Frankish rule display evidence of their organic development. Their names often reflect their Germanic origin. Lamporecchio, for example, is based on the name of the vassal Lamprecht. In the course of time, the settlements were increasingly reinforced with extensive walls and defensive fortifications. In the case of churches enlarged in the 12th and 13th centuries, there is abundant documentary evidence for antecedent structures named for the Frankish saints Martin (of Tours) and Michael. The most important consequence of Frankish rule was the spread of feudalism. Vassalage, which was governed by the personal relationship with the feudal lord – i.e. the emperor, king, count, or duke – led to a territorial and political fragmentation of Tuscany. After the death of the last margravine Mathilda of Canossa (1046–1115), who had managed to unite almost the whole of Tuscany under her rule, pope and emperor fought over her legacy. Secular and clerical barons threw up defensible castles, and in this period even monasteries and abbeys looked like fortresses. The ordinary population had to finance, through the proceeds of their labor, the knightly lifestyle, huge military costs and visible pomp and circumstance of their feudal overlords, whether on the papal or the imperial side. They used simple diplomacy – if possible – to avoid being drawn into the quarrels of the mighty: *Guelfo non son, né Ghibellin m'apello,*

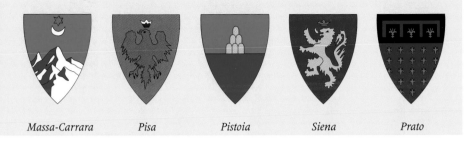

Massa-Carrara   Pisa   Pistoia   Siena   Prato

chi mi dà da mangiar, tengo da quello. ("I am neither Guelph nor do I call myself Ghibelline, I stick to the one who gives me to eat.") In about 1100, the guild system developed in Tuscany. Burghers, traders, and artisans began to smooth the path to the "free city republic" by introducing elected consuls, priors and alder-men. The descendants of the Etruscans and Romans thus to a certain extent forced the counts and feudal lords – mostly of Germanic origin – to give up their castles and manor houses and move into the cities. Tuscany was one of the first lands of the post-classical era to attempt the abolition of feudal rule and bondage.

The most important communication channels linking northern and central Europe with Rome and the south crossed the whole of Tuscany up hill and down dale. They were called Via Romea or Via Francigena, i.e., the roads to Rome or France. Settlements that lay beside them experienced rapid population growth and enormous economic prosperity. Major factors contributing to their rise to city

status were the collection of customs tolls, sales of local artisanal and agricultural products, the constant flow of custom for hostelries, and the establishment of trade connections with foreign merchants and metropolises. The more reliably the roads were policed, the safer the journey, not only for pilgrims, soldiers, and adventurers but also for merchants, kings, and emperors. The oldest, still extant churches date from this time, and their architecture reflects the coloration of Moorish and Saracen art: the patterns of cloths and silks were transferred to church walls, thanks to the skills of the stonemasons. The arts soon gained a character of their own, however. *Christus triumphans*, mostly depicted as the Pantocrator in Byzantium and the early Middle Ages, becomes *Christus patiens*, the suffering Christ on the Cross, and the Virgin Mary turns from Queen of Heaven into the caring Mother of God. Giotto shows the physical presence of man, Boccaccio the everyday life of the

Following pages: field of poppies near Pienza

13

various social classes and the problems of burgher and peasant, priest and artisan alike. Dante wrote his *Divine Comedy* in the Tuscan vernacular.

The markedly artistic sensibility of Tuscans was already perceptible at this date. In 1282, the ecclesiastical writer Ristoro d'Arezzo described the excavation of Aretine vases thus: "Their ornamentation was so superb that connoisseurs who saw them became almost foolish with delight." Two hundred years later, Savonarola said much the same: "People get so carried away by good paintings that they go wild on looking at them and almost forget themselves." A model was built for the design of the east end of the cathedral in Florence and an assessment of it left to a popular decision. On October 25, 1367, the leading citizens entitled to vote filed past the cathedral. The archives record the names of 354 members of the great Florentine families.

Florence under the Medici became a leading center of Renaissance Humanism. Under the patronage of the ruling family,

Ludovico Buti, 16th-century map of the state of Florence

Florentine school, Five Famous Men (the Fathers of Perspective), *c. 1500–1565. Tempera on wood, 42 × 100 cm, Musée du Louvre, Paris*

who put their stamp on the city like no one else, art blossomed. The eyes of men, which in Leonardo's words are "windows in the prison of the body," were allowed to see things hitherto hidden from them, the rules of central perspective were discovered, freestanding nude sculptures were produced again, topographical views of cities and landscapes, and the human world were depicted. Portraits and still lifes became independent genres. Planned scholarship – partly sponsored by the papacy – safeguarded the writings of antiquity. Knowledge of classical language and writings – now systematically studied – led to a more profound preoccupation with mythological subjects, enriching painting, sculpture and literature. The Florentine Neoplatonic theories of Marsilio Ficino (1433–1499) drank from the same well.

The heyday of science arrived, anatomical studies were begun, history became a university discipline, and the first melodrama set to music by the composer Jacopo Peri (1561–1633) was performed as an opera at the Medici court. Using the new world map of the geographer Paolo Toscanelli, Christopher Columbus (1452–1506) searched for the East Indies and found instead America, named for the Florentine seafarer and discoverer Amerigo Vespucci (1451–1512). At the Medici court, a specially created gallery in the Uffizi was fitted out to house one of the first art collections which, like collections at other European princely courts, later became the core of an important public museum. It included classical sculptures, pictures, craft works, coins and books, but also bore witness to the inventiveness of humanity in the form of scientific instruments and to the variety of nature, whose phenomena were collected as curiosities. Such things were examined and discussed among educated connoisseurs. More and more scientific

Corridor of the Galleria degli Uffizi in Florence, founded by the Medici family

investigations were proposed and financed.

Ferdinando II de' Medici sponsored Galileo Galilei (1564–1642) after his condemnation by the Inquisition, alchemy experiments were carried out in exploratory laboratories, and attempts were made using crushed rock crystal to discover the secret of porcelain-making, so jealously guarded by the Chinese. The art of inlaying semi-precious stones – the *pietra dura* technique – was developed to a standard of unparalleled excellence. The Academy of Art and, under Cardinal

Leopoldo de' Medici, the Accademia del Cimento, were established as the first scientific academies in Europe. The universities in Siena, Pisa, and Florence were expanded, agricultural experiments were undertaken with new breeds of vine and fruit, and hitherto unknown vegetables and ornamental plants were introduced. The amazing thing is that in these centuries artistic life embraced all classes. Representatives of all kinds of occupations – jewelers, cabinet makers, carpet makers, mathematicians, opticians, the city fifer, heralds, and book painters – sat on com-missions for public building works. Maintenance, conservation, and decoration were similarly placed in the care of the guilds. The Foundling Hospital (*Ospedale degli Innocenti*) commissioned from Brunel-leschi by Florence's city council in 1419 not only provided facilities for bringing up and educating often more than 1,000 children at a time but also for trying out new medicaments, vaccinations, and improving nutrition with cow's milk.

After the death of the last Medici, Gian Gastone (1671–1737), who died without issue, the Grand Duchy of Tuscany passed to the house of Lorraine. Thus in 1737 Francis Stephen, Duke of Lorraine, and later the Emperor Francis I of Austria, became Grand Duke of Tuscany. After his death in 1765 Tuscany was administered by Pietro Leopoldo (his second son in the collateral line).

Under Austrian influence, Tuscany (along with Lombardy) became a model of

Family tree of the Medici dei Cafaggiolo family, Biblioteca Riccardiana, Florence

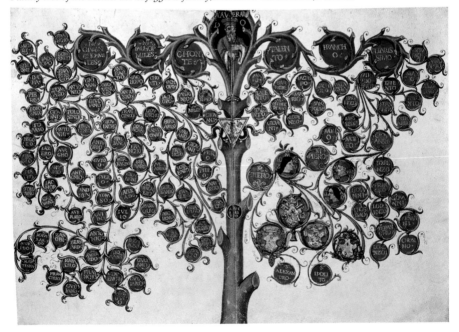

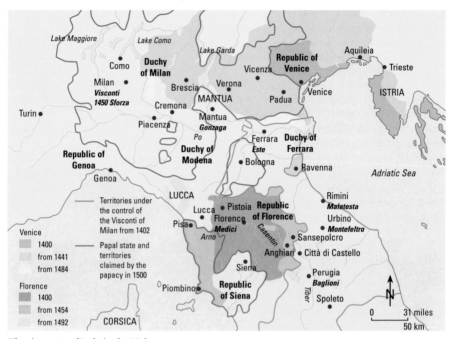

The city states of Italy in the 15th century

On the map:

Lake Maggiore

Lake Como

Lake Garda

Como

Duchy of Milan

Republic of Venice

Aquileia

Milan

Visconti 1450 Sforza

Brescia

Vicenza

Verona

Trieste

Padua

Venice

ISTRIA

Cremona

MANTUA

Mantua

Gonzaga

Turin

Piacenza

Po

Ferrara

Este

Duchy of Ferrara

Republic of Genoa

Duchy of Modena

Bologna

Ravenna

Genoa

Adriatic Sea

LUCCA

Rimini

Malatesta

Territories under the control of the Visconti of Milan from 1402

Lucca

Pistoia

Republic of Florence

Urbino

Montefeltro

Pisa

Florence

Medici

Casentin

Sansepolcro

Venice

1400

from 1441

from 1484

Papal state and territories claimed by the papacy in 1500

Arno

Anghiari

Città di Castello

Florence

1400

from 1454

from 1492

Siena

Perugia

Baglioni

Piombino

Republic of Siena

Tiber

Spoleto

CORSICA

0   31 miles

50 km

N

---

the European Enlightenment as a result of reforms in all areas. The privileges of court authorities, superannuated justiciary bodies, the right of asylum in churches, artistic corporations, and guilds were all abolished. The Church's agricultural estates and the agrarian holdings of the Medicis and Order of St. Stephen were publicly auctioned. The project to drain the Tuscan marshes led to improved soil and agriculture, and the school system was overhauled.

Medicine and anatomy were no longer taught in the lecture rooms of hospitals but at universities. Napoleon Bonaparte who transformed the nascent republic into the kingdom of Italy and had himself crowned king in Milan in 1805, continued the process of secularization and the dissolution of the religious orders and guilds.

Land registries and population register offices were set up, new roads were laid out and an imperial Scuola Normale Superiore – still an elite university – was founded in Pisa. Chambers of industry and trade were opened. During the Habsburg period, and also during a period of French influence from 1795 to 1815, national awareness arose and ideas of liberty and independence developed among the Tuscan bourgeoisie that could no longer be suppressed even after the Congress of Vienna in 1815 and the Restoration, which reimposed the rule of Grand Duke Ferdinand III on Tuscany.

During the age of *Risorgimento*, Alessandro Manzoni, Giacomo Leopardi, Ugo Foscolo, and many other patriotically minded poets, writers and politicians published their most important works and therefore influenced the struggle for freedom and the idea of unity.

The provinces of Tuscany in the 20th century

The composer Giuseppe Verdi was an ardent nationalist in his early days; the "Chorus of the Hebrew Slaves" from his early opera *Nabucco* was widely perceived to embody a nation's struggle for freedom. Other, later, choruses were further seen as expressing anti-Austrian sentiment. Indeed, nationalist feeling was even hinted at by the populace's cry "Viva Verdi!," meaning "Long live Verdi!," but also standing for "Long live **V**ittorio **E**manuel, **r**é **d**'**I**talia" ("Long live Victor Emmanuel, king of Italy").

Tuscany, thanks to its traditions, served in this heavily politicized climate as a meeting place of Italian scholars, secret societies and conspirators. The most important initiatives were the establishment in 1821 of the Gabinetto Scientifico Letterario, a literary and scientific society, and the publication of the periodical *Antologia* by the Genevan Protestant and man of letters Gian Pietro

Vieusseux from 1821–1833. Its columns were given over to history, belles-lettres and science. Nationally oriented scientific congresses took place in Florence, Pisa, and Lucca; the Accademia dei Georgofili was the scene of scientific debates about agricultural policy. Shaken by the revolutionary events of 1848, the last Grand Duke, Leopold II, reacted with draconian measures and suppression, and was only able to retain control with the help of Austrian troops. When the patriotic revolution broke out in Florence in April 1859, the Grand Duke fled, leaving the provisional government led by the Florentine Baron Ricasoli to proclaim the end of Habsburg rule in Tuscany.

In 1860, a plebiscite voted for Tuscany to join Piedmont–Sardinia, and henceforth it

Ugo Foscolo, Italian writer and literary historian, 1778–1827

Alessandro Manzoni, Italian novelist,
1785–1873.

Giacomo Leopardi, Italian poet,
1798–1837

was drawn into the political history of Italy. From 1865 to 1871, Florence was the capital of Italy.

Naturalness, moderation, and harmony are the hallmarks not only of the Tuscan landscape but also of its proud and yet amiable inhabitants. The cultural variety, artistic abundance, and geographical wealth of this region appear to have crystallized in the particular nature of its people, expressed in three very simple-sounding qualities: *genuinità* (genuineness), *gentilezza* (kindness), and *garbo* (good manners).

An impartial and at the same time self-assured relationship with past and present, with the familiar and the unfamiliar, characterize the Tuscans of today. Like the Etruscans, Romans, and people of the Middle Ages and the Renaissance, they are firmly rooted in the beautiful landscape of Tuscany, which delights both the eye and the soul with its perfect proportions.

Tuscany in a Nutshell

Dates, Figures, and Facts about the Region:

- A region of central Italy west of the Apennine range, including the archipelago around Elba. The gentle hill and mountain landscape of Tuscany shares borders with Emilia-Romagna in the north, the Marches and Umbria in the east, and Latium in the south. In the west, the 220-mile (354-km) coastline borders the Ligurian and Tyrrhenian Seas.
- Area: 8,877 sq. miles (22,992 sq. km), approximately 7.8% of Italy's total area.
- Population: 3.7 million (about 6.5% of the Italian total).
- Subdivided into nine provinces: Arezzo, Florence, Grosseto, Livorno (Leghorn), Lucca, Massa-Carrara, Pisa, Pistoia, and Siena.
- Capital: Florence.
- About 25% of Tuscany is agricultural land and about 40% woodland.
- Principal rivers: Arno (150 miles/240 km), Ombrone (99 miles/160 km,) and Serchio (64 miles/103 km).

Economy:

- Tuscany is the most important tourist region of Italy, with over 4 million visitors a year, of whom about 40% are foreign; tourism is the principal source of income for the region.
- Tuscany is also one of the leading agricultural regions of Italy, and is particularly famous for its wine, olives and olive oil, mushrooms, cheeses, and cured meats.
- Among the rich resources of mineral wealth are iron ore (Elba and Grosseto), marble (Carrara, Prato, Maremma), mercury (Monte Amiata), and lignite (north of Florence).
- Heavy industry is located along the north coast, and includes metal processing (near Piombino), oil refineries (near Livorno), and chemical and pharmaceutical industries.
- The leading center for textile production is Prato.
- Florence is famous *inter alia* for craft products (jewelry, paper, ceramics, leather goods, and basketry).
- The main fishing ports are Livorno, Marina di Carrara, Piombino, Viareggio, and Porto Santo Stefano.
- Numerous towns and cities in Tuscany have developed into modern centers of service industries.

Climate and Travel:

- Mediterranean climate with hot, mainly dry summers but frequently wet winters.
- The ideal time to visit is early summer and autumn; a visit in May is specially recommended, being mostly sunny but not too hot. The temperature is also pleasant in September and October, though be ready for rain as well.

- During Easter, the cities especially are overrun with tourists (and pilgrims).
- In the summer months of July and August it can become unbearably hot in the cities, particularly Florence. During this period the natives escape to distant regions near the sea, and countless shops, restaurants, and bars are closed. The tourist attractions are of course besieged with visitors.

Regional Wine and Cuisine Specialties:
- Tuscany is one of the most important wine-growing areas of Europe.
- Famous among the labels are the white wines of Vernaccia and the red wines of Chianti, Brunello di Montalcino and Vino Nobile de Montepulciano. A notable specialty is the sweet Vin Santo, which is drunk as an apéritif or dessert wine.
- Specialties of Tuscan cuisine: *bistecca alla fiorentina* (grilled steak on the bone), *trippa alla fiorentina* (tripe in tomato sauce), *pappardelle alle lepre* (noodles in hare sauce), *ribollita* (cabbage soup with beans and vegetables), *risotto nero* (rice with seafood), *stoccafisso alla livornese* (dried cod stewed in oil, wine, and vegetables), *bruschette* (toast with garlic, oil, and spread), *salsicce* (sausages), *pecorino* (sheep's cheese), *mozzarella di bufala* (buffalo cheese), *cantucci* (almond biscuits).

Festivals:
- General holidays include: January 1 (New Year), January 6 (Epiphany), Easter Monday, April 15 (Liberation Day), May 1 (Labor Day), June 2 (Day of the Republic), August 15 (Ferragosto, Assumption Day), November 1 (All Saints), December 8 (Conception of the Virgin), December 25 and 26 (Christmas).

Festivals and Events:
- Carnivals: notable carnivals in Arezzo, San Gimignano and Viareggio (February).
- Scoppio del Carro: historic procession and fireworks in Florence (Easter Sunday).

Climate

Average temp in °F (°C)	Jan.	Feb.	Mar.	Apr.	May	June	July	Aug.	Sept.	Oct.	Nov.	Dec.
Day	46.9 (8.3)	50 (10)	57.2 (14)	65.3 (18.5)	73 (22.8)	82.2 (27.9)	87.6 (30.9)	85.8 (29.9)	77.9 (25.5)	66.2 (19)	55.9 (13.3)	48.4 (9.1)
Night	36 (2.2)	37 (2.8)	42.3 (5.7)	48.2 (9)	54.7 (12.6)	61.5 (16.4)	66 (18.9)	65.5 (18.6)	61 (16.1)	52.7 (11.5)	44.6 (7)	38.1 (3.4)
Sunshine hrs/days	3.7	4.3	5.3	6.8	8.5	9	10.6	9.4	7.6	6	3.6	3.1
Rainy days	9	7	8	8	9	6	3	4	6	9	11	9

- Maggio Musicale: music festival in Florence (May to beginning of June).
- Regata storica di S. Ranieri: holiday and regatta in Pisa in honor of St. Rainier of Pisa (June 17).
- Calcio in costume/calcio storico: historic football in honor of St. John the Baptist in Florence (June 19, 24 and 28).
- Corsa del Palio: historic horse race in Siena (July 2 and August 16).
- Festival Pucciniano: music festival at Torre del Lago Puccini (mid-July to mid-August).
- Settimana Musicale Senese: music festival in Siena (last week in July).
- Bravio delle Botti: barrel rolling in Montepulciano (2nd Sunday in August).
- Mostra Mercato Internazionale dell'Antiquariato: antiques fair in Florence (September–October).
- Giostra del Saracino: historic processions and jousting contests in Arezzo (1st Sunday in September).
- Luminara di Santa Croce: torchlight procession in honor of the Volto Santo in Lucca (September 13).
- Rassegna del Chianti Classico: wine festival in Greve in Chianti (2nd week in September).

Traveling to Italy:

- By car: from the north by toll *autostrada* via La Spezia or Bologna along the coastal routes or via the central A1 section (Milan–Bologna–Rome) to Florence. The historic centers of many cities are closed to cars (*zona blu*).
- By train: the main rail connection from the north leads to Florence, from where all parts of Tuscany can be reached by branch line.

- International airports: Aeroporto Amerigo Vespucci at Peretola (Florence) and Aeroporto Galileo Galilei (Pisa).
- Ferries to the Tuscan islands from the ports of Livorno, Piombino, and Porto Santo Stefano.

Addresses for Travel Arrangements:

- ENIT – Italian State Tourist Office :
  639 Fifth Avenue, Suite 1565, New York, NY10111, U.S.A. Tel. (212) 245-4822. Fax (212) 586-9249.
  500 North Michigan Avenue, Suite 2240, Chicago 1, IL60611, U.S.A. Tel. (312) 644-0996. Fax: (312) 644-3019.
  12400 Wilshire Boulevard, Suite 550, Los Angeles, CA90025, U.S.A. Tel. (310) 820-1898. Fax: (310) 820-6357. E-mail: enitla@earthlink.net.
  1 Princes Street, London, W1R 8AY, U.K. Tel. (020) 7408 1254. Fax (020) 8493 6695.
  1 Place Ville Marie, Suite 1914, Montreal, Québec, H3B 2C3, Canada. Tel. (514) 886-7668. Fax (514) 392-1429. E-mail: initaly@ican.net.
  c/o Italian Embassy, 61–69 Macquarie Street, Sydney 2000, N.S.W., Australia. Tel. (02) 9247 8442.
  c/o Italian Embassy, 36 Grant Road, Thomdon, Wellington, New Zealand. Tel. (04) 736 065.
  c/o Italian Cultural Institute in Pretoria, 165 East Avenue, Arcadia 0083, Pretoria, Gauteng, RSA. Tel (012) 343 6678.

Internet:

- www.turismo.firenze.it.

Opening Times of Important Museums and Churches:

Florence

Bargello: 8.30–13.50, closed Mon.

Campanile di Giotto: summer 9.00–18.50, winter 9.00–16.20.

Cupola del Duomo: 8.30–18.20, Sat. 8.30–17.00, closed Sun.

Galleria d'Arte Moderna e Galleria del Costume (Palazzo Pitti): 8.30–13.50, closed 1st/3rd/5th Mon. and 2nd/4th Sun. in month.

Galleria degli Uffizi: 8.30–21.00, Sat. 8.30–24.00, Sun. 8.30–20.00, closed Mon.

Galleria dell'Accademia: 8.30–18.50, Sat./Sun. 8.30–13.50, closed Mon.

Galleria dell'Ospedale degli Innocenti: 8.30–14.00, closed Wed.

Galleria Palatina (Palazzo Pitti): 8.30–18.50, Sat./Sun. and holidays 8.30–13.50, closed Mon.

Museo di S. Marco: 8.30–13.50, closed Mon.

Museo e Chiostro di S. Maria Novella: 9.00–14.00, closed Fri.

Museo Marino Marini (P S Pangrazio): 10.00–17.00, Sun. and holidays 10.00–13.00, closed Tues.

Museo Nazionale Archeologico: 9.00–19.00, Sat. 9.00–14.00, Mon. 14.00–19.00

Palazzo Vecchio: 9.00–19.00, Thurs. 9.00–13.00, Sun. and holidays 8.00–13.00.

Pisa

Battistero: spring 10.00–19.40, summer 13.00–19.40, winter 9.00–16.40.

Camposanto: spring 9.00–17.40, summer 8.00–19.40, autumn 9.00–17.40, winter 9.00–16.40.

Duomo: spring 10.00–19.40, summer 13.00–19.40, winter 10.00–18.45, Sun. and holidays 15.00–16.45.

Museo dell'Opera del Duomo: spring 9.00–17.20, summer 8.00–19.20, autumn 9.00–17.20, winter: 9.00–16.20.

Museo Nazionale di Palazzo Reale: 9.00–13.00, Sun. closed.

Museo Nazionale di S. Matteo: 9.00–19.00, Sun. and holidays 9.00–14.00, Mon. closed.

Siena

Duomo Libreria Piccolomini (in the cathedral)/Battistero di San Giovanni (below the cathedral): Mar. 16–Oct. 31: 9.00–19.30; Nov. 1–Mar. 15: 7.30–13.00, 14.30–17.00.

Museo Civico: Mar. 16–Oct. 31: 10.00–19.00; July/Aug: 10.00–23.00; Nov. 1–Mar. 15: 10.00–18.30.

Museo dell'Opera del Duomo: Mar. 16–Sept. 30: 9.00–19.30; Oct.: 9.00–18.00; Nov. 1–Mar. 15: 9.00–13.30.

Museo e Santuario di S. Caterina: summer 9.00–12.30, 14.30–18.00, winter 9.00–12.00, 15.30–18.00.

Palazzo delle Papesse: 12.00–19.00.

Pinacoteca Nazionale: Mon. 8.30–13.30, Tues.–Sat. 9.00–19.00, Sun. and holidays 8.00–13.00, winter 8.30–13.30.

S. Maria della Scala: Apr. 1–Oct. 31: 10.00–18.00 Nov. 1–Dec. 24 10.30–16.30; Dec. 25–Jan. 6: 10.00–18.00.

Torre del Mangia: Mar. 16–Oct. 31: 10.00–19.00; July/Aug: 10.00–23.00; Nov. 1–Mar. 15: 10.00–16.00.

Massa

Massa

The dominant feature of the province of Massa-Carrara is the Apuan Alps, a massif which stretches from the Tuscan border with Liguria in the north-west to Lucca in the south-east. Its extensive marble deposits have for centuries sustained the economy of this province, which is centered on the twin towns of Massa and Carrara. The capital, Massa, is made up of two parts: Massa Vecchia, dominated by the medieval fortress, and Massa Nuova, the ornate 16th-century lower town. The central square, Piazza Aranci, is dominated by the Baroque ducal palace, and is still lines by its double-rowed avenue of attractive orange trees.

Massa is first documented in 882, and in the 10th century was the seat of the Bishops of Luni. A century later, the settlement was a possession of the Obertenghi counts, who constructed the first castle. The presence of marble deposits led to successive takeovers by Lucca, Pisa, the Medici of Florence, and the Visconti of Milan, but after the city joined Carrara under the control of the Malaspina counts in 1442, a period of continuity ensued.

Later, Alberico I Cybo gained control through marriage.

In 1741, both cities passed to the dukes of Este, who remained in charge – except during the Napoleonic occupation – until the accession to the Kingdom of Italy in 1861.

View of Piazza Aranci and the ducal palace

Duomo SS. Pietro e Francesco

Massa Cathedral has a long building history, as is immediately apparent from the façade, which dates only from 1936. Fascist architects had a predilection for showy materials and so, given the proximity of the marble quarries, it was a matter of course at the time that the façade should be constructed of valuable Carrara marble. The end result is a homogeneous structure with motifs from Renaissance architecture and borrowings from classical Roman models. The central section of the façade is opened up by two rows of large arches, three forming a portico at ground level and three forming a loggia above. A classicizing pediment surmounts this west front, completing the triumphal arch motif in a cold, dry architectural style that is an expression of power but lacks excitement, despite the glossy marble.

The Interior

The interior with its undivided nave reveals more of the history of the church, which is dedicated to Saints Peter and Francis. A small church was established here in 1389, and extended by Jacopo Malaspina in 1447. The church attained its present dimensions after further rebuilding in 1616. Architecture and furnishings alike radiate Baroque splendor. Numerous altars and altar paintings, painted in the 17th century largely by local artists, convey an impression of the church in its heyday. When Massa became a separate diocese in the 19th century, the church acquired cathedral status.

the Cybo Malaspina family. Directly above it is the chapel of the Holy Sacrament, erected in the right transept at the behest of Carlo II. In the center is a lavish Baroque altar built to the design of Alessandro Bergamini.

Pinturicchio (c. 1454–1513), *Madonna*, 1489–1492
Fresco (fragment)

The fragment of fresco of the Madonna built into the altar is the work of one of the most important Umbrian painters of the second half of the 15th century, Bernardino di Betto Biagio, known as Pinturicchio. After training in the workshop of Perugino, he accompanied the latter to Rome, where both worked for the Pope in the Sistine Chapel. As Pinturicchio was considered a talented decorative artist with an elegant, detailed narrative style, he was also employed by leading Roman families to decorate their chapels.

Alessandro Bergamini and Giocanni Francesco, Cappella del S. Sacramento, Baroque altar, 1694
Marble

In 1695, Alberico II Cybo Malaspina and his brother Cardinal Alderano commissioned architects Giovanni Francesco and Alessandro Bergamini to construct a subterranean crypt as a burial chapel for

This Madonna was commissioned for the Cybo family's chapel in the Roman church of S. Maria del Popolo. It was later transferred from there to Massa.

La Rocca

The older part of Massa – Massa Vecchia – grew up around the first castle founded by the feudal lords, the Obertenghi. As the castle changed hands, new parts were constantly added. Now called Castello Malaspina or La Rocca, it stands on a steep rocky promontory and is surrounded by a defensive wall with four gateways. The extensive layout within the walls was fashioned by the ruling Malaspina family, who transformed it in the 16th century into a princely residence, building a Renaissance palace in the southern part. This new palace was linked to the medieval part by an elongated loggia and was largely built according to the plans of the renowned architect Niccolò Civitali (1482–1560) from Lucca. The fine façade is decorated with costly polychromatic inlays of various types of marble. The walls surrounding the castle have ramparts that can be walked for their entire length, offering fantastic views of the city and the sea.

Sala della Spina

The ground floor contains a number of rooms painted with frescoes, the decoration of the Sala della Spina being particularly notable. The room is vaulted with an umbrella dome and completely decorated with *trompe l'œil* paintings. Above the painted marble panels are large, similarly *trompe l'œil* loggia windows providing a framework for an imaginary Arcadian landscape.

The White Gold of the Apuan Alps

Ruth Strasser

At the end of the 19th century, an Englishman wrote of his travels in Tuscany: "I have seen incredible things, splendid cathedrals, magnificent palaces, delightful Madonna paintings, and have drunk good wine and bathed in a blue sea. But the finest experience was the marble quarries of Carrara: the workers began to sing and the marble moved." He was referring to the *cantilena*, the traditional rhythmic singing of the marble workers accompanied by voluble profanities as they lifted the massively heavy blocks with iron levers and pushed them forward.

If you approach the towering massif of the Apuan Alps from the sea on a clear afternoon, you are almost blinded by the gleaming white of the precipitous slopes. The sharp-edged, smooth marble quarries, called *tagliate* (cuts), gleam in the afternoon sun like glaciers, as do the *ravaneti*, the extensive slopes of marble scree created by the blasting.

It was the Greeks who called this noble white rock *marmaros*, the "gleaming, glistening" stone, and the mountains behind Carrara contain the largest deposits worldwide of this high-value material. The mountain range, the Apuan Alps, begins in the north where the three regions of Liguria, Emilia-Romagna and Tuscany meet, and covers 417 square miles (1,080 sq. km) in a north-west–south-east direction across Tuscany. Its geological history differs from that of the Apennines. At the end of

the Triassic and beginning of the Jurassic era, when this region was still under water, all limestone, shell and alluvial deposits were compressed at high temperatures by shock waves caused by the rise in the sea level, thereby undergoing transformation into crystalline marble. This shares a chemical formula, $CaCO_3$ (calcium carbonate), with eggshells, but not its metamorphic, constant-grained crystalline form – in its purest state it is snow-white like a sugar cube and only colored with patches or veins through impurities. Over 100 million years later, when the water level sank in the Tertiary as a result of continental shift, these marble deposits came to the surface, reaching heights of about 6,500 feet (2,000 m). The original Ligurian inhabitants of the Apuan Alps called the rock *car*, which later developed into Carrara.

However, it was the Romans who first started systematic quarrying of marble. Some 10,000 captives and slaves, including Ligurians and, later on, deported Christians, provided the forced labor for this heavy work: iron wedges had to be driven with large hammers into pre-chiseled cracks before the block came away. Because marble is relatively easy to split compared with other rocks, an amazingly simple but slow technique could be used. Wedges of dry wood were driven into the preliminary cracks and then soaked in water. The wood swelled, and the expansion of the capillaries was so great that the wedges split the stone. The blocks, weighing between 15 and 20 tons, were abseiled down the steep slopes on a kind of wooden sledge (*lizza*) over logs smeared with soap. The block, which had been roughly pre-chiseled on the spot, was accompanied by a 16-strong team of workers alongside, behind and (sometimes life-threateningly) in front of the block. Once the block reached the foot of the slope, transport continued by oxcart to the port of the Roman city of Luni, north of the present-day resort of Marina di Carrara, from where it went under sail to Rome. The declared intention of the Roman emperor Augustus (63 B.C.–A.D. 14) – "I found Rome in brick. I will leave it in marble" – was carried out mainly in the imperial era. Only with the economic crisis of the Roman Empire from the 4th century onward was there a decline in marble quarrying, although extensive workings resumed in the Romanesque and Hohenstaufen periods.

The introduction of explosives in the 16th century offered a simpler way to open new cracks, but its use was soon greatly reduced as it produced a lot of worthless rubble. Thus for 2,000 years the same laborious methods of cutting the stone and the same dangerous

View of a marble quarry near Carrara

means of transporting it were used. The working day of the laborer was measured from "moon to moon." He had to leave his house at the foot of the mountains at a nocturnal hour to reach the quarries by daybreak. He did not leave again until twilight, with the long climb down still ahead of him. It was only about 100 years ago that a radical innovation was introduced for cutting. A spiral cable made of three intertwined steel wires was drawn over special running gear and wrapped round the marble block like a sling. In its grooves it carried a mixture of water and pure quartz sand, the mechanical friction of which cut the stone. Of course, the technique required a precise calculation of where to place the running gear and at the same time an accurate knowledge of the direction and layering of the rock. Although marble is a material that inherently lasts millennia, once it is cut on the wrong side it is no longer weatherproof. "But we are born with marble eyes, the skill is in our genes," the marble workers still say today, proud of their occupation. Even in Roman times, each stage of the work required high specialization.

Very different types of marble are quarried in Carrara. The most valuable is *statuario*, a rare, pure white to ivory-colored stone that was used for statuary even in antiquity and of which only small reserves are left. Also highly regarded are *venato* (white with green veining), *calacata* (white or ivory-colored with creamy yellow veining), the mainly gray *bardiglio*, the *cipollino* with gray-green graining, the *verde Apuane* (a green to dark green serpentine), and the bluish-violet *paonazzo*. In the three clefts of Colonnata, Miseglia and Torano that open into the mountainside above Carrara there are 190 quarries, up to a height of nearly 4,600 feet (1,400 m). Annual output is 1 million tons, or about 60 per cent of all quarries in the Apuan Alps. In the 1970s, modern operations were introduced – mainly opencast mining. Horizontal and vertical channels are bored along the planned edges of the block, along which a diamond-studded cutting cable is inserted. The still risky transport is now done exclusively by trucks, which drive up winding tracks of marble gravel to dizzying heights. Sometimes there is no turning room and the trucks have to reverse, which not infrequently leads to accidents even today. The Roman writer Livy (59 B.C.–A.D. 17) called the population of Carrara *gens marmoris*, a race made of marble. Modern Tuscans call them "marble skulls," constantly dealing with marble having presumably affected their character. It is no mere chance that in the

Marble being transported by oxcart

early 20th century Carrara was the hotbed of the most radical but non-violent European workers' movement, the anarcho-syndicalists.

Their work in earlier times provided the raw material for another notable "blockhead" – Michelangelo Buonarotti (1475–1564). He rented a room in Carrara and often rode a mule into the mountains to choose his marble for himself. What distinguished the true sculptor in his view was cutting the sculpture from the stone, not shaping by adding, as with clay, for example. The finished sculpture lay concealed in the prime matter, with the idea of it as a copy in the artist's head. The artist's job was to unite the two. Unhewn marble is a formative element of many of Michelangelo's sculptures, eloquent of his concept of the *non finito*, the work of art intentionally left unfinished.

As the Italian poet Giosuè Carducci said of the peaks of Carrara, this mountain is something special because we have not just its natural appearance but also the constant process of change by man before our eyes. Whole mountain tops have already been carried away, and it has been calculated that reserves are enough for another thousand years. Will the eternal marble mountains have wholly disappeared by then?

Michelangelo Buonarotti (1475–1564), Lorenzo de' Medici, Duke of Urbino, c. 1525 (detail), marble, Sagrestia Nuova, S. Lorenzo, Florence

Carrara

The Romans began to excavate the marble from the Carrara quarries from about 70 B.C. The marble was shipped from the port of Luni, north of Carrara, and Carrara itself at the foot of the mountains was actually only a settlement beside the Carrione river where the marble workers lived. The place was first documented in 963, when Emperor Otto I gave it to the Bishops of Luni. In the 12th century, the Pisans resumed operation of the quarries abandoned in the early Middle Ages. From 1322, a succession of rulers – the Spinola from Genoa, the Rossi from Parma, the Scaligeri from Verona, the Visconti from Milan and the Guinigi from Lucca – quarreled about the marble. Finally, in 1442 the town, together with the neighboring Massa, were captured by Malaspina counts, since when the history of the two cities has run in tandem.

Palazzo Cybo Malaspina

The Palazzo Cybo Malaspina, which houses the Accademia di Belle Arti, dates from the 16th century when the Duke Alberico I had it built to replace the medieval castle, remains of which are preserved in the tower. Another major initiative of Alberico's was the city wall, which encompassed the new parts of the city and – as the focus of his urban scheme – the Piazza Alberica, named for him.

Maria Teresa Cybo Malaspina d'Este, the wife of the Duke of Modena, founded the Accademia di Belle Arti in 1769, uniting a museum and school of sculpture in a single institution. In 1805, during her reign, Napoleon's sister Elisa Baciocchi, the Princess of Lucca, presented the Palazzo Cybo Malaspina to the academy as its new accommodation.

The Palazzo is at the end of the Piazza Gramsci, which once contained a garden belonging to the palace and is now a busy focal point of the city. The building has a fine interior court with a Renaissance portico that still displays remnants of the original wall paintings.

Finds from antiquity are also on display here – sculptures from the Roman theater at Luni, tomb stelae and a Roman marble relief from Fantiscritti, brought here from the quarry of that name in 1863. It dates back to the reign of the Emperor Septimius Severus (193–211) and features three classical figures as youths (fanti) – Jupiter in the middle, with Hercules and Bacchus on either side. Interestingly the work also features the signatures (scritti) of Michelangelo, Giambologna and Canova, testifying – according to an old tradition – to visits by these famous artists to this area.

Carrara

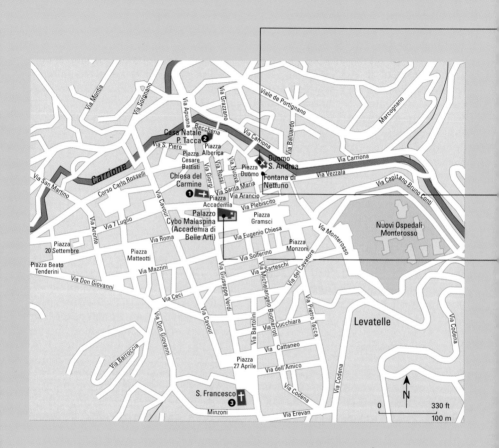

Duomo S. Andrea, Piazza Duomo, p. 46

Fontana di Nettuno, Piazza
Duomo, p. 49

Palazzo Cybo Malaspina
(Accademia di Belle Arti),
1 Via Roma, p. 43

Other sights of interest
(not covered elsewhere in
this book):

1   Chiesa del Carmine, Piazza
    Accademia

2   Casa Natale P. Tacca, Piazza
    Alberica

3   S. Francesco, Piazza 27 Aprile

Duomo S. Andrea

Work was begun on Carrara's most important building, the cathedral, in the 11th century. It is built entirely of marble. In the 13th century, the site was extended eastwards when the apse was rebuilt, giving the church its present dimensions. Gray and white stripes enliven the whole exterior of the basilica, recalling the Romanesque style of Pisa. The lower part of the façade is also reminiscent of the cathedral there, being articulated with Romanesque blind arcading, though unlike Pisa only alternate consoles are continued down in a flat pilaster, which contributes to creating a rhythm that is more open and that makes the façade look relatively broad.

The upper story was added only in the 14th century, this time in Gothic style. A rising flight of columns encloses a lavishly decorated rose window, which is inscribed in a frame of fleurons of the same date. Beside the apse is a bell tower in the Ligurian style, with a stumpy spire and corner pyramids of a late 12th-century date.

West Doorway

Both the figured decoration on the west door and acanthus frieze on the north door betray the influence of Emilian and Veronese work. Possibly the Veronese ruler of Carrara at that date brought workmen from his homeland with him.

The main west doorway is bordered with pilasters, while the lintel and archivolt are decorated in flat relief with floral tendrils and animal figures. A 12th-century frieze features animals grouped around an eagle at the vertex, though individual animals are hardly identifiable because of weathering.

Some 100 years after these sculptures, i.e., around 1350, the façade area above the west doorway was expanded to include the rose window and gallery of columns. The architectural decoration of the building is completed by the arcaded frieze along the exterior walls north and south. It rests on sculptured brackets featuring creatures such as lions and oxen. Animal consoles of this sort are common mainly in Ferrara or Verona, where hunting friezes also display wolfhounds baring their teeth, as below the arch here.

The Interior

The plain interior reflects the building history of the church over the centuries. In the Romanesque period, the basilica – with a nave and two aisles plan – was vaulted. The highly varied capitals of the nave arcade date from this period, showing numerous hunting and animal scenes. The style is reminiscent of the sculptures on the west doorway. From the 14th century the nave walls were frescoed, though this painted decoration survives only in fragments. The marble furnishings date almost entirely from the Cinquecento, the period when the Malaspina had consolidated their rule. Examples include the main altar and the 16th-century pulpit of variegated marbles, which is attributed to the Carrara sculptors Domenico di Sarto and Nicodemo. The marble choir stalls, made by Francesco Bergamini, are somewhat later in date.

The church is richly furnished with statues. The oldest examples are the altar of Divine Providence on the inside of the façade, probably the work of Giroldo da Como (14th century), and the marble Annunciation group in the south aisle, dating from 1310 and revealing French influence. There is also a 15th-century altar here that contains the relics of S. Ceccardo, the patron saint of Carrara.

Fontana di Nettuno

Besides the cathedral is a large, somewhat weathered fountain figure that was not originally intended for this spot but proves at least that over the centuries Carrara was where many sculptors worked. The figure was commissioned by the burghers of Genoa from the Florentine sculptor Baccio Bandinelli (1493–1560). The famous Genoese admiral Andrea Doria (1468–1560), the naval commander of the Emperor Charles V's fleet and inventor of the first armored ship, had defeated the French after a century of foreign rule and liberated his city. The statue was intended to honor him as ruler of the seas of the world. After the death of the sculptor, the fountain figure remained, in its rough unfinished state, in Carrara, and in May 1563 was set up on its present site, as the inscription notes.

The artist gave his figure of the ancient sea god Neptune the facial features of Andrea Doria. For the first time, a real historical personage was immortalized in a nude figure. With a rigid and immobile upper body, the ponderous figure remains precariously upright on the heads of two dolphins. This unstable and unbalanced pose dispenses with classical *contrapposto*, and is typical of the Mannerist sculpture of Bandinelli.

A Bohemian and His World – Giacomo Puccini

"He was the handsomest man I ever met." As to Puccini's looks there was no doubt, not for Alma Mahler anyway, whose view was shared by many women. Views about his achievements as a composer were not so unanimous. Adolf Weissmann opined in 1925 that Puccini's great achievement was to create operas about ever-

Group photo with (l. to r.) Giacomo Puccini (1858–1924), Giuseppe Giacosa (1847–1906) and Luigi Illica (1857–1919)

yday life, but in 1951 Benjamin Britten wrote: "When I heard *La Bohème*, the cheap vacuity of its music made me ill." However, by 1904, with the premiere of his opera *Madama Butterfly*, Puccini had become a huge success.

Ever since a Puccini forebear had been appointed as organist and music director at the cathedral of his home town Lucca, the city's music life had been in the hands of the Puccini family. They were music teachers, composers, organists, and directors of music. Giacomo was born on December 22, 1858 as the fifth child of Michele and Albina Puccini. The father was the head of the conservatory in Lucca. When he died in 1864, it was stipulated in a contract that "Signor Giacomo," then six, should take over his father's job as organist and music director as soon as he was old enough.

Not much is known about young Giacomo's school days, only that he was a moderate achiever. However, he soon contributed to his family's meager income by playing the piano in taverns and at popular festivals and public dances in the nearby coastal resorts, and by playing the organ in Lucca. However, church music did not interest him. When Giuseppe Verdi's *Aida* was performed to great acclaim in 1876, his composition teacher at the Lucca conservatory sent Puccini and two friends to the opera in Pisa – a twelve-mile walk each way. But it was worth the trouble. "It was as though the gates of music had opened to me."

Milan and the opera stage was now Puccini's declared objective. That is where the Teatro della Scala, the major music publishers, and the famous Conservatorio Reale all were.

But studying in Milan was prohibitively expensive for the family. Nor was the city of Lucca willing to invest in a musician no longer under consideration for the promised post of organist. In the end, Puccini was accepted at the Milan conservatory in 1880 thanks to a royal scholarship and financial support from a relation. There he led a rather impoverished but already relatively wild life. In pursuit of his vocation, which he explained in typically histrionic terms – "God touched me with his little finger and said: Write for the theater! Mind – only for the theater!" – Puccini remained in Milan even after completing his studies. In the space of only three months, he wrote his first one-act opera *Le villi* for a music competition. It was rejected by the music publishers Sonzogno on the grounds that the musical notation was illegible.

La Bohème, *title page of the Ricordi first edition*

But when Puccini managed, with the help of influential patrons, to get the influential publisher Ricordi interested in his work, the foundations were laid for a lifelong friendship and collaboration. The reworked version of *Le*

Hein Heckroth, La Bohème, *set design for the production by Wolf Völker at the Städtische Bühnen in Essen, 1930/1931*

villi was a *succès d'estime*, and was applauded by the critics.

In the meantime he had had a son by his mistress, a married Lucchese woman, which raised considerable dust in the small town and led to a scandal. But no sooner had Puccini scored his first success in 1884 than he retired to the inaccessible marshland of Torre del Lago near Viareggio. There he was able to work, drink with the villagers, fish in the lake, and shoot duck. Initially he rented only simple accommo-

dation, but later acquired a villa situated near the lake.

With his unconventional lifestyle, Puccini himself led the existence of a bohemian, thus conforming entirely with the *fin de siècle* artistic convention. Oscillating between moods of melancholy and euphoria, he often whiled the night away composing at the piano. If he had a sudden idea in the tavern, he carried the whole jovial company back home with him. During the long work on *La Bohème*, whose subject was close to Puccini's heart, a club of the same name was founded, and celebrated its completion in boisterous fashion. In 1900 came the composition of *Tosca*, and in 1904 the triumph of *Madama Butterfly*. The premiere of *La Fanciulla del West* (The Girl of the Golden West) followed in New York in 1910.

Puccini was the first Italian composer to achieve fame in the U.S.A. during his own lifetime. The premier of his "American" opera, *La Fanciulla del West*, was a sensational social occasion, reported internationally. The two male leads were Enrico Caruso and Pasquale Amati, the conductor was Arturo Toscanini. The opera was later staged in Chicago, Boston, and London, before its Italian debut in Rome.

Even during his numerous stays abroad and despite many changes of residence, Puccini constantly returned to the area around Lake Massaciuccoli. To the chagrin of his wife Elvira, he pursued not only field sports but also other pleasures, which of course did not remain unknown to her. Furious at his countless affairs, rendezvous, and escapades, she once waylaid a carriage on the open road which she presumed contained the miscreant, thinking to catch him *flagrante delicto*. Finding only her rival inside, she set about her with an umbrella. When her husband returned home, she asked him what he had caught. "Oh just a dumb chicken," was his laconic answer. Eyewitnesses reported that the domestic storm that erupted over his head at that point lasted three days.

His ever greater fame and success with the public ensured for the musician and his family a life of luxury and comfort, and also allowed him to travel frequently. The first signs of a fatal illness appeared in 1922, and Puccini was unable to complete his final opera, *Turandot*. When he took himself off to Brussels for an operation in 1924, the residents of his village, and with them the whole world of music, came to say goodbye. It was assumed that he would not survive the forthcoming operation. And Puccini did indeed die in Belgium, on November 29, 1924, a long way from home. He was buried near his villa in Torre del Lago.

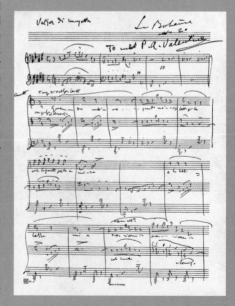

Giacomo Puccini (1858–1924), handwritten score of La Bohème, *1896*

Lucca and Region

Lucca

In the fertile plain of the Serchio between the Apuan Alps and Monte Pisano lies one of the most engaging of Tuscan provincial capitals. Confined within 16th- and 17th-century walls and bastions, it is the very image of an enclosed city.

Ligurians and Etruscans settled here, and in the 3rd century B.C. there was a Celtic Ligurian settlement called *Luk* (marsh). The name was taken over by the Romans as the colony of *Luca* in 180 B.C. It lay at the junction of important long-distance roads, and a town grew up with a grid layout that is still evident. Here, Caesar, Pompey, and Crassus met in 56 B.C. to form the Triumvirate.

In 571, the Lombards made Lucca an episcopal seat. Under the Franks, the town remained the center of the county of Tuscia. Its position on the Via Francigena, together with maritime trade via nearby Pisa, promoted commercial growth. Lucca was mainly a center for luxury goods – gold leaf, brocades, and silk – distributed throughout Europe and in the Orient. Until the late 11th century, the prosperous city contained the only royal mint in central Italy.

Ambitions for independence first surfaced in 1080 with the election of the city's own consuls, and were finally realized under Frederick Barbarossa in 1162.

There followed a period of economic prosperity and peace, during which the main Romanesque buildings of Lucca were constructed.

In the 13th and 14th centuries, intense rivalry between Florence and Pisa led to economic and political difficulties. A state of near civil war resulted, inducing local craftsmen to emigrate to Florence or Venice, taking their craft skills and experience with them.

From 1316, the city was weakened by the over-ambitious territorial claims of its ruler, Castruccio Castracani, and after his death in 1328 Pisa took control. Forty years later, Emperor Charles IV gave Lucca a charter of independence. From 1400, peace and commercial growth returned under the *signoria* of the merchant Paolo Guinigi, whose family built the tower with the seven holm oaks – one of the emblems of Lucca – growing on its top.

After the restoration of the republic in 1430, Lucca remained the only independent Tuscan city until the French invasion in 1799. Napoleon gave it to his sister Elisa Baciocchi as a principality in 1805. The Congress of Vienna subsequently installed Maria-Luisa of Bourbon-Parma as regent. In 1847, not long before Italy was united, her son Lodovico ceded the city to the Grand Duchy of Tuscany.

Aerial view of the Piazza Anfiteatro

Lucca

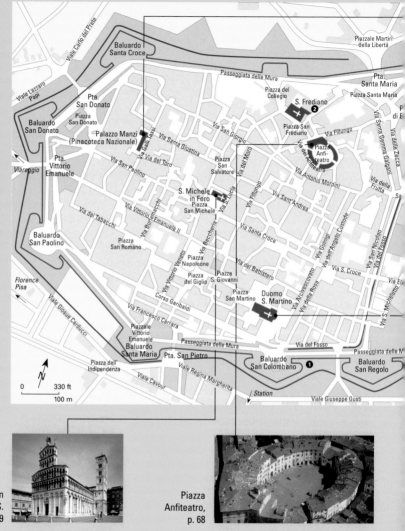

S. Michele in Foro, Piazza S. Michele, p. 69

Piazza Anfiteatro, p. 68

Palazzo Mansi (Pinacoteca Nazionale), 43 Via Galli Tassi, p. 77

Villa Guinigi (Museo Nazionale), Via della Quarquonia, p. 78

Duomo S. Martino, Piazza S. Martino, p. 70

Other sights of interest

1 Le Mura, city walls, p. 60

2 S. Frediano, Piazza S. Frediano, p. 61

Le Mura – the City Walls

The massive, still completely intact fortified wall of Lucca is the fourth in the history of the city, following the previous Roman, Lombard and "communal" walls. As previous walls were rendered inadequate by the invention of new weapons of war, further bastions (*baluardi*) for cannon were erected forward of the walls at regular intervals in the course of the 15th century. When the best-known military architects subsequently began constructing a new wall in the mid-16th century, these bastions were incorporated in the layout. The work was completed in 1650, after enormous financial expenditure and the use of about 6 million bricks.

The walls total over $2^1/_2$ miles (4.2 km) in length and consist of 11 earthworks that are up to 98 feet (30 m) wide at the base and are defended by 40-foot (12 m) high external brick walls. Beyond that is a 115-foot (35 m) wide moat once filled with water, and beyond that again an external earthwork for the gunners. These walls were never put to the test – except when the Serchio flooded in 1812. The Lucchesi are very proud that their city never came under the control of the Medici grand dukes, and still distinguish between those born *fuori* (outside) or – like real Lucchesi – *dentro le mura* (inside the walls).

S. Frediano

The first church was established in the 6th century by Fredianus (Frigdanius), a bishop of Irish origin and now patron saint of Lucca. His simple building near the ancient amphitheater was rebuilt in the Romanesque style in the early 12th century and rededicated in 1147.

In order to avoid the façade facing the city wall, the west end was, exceptionally, moved to the east. Three plain doorways with high semi-circular hoods show the original layout of Fredianus's basilica. When side chapels were later added, a further span was added at each end.

In the 13th century, the nave roof was raised to create a lofty gable end that – unusually for Tuscany – is decorated with a gold mosaic. This was carried out in the Byzantine style in around 1230 by artists from the celebrated Lucchese workshop of the Berlinghieri.

The mosaic depicts the Ascension. In the upper part, the risen Christ sits in a mandorla, borne by two angels. Below are the twelve apostles wearing classical robes, visibly excited. Their symmetrical arrangement lacks its former centerpiece, a figure of the Virgin, which was later removed to make a pointed window.

The Interior

Inside is a nave and two aisles layout with no transept. Despite later extensions, the church is one of the finest examples of Lucchese Romanesque. Twelve pairs of columns – matching the number of apostles – carry the well-proportioned nave arcade. Some of the remarkable Composite capitals are 4th-century Roman spoil; the other capitals date from the 12th or 15th century.

Now plain, the nave walls were presumably once painted with frescoes. The lofty clerestory with its evenly spaced windows springs from a band molding. In the 13th century, the clerestory wall was raised by nearly 11 feet (3.30 m). The original proportions had matched those of an early Christian basilica. With the extra height, the ratio of width to height (1:2) matched that of the cathedral in Pisa. The side chapels added between the 13th and the 16th century are burial chapels of the great Lucchese families, and are therefore expensively decorated with sculptures and paintings. The Zita Chapel contains the relics of a local serving-maid saint (St. Sitha). The church originally had a large monastery, which in the 16th century became a center for the Reformers, who were initially tolerated. Later, most of them moved to Geneva to escape persecution by the local Inquisition.

Font, c. 1150
Marble, h. 330 cm, diam. 255 cm

In front of a lunette of the *Annunciation* made c. 1510 of color-glazed terracotta at the workshop of the Florentine della Robbia family of sculptors stands the large Romanesque font, which was removed in the 18th century and restored only in 1952. It dates from the mid-12th century, and consists of a round basin with a central pier decorated with a stylized representation of flowing water from which a naked youth and a sea monster are emerging. Above this is a bowl decorated with masks, with openings through which water streams out. On this perches a cover standing on columns, adorned with scenes of the months and symbols of the four evangelists.

Several artists were involved in the creation of this work. The figures on the cover were made by a classically trained Tuscan sculptor. The crowded scenes on the lower basin are in the histrionic style of a Lombard artist, and show events in the life of Moses. Particularly fine is the relief of the *Passage through the Red Sea*, where Pharaoh's soldiers look like medieval knights. The figures of Christ as the Good Shepherd, with a lamb on his shoulders and surrounded by apostles, saints, and prophets, are the work of a Byzantine-influenced artist who records his name as "Robertus Magister."

Between Papacy and Empire – the Interminable Conflict between Guelphs and Ghibellines

Ruth Strasser

The modern visitor to medieval Tuscan towns who happens to glance upwards cannot help noticing the different battlements on city walls, city halls and palaces: rectangular merlons with a straight edge (Guelph) or horned in the shape of a swallow-tail (Ghibelline). These indicate which of the two warring parties (supporting, respectively, the pope or the emperor) once held sway in the locality, or community, or even family – except where later restoration work has led to the telltale symbol being switched.

Guelph and Ghibelline as historical concepts make their first appearance in documents from 1240. At the time, Tuscany was a long way from constituting a political unit, being split into individual city states which feuded with each other violently at the slightest excuse and were involved in the power struggles between the emperor and the papacy. Thus cities that cultivated pro-papal policies were also labeled Guelph, and defended themselves against interference by the emperor and empire in communal affairs, tolerated no imperial clerics within the city gates and likewise wished to pay no taxes to the emperor. The Ghibellines included the historical landed nobility, who had of course long exchanged their landed estates for fortified urban palaces and lived off rents and tolls. They looked to the emperor to back

Campanile of the Palazzo Vecchio, Florence

their endeavors to sustain obsolete ideals such as feudal rule and vassalage against the new economic and political strength of an increasingly powerful mercantile and commercial class. The conflict between emperor and pope dated back to the 11th century, when the former Bishop of Florence, Hildebrand, was elected Pope Gregory VII and banned lay investiture, i.e. the right to appoint bishops and abbots that emperors, as God's anointed, had enjoyed since Charlemagne. Linked with this was the abolition of the right of secular landlords to collect taxes from churches and monasteries. The historical outcome is well known. In 1076, the Salian German king and later Emperor Henry IV declare the pope deposed, with the words; "I, Henry, by the grace of God king, say to you with all my bishops, come down, come down." Gregory excommunicated the king in 1077, who was forced to humble himself barefoot in the snow before the pope at Canossa, in a temporary reconciliation. The struggle over investitures grew more bitter during the reigns of the Hohenstaufen emperors Frederick Barbarossa, his son Henry VI and grandson Frederick II, who rejected any papal supremacy. After Pope Innocent III had come out in 1201 in support of rival candidate Otto IV, son of Henry the Lion and a Welf, the naming of the two factions was just a matter of time. The imperial party were called Waiblinger – after the main seat of the Hohenstaufen family. This was corrupted to Ghibellini in Italian. The equally Germanic Welf dynasty also became henceforth in Italy the pro-papal Guelfi.

Campanile of the Palazzo Pubblico, Siena

The Tuscan cities were in any case at each other's throats. As populations grew with the expansion in the 13th century of long-distance trade, bringing with it the development of a northern Italian banking system hitherto unrivaled in the west, the foreign policy split between emperor and pope was formalized in city statutes. This meant for a Florentine or Sienese that the most important thing was not what city they were born in but whether their family belonged to the Guelph or Ghibelline faction, and where the loyalties of the current city council lay. Only later in the course of things did individual cities explicitly take sides politically. As centers of the great mercantile houses Florence and Lucca were on the side of the Rome-oriented Guelphs, whereas Pisa, Siena, and Pistoia were ruled by imperially-minded Ghibelline families who, when the Emperor crossed the Alps, accommodated him and his retinue in their palaces, often for months. Yet the political situation in Tuscany became still more complicated. During a game, the small son of the powerful Cancellieri family from Pistoia slightly injured a related child with his sword. When the little miscreant was sent by his father to the parents of the injured child to ask forgiveness for his carelessness, the Cancellieri child there and then had his hand chopped off on a butcher's table. The hand was returned with the message: "Sword wounds are healed with steel, not words." The Ghibelline families in Pistoia divided into opposing camps, which later became known as the Whites and the Blacks. This internal dispute also spilled over into neighboring Guelph Florence, where similar strife broke out when a certain Buondelmonte dei Buondelmonti, a friend of the long-established Donati family, failed to redeem a pledge of marriage to a member of the family, and was murdered by the girl's relatives. Corso Donati, one of the most influential men of Florence and a direct relative of the Black Cancellieri from Pistoia, thereupon established the Black Guelph faction in Florence. At that, the Donati family's enemies, the rich newcomer mercantile family of Cerchi, suddenly became representatives of the White Guelphs. Alliances of all sorts were concluded. Political adversaries in exile in other Italian cities signed up mercenary leaders, interested parties from abroad became involved in the division of power, and defeated cities were sold to the highest bidder. Treachery on the part of relatives or friends left behind by the exiles was common. Curfew was imposed at dusk. "Blood flows in the streets, and the dogs drink it from the gutters," wrote Dante impressively of the dangerous conditions in Florence in his day. As a White Guelph member of the city council, in the end he too fell victim to the hostilities, and in 1302 had to leave Florence for good when the papal troops entered Florence.

During the period when the Guelphs had the upper hand in Florence, artisans and small traders, the *popolo minuto*, took part in government, not only was property of the Ghibelline families confiscated but also a law was passed barring noblemen from political office and releasing rural workers from their obligations to landowners. A law in the Florentine state archives of August 6, 1289 prohibits the purchase and sale of people for the purpose of exploiting their labor, and deals with the liberty and self-determination of man – the first attempt at a constitution of human rights independent of divine laws or imperial regulation.

After the Hohenstaufens had died out in the mid-13th century, the Ghibelline faction gradually lost its followers. The young Luxembourg emperor Henry VII, who tried to depose the pope with the help of his Pisan and Sienese allies, failed to achieve his object because he died on the way to Rome in 1313. The inhabitants of the Tuscan cities increasingly organized themselves into guilds, and clamored for the city councils to be popularly elected.

Giorgio Vasari (1511–1574), Prospect of Florence during the Siege by the Imperial Army in 1529 *(detail). Sala di Clemente VII, Palazzo Vecchio, Florence*

Amphitheater – Piazza Anfiteatro

The Roman amphitheater, which dates from the 2nd century A.D. and whose floor level was about ten feet lower than today, was elliptical in ground plan, and was surrounded by two superimposed rows of arches on piers. The whole building was destroyed during the barbarian invasions and subsequently used as readily available building material as in, for example, the columns of Lucca's Romanesque churches. Unconcerned, later residents built new houses on the ruins, of necessity following the elliptical building line of the ancient amphitheater, the shape of which is still evident in the piazza. After the whole area was subsequently built over, in 1830 Maria-Luisa of Bourbon-Parma had the piazza cleared. Four arches, through which you still enter the square, indicate the entries to the ancient amphitheater.

S. Michele in Foro

Though it took 200 years to build, the Romanesque basilica of S. Michele in Foro never attained the height originally planned. This is why the nave and right aisle are so ill matched to the projecting marble west front with its imposing colossal statue of the archangel Michael. The *in Foro* cognomen derives from the square, which was once the forum of the Roman colony. The wall of the lowest story of the church is articulated by arcading, into which colored rhomboid patterns are inserted. On the west front, freestanding columns support the richly ornamented blind arcading of the upper levels and gable. The stonework emphasizes the unity of the façade decoration, the originality of which lies in the lavishly sculptured arcade shafts, capitals, and consoles. The 13th-century decorative scheme was executed by Guidetto da Como's workshop, combining motifs from Lombardy and Pisa.

Duomo S. Martino

Founded in the 6th century, upgraded to an episcopal seat in the 8th century and rebuilt from 1060, the cathedral underwent considerable reconstruction between the late 12th and the 14th century.

Before Guidetto, the celebrated master from Como who has immortalized himself in an inscription beneath the right-hand column in the first gallery, could complete the marble façade in 1204, he had to tailor his decorative scheme to the already existing 226-feet (69 m) high campanile. This accounts for the asymmetry of the delicately articulated façade, which looks as if it is leaning against the defiant, two-colored tower of travertine marble and brick. The façade is divided into two zones: at ground level, three large arches open into a portico; above this are three gallery arcades, with the top one possibly intended originally as a gable in the style of S. Michele in Foro. Each column is differently sculpted, with reliefs of dragons, lions, human figures, and geometrical patterns alternately in black and white marble. Above the arcades vegetable ornamentation and animal motifs are visible: their design is reminiscent of patterns on the famous Lucchese silks.

The doorways have remarkable reliefs with scenes from the lives of St. Martin, St. Regulus and Christ.

Lucchese artist of Lombard origin,
***St. Martin and the Beggar*, c. 1240**
Marble, lifesize

Among them is one of the rare freestanding equestrian sculptures of the Italian Middle Ages. It was created in 1240 for the façade of the cathedral, where it is now replaced by a copy. The slightly bent leg posture and bowed back of the beggar, expressing both humility and respect for the noble knight, are strikingly lifelike.

North Doorway of West Front

The layered decoration and its coloring give the doorway a closed-in appearance. The sculptural parts are particularly interesting. As with the other two doorways, reliefs dating from around 1260 adorn the lintel and tympanum.

The lintel contains scenes of the *Annunciation*, the *Birth of Christ,* and the *Adoration of the Magi*. As lifelike and expressive as these linked events from the childhood of Christ are the figures of the *Deposition* in the tympanum.

In accordance with Christian iconography, the three Marys and male believers have gathered around the Cross. Christ's arms have already been freed and Nicodemus is releasing the feet, while Joseph of Arimathaea grasps the upper part of Christ's body.

The sculptor, who has been identified with Nicola Pisano's circle, has achieved a miracle of emotional expressiveness with the arrangement of the figures in the tympanon. The narrowness of the frame, for example, intensifies the weight of the dead Christ. The Lord's face appears peaceful, almost smiling. The face of Joseph of Arimathaea is strained and yet loving. The soldier on the right raises his head, both curious and as if witnessing a vision.

**Master of St. Regulus, reliefs on west front,
showing scenes from the life of** *St. Martin,*
The Labors of the Months, July to December
(detail), 13th-century
Marble

The sculptor of the south doorway, the
Master of St. Regulus, also carved the
reliefs between the doorways in the mid-
13th century. Below the scenes from the
life of St. Martin is a series of labors of the
months, which shows small figures at
work in an evenly spaced arcade. The
scenes are very appealing presentations of
each monthly labor: in January, the fire is
guarded, February is for fishing, March for
pruning the vines, April is for sowing, in
May the knight goes wooing with flowers,
in June the wheat is harvested, July is for
threshing, August is the fruit harvest, the
grapes are pressed in September, and the
wine barrels filled in October. Plowing is in
November, and slaughtering in December.
The spandrels of the arcade contain the
relevant Zodiac symbols.

A special charm of this relief is the
contrast between the almost turquoise
gleam of the background and the white of
the active figures in the foreground.

Duomo S. Martino

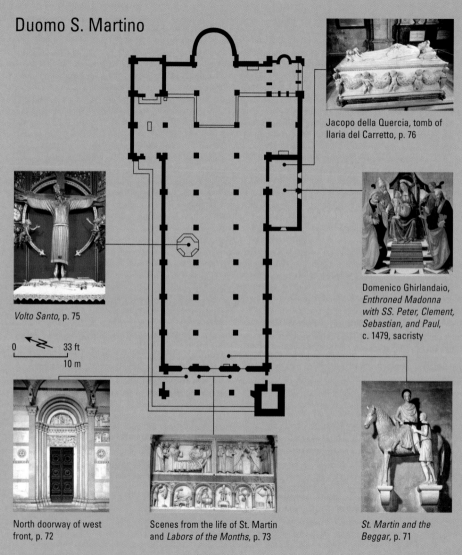

Jacopo della Quercia, tomb of Ilaria del Carretto, p. 76

Domenico Ghirlandaio, *Enthroned Madonna with SS. Peter, Clement, Sebastian, and Paul*, c. 1479, sacristy

Volto Santo, p. 75

0   33 ft
10 m

North doorway of west front, p. 72

Scenes from the life of St. Martin and *Labors of the Months*, p. 73

St. Martin and the Beggar, p. 71

Volto Santo, between 1170 and 1220
Wood, h. 250 cm

An elegant octagonal tempietto, the work of one of Lucca's most important Renaissance sculptors, Matteo Civitali (1436–1501), contains the *Volto Santo*, the Holy Countenance. It is a Christus Pantocrator, showing Christ as an all-sovereign ruler. Face, hair and beard are severe and symmetrically arranged. A long girdled tunic called a colobium and the horizontally spread arms emphasize the axial symmetry of the figure. It shows not physical suffering but triumph over death and the belief in the Resurrection. According to legend, Nicodemus carved a wooden crucifix of cedar of Lebanon in order to possess a *vera ikon*, a true image of Christ. After it had long been hidden, the crucifix is supposed to have been brought in 782 in a crewless ship to Luni on the northern coast of Tuscany and then carried in a driverless oxcart to Lucca.

This walnut effigy of the *Volto Santo* is one of a group of large-scale Romanesque crucifixes dating to between 1170 and 1220, though its style may derive from a now lost earlier cross that reached Tuscany from Syria.

The legend of the Lucchese Cross had spread throughout Europe in the early Middle Ages. For example, William Rufus of England affirmed his oath in 1087 with the words *per sanctum Vultum de Lucca*. A "Saint Vaudeluc" crops up in French medieval love songs. The image appears on seals of Flemish merchants, and Dante mentions it in Canto XXI of the *Inferno*. Every year on September 13 the *Volto Santo* and its precious ornaments are carried through the city. All windows and arcades are then lit with countless little lanterns.

**Jacopo della Quercia (c. 1374–1438),
tomb of Ilaria del Carretto, c. 1406–1408**
Marble, 88 × 205 cm

On December 8, 1405 Ilaria del Carretto, second wife of Paolo Guinigi, "Signore" and lord of Lucca, died giving birth to her second child. Her husband commissioned the young Sienese sculptor Jacopo della Quercia to make her effigy, between 1406 and 1408. Now in the sacristy, it is one of the finest works of the Quattrocento. The Sienese artist and his colleague Francesco di Valdambrino managed to capture the youth and beauty of the dead woman in marble with great expressiveness. Ilaria lies on a freestanding sarcophagus; at her feet a small dog is on guard, an emblem of

fidelity beyond the grave. Ilaria wears a robe fastened high around the neck, the delicate folds of the gown emphasizing the natural grace of the figure. Particularly impressive is the way della Quercia captures her fresh, youthful countenance.

The still wholly Gothic style that marks this early work of della Quercia blends harmoniously with the decoration of the *tumba*, which dates from not much later but already heralds the early Renaissance. Ten naked, cheerful putti surround the death bed carrying bulging garlands of fruit, depicted on a scale and with an autonomy unseen since antiquity.

Palazzo Mansi – Pinacoteca Nazionale

The original 17th-century palace with its plain exterior was rebuilt a century later by its owners, the Mansi family. The interior was furnished in the grand manner, with an ornate ballroom and luxurious bridal chamber.

These days the Palazzo Mansi houses the Pinacoteca Nazionale. The gallery has particularly good collections of 16th-century Venetian painting and Dutch and Florentine painting of the 18th century. Most of these works were given to the city of Lucca by Grand Duke Leopold II when it was incorporated into the Grand Duchy of Tuscany.

Pontormo (1494–1557),
portrait of a young man, c. 1522/1525
Oil on wood, 85 × 61 cm

The half-length portrait shows the subject in a classic grand pose. Standing erect, one hand on his hips, the other resting on a parapet, the youth looks at us haughtily. Despite this pose, the body almost seems the disappear in the voluminous mantle and the black background. Only the breadth and dominant color of the mantle lend the young man solidity. His gaze and facial expression and the way he holds his head reveal youth and self-assurance, but also a degree of uncertainty. The conflict between the treatment of the dress and that of the facial expression are characteristic of the anti-classical, Mannerist style of Pontormo.

In his *Vita* of Pontormo, Vasari reports that this is a lifelike portrait of the young Alessandro de' Medici, an illegitimate son of the Medici pope Clement VII who was about 13 at the time of the portrait. In 1537 Alessandro, a tyrannical ruler of Florence, was murdered by his cousin.

Villa Guinigi – Museo Nazionale

Paolo Guinigi, who ruled Lucca for 30 years at the beginning of the 15th century and already possessed a large palace in the center of the city, the Palazzo Guinigi, built a second residence surrounded by a lovely garden outside the medieval walls. Following a very successful restoration in 1968, this Villa Guinigi now houses the Museo Nazionale. In the extensive, two-tone brick complex with colonnades on the ground floor and triforium windows on the upper floor carried on white supports, there is a comprehensive collection of ancient classical items and fine pieces of all kinds from the Middle Ages to the 18th century.

Etruscan Grave Goods

Of special importance within the extensive collection of the Museo Nazionale are the finds of burial gifts from an Etruscan tomb unearthed in 1892 near the Rio Ralletta in the former marshland of Bientina south of Lucca. They include an Attic crater and high-quality gold work: earrings, large pins, fibulae used as fasteners for clothing, various pendants, and beaten plates. To produce the *granalia*, the fine gold nuggets for granulation, the Etruscans melted gold particles in pulverized charcoal at around 2,000 °F (1,100 °C) and then washed them with lye from ash and rainwater and sorted them – often they were under 0.1 mm in diameter. Only the finest animal hair was used to compose these tiny grains into a variety of ornaments and figures, without the usual aids of soldered-on wire or incised grooves. A basic copper carbonate called chrysocolla, that is contained mainly in malachite, an emerald green mineral, was used as a "gold adhesive" for the subsequent soldering.

**Berlinghiero Berlinghieri
(c. 1175/1180–pre-1236),
crucifix panel, c. 1220**
Tempera on wood, 175 × 140 cm

The painted wood crucifix by the Lucchese artist Berlinghiero Berlinghieri is particularly well preserved. It is signed *Berlinghieri Me Pinxit*. Berlinghiero shows Christ on the Cross in upright pose with a highly decorated green loincloth. The face is framed by a halo studded with rock crystal, and the large open eyes gaze straight at the viewer. This erect pose does not depict the agony of the suffering Christ on the Cross (*Christus patiens*) but the Christ who has overcome death (*Christus triumphans*). In early Christianity, the Crucifixion and Passion were symbolized by such emblems as the Cross and the Lamb. A council called by the Emperor Justinian II in 691 advocated the direct depiction of Christ, with the Crucified Christ himself being shown. It would be the job of the painter to attract the viewer to the picture by bringing before him the living Christ, who redeemed the world through his suffering. Panel crucifixes of this type were incorporated into the iconostasis (a screen separating the sanctuary from the body of the church) adopted by the eastern Orthodox Churches. The iconostasis, which was covered with icons and pierced by three doorways, remained common until the 14th century.

Mighty Trees, Paintings, and Bubbling Water – the Tuscan Villa

Ruth Strasser

Humanistically educated citizens of 15th-century Florence became familiar with the lifestyle of their forebears in part by reading works by the classical authors. There were thereby not only improving their knowledge of Latin, but were at the same time discovering the Romans' much-prized division of life into the *vita activa,* a busy professional life as a merchant, politician or banker, and the *vita contemplativa*, the temporary withdrawal into rural seclusion, to devote time to the Muses and the arts. This meant that the close link between city and country that is a feature of Mediterranean culture generally remained intact.

Abandoning the feudal and county system preferred by the Franks, the free urban communes reincorporated the surrounding lands into their ownership and made city-dwellers into landowners. The well-conceived system of the *civitas,* or city republic, was transferred to the country and landscape, so that nature lost the threatening aspect it had had for medieval people. In the council chamber of the Palazzo Pubblico in Siena, a fresco by Ambrogio Lorenzetti (c. 1293–c. 1348) from the mid-14th century depicts the freedom of unhindered intercourse between city and country. Around 1400, most of the urban population had a piece of land in the *contado*, the

Villa di Castello, Florence

countryside surrounding the city, and *villeggia-tura* flourished – temporary residence in the country, which also raised the status of agriculture and farming. The villa became the summer residence. It was distinct from a mansion or castle in that its owner was not independent but a citizen subject to urban justice, and different from an estate in that its owner was there only temporarily. Even so, the villa was always associated with agriculture, and was integrated into a larger system of semi-smallholdings.

Exemplary of this relatively new cultural institution and way of life in every respect was the Medici family from Florence. The villas of the progenitor, Cosimo Vecchio (1389–1464), Caffagiolo and Il Trebbio, were constructed or rebuilt in the style of medieval castles or fortresses, with fortified towers and gateways, ramparts, and rain spouts. But with the appearance of theoretical treatises on the architecture of the villa imbued with the ideals of antiquity, the villa became the location of *otium*, educated leisure. Time was given over to studying, philosophizing with friends, writing, making music, hunting, growing oranges and lemons, and experimenting with vines. It also meant healthy eating and escaping the oppressive summer heat of the city.

In the *Decameron*, Boccaccio (1313–1375) depicted the villa as the ideal refuge from the horrors of the 1348 plague that raged mainly in the cities. Petrarch (1304–1374) described country living as the appropriate way of life for members of the intellectual elite, while the Renaissance architect and architectural writer Leon Battista Alberti (1404–1472) recommends it for "simple pleasures, to be able to enjoy to the full all the advantages that a landscape has to offer – light, air, distant views, and panorama."

Alberti wrote four treatises about the appearance and significance of a country residence, the choice of the site on geographical and climatic grounds, and the architectural design – each villa should have a large room (*sala*) and interior court (*cortile*). Alberti also discusses questions of interior furnishing, and cites the rediscovered benefits of agricultural activity for the owners' physical and spiritual well-being. In 1598, Flemish painter Joost Utens was commissioned by Grand Duke Ferdinando de' Medici (1549–1609) to paint a series of lunettes in the grand room of the Villa Artimino, in which the villas of the de' Medicis are faithfully depicted in detail. We see here not just their variety but also their typology: clear, light façades, wall surfaces and windows in harmonious relationship, the structure relieved by a portico, a loggia, or terraces. Internally as well, plainness rules: a simple tile or stone-flagged floor, ocher-colored walls with sparse fresco decoration, little furniture – for example, a large wooden table with benches and stools, rustic seats, wall cupboards, a large fireplace, and a tiled kitchen with an oven. The lack of ostentation and a measure of restraint in the decoration and furnishing have always remained characteristic of the Tuscan villa. The same simplicity marks the garden: flower beds laid out along a central axis, with wild flowers and fruit trees, and paths framed by baskets. The disposition of flower pots and orange and lemon trees in terracotta tubs corresponds to

Villa Medicea, Poggio a Caiano

the laws of symmetry. Arbors and pergolas of vines and climbing plants provide shade, fountains mark the junctions of paths, mazes and artificial grottos made of tuff, shells, and colored pebbles provide surprising views inside and out. An era that discovered the laws of perspective, harmony of proportion, and the rules of classical mathematics applied these concepts of order to both architecture and garden design. Variety and differentiation are achieved with sundry shades of green and the creation of light and shadow effects, and by ringing the changes on geometrical shapes such as circles, squares, spheres, cones, and cylinders. In his diary for 1459, Florentine merchant Giovanni Rucellai describes an impressive example of *ars topiara*, the art

of cutting hedges and bushes to shape. In the garden of his villa, he had cut from evergreen box, laurel, and holm oaks the shapes of ships, giants, dragons and other fabulous beasts, temples with columns, a pope and cardinals.

During the 16th and 17th centuries, rising profits from commerce and banking led to ever greater investment in landed estates. "It is a general obsession with the Florentine," wrote a Venetian diplomat, "that he makes 20,000 ducats in profit and spends 10,000 of it on a country house." In time, the garden became something more constructed than planted, with embankments, terraces, enclosing walls with sculptural niches, symmetrically disposed double flights of steps and artistic balustrades,

Villa Medicea di Careggi, Florence

making as it were an extension of the villa. Stone worked in many shapes and water became increasinbly popular: along with evergreen plants, stone, and water were the core elements of the Tuscan Renaissance garden. Surprise effects and lavishly designed and hydraulically engineered attractions were important components: resounding waterfalls, foaming cascades, artificial rain, automatically generated birdsong, and organ music – and artificially moving dragons. The more lavish the setting, the more amusing the entertainment. Exotic plants from overseas were bred, and continual arabesques were created in geometrically arranged flowerbeds, the *parterres de broderie*. Once a small open-air theater was added, the villa could host a delightfully

magical *festa*. Outstanding examples of villa complexes from this period are found especially in the Lucca and Pistoia areas. When the Medici family died out, all the villas were put up for sale by the new Habsburg-Lorraine rulers, especially to English buyers, who transformed the buildings into pseudo-medieval knightly castles and transformed the Tuscan gardens into English parks.

Barga

Duomo S. Cristofano

West Doorway

Barga is a picturesque little hilltop town in the central Serchio Valley. It has been an important agricultural and craft center since the Middle Ages, and is celebrated for its silks. High above the town is the cathedral of S. Cristofano, on a large vantage point called the Arringo. A small aisleless church was built here in the 10th century, and in the 14th century it became the vestibule of the present cathedral. At the same time, the former north wall beside the battlemented bell tower was turned into a façade. The fine travertine masonry and its plain ornamentation still date from the 11th century. The decoration of the arches springs from flattened consoles that are sculpted as human figures and animals. Inside the church, the marble pulpit is well worth noting; it was made in about 1250, before Nicola and Giovanni Pisani appeared.

The fine doorway, reached up six semicircular steps, was inserted in about 1200. Particularly remarkable is the decorated lintel, which depicts a wine harvest and stands between two lion brackets.

Guido Bigarelli (workshop), pulpit, c. 1250
Marble

The interior of San Cristofano has a nave and two aisles, the nave itself having a richly decorated Romanesque *ambo*, i.e., a pulpit linked with the choir stalls and adorned with reliefs and figures. The quality of workmanship makes it one of the most important of all pre-Nicola Pisano pulpits in Tuscany. It was probably made by a Lucchese artist from the workshop of Guido Bigarelli (c. 1250–1256), when the church was elevated to the status of a parish church with baptismal rights.

The four columns of red marble rest on impressive lions and an atlantes. Their classicizing foliage capitals and an eagle capital carry the breastwork of the pulpit which possesses three lecterns: the one on the left is supported by an eagle, the symbol of St John the Evangelist. Below, the symbols of the other evangelists complete the Tetramorph: in the center, the angel of St. Matthew, the ox of St. Luke on one side and the lion of St. Mark on the other.

The lectern on the chancel side rests on a sculpture of St. Christopher, the one on the right on a figure of St. John the Baptist.

Guido Bigarelli (workshop),
Annunciation and *Birth of Christ*
(detail of pulpit)

Scenes of the childhood of Christ are executed on the other panels of the breastwork of the pulpit in the same vigorous three-dimensional style.

Particularly impressive is the panel relief facing the nave. Beneath deeply recessed arcades are the *Annunciation* and the *Birth of Christ*. A heavy, blocklike physicality and severe physiognomies characterize the

figures, which overflow out of the arcaded framework. Their restrained gestures and body language make clear what is happening. The sculptor lovingly shows the ox and ass sniffing the child in the crib, and even the scene in which the maids prepare the first bath for the newborn Christ is prominent in the foreground and not relegated to the background as a mere triviality.

The composition, arrangement and frontality of the figures recall scenes in contemporary book illuminations.

Pistoia

Pistoia

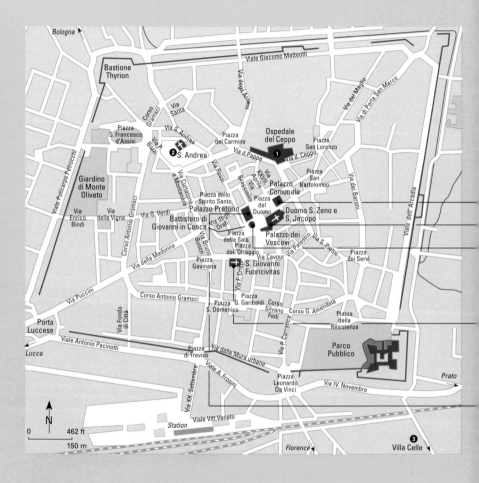

Palazzo Comunale, 1 Piazza del Duomo, p. 92

Duomo S. Zeno e S. Jacopo, Piazza del Duomo, p. 94

Battistero di S. Giovanni in Conca, Piazza del Duomo, p. 101

S. Giovanni Fuorcivitas, Via Cavour, p.102

Palazzo Pretorio, Piazzetta Scuole Normali, p. 93

Other sights of interest

1   Ospedale del Ceppo, Piazza Giovanni XXIII, p. 114

2   S. Andrea. Via S. Andrea, p. 108

3   Villa Celle, Santomato (south-east of Pistoia), p. 114

Pistoia

The provincial capital of Pistoia lies on the river Ombrone between the foothills of the Apennines and, to the south, the hills of Montalbano. Evidence of Etruscan habitation has been found in the area, and in the 2nd century B.C. the settlement of "Pistoria" was founded by the Romans as a supply base for their wars with the Ligurians. The regular chessboard layout typical of the Roman streets was later incorporated into the town's coat of arms. The Langobards made Pistoia their royal capital. However, it was not until after the death of Countess Matilda of Canossa in 1115 that the economy began to flourish, fueled by trade and the manufacture of cloth. Pistoia's citizens wanted independence, and in 1177 it was one of the first towns in Italy to have its own constitution.

Between the 12th and 14th centuries the town enjoyed a period of renewal, the circle of the town wall was extended outwards, the early medieval parish churches embellished, and a large number of new

Palazzo Comunale

secular and sacred buildings erected. During this period many artists moved to Pistoia from the neighboring towns, particularly Pisa and Florence. The heart of the present day city has retained the historical character of the independent municipality in its heyday.

Traditionally loyal to the emperor, Pistoia was in the end too weak to stand up to the constant pressure from the towns of Lucca and Florence, and in 1324 it came under Florentine rule. The inhabitants maintained a certain autonomy, however, and in the 14th century the third wall ring – still largely preserved – was erected.

Pistoia had been known since Roman times for its metalworking, and indeed the word "pistol," originally meaning a kind of dagger, is supposed to have been derived from "Pistoia." In the Art Nouveau period its metalworking industry experienced a renaissance, while in the course of the 20th century the town developed into one of the most important centers for plant nurseries.

The Piazza del Duomo, the town's principal square in both secular and spiritual terms, is dominated at its eastern end by

Palazzo Pretorio, inner courtyard

the elegant Palazzo Comunale. This was built in 1294, extended in the 14th century and now houses the Museo Civico. Directly opposite is the Palazzo Pretorio (Palace of Justice) erected in 1337, which today still accommodates the *tribunale*, the district court. In the inner courtyard, which is mainly original, the judge's bench, the seating and the colorful coats of arms recall the many *podestà* who have lived and passed judgment here over the centuries.

Duomo S. Zeno e S. Jacopo, Campanile and Palazzo dei Vescovi

The Campanile rises boldly and defiantly 220 feet (67 metres) high next to the façade of the cathedral. At the time of its communal independence in 1199 the first three stories were built as the official seat of the *Capitano del popolo* and it was known as the "Fortezza del Campanile." It was not until 1300 that the three, visually striking upper tiers were added, with their striped marble incrustation, dwarf galleries, and swallowtail battlements. The spire was erected in the 16th century.

At the southern end of the cathedral square stands the Palazzo dei Vescovi, the Bishop's Palace, which now houses the cathedral museum. In 1143 Bishop Atho of Pistoia managed to obtain precious relics of St. James the Elder from his tomb in Santiago de Compostela. This made Pistoia into an important stage on the pilgrims' route to Compostela. To house the relics, Atho built a chapel in the south aisle of the Duomo, with a separate entrance. The chapel was demolished in the late 18th century but the sacristy next to it, housing the relics, is now incorporated into the cathedral museum. Today there is access from the Bishop's Palace to a subterranean archaeological trail, which leads past finds from excavations of the early Christian and Roman town down to the lower layers where there are Etruscan grave stelae.

The contrast with the powerful campanile makes the façade of the cathedral appear extremely delicate. The structure of its upper level is created by dwarf galleries and striped marble décor. The clear articulation of the façade, together with its porch that was added in 1311, and the absence of small-scale decoration, give it an appearance of overall unity. The combination of Pisan and Florentine styles is interesting. The stripes of the arches repeat the pattern in the upper colonnaded galleries, and are reminiscent of the cathedral in Pisa. On the other hand the square fields in the attic floor are influenced by Romanesque marble incrustation in Florence. The porch has a pattern of semicircular and horseshoe-shaped arches. The stilted central arch is surmounted by a vault with glazed coffering by Andrea della Robbia, who is also responsible for the terracotta relief of 1505 depicting the Virgin and Child and two angels in the tympanum of the central portal. In the lunettes of the arcaded walkways the remains of frescoes have recently been discovered during restoration work in the porch.

The gable is crowned by two 18th-century sculptures: on the left is S. Zeno, Bishop of Verona and patron saint of Pistoia until the arrival of the relics of the new patron S. Jacopo. The latter stands on the right and each year on July 25, his name day, he is festively decorated and honored with a jousting tournament in medieval costume, the "Giostra dell'Orso."

Duomo S. Zeno e S. Jacopo

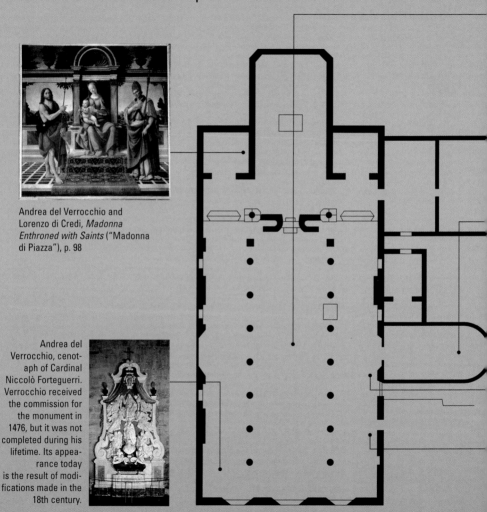

Andrea del Verrocchio and Lorenzo di Credi, *Madonna Enthroned with Saints* ("Madonna di Piazza"), p. 98

Andrea del Verrocchio, cenotaph of Cardinal Niccolò Forteguerri. Verrocchio received the commission for the monument in 1476, but it was not completed during his lifetime. Its appearance today is the result of modifications made in the 18th century.

Nave, p. 98

Silver altar of St. James, p. 100

Coppo di Marcovaldo and his son Salerno, painted Crucifix, c. 1275. On either side of the crucified Jesus on the signed panel Crucifix, the following scenes are portrayed: the Kiss of Judas, the Flagellation, Descent from the Cross, Christ before Pilate, the Entombment, and the Resurrection.

The tomb of the lawyer Cino da Pistoia, with the seated figure of the dead man between the patron saints Zeno and James, c. 1337.

0   33 ft
     10 m

upper parts it is possible to make out traces of the fresco painting that once covered them. Directly under the open roof truss with its original beams, the clerestory windows provide light for this most impressive space. The capitals with their many different designs are outstanding examples of Romanesque architectural sculpture.

The remaining decoration is also very rich. On the right wall there is the 14th-century gravestone of the lawyer and poet Cino da Pistoia, an early example of bourgeois interment within a cathedral. This contemporary of Boccaccio and Petrarch, as the inscription informs us, taught the children of well-to-do families. The large Crucifix of 1275, with its fine miniature representations of the "suffering Christ" and six scenes from his life, is by Coppo di Marcovaldo, one of the first Tuscan painters known by name.

Andrea del Verrocchio (1436–1488) and Lorenzo di Credi (1459–1537), *Madonna di Piazza*, after 1475
Oil on wood, 189 × 191 cm

In the chapel at the choir end of the north aisle, which used to open out on to the town hall square, there hangs the *Madonna di Piazza*, a major work of late Quattrocento painting. On the occasion of the burial of Bishop Donato de' Medici in this chapel the Florentine Andrea del Verrocchio was commissioned to paint this *Madonna and Child Enthroned with*

The Interior

On either side of the nave, seven columns and one pillar lead up to the choir, glowing in its Baroque splendor behind the powerful triumphal arch. The nave walls rise above uniform arcades, and on the

SS. Donatus and John the Baptist," but responsibility for the execution of the work was soon taken over by his pupil Lorenzo di Credi. The picture is an example of a "Sacra Conversazione," the representation of the Virgin Mary with saints.

The silver altar of St. James, 1287–1456
Silversmith work, w. 346 cm × h. 215 cm

The silver altar of St. James is an outstanding example of the art of Tuscan goldsmiths, of which several generations worked between 1287 and the middle of the 15th century. The altar consists of a dossale and a mensa, the antependium of which shows the story of Christ. On both sides there are depictions of the story of the Creation (right) and of scenes from the life of St. James (left). The dossale is decorated with figures in niches, arranged in horizontal layers. The 628 figures, which were partly cast using the *cire-perdue* ("lost wax") process, and were partly hammered out of sheets of silver, and gilded, have style elements ranging from Gothic to early Renaissance.

The starting point was a small altar table with a Byzantine-effect Maria, surrounded by apostles gathered around St. James holding a book and a pilgrim's crook. Little by little it was adorned with an annunciation scene and the scenes on the sides of the antependium and the mensa. The statuettes of St. Gregory and the prophets Isaiah and Jeremiah posed dramatically in quatrefoil panels were ascribed to the young Brunelleschi, who had been trained as a goldsmith.

Battistero di S. Giovanni in Conca

Opposite the west façade of the cathedral is the baptistery started by Cellino di Nese by 1338 to designs by Andrea Pisano as a tall, octagonal cupola construction with a cupola, and decorated with white and green marble stripes. The blind arcades with trefoil arches and mounted by crockets, the tabernacle, and the pinnacles on the corner pillars are in keeping with the contemporary Gothic stylistic repertoire.

A triangular gable and a rose window with simple tracery crown the main entrance. The stepped recessed portal has finely worked capitals and an architrave with reliefs portraying the life of St. John the Baptist. On the tympanum above it John the Baptist, St. Peter and the Madonna and Child stand in front of a stone inlaid background. The Madonna and Child, depicted with great Gothic vitality, are the work of Tommaso and Nino, the sons of Andrea Pisano.

Immediately next to the portal there is a small Gothic external pulpit which was intended for outdoor sermons.

In contrast to the fullness of the decoration on the exterior structure, the interior of the baptistery appears surprisingly plain and spacious. The font, worked from multi-colored marble, was created by the sculptor Lanfranco da Como in 1226.

ping, and a high blind arcade on the ground floor with two blind galleries above it, in decreasing height. Recessed rhombuses, narrow windows, and above all the irregularity of the blind arcades, provide variety. Some Small geometrical ornaments in countless variations decorate the arches.

The steeply proportioned portal has a relief depicting a scene from the Last Supper on the high lintel and bears an inscription dating from the year 1162: *Gruamons Magister Bonu fec[it]. hoc opus* (Master Gruamonte carried out this work). The disciples sit round the table in strict order. The only movement is provided by the figures of St. John the Apostle, who is leaning on the shoulder of his Lord, and Judas Iscariot, who is cast under the table as the villain and portrayed on a much smaller scale.

The Interior

The interior of S. Giovanni reveals it to be one of the rare single-aisled churches. Under this roof truss, which is still open today, the council of elders held its meetings in the 13th century.

S. Giovanni Fuorcivitas

The church of San Giovanni Fuorcivitas is endowed with a very richly designed façade. The first church was built here in the 8th century on a site that was outside the town wall – hence the name. When the town was undergoing renewal and reconstruction in the middle of the 12th century, it was replaced by a new Romanesque building. The north side, which faces the town center, was therefore designed as the main façade.

The church has a delightful overall appearance with its broad front, even stri-

The pulpit was reworked by the oldest employee of Nicola Pisano, the Dominican monk Fra Guglielmo, in 1270. Created in the comparatively old-fashioned, rectangular form, the front shows scenes of the *Washing of the Feet, Crucifixion,* and *Lamentation* as well as the *Descent into Limbo.* On the left are the *Annunciation, Visitation, Birth of Christ,* and *Adoration of the Magi,* while on the right the *Ascension, Virgin Mary and the Apostles, Pentecost,* and *Death of the Virgin* are depicted. The lectern in the center is supported by an ox, lion, eagle, and an angel, the symbols of the four evangelists.

The holy water stoup is the work of Nicola Pisano (*c.* 1225 to 1278 or later). Its supporting pillar is made up of the personification of the three Christian virtues – faith, hope, and charity – while the four cardinal virtues – prudence, temperance, fortitude, and justice – are woven, as it were, into the stoup. The impressive 14th–century polyptych depicting the *Madonna and Child with Saints* was painted by the pupil of Giotto, Taddeo Gaddi (c. 1300–1366). The group of the *Visitation* made of glazed terracotta by Luca della Robbia (1399/1400–1482) is particularly expressive, especially in the way it represents the difference in age between the two pregnant women.

In a Colored Robe of Marble – Tuscan Incrustation

It is impossible to imagine Tuscan churches without the stripes, without the ornamentation, without the wonderful marble facing of the interior and exterior. Nowhere else does one find such a concentration of marble-incrusted buildings. The beauty and opulence typical of altars or chapels is to be found throughout the whole space of a church, even on its outside walls. The exotic patterns, Lombard animal motifs, strict geometric forms, and imaginative décor in marble that characterize Tuscan churches, create a profound and lasting impression. The fine stone-built medieval churches and the great structures of the Renaissance pale in comparison.

The raw stone or brick walls of these Romanesque churches were faced with precious stone, mostly marble, which was inlaid in a similar fashion to the technique of wood inlay. There are two distinct styles, one predominating in and around Florence and and the other in and around Pisa. Dark green marble is laid between the light slabs of the Baptistery in Florence and the church of San Miniato al Monte. Horizontal stripes, vertical lines, frames, and arches take up the constructional motifs of the architecture and articulate the wall surfaces – a function which elsewhere is fulfilled by sculptural decorations, arches, columns, pillars, or cornices. This "architectonic" application of decorative elements spread throughout the area around Florence from the 11th century onwards and is to be found in the churches of SS. Apostoli and S. Stefano al Ponte in Florence, at the Badia in Fiesole, and the collegiate church of S. Andrea in Empoli.

This variable blend of architecture and décor, indeed the rediscovery and application

Collegiata S. Andrea (façade), Empoli

of these building forms in uniform harmony, is attributable to Classical antiquity. This leads on to the idea of a proto-Renaissance, in which Classical antiquity was reborn, heralding the actual Renaissance. In the age of the poet Dante the Florentine Baptistery was indeed seen as belonging to Classical antiquity. This form of marble facing still lives on in the late-15th-century "Classical" Renaissance church of S. Maria delle Carceri in Prato.

This Pisan-Romanesque style, on the other hand, springs from quite different influences. The cathedral in Pisa is striking for its stripe pattern, ornamental rhombuses and medallions which have no formal relationship to the architecture, unlike the

Detail of the marble floor with the Sienese she-wolf, Duomo S. Maria Assunta, Siena

ornamentation in Florence. The decoration ignores the elements of the architecture, or at best emphasizes their rhythm or supports their form. Many elements of the Pisan decorative style, such as the varying color of the arches, are reminiscent of the northern Alpine churches of the Ottonians, while certain ornamental motifs, such as the medallions or the pattern over the blind arcades of the west façade, are redolent of oriental designs. In the buildings which followed Pisa, such as the façade of the church of S. Michele in Foro in Lucca, we can see the addition of Lombard influences.

The highly decorative style of Pisa cathedral is much more widespread in Tuscany than the strict Florentine proto-Renaissance style. The awe-inspiring interior decoration of the cathedral at Siena probably represents the last creation conceived in the Pisan mold. French Gothic influences such as in S. Maria della Spina in Pisa and demands of the mendicant orders for simpler buildings caused later architectural developments to take different routes.

Ospedale del Ceppo

According to legend an angel is supposed to have instructed a married couple from Pistoia to erect a hospital in the place where they would find a tree stump flowering in winter. Indeed a hospice and a religious fraternity were founded here. There are records of a hospital and a pilgrims' lodge on this spot going back to 1287. The name "ceppo" is derived from the tree stump or hollowed-out root in which alms were collected for the upkeep of the social institution.

At the beginning of the 16th century the Florentine hospice took over the running of the Ospedale del Ceppo. Financial problems and the dominance of Florence had led to this change, and it was only under the management of the Florentine Carthusian Leonardo Bonafede that the construction of the site was finally completed.

Like Brunelleschi's architecture of the foundlings' home in Florence, the building in Pistoia received a new ent-rance hall. Here six semicircular arches rest on slim pillars. Instead of a cornice, there is a terracotta frieze which groups the arcade together. Colorful medallions deco-rate the spandrels between the arches. The entrance hall has a lighter and less concentrated effect than the work of Brunelleschi, although the influence of this significant model is very noticeable. The frieze and the tondi with the representations of the Virgin Mary, the coats of arms of Pistoia, the hospital, and the Medici are the work of Santi Buglioni, an artist who came from the workshop of Luca della Robbia. The last panel was created by a successor who clearly had not acquired the secret of the famous glazing.

Santi Buglioni (1494–1576),
***Feeding the Hungry* (detail), 1522–1576**
Majolica, c. 500 cm

The "Seven Works of Mercy" are the subject of the frieze: clothing the naked, taking in strangers, caring for the sick, comforting the prisoner, burying the dead, feeding the hungry, and giving water to the thirsty. The single scenes are reproduced with great liveliness and a wealth of anecdotal detail. Of partic-ular note are the accurate observation of the clothing, the concise characterization of the faces and the detailed representa-tion of the gifts and the décor. The bene-factor in each case is Leonardo Bonafede, the head of the hospital, who can be iden-tified in the middle of the scenes wearing the costume of the order.

S. Andrea

Gruamonte (active around 1166),
Journey of the Magi (detail), 1166
Marble

As with almost all churches in Pistoia, S. Andrea originated in the mid-12th century and was converted from what was originally a basilica, dating from the 8th century. In documents it is mentioned as a "pieve suburbana," since it lay outside the inner ring of the city wall that enclosed the Langobard-Frankish settlement.

The façade is in the 12th-century Pisan style. The gable floor remained incomplete, with the customary rows of arches missing. On the lower floor the façade is articulated with five very steep, irregular blind arches. The striped pattern, the recessed rhombi, and the panels composed of small geometrical figures are the kind of decorative elements normally to be found on floors or as the backgrounds to reliefs, and are particular to the sculptor Gruamonte. He was active here as an architect between 1160 and 1170, and introduced the steeply proportioned façades and tall, narrow naves typical of Pistoia, of the kind that are found inside this columned basilica.

The main doorway is decorated with Romanesque figures. The Magi appear twice on the architrave: on the left they are on their journey, while on the right they are standing before the Madonna and Child. King Herod is depicted in the center. The sculpturally worked figures are very lifelike, the folds of their garments creating a free-flowing play of light and shadow. Nevertheless there is a very strict underlying order, a mixture of ceremonial and individual expression, characteristic of the sculptural works of Gruamonte, who created this relief in 1166 together with his brother Adeodato.

The door lintel rests on capitals, which are also decorated with sculptures. Another artist, Henricus, created the scenes of the *Annunciation to Zacharias* on the left, the *Visitation*, and, on the right, the *Annunciation to Anne*. Two lions, one with a person, the other with a fabulous beast between its claws, support the archivolts and complete the portal.

Pescia

S. Francesco

The village of Pescia, on the river of the same name, was rebuilt in the 14th century after its complete destruction by the rulers of Lucca. Under the Medici family it became a town and the seat of a bishop. The simple church of S. Francesco was built in about 1300 as a Gothic hall church with an open roof truss and three vaulted apsidal chapels.

Bonaventura Berlighieri (c. 1207–1274), panel of St. Francis, 1235
Tempera on wood, 160 × 123 cm

The most important decorative feature of S. Francesco, which served as the burial church for the rich merchants of Pescia, is the large altarpiece by the Luccan painter Bonaventura Berlinghieri. In an inscription beneath the feet of St. Francis he signed and dated his work 1235, only nine years after the saint's death. The panel is the oldest surviving example of this type of picture, portraying the saint in a central position surrounded by scenes of his life and works, a format which until then had been reserved for the Madonna and Child.

The proportionately over-large figure of St. Francis stands on the central axis. The six scenes from his life arranged on either side of him include, in the central position, the *Sermon to the Birds* and the *Healing of Bartholomew of Neri*, two events which encapsulate the saint's love of man and nature. The *Receiving the Stigmata*, as the most important stage in his life, shows St. Francis as a disciple of Christ.

The artist presents a comprehensive repertoire of healing deeds and miracles a very short time after the monk's death and canonization, and it is probable that he received instructions from his patrons, the Franciscans, about the choice of scenes to be represented.

Collodi

Villa Garzoni

A few miles west of Pescia lies the picturesque village of Collodi, perched on a hill ridge. The Villa Garzoni stands in a prominent position at the lower end of the village, at the entrance to the narrow river valley. This building, an impressive Baroque, four-story building with belvedere tower and roof statues, was converted between 1633 and 1652 by the Garzoni family from the earlier medieval castle. The garden, originally in Italian style, was laid out at the same time, and forms an impressive backdrop on the steep slopes. In the 18th century it was embellished with the addition of terraces, balustrades, mazes, waterfalls, fountains, grottoes, and statuary, from plans by the architect Ottaviano Diodati. The garden's reputation spread all over Europe and influenced the designers of the gardens of Versailles, Fontainebleau, and Potsdam.

Collodi, Villa Garzoni

is a group of bronze sculptures designed by Emilio Greco, representing the story of Pinocchio, the stubborn wooden puppet whose long nose was a punishment for telling lies. The sculptures represent the tree from whose wood Pinocchio is carved, then Pinocchio looking at the blue fairy, and the falcon, which, hovering above the oak tree, frees him from the noose. A path leads through the park past 21 bronze sculptures by Pietro Consagra, portraying the main episodes and characters from the various adventures of the little hero. At the end Pinocchio reappears to take his leave of the visitor.

Emilio Greco (1913–1995), Pinocchio and the Fairy, *1956, bronze, h. 500 cm*

Parco di Pinocchio

The writer Carlo Lorenzini (1826–1890), author of the famous children's story of Pinocchio, took his pen name Collodi in honor of his mother's birthplace. As a memorial to him a Pinocchio Park was created in the 1950s. At the entrance there

Pietro Conagra (b. 1920), Pinocchio Waves Goodbye, *1972, bronze*

Villa Celle

In Santomato near Pistoia there is one of the few Tuscan important collections of contemporary art. The collection, owned by the entrepreneur Giuliano Gori, consists of works of "environment art," and is regarded as one of the finest of its kind in Europe. Gori invites major international artists to his estate, the Fattoria di Celle, to create works specially for the place. They work and live at the villa, in many cases for several months, and receive free board and lodging and payment in kind. The 50-acre (20-hectare) site, laid out in about 1800 as an English landscape park with glades, lakes and cascades, has now been turned into a quite unique "Gesamtkunstwerk" and museum of modern art.

The visitor walks along Bukichi Inoue's meditation path into the earth's interior, encounters the "death of Ephialthes" by Anne and Patrick Poirier at the waterfall, stands before the "endive" made by Ulrich Rückriem, and wanders between magical places like the one created by Olavi Lannu and futuristic works such as the metal techno-arsenal by Dennis Oppenheim. There is a sound installation by Max Neuhaus and a labyrinth created by Robert Morris that is reminiscent of the marble decoration of Tuscan churches. A temple of Venus stands in the middle of a circle of stone benches, trees, and shrubs, and around the whole area the American Joseph Kosuth has built a 6-foot (2-meter) high glass wall so as to divide the area into one part that is accessible and another that is permanently closed off.

The sculpture park has spilled over into the surrounding agricultural land, so that a bronze fruit basket by Ian Hamilton Finlay is to be found in the middle of an olive grove, for example, and a collection of bronze hollow bodies created by the Polish artist Magdalena Abakanowicz stands in a nearby meadow, a monument to the people who have worked this land for centuries. Giuliano Gori calls this type of artistic creation "site-specific works," an echo of earlier times when artists regularly executed their works for villas and palaces "on site."

The Interior – Michelangelo Pistoletto (b. 1933), *The Tail of Arte Povera*, 1980
Installation

As well as commissioning works of art, in the long tradition of patronage, Gori also buys at exhibitions and from studios and galleries. The many rooms of his villa, as well as its outbuildings, are filled with numerous works of art, and the paintings alone would be enough to stock a whole museum. As in the case of the outdoor works, the owner allows the artists to select the appropriate room or corridor for their works and installations. So, for example, Sol LeWitt has covered the wall areas in the attic with geometrical drawings, while in another room Michelangelo Pistoletto has created a memorial to "Arte Povera."

Arte Ambientale – Twentieth-Century Art in Tuscany

Lorenzo Bruni

Daniel Spoerri (b. 1930), Unicorns – Navel of the World, *1991, bronze, 280 × 90 × 50 cm, diam. 9.30 m, Sculpture Park, Seggiano, Monte Amiata*

One of the essential properties of art is its ability to create a world beyond reality in its works. Even a particular geographical location may acquire an unmistakable character of its own through art, and this phenomenon can be observed especially clearly in many places in Tuscany. However, in its search for an international artistic language the early 20th-century avant garde pursued a self-referential art without location or topography. From that time, the specific quality in the way localities, squares or even whole cities were laid out artistically and aesthetically rather vanished. For much of the 20th-century, the artistic shaping of environments in modern art was restricted to functionality and function and defined by the fundamental antithesis of art and space.

Only towards the end of the 1950s did attitudes change as efforts were made to liberate art from the obligatory rounds of museums and galleries and to relocate it in reality, in all its influence and power, so that art could again leave behind visible traces and unmistakable signs in the environment.

Pioneers of this kind of contextual art were the American exponents of Land Art (or Earth Art), who integrated their works in nature as "site-specific work" in order to emphasize the character of a particular landscape. Tuscany is especially suited to this approach, for nowhere else does the enduring intervention of mankind over the centuries – visible at a geological and an archaeological level – show such respectful accord with the natural environment. Moreover, in Tuscany the relationship between town and country has been completely reversed compared with earlier times. In most parts of the world, since the Middle Ages, it has been the towns which have dominated and after a fashion ennobled the surrounding countryside. In Tuscany, it has been the other way round. In terms of our present-day aesthetic values and lifestyle, it is the Tuscan landscape that has enriched the towns. It is no coincidence that there are more sculpture parks here than anywhere else in Italy – parks that are directly reminiscent of the landscape backgrounds of the great fresco cycles, and in which Renaissance-style artistic patronage lives on.

When we look at a selection of site-specific works of art in the region, we find a noticeable trend towards developing new artistic forms of expression beyond painting and sculpture that can be generally classified as "installations." In line with a change in the concept of art, the interest of the installation artist concerns the physical presence of the artistic object rather than its mimetic or illusionist function. It is thus art that enters real space, not reality that is elevated into art.

Mauro Staccioli, Tower of Luciana '92, *1992, cement and metal, Torre di Luciana near San Casciano in Val di Pesa*

This crossing of artistic frontiers into the surrounding space began with painting, which had cast off its chains by exploring non-painterly concepts. Around 1960, American Neo-Dadaists and French Nouveau Réalisme began to incorporate real everyday objects into their pictures, thereby breaking up the essentially flat, two-dimensional nature of the works.

In 1996 and 1998 respectively, Daniel Spoerri and Niki de Saint Phalle (both born in 1930, and adherents of the Nouveau Réalisme school) created sculpture parks in Tuscany. Saint

Phalle's is in a wood near Capalbio. In close collaboration with her partner Jean Tinguely (1925–1991), she created works that are a cross between sculpture and architecture and that the public can walk through, bathed in a sea of light from gleaming mosaic stones.

Spoerri meanwhile laid out a sculpture garden in the park surrounding his house in Seggiano at the foot of Monte Amiata (now the home of the Spoerri Foundation), to accommodate his own and his artist friends' works. The bronze assemblages made of everyday objects are animist "sculptural situations," demonstrating that all things have souls. Like an initiation rite, they describe a course intended to drive out human fear, protect humanity from self-loss and steer it towards a reunion with itself and with nature.

Having mastered everyday objects, at the end of the 1960s art developed into Minimalist Art and Land Art, and began to probe areas which until then had been the sole preserve of man and nature. The principal results of this reconnaissance are in the romantic park of the Celle estate near Pistoia.

The ambitiousness of these years is immediately apparent here: not only did it involve artistically reshaping "locality," whereby works of art had to hold their own against everyday reality, but it also meant redefining art's relationship with nature. It was a time of radical change, in which ideas were formed in

Eliseo Mattiacci (born 1940),
Compressed Balance, *1994,*
metal, San Gimignano

Mario Merz (born 1925), Untitled, 1997–1999, aluminum and neon, San Casciano in Chianti

nature itself by the landscape, and the direct experience of nature took the place of the image of nature.

Famous examples of the development of such spatially referential art are to be found outside the Museo per L'Arte Contemporanea Luigi Pecci in Prato, not far from Florence. They are remarkable not for their confrontation with space but for the attempt at a dialogue via a new materialization and definition of space such as we find in the works of Anne and Patrick Poirier and Mauro Staccioli as well. These all plumb the possibility of a more precise definition of location. Indeed, the Poiriers (both born in 1942) achieved a harmony between figurative metaphorical symbols and the architecture of the Medici villa in Pratolino (now Villa Demidoff).

Staccioli (born in 1937) himself created a link between material symbols and the Tuscan landscape in Torre di Luciana near San Casciano in Val di Pesa, not far from Florence. The latter highlights the contrast between clear basic forms (in this case a crescent) in his work and the natural environment, marked by a provocative lack of balance and emphasized by the use of concrete, a material typical of modern civilization.

Marking another step towards a newly constituted relationship between art and space is Arte Povera ("poor art"), which limits itself to using the most basic materials, with the aim of fathoming the true nature of things. Arte Povera was an important prerequisite for Conceptual Art, which shifts the focus from the object itself to the idea. The works of artists who sought to integrate their works not just into nature, but also into existing locations such as churches, urban neighborhoods or areas, must be considered particularly remarkable and courageous in such a period of exploration. These qualities became evident in an event organised by the Museo all'Aperto (Open-air Museum) in San Gimignano called *Affinità Elettive* (Elective Affinities). Of the five participating artists, the Greek Jannis Kounellis (born in 1936) emphasizes the chronological continuity of the site by including the campanile of S. Jacopo and its dimensions, but also refers to alienating, almost abstracting forces by muting a small bell with an iron rod. Similarly, Eliseo Mattiacci places a railway sleeper on a metal ball in a seemingly impossible balancing act.

The disparity between these two items echoes the contrast between the medieval fortifications and the broad landscape opening out before them, thus underlining the physical risk inherent in this tension.

A similar re-evaluation of ambience by means of programmatic alienation is the hallmark of an initiative at Peccioli in the province of Pisa, where since 1991 international artists such as Hidetoshi Nagasawa, Vittorio Messina and Vittorio Corsini have been invited to create long-term installations.

One of the artists is Fortuyn O'Brien, who erected "unusable" stone benches on cylindrical rollers at the entrance to a church outside the village. They are visible, yet not real resting places.

Among the various activities manifesting a degree of continuity is an exhibition organized annually by five communities in the Sienese Chianti called Arte all'Arte, which has likewise produced permanent installations such as the work of Ilya Kabakov (born in 1933) in Colle Val d'Elsa and the beautiful work by Mimmo Paladino (born in 1948) at the 12th-century Fonte delle Fate fountain in the industrial town of Poggibonsi. Its basin brings together various clay-made forms of primeval life – including humans and reptiles – in foetal position, as though the basin were a uterus.

Another interesting initiative is the biennial Tuscia Electa, which takes place in various communes between Florence and Siena and encourages dialogue with places whose onetime importance has been forgotten even by the local inhabitants of the area.

On the medieval town wall of San Casciano in Val di Pesa there is a symbol of natural freedom, still visible today, created by Mario Merz (born in 1925): deer followed by a Fibonacci number sequence, symbolizing human will regulating and controlling nature.

Common to all the developments mentioned here that involve the environment is an approach to artistic expression that functions according to the rules of nature, prefers natural materials and thus tends to follow natural aesthetic criteria rather than experimental arrangements. The same applies to

Dopopaessaggio (Imitating Landscape) at the Castello di Santa Maria Novella at Tavernelle.

These are all contemporary examples of the interdependent relationship of art and landscape in Tuscany, which in the past provided exemplary solutions and over the last fifty years were regarded not as a burden but as a challenge. Here mutual reference, dialogue and the present are all consciously permitted, made possible and even promoted.

Mimmo Paladino, The Sleepers,
25 elements in bronze on iron plates, installation in the fountain basin of the 12th-century Fonte delle Fate for Arte all'Arte 1998, Poggibonsi

Prato

Prato

Prato, today the third largest town in central Italy, was able to break away from the domination of Florence in 1992 when it became the capital of a newly created province. After centuries, Prato was once again an independent city. Situated on the banks of the river Bisenzio, it has no evidence of an Etruscan or Roman past, but in Roman times there was a commercial center in the nearby countryside, known as "Pagus Cornius." This developed in early medieval times into a settlement named "Borgo al Cornio," but it had no city rights and therefore, at that time, no chance of becoming a bishop's seat.

During the Lombard period, Prato was under the protection of Count Hildebrand. His son Alberto founded the powerful Alberti family, whose members were to become some of the most important feudal lords of Tuscany. The name "Prato" (Latin *pratum*), meaning meadow, derived from a a piece of land where a market was held, between the fortress and the town, and was later transferred to the settlement itself. Civic development followed a similar pattern to that of other Tuscan towns: in 1187, Prato received imperial recognition as a free commune; ten years later, it replaced the consul with the *podestà*, who was in turn replaced by the *capitano del popolo*. From 1248 onwards, Prato was an

Castello dell'Imperatore, Prato

imperial base on the road to Apulia. Today, the only remaining evidence of this period of imperial power is the "Castello dell'Imperatore," fortified with Ghibelline battlements, which Emperor Frederick II had built on the foundations of the old castle of the Alberti. It lies outside the contemporary – 12th century – fortifications, but within the later ring of walls dating from the 14th century, which are still well preserved. The fortress is the only Hohenstaufen castle in northern and central Italy built to the design of the imperial castles of Apulia.

After the end of Hohenstaufen rule, internal strife broke out, which was increased by pressure from other Tuscan cities, whether Guelph or Ghibelline. In 1313, the civic government sought the protection of the French royal house of Anjou from Naples, but the latter sold the *signoria* of Prato to Florence in 1351. Florence now enjoyed control of a town whose finely worked textiles and excellent goldsmiths' products had been traded and famed throughout markets of Europe since the 13th century.

During the Cinquecento the arts flourished thanks to the patronage of the Medici, but afterwards the economy went into decline. It was not until the 19th century that Prato became a prosperous textile center, referred to as the "Manchester of Italy."

Prato

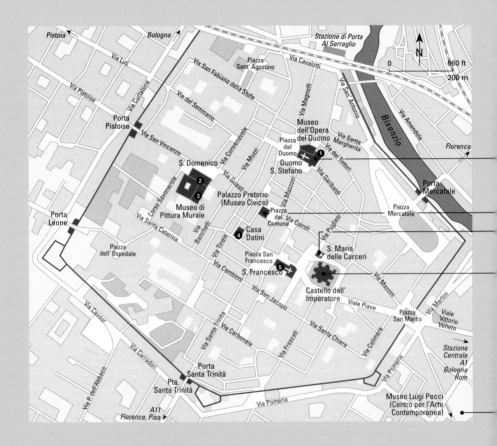

Duomo S. Stefano, Piazza del Duomo, p. 128

Palazzo Pretorio (Museo Civico), 1 Piazza del Comune, p. 136

S. Maria delle Carceri, Piazza S. Maria delle Carceri, p. 142

Castello dell'Imperatore, Piazza S. Maria delle Carceri, p. 124

Other sights of interest
(not covered elsewhere in this book):

1 Museo dell'Opera del Duomo, 49 Piazza del Duomo

2 S. Domenico, Piazza S. Domenico

3 Museo di Pittura Murale, 8 Piazza S. Domenico

4 Casa Datini, 33 Via Ser Lapo Mazzei

5 S. Francesco, Piazza S. Francesco

Museo Pecci (Centro per l'Arte Contemporanea), 277–291 Viale della Repubblica, p. 146

Duomo S. Stefano

Prato developed from the settlement that grew up round the former parish church of S. Stefano, first mentioned in 998. The church was raised to the status of cathedral in 1653 when Prato became a bishopric – a privilege which the city had to share with Pistoia for 300 years to come.

Construction of the present building began in 1211 and continued for several centuries. The Lombard architect Guidetto da Como supervised construction of the nave walls with their blind arches, derived from the design of the cathedrals of Pisa and Lucca. From 1317 onwards, the structure was extended to the east, and in 1340 the Gothic-inspired, six-story campanile was added. After these alterations, the western side was no longer in tune with contemporary taste: from 1385 to 1457 the present tall, elegant façade was added. Traditional elements, including the green and white marble incrustations, were effectively employed and were combined with modern Gothic forms such as the tracery above the gable.

On the left-hand side of the Duomo, a small chapel with a star-shaped window adjoins the façade. It was built between 1385 and 1395 to hold the "Sacro Cingolo," the Sacred Girdle of the Virgin, one of the most precious relics of the cult of the Virgin Mary. The Mother of God is supposed to have handed the Girdle to the apostle Thomas on her Assumption into Heaven, and Thomas in his turn presented it to a priest. According to legend, a merchant from Prato, called Michele Dagomari, received the Girdle as part of the dowry at his marriage to a girl called Maria in Jerusalem in 1141. Shortly before his death, he left it to the church of S. Stefano. Today this relic is still displayed on church and secular holidays.

Michelozzo (1396–1472) and Donatello (1386–1466), exterior pulpit, 1428–1438
Marble and bronze, relief panels, 73.5 × 79 cm

The festive appearance of the cathedral façade is heightened by the exterior pulpit at the right-hand corner. It is from here that the Sacred Girdle is displayed: as early as the 13th century there was a wooden balcony on this spot for the presentation of the Girdle. The pulpit is a masterpiece created during the period 1428–38 by the Florentine sculptors Michelozzo and Donatello. It consists of a baldachin supported by a central column and a round pulpit body resting on handsomely worked consoles and a bronze base. The Classically inspired architecture, which makes use of impressive proportions to link the body and baldachin of the pulpit with the main building, is the work of Michelozzo.

Donatello probably began his part of the task, a frieze of dancing putti, in 1433. The frieze consists of seven rectangular reliefs, each divided from the other by two fluted pilasters. The scenes of the reliefs are sculpturally worked from their gold mosaic background. The artist clearly demonstrates the experience gained on his recent trip to Rome. The design of the relief panels, for instance, is reminiscent of Roman sarcophagi, the putti inspired by Classical genii. With flying garments, half-naked, and full of the joys of life, the plump *amorini* are dancing and playing music in praise of the Virgin Mary. Their unrestrained lively movement makes them almost seem to burst out of the containing architectural framework. To protect them from environmental damage, the original reliefs have been moved to the cathedral museum and replaced on site by copies.

Duomo S. Stefano

Cappella del Sacro Cingolo (Chapel of the Sacred Girdle): Giovanni Pisano, *Madonna del Sacro Cingolo*, c. 1317. The Madonna and Child, with its dynamic folds of drapery, is one of the sculptor's last works.

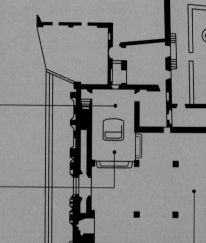

Cappella del Sacro Cingolo (Chapel of the Sacred Girdle): Agnolo Gaddi's fresco cycle on the *Life of the Virgin* and the legend of the relic, still honored today, of the Virgin's Girdle, was created in 1392–1395.

Interior, p. 132.

Benedetto da Maiano, *Madonna dell'Olivo*, c. 1480. The sculptor originally created the enthroned terracotta Madonna and Child for a private owner. The stone tabernacle and the marble relief with its *Pietà* are attributed to his brother.

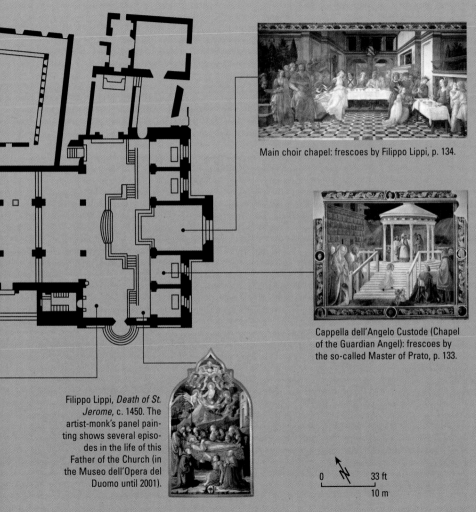

Main choir chapel: frescoes by Filippo Lippi, p. 134.

Cappella dell'Angelo Custode (Chapel of the Guardian Angel): frescoes by the so-called Master of Prato, p. 133.

Filippo Lippi, *Death of St. Jerome*, c. 1450. The artist-monk's panel painting shows several episodes in the life of this Father of the Church (in the Museo dell'Opera del Duomo until 2001).

0   33 ft
10 m

The Interior

The various phases of construction can also be distinguished in the design of the interior: the broad arches are Lombard, but the green and white marble bands, on the other hand, show Pisano-Romanesque influence. The roof beams, originally exposed, were vaulted in 1676. The dark gleam of the *verde di Prato* of the columns, a blackish-green serpentine from the Prato area, is impressive. The broad transept opens up before us, with its Gothic ribbed vaulting, colorful glass windows and the flat end-wall of the choir chapels, which follows the design of Cistercian churches.

The "Cappella del Sacro Cingolo," which lies to the left of the entrance, was built in 1385 for the safekeeping and veneration of the Sacred Girdle of the Virgin Mary. The frescoes on the chapel walls, executed by Agnolo Gaddi between 1392 and 1395, describe the life of the Virgin and portray scenes from the legend of the Sacred

Girdle. On the high altar is the marble sculpture of the *Madonna and Child* (1317) by Giovanni Pisano. The attractive, skillfully worked bronze screen dates from the middle of the 15th century. The chalice-shaped pulpit is the work of two Florentine Renaissance sculptors during the years 1469–1473: Mino da Fiesole was responsible for the reliefs of *Herod's Feast* and the *Beheading of St. John the Baptist*; while the *Assumption of the Virgin*, the *Stoning of St. Stephen* and the entombment of the church patron are by Antonio Rossellino.

Paolo Uccello (c. 1397–1475), *Birth of the Virgin*, c. 1435
Fresco

In the "Cappella dell'Assunta" (Chapel of the Assumption), which lies to the right of the main choir, the walls are completely covered with frescoes. Here, in the 1530s, Paolo Uccello painted the four saints Paul, Jerome, Francis, and Dominic, and also the virtues of *Faith, Charity, Hope,* and *Fortitude* in the vaulting, the *Dispute of St. Stephen*, the *Birth of the Virgin,* and the *Presentation of the Virgin in the Temple* in the lunettes, together with the 15 portraits in the tondi of the frieze. Further scenes from the life of St. Stephen were completed by Andrea di Giusto around 1450.

The compositional structure of the scene in the *Birth of the Virgin* is perfect. Using his own individual perspectival structure, Uccello evenly distributes the people and the architectural elements in the space. The individuation of each figure is achieved by special characterization. Also remarkable is the narrative expression in the description of details, and the strong colors, skillfully combined even in the geometric decoration.

Filippo Lippi (c. 1406–1469),
Herod's Feast, **c. 1461–1465**
Fresco

In the main choir chapel Filippo Lippi painted, between 1452 and 1468, with interruptions, one of the most important fresco cycles of the early Renaissance. Of the scenes from the life of St. John the Baptist, *Herod's Feast* is surely the most fascinating. Inside a hall, presented in central perspective, a crowd of guests is sitting at a banquet. The structure of the architecture, the breadth of the room and the painted views out over the landscape point to links with the Florentine architect Filippo Brunelleschi. The many portrait-style heads, in particular the powerful

male figure standing directly in the fore-ground, are reminiscent of Piero della Francesca from Arezzo. Filippo Lippi was an eight-year-old orphan when he was taken in by the Carmelites of S. Maria del Carmine in Florence. In 1421 he took his vows and began, under the influence of the frescoes of Masaccio, to paint in the Brancacci chapel in Florence.

Filippo Lippi, *Salome Dancing*
(Detail of *Herod's Feast*)

Characteristic of, and a new feature in, the painting of Filippo Lippi is the conception of the figures, with their gentle movements, the delicate lines of the drawing and the exceedingly light appearance of

the fabrics. This can be seen in all its perfection in the figure of Salome dancing. Her gracefully arched body seems to float above the paving of the floor – even her garment flutters as if it had been released from the laws of gravity and, in subliminal eroticism, it allows the forms of the body to be made out under the thin material. The head is inclined gracefully.

An entire generation of artists was influenced by this Salome. In his works of Botticelli, his pupil, and of Filippino, the son of Filippo Lippi, and even of Leonardo, the figure turns into graceful figures of Spring or angels of the Annunciation. Filippo Lippi is supposed to have portrayed his beloved, the nun Lucrezia Buti, in the figure of Salome. In 1456 he eloped with Lucrezia, whose features from that date also determined the faces of his Madonnas. In 1461, Cosimo il Vecchio de' Medici arranged a papal dispensation for the couple, so that they could marry.

Palazzo Pretorio – Museo Civico

The Palazzo Pretorio developed from a Romanesque brick building. The tower, originally designed as a residential building, became the property of the *capitano del popolo* in 1284, and he set up his offices there. In the mid-14th century the palace was enlarged and modernized, and an extension built of ashlar was added to the old residential tower.

An interesting feature is that the two styles of building remained visibly separate, side by side. One can still note today the different stages of con-struction by the variations in material. Even the various shapes of the win-dows were not adjusted to match each other: Romanesque round-arched windows contrast with beautiful biforate Gothic windows.

Since 1850, this palazzo has also housed the Museo Civico, which has an inte-resting collection of 14th to 18th century art.

The "Self-Made Man" of the Middle Ages

Statue of Francesco di Marco Datini in Prato

"In the name of God and of profit" was the motto Francesco di Marco Datini wrote on his ledgers. The life of this merchant, whose more than life-size statue stands in the Piazza del Comune in Prato, could surely not be summed up more fittingly. Together with his entire fortune, he left to the city over 100,000 private and business letters, more than 500 ledgers, and thousands of miscellaneous business documents such as contracts, bills of exchange, and bank drafts. It is through these that posterity has learned about his business deals, his social relationships with relatives and friends, his tormented anxiety about goods, ships, health, and his own soul's salvation.

Born in 1335 as the illegitimate son of the Prato innkeeper Marco di Datini, the enterprising Francesco, after the death of his parents, went to take up an apprenticeship in Florence in 1348, the year of the Great Plague. Having heard stories from Tuscan merchants about the golden opportunities for advancement in Avignon, he left for the flourishing trading city on the Rhône with only 150 florins in his pocket – and also with the dream of wealth and a free life, and the intention of becoming a merchant.

It was customary for the sons of great merchant families to be trained first in the trading houses of their home cities, then in

Master Biadaiolo, Distribution of Grain to the Needy at Or San Michele, *1335–1340, miniature, codex* Il Biadaiolo, *Biblioteca Medicea Laurenziana, Florence*

offices it was just as necessary to learn foreign languages, laws, and customs as it was to be politically sensitive and have diplomatic skills.

Francesco Datini, who did not have these advantages, probably at first lodged in the Avignon apartment and office of one of the Tuscan merchants who had settled in large numbers in the overcrowded city, in the area between the luxurious papal palace and the narrow quarters of the artisans and the poor, hoping for profitable business.

A few years later, Datini was already independent. Active in the weapons trade, he was earning so much that he was able to send for his brother to join him. With a series of changing Tuscan partners, he founded profitable trading companies for extensive import and export transactions. He dealt in salt, wine, oil, vinegar, honey, and spices, in dyes, Catalonian leather goods, French enamel work, linen from Genoa, silk, taffeta, and costly liturgical robes from Lucca, in painted marriage chests and silverware from Florence and, most importantly, in the newly fashionable foldable altar panels for private worship. "I could make as much money as I wanted," he said later, and for the time being he ignored the constant pleas for him to

branches elsewhere in Italy, and finally in France, Flanders, or England, because in order to build up and direct the network of family-owned foreign banking and trading branch

return home and settle down into a more ordered way of life. Even after his return to Prato in 1382, the man who (according to his best friend Lapo Mazzei) "always had women, ate nothing but partridges, worshipped art and money as idols and thereby forgot the Creator and himself" spent almost all his time on business journeys. In his letters he gave his young wife Margherita precise instructions for the preparation of his favorite dishes: a good soup with creamy cheese, fresh eels and other fish, delicate meats such as veal, pork, goat, lamb, and game, large beans and chickpeas, flavored with mint, rosemary, thyme, and marjoram, and fresh figs, peaches, and nuts.

With increasing age, he too fell under the influence of the fear, widespread among merchants in particular, that he had not given enough care to the life to come. In 1252, a gold coin was minted in Florence, which as the florin rapidly became the main currency in European trade. Now that money had become the equivalent of time, deals involving interest and even outright exploitative usury flourished. The church indeed condemned the sale of time, but there was not a single businessman who did not increase his wealth with percentages and interest by dealing in exchange and payment by installments. In order to buy his freedom from the feared tortures of hell, Datini, whose exchange office in Avignon had been one of the best addresses in the city, left his entire wealth – except for a sum to support his wife and daughter – to his own, secular charitable foundation. His distinctive individualism foreshadowed the character of the Renaissance man of around a hundred years later, a man such as Giovanni Rucellai, who said of himself: "For 50 years now I have done nothing but make money and spend money. And it has become clear to me that spending money brings even greater pleasure than making money."

Niccolò di Pietro Gerini,
The Story of St. Matthew *(detail), c. 1395, wall fresco,*
S. Francesco, Prato

Her porcelain–colored face still bears signs of the late Gothic aloofness which in Lippi's work was not transformed into characteristic liveliness until he fell in love with Lucrezia Buti. Francesco di Marco Datini, merchant of Prato, is kneeling in front of the throne: he has left his fortune to the charitable "Ceppo" foundation he has established. He is leading four *buonuomini,* meaning voluntary helpers, towards the blessing of the Christ Child and the intercession of the saints.

Giovanni da Milano (active c. 1346–1349), *Polyptych,* 1360
Tempera on wood, 166 × 166 cm

With its intensive coloring and austere forms, this polyptych by Giovanni da Milano, a painter who came from Como, introduces northern Italian elements into the Tuscan painting of the Trecento. The work was created in 1360, and the artist has signed it below the centrally enthroned Mother of God. On her left are St. Catherine of Alexandria and St. Bernard, on her right SS. Bartholomew and Barnabas. The predellas with scenes from the life of the saints are noteworthy in particular for the miniature-like, finely painted landscapes.

Filippo Lippi, *Madonna del Ceppo,* 1454
Tempera on wood, 187 × 120 cm

Flanked by St. Stephen and St. John the Baptist, the Virgin is enthroned in front of a gleaming gold background.

S. Maria delle Carceri

An image of the Virgin Mary on the wall of a prison which stood outside the first city wall next to the Castello dell'Imperatore had since the Middle Ages possessed the reputation of working miracles. In its honor the church of S. Maria delle Carceri was commissioned from Giulano di Sangallo (c. 1445–1516), and construction began in 1484. Giuliano created a central-plan building, the ideal form of the Renaissance, with four arms. He based it on Brunelleschi's Pazzi chapel in Florence, but developed the latter's design further to achieve perfect symmetry: the area of each arm was to equal half that of the central square chamber. The decorative white and green marble incrustation of the exterior structure is derived from early Romanesque Florentine buildings. The simple, geometrical austerity of the decoration merges with the actual structure in a highly successful synthesis. The campanile dates from the 18th century.

The Dome

Inside the church the relationship with Brunelleschi's architecture becomes even clearer. Just as the latter had done in the Old Sacristy of San Lorenzo, Sangallo accentuated the structure in this building by using architectural divisions formed by sturdy pilasters of *pietra serena*, gray sandstone, which contrast sharply with the plastered walls. However, Sangallo intensified these structural elements, thus creating the monumental effect of the interior. In the central crossing, pendentives – vault spandrels – lead from the barrel-vaulted side chapels to the crowning melon-shaped dome. The blue and white medallions of the evangelists and the glazed terracotta frieze by Andrea della Robbia, dating from 1492, lend to the clearly defined, evenly arranged design a touch of color. The architect's brother, Antonio da Sangallo, used this church in 1518 as a model for the construction of S. Biagio near Montepulciano.

City Republic and the Haute Bourgeoisie

Ruth Strasser

"Viva il popolo!" In nearly all Tuscan towns in the 13th century an urban upper middle class had developed, due to the rapidly increasing population, the opening up of new markets for local and long-distance trade, and also the beginnings of the division of labor and specialization in individual guilds. This new class no longer wanted to be a ball tossed between the emperor and the pope. The members of this social group of judges, lawyers, bankers, merchants, and traders, who had risen up the social scale as a result of their enterprise, commercial skill, wealth, and ruthlessness, created a republican type of government known as *primo popolo* (first people). All citizens were divided up into *gonfaloni*, neighborhood associations – a sort of militia for internal and external security, in which every male citizen between the ages of 15 and 70 had to serve. At the head of these associations was the *capitano del popolo*. For reasons of impartiality and as a protection against corruption, he was always appointed from outside, and was responsible for upholding the constitution and the new civic rights. At his side stood the highest governmental authority, the *consiglio degli anziani*, a council of elders which decided on every plan, every expenditure, every military expedition, and every alliance. The highest official of justice was the *podestà*, who pronounced legal judgments with the aid of a staff of lawyers and notaries. These posts were always occupied for only two to six months, those elected were never allowed to leave their official headquarters – town hall or law courts – and the nobility were excluded from election.

Domenico Lenzi, Specchio Umano, *miniature, Biblioteca Medicea Laurenziana, Florence*

There were also other councils and administrative structures for organizing the tasks of the newly arisen *civitas*, such as security, public order, tax collection and the 21 guilds in which every full citizen had to be registered in order to carry on a profession. Among the seven *arti maggiori* were the textile guilds such as the *arte della lana*, the wool producers, in whose workshops along the Arno countless waged workers processed wool into the finest cloth.

The Florentine chronicler Giovanni Villani wrote in 1338: "There are more than 200 workshops for the wool guild, which produce 70–80,000 pieces of cloth to a value of 1,200,000 florins. More than 30,000 people make their living from this work." Manufacture was divided into different specialized procedures: sorting, washing, beating, carding, winding, spooling, fulling, smoothing, tentering, drawing, drying, pressing, folding, and packing. Another textile guild was that of the *calimala*, the wholesalers, who imported raw wool and plain cloth from England and improved it, dyed it, and exported the extremely valuable end product.

There were also the silk manufacturers and the guild of furriers. The former noble families, often living impoverished lives in the city and excluded from the rights of the urban patricians, looked for new ways to take part in the profitable trade of the city. Often they would

Ambrogio Lorenzetti (c. 1293–1348), St. Nicholas Raising a Child from the Dead *(detail), c. 1332, tempera on wood, Galleria degli Uffizi, Florence*

return, after living many years in some other region, with new "de-ennobled" names, or they tried to join the upper middle class by marrying their sons and daughters into it. Often these merely practical connections gave rise to huge family concerns which had a powerful presence in trade all over Europe.

Greater guilds (l. to r.): horse dealers, silk makers, cloth dealers, doctors, and apothecaries

Lesser guilds (left to right): carpenters and woodcutters, wine dealers, locksmiths, innkeepers

Centro per l'Arte Contemporanea Luigi Pecci

Anne and Patrick Poirier (b. 1942),
Exegi monumentum aere perennius, **1988**
Installation of several stainless steel bodies of
varying size, 600 × 1800 cm

High-quality 20th-century art in public places – such as, for instance, the monumental sculpture by the British sculptor Henry Moore in the Piazza S. Marco – is a feature of Prato which demonstrates that it is also a modern city. This impression is reinforced by the "Centro per l'Arte Contemporanea Luigi Pecci," a center for contemporary art on the outskirts of the

city. In front of it, Anne and Patrick Poirier have made their highly visible mark with their collapsed pillar of shining steel. The French artist couple see themselves as tracking the thoughts and remnants of the past, and their portrayal of fragments and ruins is in-tended to help the eye to see the interrela-tion between history, lived and recorded, and between memory and forgetting.

This museum of modern art – which is quite unusual in the Tuscan context – was opened in 1988 by the city council with the backing of the foundation set up by the textile manufacturer Enrico Pecci in memory of his son Luigi. The fan-like structural complex was designed by the Florentine architect Italo Gamberini (1907–90). Exhibitions of works by well-known national and international artists are held here, displaying a broad spectrum of trends in contemporary art since the 1970s. It also houses an information and records center, with a public library containing a magnificent collection of exhibition catalogues and artists' biographies, as well as an art database which can provide further information.

Exhibition Hall

After the "Centro" had been in existence for ten years, the exhibition became a reality. Since June 1998, the center's permanent exhibition of international art, in the new building designed by the architects Bacchi and Sarteanesi, complements the regular temporary exhibitions. Among the permanent exhibits are works by Enzo Cucchi, Michelangelo Pistoletto, Mauro Staccioli, Alberto Burri, Mario Merz, Sol LeWitt, Yannis Kounellis, Anish Kapoor, and Julian Opie. There have been temporary exhibitions by, among others, Barbara Kruger, Tadashi Kawamata, Gilberto Zorio, Alberto Burri, and Lucio Fontana.

Poggio a Caiano

Villa Medicea

Pontormo (1494–1557),
Vertumnus and Pomona (detail), 1519–1521
Fresco

In about 1480, Lorenzo il Magnifico purchased the villa on the river Ombrone in Poggio a Caiano from the Rucellai family of Florence. Lorenzo commissioned a new building, planned by Giuliano da Sangallo. The result was the very archetype of the Renaissance villa, which became the model for later country houses. A symmetrical structure with a plain façade, the villa is surrounded by a broad terrace at the *piano nobile* level, above the arcade-supported lowest floor. The entrance is approached via a stairway, originally rectangular but replaced by a curved free-standing stairway in the 18th century. The portico is crowned by a Classical-style pediment with a terracotta frieze – the first appearance of this type of element in Renaissance architecture.

The first Medici pope, Leo X, had the great hall decorated by well-known artists: Pontormo, Franciabigio, Andrea del Sarto, and Alessandro Allori. Particularly impressive is the lunette fresco *Vertumnus and Pomona* by Pontormo which portrays a legend from Ovid's *Metamorphoses*. In the fresco on the right-hand wall, re-worked by Allori, del Sarto made reference to a treaty made by Lorenzo il Magnifico.

Villa Medicea, view of the hall with frescoes by Pontormo

Carmignano

S. Michele

The village of Carmignano lies in the hills of Monte Albano, to the west of Florence and not far from Vinci, the birthplace of Leonardo. Its medieval fortress, a strategically important point between Lucca and Florence, was fought over for a long time. In the late 13th century the Franciscans founded a monastery here – the parish church of the monastery has been preserved in its Gothic form, while the cloisters were rebuilt in the Renaissance.

Jacopo Pontormo (1494–1557),
Visitation, **c. 1528–1529**
Oil on panel, 202 × 156 cm

S. Michele is home to a remarkable painting, Pontormo's *Visitation.* From 1528 to 1529 the painter, who was a local man, worked on this portrayal of the meeting of Mary, the mother of Jesus, and Elizabeth, the mother of St John the Baptist, both shown as pregnant. The unreal-seeming surroundings in which the scene is taking place, the use of magical, shrill and glistening colors, the interlinking gestures and the intense gaze exchanged by the two protagonists, combine to give this picture a visionary character. The figures of the other two women in the picture, standing in the background, facing the front and looking straight at the viewer, are a puzzle. They could be described as maids, but this would not account for their expressive gaze; they seem rather to be a variation, another aspect of both Mary and Elizabeth who, standing here, despite the fullness of their bodies, appear to glide towards one another as if in the circle of a dance.

Florence and Region

Florence

"Daughter and creation of Rome that was destined for great things in its rise," wrote the historian Giovanni Villani in the *Cronaca* of his native Florence in 1338. Founded in 59 B.C. as a Roman veterans' colony in the fertile Arno Valley, "flowering" Florentia developed over the course of its history into the almost absolute ruler of Tuscany, and is even today a capital, administrative center and art metropolis.

Laid out under the Emperor Augustus (27 B.C.–A.D. 14), the city later acquired a temple for the Capitoline gods, three thermal baths, a theater, and an amphitheater. Because of its favorable position astride routes in every direction, Florence flourished commercially even in Roman days. The city's coat of arms reflects this: the flowering lily is still found growing wild at the roadside. In the beginning of the 4th century A.D., the Emperor Diocletian made Florence the capital of the Seventh Region, i.e., Tuscany and Umbria.

Along the Via Cassia, which crossed the Arno on its way from south to north through Florence, the first small Christian communities and churches sprang up as Syrian traders settled there. In 393, the Bishop of Milan and Father of the Church Ambrose dedicated the church of S. Lorenzo as the first episcopal seat.

Palazzo Vecchio (detail of the façade and main doorway), Florence

With the dissolution of the western Roman Empire and the struggles between Goths and Byzantines, a time of destruction and decline set in. Things remained thus during the early Middle Ages, as both the Lombards and the Frankish margraves who ruled Tuscany based themselves in Lucca. Only with the last margravine Mathilda of Canossa, who had chosen Florence as her seat of government, was there a new cultural burgeoning. From the mid-11th century, the city was the center of an ecclesiastical revival, and buildings such as the baptistery and church of S. Miniato al Monte are indications of this Proto-Renaissance. After the death of Mathilda in 1115, Florence obtained its civic independence. In the following 200 years, during which the number of residents rapidly rose to over 100,000, energy was mainly focused on political and commercial expansion. The neighboring rival Fiesole was destroyed, the position of the landed aristocracy was challenged. *Terre murate*, i.e., fortified settlements, were constructed as outposts – "... and so the commune of Florence began to expand, more from strength than right. It extended the *contado* [hinterland] and subjected all the country people to its laws and destroyed their forts" (Giovanni Villani, 1348). In the subsequent period, Florence's drive for hegemony in the *contado* ended with

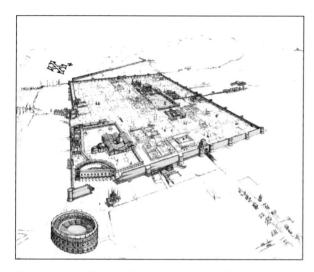

Reconstruction of Roman Florence, drawing, 1992

the capture of most of the Tuscan cities – except that of Lucca.

In the early 13th century, urban life was plagued by conflict between the Guelph and Ghibelline factions, leading to near civil war conditions. In 1250 the first government consisting of the *primo popolo* (artisans and merchants) was formed. Bondage was abolished, the textile industry flourished and a euphoric era of building set in that stamped a distinctive shape on the city. Cathedral, city hall, palace of justice, and monastic churches sprang up.

From 1284, following previous extensions, the city walls were finally completed. Just over 5 miles (8.5 km) long, with 73 towers and 15 gates, they remained intact until they were demolished in the late 19th century.

In the early 14th century, the pioneering works of Giotto and Dante Alighieri ushered in a new fruitful period in art and literature. However, along with the devastating Arno floods of 1333, the horrors of famine and recurrent plague epidemics (in 1348, for example), the Trecento was also a century of catastrophes. Growing social tensions finally burst out in the uprising of the *ciompi* (woolcarders). A group of leading Florentine families promptly took over the city and formed the *signoria*. However, the popular revolt was not without influential support – from the young, nouveau-riche family of the Medici. Though Cosimo Medici, the head of the family, was banished, he returned only two years later in triumph as the *pater patriæ*, father of the country. This was the start of the unparalleled, (almost) unbroken political career of the Medici family, whose patronage fashioned the artistic and intellectual temper of Florence for nearly 300 years.

Under Cosimo Vecchio (Old Cosimo), his son Piero Gottoso (the Gouty), and especially his grandson Lorenzo il

Magnifico (the Magnificent), Florence became the cradle of the Renaissance, an era that lasted from 1420 to about 1550, and brought forth artists such as Masaccio, Donatello, Brunelleschi, Leonardo, and Michelangelo.

From 1494 until his execution in 1498, politics were dominated by the preachings of the Dominican monk Savonarola. The Medici family were driven out of the city once again, the constitution was amended, and a Great Council with 1,500 members was set up, lasting until the Medici finally returned in 1512.

They provided two popes, Leo X and his nephew and successor Clement VII, and after a brief republican interlude the family were able to consolidate their rule again with imperial and papal assistance.

In 1531 they became the Dukes of Tuscany, and in 1569 Cosimo was named Grand Duke. In 1737, following the death of the last Medici, Gian Gastone, the title passed to the house of Habsburg-Lorraine. After the city joined the new kingdom of Italy in 1861, the city was temporarily (from 1865–1871) the capital of Italy, which brought profound changes in the historic city center, including the construction of a great ring road to replace the medieval walls. This now marks off the historic city center.

Veduta *of the city of Florence (the Chain Map) c. 1472, Museo di Firenze com'era, Florence*

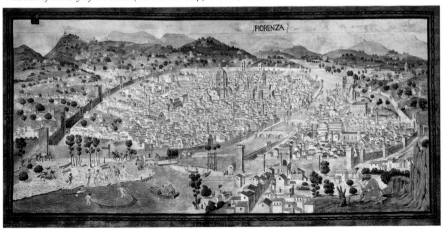

Florence

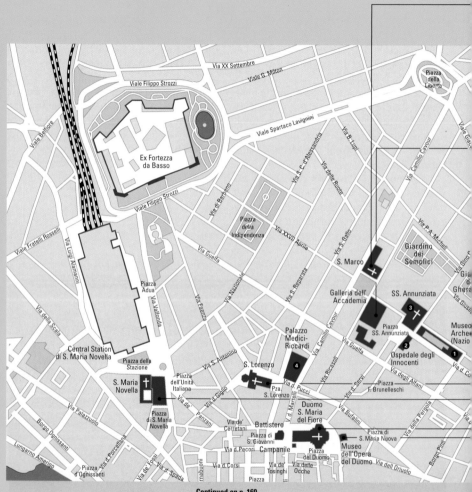

Continued on p. 160

S. Marco, Piazza
S. Marco, p. 250

Galleria dell'Accademia, 60 Via
Ricasoli, p. 259

S. Lorenzo, 9 Piazza S. Lorenzo,
p. 240

S. Maria Novella, Piazza
di S. Maria Novella, p. 234

Duomo (S. Maria del Flore),
Piazza del Duomo, p. 169

Battistero and campanile,
Piazza del Duomo, pp. 162, 168

Museo dell'Opera del Duomo,
Piazza del Duomo 9, p. 174

Other sights of interest

1   Museo Archeologico (Nazionale),
    38 Via della Colonna, p. 262

2   Ospedale degli Innocenti, Piazza
    della SS. Annunziata, p. 262

3   SS. Annunziata, Piazza della SS.
    Annunziata, p. 260

4   Palazzo Medici-Riccardi,
    1 Via Cavour, p. 248

Florence

S. Maria del Carmine, Piazza del Carmine, p. 226

S. Spirito, 29 Piazza S. Spirito, p. 228

Duomo (S. Maria del Fiore), Piazza del Duomo, p. 169

▲ Continued on p. 158 ▲

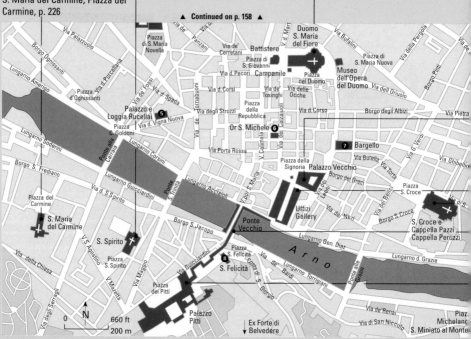

Palazzo Vecchio, Piazza della Signoria, p. 182

Galleria degli Uffizi, Loggiata degli Uffizi, p. 184

S. Croce and Cappella Pazzi, Piazza S. Croce, pp. 200, 208

Ponte Vecchio, p. 216

Palazzo Pitti, Piazza dei Pitti, p. 221

Battistero S. Giovanni

The harmoniously proportioned baptistery is the oldest building on Florence's most important religious site, which covers the extensive area once occupied by a Roman palace complex. A building that preceded it was first mentioned in 897. The foundation stone for the new baptistery was dedicated by Pope Nicholas II in about 1060; the building was in use by 1128, and the lantern was completed in 1150.

The octagonal central plan has two stories, with an attic above capped by a pyramid roof that hides a dome. The design is an ingenious mixture reflecting similar earlier buildings in Ravenna and Rome, and was itself an influence on the Renaissance architect Filippo Brunelleschi when it came to building the dome for the cathedral. The unknown architect derived the orders in the pilasters and columns of the floors, the precise semi-circular arches, and the "attic windows" in the upper floor from antiquity. The marble facing of the exterior is an innovation, giving the appearance of three-dimensional decoration applied to the flat surface, and the slight transposition of the arches creates the impression of a sculptural blind arcade.

The Romanesque building was altered twice: in 1202 the round choir chapel was replaced by a polygonal one, and in 1339 Arnolfo di Cambio assimilated the stone corner piers to the exterior decoration of the cathedral by facing them with green and white stripes. There are three, partly gilded bronze doors, on the south, north, and east sides. That of the south door by Andrea Pisano dated 1330–1336 is the oldest. The quatrefoil reliefs show scenes from the life of Florence's patron saint St. John the Baptist.

Lorenzo Ghiberti (1378–1455), north doorway, 1403–1424
Bronze (partly gilded) h. 450 cm (with frame), quatrefoils 39 × 39 cm each

In the famous competition in 1401 for the commission for the bronze doorway, Lorenzo Ghiberti with his test piece beat off rivals who included Brunelleschi and Jacopo della Quercia. His doorway on the north side features 20 scenes from the life of Christ in the upper fields, plus representations of the four evangelists and the four Fathers of the Church at the bottom. At the intersections of the frames of each scene Ghiberti added portrait heads, including a self-portrait. The door frame displays some fine and very natural-looking details such as a frog, a squirrel, and a snail.

Lorenzo Ghiberti,
Porta del Paradiso, 1425–1452
Bronze (partly gilded), 521 × 321 cm (overall), reliefs 80 × 80 cm each

After Ghiberti had finished his first door, he was commissioned to do a second. The result, dating from 1425–1452, consists of only ten square gilded bronze panel reliefs that show Old Testament scenes selected by the Humanist scholar Leonardo Bruni. This famous and newest door was installed on the east side so that it faced the cathedral entrance. Michelangelo was so taken with its beauty that he called it the Porta del Paradiso – the Gate of Paradise – a reference also to the function of the building, because the door leads to "saving baptism." The door is now replaced by a copy, the original panels having been restored and placed on show in the Museo dell'Opera del Duomo.

The frame of the Paradise door is also richly decorated with 48 niche statuettes and portrait medallions, which include sibyls, prophets, and other biblical figures, couched between delicate foliage motifs. Prominent in the middle is the solid bald head of Ghiberti himself. Beaming and with raised eyebrows, he appears to radiate satisfaction with his work. As there are only ten scenes depicted, the artist had larger areas in which to present the narrative, and he was able to include more episodes in each field.

Lorenzo Ghiberti, *Genesis*
(detail from the *Porta del Paradiso*)

Prompted by Donatello and Brunelleschi, Ghiberti opens up the depth of the relief, to give the scene more atmosphere.

Paradise	Cain and Abel
Noah	Abraham and Isaac
Jacob and Esau	Joseph
Moses	Fall of Jericho
David	Solomon and the Queen of Sheba

Moving from the flat relief to high relief, he displays superb mastery in his handling of proportions, linear momentum, and the interplay of light and shadow. Each panel includes several scenes, in this case the creation of Adam and Eve, the Fall and the Expulsion from Paradise.

Despite the sumptuous richness, the decoration is still entirely subordinate to the architecture.

The tomb of the Antipope John XXIII, Baldassare Coscia, is fitted in between two wall columns. This was created by Donatello and Michelozzo between 1424 and 1427, and is the first canopied tomb of the Renaissance.

Dome mosaic, c. 1225–1320

The light gleams mystically on the gold background of the great dome mosaic. Inspired by the mosaics of S. Marco in Venice and presumably built with the help of mosaicists from there, it was put together by a variety of artists supervised by the Franciscan monk Fra Jacopo da Torrita. It depicts God's saving grace and the life of John the Baptist. The main subject on the chancel side is the Last Judgment: Christ displaying his stigmata, sitting on a rainbow as judge, while advocates sit on a level with him and underneath him the Resurrected climb out of tombs and coffins.

The Interior

The interior walls of the baptistery are also divided into two stories, above which there is a low mosaic-decorated attic and the vault. Corinthian columns and corner pilasters in the lower story carry a massive entablature – the arrangement and niches are derived from the Pantheon in Rome. On the upper floor, a gallery opens up through evenly spaced double-arched windows framed by pilasters.

The decoration is conspicuously lavish. The interior is assembled like a precious shrine, with variegated marble patterns on the floor, gilded capitals dating from antiquity, glowing mosaics, rectangular inlays, and green and white marble facings.

Campanile

In 1334, Giotto di Bondone (1267–1337), already celebrated as a painter, was appointed cathedral architect in succession to Arnolfo di Cambio. In his term of office, which lasted barely four years, he concentrated on the campanile, completed after his death by Andrea Pisano and Francesco Talenti. The 290-foot (89-meter) bell tower is a satisfying blend of architecture, sculpture, and colored decoration on a square ground plan, crowned with a projecting cornice and balustrade.

The molded plinth supports a double story divided into portrait-format wall panels. The reliefs in these depict human occupations and activities, grouped according to concepts such as *Necessitas, Virtus,* and *Sapientia* (Necessity, Virtue, and Wisdom), accompanied by the Christian virtues, sacraments and liberal arts plus Old Testament and Classical figures. The narrative begins on the west side and runs round the plinth in an anticlockwise direction. The sculptural program was devised by Giotto, with the reliefs executed largely by Andrea Pisano, Luca della Robbia, and Andrea Orcagna. Directly above plinth level is a series of sculptures by Andrea Pisano and Donatello, though the ones there now are in fact copies, and the originals are preserved in the Museo dell'Opera del Duomo.

Duomo S. Maria del Fiore

Along with St. Peter's in Rome and Milan cathedral, S. Maria del Fiore is one of the biggest cathedrals in the Christian world. Dedicated to the Virgin Mary, it was begun in 1296 by Arnolfo di Cambio (c. 1245 – 1302). From 1417 at the latest, Brunelleschi (1377 – 1446) was recorded at work on the dome. The gold ball at the top was in place by 1471, but the marble cladding of the façade was added only in the 19th century.

The view along the south wall presents an expanse of white, green, and pink marble. The clear articulation and blind arcades in the choir chapels are based on the decoration of the baptistery. The ground plan is a Latin cross with a nave and two aisles. The giant dome (rising to over 380 feet – 116 meters – overall) on its lofty drum stands above an octagonal crossing, which is flanked on the east, north, and south sides by apses, interspersed with sacristies. The smaller domes on the choir chapels and the "exedras"

over the sacristies help to support the weight of the drum. Eight marble ribs run from the corners of the drum up to the lantern, their weight being carried downwards by respond buttresses. The combination of structural and aesthetic features looks obvious to modern eyes, but was absolutely innovative in its day.

Duomo S. Maria del Fiore

Domenico di Michelino, *Dante and the Divine Comedy*. The mural was commissioned in 1465 to celebrate the 200th anniversary of Dante's birth, and shows the famous poet outside the gates of his native city together with scenes from his work.

Paolo Uccello, painting depicting equestrian sculpture of Sir John Hawkwood, p. 173

Interior, p. 172

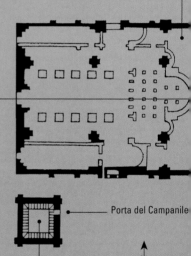

Campanile, p. 168

Porta del Campanile

0   65 ft

20 m

N

Porta della Mandorla. Made in marble 1414–1421, the huge gable relief on the north wall of the nave shows the *Assumption of the Virgin* and *Doubting Thomas*. It is considered the most important work of Nanni di Banco.

Entrance to Brunelleschi's dome

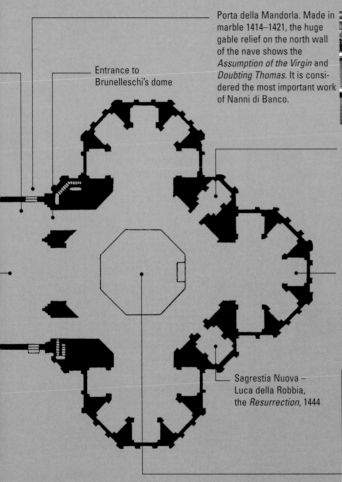

Luca della Robbia, lunette over the door to the Sagrestia Vecchia, 1442–1445. Executed in painted and glazed terracotta, the relief of the *Ascension* shows the Risen Christ surrounded by worshiping angels, while sleeping soldiers are arranged round the coffin.

Lorenzo Ghiberti, Reliquary of St. Zenobius. The reliefs from the front and sides of the rectangular bronze work dating from 1434–1442 depict scenes from the life of the Florentine saint.

Sagrestia Nuova – Luca della Robbia, the *Resurrection*, 1444

Apses and dome, p. 169

The Interior

The cathedral consists of a nave and two aisles, with a total length of 500 feet (153 m) and a width of 125 feet (38 m). The overall impression is determined by the coloration and plain, severe design. The generous proportions lend the rib-vaulted interior the character of a hall.

Large pointed arches on sharply articulated piers provide a longitudinal rhythm. Above the arcades, a passage supported on heavy consoles like a prominent entablature links the nave to the chancel, apses, and the huge octagonal drum, creating thereby a unifying horizontal axis. The massive wall surfaces of the octagon, which right from the start were intended to carry the two-layer dome, have a functional appearance. Much of the once-rich decoration has been lost, having fallen victim to numerous restorations or else been transferred to the Museo dell'Opera del Duomo, but the unique spatial impression of Florentine Gothic architecture has survived the centuries.

The stained glass in the drum was executed to designs by Donatello, Uccello, Ghiberti, and Castagno. The clockface on the inside above the main doorway, painted by Uccello in 1443, displays 24-hour numerals in Roman style, and has only one large hand, which gives the hours in anticlockwise direction.

The dome fresco of the Last Judgment was designed by Giorgio Vasari and begun in 1572. After Vasari's death it was completed in 1574 by the Roman Mannerist master Federico Zuccaro (c. 1540–1609) and his assistants.

Paolo Uccello (c. 1397–1475), painting of equestrian statue of Sir John Hawkwood, 1436

Fresco (transferred to canvas), 820 × 515 cm

Paolo Uccello, a native of the Arezzo area, was commissioned by the city council to paint an equestrian portrait. It is in memory of one of the best-known mercenaries of the 14th century, the Englishman Sir John Hawkwood (or "Giovanni Acuto"), who served in the Florentine army and had become an honorary citizen. Originally, Hawkwood had been promised that a statue would be erected after his death, but – as a cost cutting exercise – the city opted instead for a fresco.

Uccello's portrait is notable for its clarity and use of monochrome *terra verde*, which gives a remarkably sculptural look of patinated bronze. The illusion of an equestrian figure standing on a plinth – proudly signed *Pauli Ucielli opus* by the artist – initially seems perfect. However, though the plinth is shown in pronounced perspective as though viewed from below, the rider is in fact seen in straight profile.

Museo dell'Opera del Duomo

Luca della Robbia (1399/1400–1482), choir loft, 1431–1438
Marble, 328 × 560 cm

Beside the one-time workshop of Donatello opposite the cathedral choir is the entrance to the recently restored and newly fitted-out Museo dell'Opera del Duomo. A works office or *opera* was first mentioned in 1390, and was moved by Brunelleschi to its present position. It used to be the center of all cathedral construction work. In 1891, the former long-standing art depository was turned into a museum. It houses outstanding works of the Middle Ages and Renaissance which, for reasons of fashion or conservation, have been banished from their original positions in the cathedral, baptistery, or campanile.

The choir lofts were originally installed over the sacristy doors in the cathedral, but were removed in 1688 on the occasion of the wedding of Ferdinando de' Medici to Violante of Bavaria.

The scenes on the marble loft of Luca della Robbia refer to Psalm 150: "Let every thing that has breath praise the Lord." Child angels "praise him with the timbrel and dance, ... the sound of the trumpet, ... psaltery and harp, ... stringed instruments and organs and loud cymbals." An amazing number of moving figures are packed into tiny spaces and subordinated to the architectural framework.

**Donatello (1386–1466),
choir loft, 1433–1438**
Marble, 348 × 570 cm

Donatello's counterpart shows a frieze of dancing putti behind columns that stand on tall brackets. Unlike della Robbia's loft, Donatello's dispenses with the strict architectural frame and puts more emphasis on depicting movements, the liveliness of the figures, and their almost completely three-dimensional quality. It is a bold move to carry the composition across the whole width of the loft. Equally daring is the idea of a roundelay of putti behind the mosaic columns, giving the impression of great spatial depth. Although the same subject is treated, here childlike boisterousness and an impressive realism in representing the human body are the key characteristics.

The ornamental elements of the pulpit are also admirable. The scrolls on the consoles, acanthus leaves, classical vases, shell patterns, and other Classical motifs indicate, like the dancing putti, the Cinquecento's great interest in the art of Classical antiquity.

Donatello, *Habakkuk*, 1423–1426
Marble, h. 195 cm

Donatello's statue of Zuccone ("Bald Head"), as the prophet Habakkuk was nicknamed, is riveting. It was made, like a number of other figures, for the niches of

the campanile. The slightly inclined, bald head and expressive physiognomy, particularly the eyes and projecting ears, give the prophet a sense of presence which reminded Vasari of a portrait. Tension and energy characterize the man's posture. The voluminous toga underlines the impression of an emaciated but energetic man. Physicality and facial expression suggest the image of the "charismatic seer."

Donatello,
***St. Mary Magdalene*, c. 1455**
Wood (painted in color),
h. 188 cm

The wooden statue of Mary Magdalene was originally created by Donatello around 1455 for the Battistero in Florence. In this moving late work, the beautiful Mary Magdalene appears emaciated and close to death. It is a brilliantly realized representation of the story of the saint's life as a penitent in a cave in southern France. The wasted body is clad only in her hair; the face looks like a skull, the eyes seem at the point of death – their asymmetry just seems to intensify her

expression. Only in the hands raised in prayer is the youth and former loveliness of the saint discernible.

him upright and clasps him to her. The heads touch – at this moment, faith means immersion in pain and death.

Michelangelo Buonarroti (1475–1564),
Pietà, **1550–1553**
Marble, h. 226 cm

This famous late *Pietà* by Michelangelo, which was in the cathedral from the 18th century until 1981, is one of the most moving works from the High Renaissance. Michelangelo worked on the marble group, which was originally intended for his own tomb, from 1550 until 1553. But the stone broke, the figure went wrong and Michelangelo smashed it. A pupil of Michelangelo's, Tiberio Calcagni, put it together again and so completed the Magdalene figure. The difference in the workmanship is very obvious.

Michelangelo's statue combines the subject of the *Deposition* with those of the *Lamentation* and *Pietà*. Christ collapses in a broken movement, with the Pharisee Nicodemus holding the dead body. Mary holds

Orsanmichele

In 1336 a grain store above an open hall replaced the small 8th-century church of San Michele in Orto (a vegetable garden). It had an oratory attached, the Orsanmichele, whose arcades were decorated with the typical filigree tracery of late Florentine Gothic.

In the 14th century, the building became a center for the guilds, 14 of which, together with the merchants' tribunal, were allowed to display their

patron saints in the exterior niches. The sculptures were made in the early 15th century, and form a stylistically homogeneous ensemble of the Early Renaissance art, with outstanding works by Ghiberti, Verrocchio, and Donatello, some of which are exhibited on the upper floor.

The Interior

The previous building already had a miracle-working picture of the Virgin hanging on a pier, but it is presumed to have been destroyed in a fire at the beginning of the Trecento. In 1347 it was replaced by the large Madonna by Bernardo Daddi (c. 1290–1348), clearly a follower of Giotto. The faithful streamed into the two-aisle hall to pray, and the merchants to buy. After the great plague of 1348, the survivors gave enough money to commission from Andrea Orcagna (1315/1320–c. 1368) a costly tabernacle for the Madonna. The result was a sumptuous ciborium with apostle figures, gables, and finials, which seemed too precious for an ordinary market. In 1380 the cornmarket had to move, the arcades were enclosed, and the market thus became a church again. Even today, however, you can see the openings in the northern wall piers where grain was poured in and drawn off.

Orsanmichele

Donatello, *St. George*, copy (original in the Bargello), c. 1416–1417. This statue was already much lauded in the Renaissance, and is impressive in its depiction of the brave warrior, while the socle relief showing the encounter with the dragon is executed in flat relief (*rilievo schiacciato*).

Interior, p. 178

Donatello, *St Mark*, 1411–1413. The marble evangelist stands on a cushion with slightly turned body, balancing his weight on one leg, while the other is bent and relaxed.

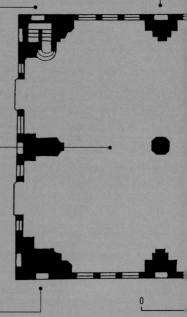

0

Nanni di Banco, *Santi Quattro Coronati* (Four Crowned Saints), c. 1410–1415. The four patron saints of the stonemasons' and carpenters' guild are elegantly housed in a niche. The socle relief shows the occupations of bricklayer, stonemason, architect and sculptor.

Andrea del Verrocchio, *Christ and Doubting Thomas*, 1467–1483. The sculptor cleverly overcame the problem of fitting two figures into a niche originally intended for only one, which was Donatello's St. Louis of Toulouse.

Tabernacle by Andrea Orcagna (1359) with the *Madonna delle Grazie* by Bernardo Daddi (1347).

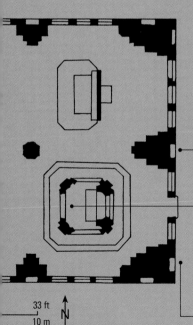

Lorenzo Ghiberti, *St. John the Baptist*, 1413. The guild of great merchants commissioned this first over-lifesize bronze statue to be erected in Florence.

33 ft
10 m

Piazza della Signoria and Palazzo Vecchio

The Palazzo dei Priori was begun in 1298 to plans by Arnolfo di Cambio. It was intended as the magistrate's seat, but was later called the Signoria. Since then, the Piazza della Signoria has been the center of political life. The large Neptune fountain was erected by Bartolommeo Ammanati in 1565 for the wedding of Francesco de' Medici, son of Cosimo I, to Joan of Austria. At the time, the palace, which had been extended in Savonarola's day, served the Medici dukes as a palace, and only became the Palazzo Vecchio when they moved to the Palazzo Pitti. Dressed-stone blocks and Gothic biforate windows shape the façade and, together with the massive crenellated battlements above the heraldic frieze, give it its fortified appearance. The slender tower rises from the fortress block as a symbol of secular power.

Statues were erected in front of the façade. In contrast with the equestrian statue of Cosimo I by Giambologna, the statue of *Judith*, the heraldic lion by Donatello, Michelangelo's famous *David,* and Baccio Bandinelli's *Hercules and Cacus* (most now replaced by copies) symbolize the commune's desire for liberty.

The Loggia dei Lanzi was built in 1374–1381 for the city council's public ceremonies, and today contains many outstanding sculptures.

Galleria degli Uffizi

In 1560, Cosimo I commissioned Vasari to build a further suite of buildings for the offices of the magistrate's administration, the *Uffizi*. The end of the complex, which runs down towards the Arno like a grand avenue, is an elegant portico screen. With the exception of the Zecca, the old mint, which was incorporated into the new Palazzo, the ground floor is comprised of open colonnades. Above a mezzanine with blind windows there are two stories that are of equal height.

The top story was used to house the Medici family's continually growing art collection. Under a provision of the family will, in 1743 it passed into the ownership of the city. Besides classical sculptures, the Uffizi contains masterworks of painting dating from the Middle Ages to the 18th century, especially of the Italian and the Netherlandish schools.

Medici Venus
Marble, h. 153 cm

Classical sculptures found during excavations in Rome, bought by the Medici and originally installed in the garden of the Villa Medici in Rome, were subsequently transferred to Florence to form the basis of the sculpture collection in the Uffizi, including the famous Medici Venus found in 1618 in the villa of the Roman emperor Hadrian. The marble figure is of the *Venus*

pudica (Modest Venus) type, and goes back to an Greek original by Praxiteles in the early 4th century B.C.

Galleria degli Uffizi

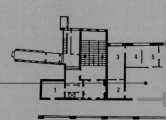

Piero della Francesca's
Federico di Montefeltro,
Early Renaissance gallery,
p. 190

Giotto's *Ognissanti
Madonna*, 13th-century
Tuscan painting and
Giotto gallery, p. 188

Filippo Lippi's
*Madonnna with Child
and Two Angels*, Filippo
Lippi room, p. 191

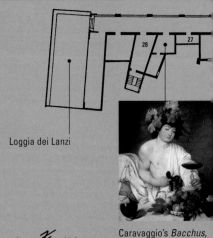

Loggia dei Lanzi

Caravaggio's *Bacchus*,
Caravaggio room, p. 199

0   65 ft
20 m

Botticelli's *Birth of Venus*,
Botticelli gallery, p. 192

Michelangelo's *Doni
Tondo*, Michelangelo
and early 16th-century
Florentine painting gallery, p. 196

Piazzale degli Uffizi

Titian's *Venus of Urbino*, Titian
gallery, p. 198

Giotto di Bondone (1267–1337),
Madonna in Maestà **(Ognissanti Madonna),**
c. 1310
Tempera on wood, 325 × 204 cm

Painted around 1310, Giotto's altarpiece
for the Florentine church of Ognissanti is
exhibited with the panels of the Madonna
Enthroned by the older masters Duccio
and Cimabue. Their proximity highlights
the innovative nature of his style. Giotto
gives his bodies volume, almost gravity.
The clear interest in perspective painting is

specially noticeable in the tabernacle,
where the eye is directed at the central
figures. Surrounded by angels, the mother
of God sits enthroned in majesty. Like
Christ's garment, her light undergarment
is much plainer than the materials in the
pictures of the earlier masters. The vigorous Christ sits like a child yet with great
earnestness in his mother's lap. The
novelty of Giotto's *Maestà* lies in its combination of statuesque sublimeness and
living naturalness.

Gentile da Fabriano (c. 1370–1427),
Adoration of the Magi, **1423**
Tempera on wood, 173 × 220 cm

Gentile, who came from the Marches,
painted this panel for the chapel in the
church of Santa Trinità belonging to his
client Palla Strozzi. The great variety of
detail in the design of landscape and
figures distinguishes Gentile's style. He
decorates his composition with details,
giving it a sense of fairy-tale magic. A thief
steals the spurs from the young magi,
while in the left background a traveler is
fatally stabbed in the throat. Tame
monkeys, lions, and cheetahs accompany
the figures clothed with oriental robes and
head coverings. With its lavish use of gold
and fine elegance of line, the altar painting
is a masterly example of the International
Gothic style.

**Piero della Francesca
(c. 1415–1492),**
Federico di Montefeltro,
c. 1465 (right side of a diptych)
Tempera on wood, 47 × 33 cm

In this diptych portraying the ruling couple of Urbino, the Uffizi possesses perhaps the finest double portrait of the Early Renaissance. Piero della Francesca came from Borgo Sansepolcro. He painted Federico di Montefeltro in about 1465, while the portrait of the duke's wife Battista Sforza was painted only in 1472, after her death.

Water, hills, and arable land of the ducal estates are shown with calm clarity in the background. The landscape is suffused with a transparent atmosphere that is still to be experienced from the tower of the Ducal Palace in Urbino. The severe profile of the duke and duchess in the foreground, painted after the style of classical medallions, are shown – in the duke's case, at least – in a realistic and truthful manner. The face is caught almost photographically, with hooded eyes, a number of warts, a hooked nose broken probably in sporting combat, and fine curly hair. The color of his robe contrasts with the surroundings, and emphasizes his superiority as a ruler.

Filippo Lippi (c. 1406–1469),
Madonna and Child with Two
Angels, **c. 1460**
Tempera on wood, 92 × 63 cm

The Madonna panel is a late work and one of the best-known by the Carmelite monk and painter called Fra Filippo Lippi, whose emotional and lyrical style cannot fail to captivate. The figure group stands out almost sculpturally against the background, which is visible through a window frame looking on to a wide landscape with cliffs and fields, and the sea and a town in the distance. The figures are suffused with glowing light.

The entranced expression on the graceful Madonna with girlish features contrasts with the cheerful roguishness of the two angels, who busy themselves holding up and supporting the curly-haired blond Christ, who is wrapped in an ultra-fine cloth. This ideal of female beauty is a trait of almost all works by Lippi, and was imitated more than once by his most talented pupil Sandro Botticelli. According to Vasari, Lippi was "always obsessively in love," and in this picture once again he immortalizes the features of his beloved, the Prato nun Lucrezia Buti.

Sandro Botticelli (1445–1510), *Birth of Venus*, c. 1485

Tempera on canvas, 172 × 278 cm

This famous painting was commissioned around 1485 by Lorenzo di Pierfrancesco de' Medici for the family's Villa di Castello. The title of the picture is misleading, because Botticelli shows not the birth but the arrival of Venus. The Classical goddess of love, born out of the foam of the sea, is driven ashore by zephyrs. One of the Horae, a flower-bedecked goddess of spring, hurriedly approaches with a gown for the naked beauty.

Botticelli was among the favorite painters of the leading families of Florence. Especially the Medici admired the "master of the swirling line." Many of his paintings are difficult to interpret, being inspired by ideas of Neoplatonic theory and the Humanistic circle associated with philosopher Marsilio Ficino (1433–1499), where Venus was considered the embodiment of divine love.

Botticelli's favorite model for his Venus and madonna faces was Simonetta Vespucci, the paramour of Giuliano de' Medici whose beauty also featured in contemporary songs.

Hugo van der Goes (c. 1440–1482),
Portinari Altarpiece (center panel), c. 1475
Oil on wood, 253 × 304

When the altarpiece by the Flemish painter Hugo van der Goes arrived in Florence in 1483, it was a sensation with local artists. The monumental triptych, showing the Adoration of the Shepherds, had been commissioned by Tommaso Portinari, head of the Medici bank in Bruges, who sent it by sea to Florence. The side panels depict the donors with three of their ten children. The empirical rules of proportion are here neglected in favor of an old-fashioned perspective of hierarchy, with the sizes of the subjects corresponding to their notional status.

However, faces and fabrics are rendered thoroughly naturalistically, with equally patient and painterly devotion to even the smallest details of landscape and architecture. As a result, Hugo van der Goes's picture was to exercise a considerable influence on late-15th century Florentine painting.

in the work, as the stylistic differences in the execution of the two figures suggest.

The figure of Mary combines majesty and youthful tenderness. She sits in the corner besides a building of undefined function, at a lectern richly decorated with classicizing decorative elements. The angel of the Annunciation, raising a

Leonardo da Vinci (1452–1519),
Annunciation, **c. 1437–1475**
Oil and tempera on wood, 98 × 217 cm

The wide-format *Annunciation* has been in the Uffizi since 1867. It was presumably laid out by Leonardo around 1470 during his time in the workshop of Andrea del Verrocchio. Possibly several apprentices in Verrocchio's workshop were involved

hand in blessing, kneels on a flower-strewn meadow. The handling of the garments is marvelous, with the thin white material shown in delicate folds, the ribbon fluttering, and the warm-toned mantle billowing. Behind the figures, the eyes rests on a distant, atmospherically dense landscape beyond the sharply delineated cypresses in remote waters and mountains.

Michelangelo Buonarroti (1475–1564),
Holy Family **(Doni Tondo), c. 1504**
Tempera on wood, diam. 120 cm

The *Doni Tondo* is the only surviving panel
painting by Michelangelo. It was commissioned for the wedding of Angelo Doni and

Magdalena Strozzi in 1504, and is unusual
in the composition of a very sculptural
Holy Family within a tondo frame. Mary
kneels on the ground, leaning against
Joseph's knee for support, and takes the
naked, vigorous Christ child from his
secure grasp. Behind the separating wall

on which Joseph sits, the infant John the Baptist can be seen. With a look of admiration and at the same time melancholy, he seems to be turning to leave. He is left behind in the Classical-looking world of the handsome naked youths in the background.

The cool, brilliant colors and sweeping, interlocking gestures were to be a source of inspiration for the Mannerists, but it was only Michelangelo who captured the profound, Christ-focused intimacy of the scene with them.

Raphael (1483–1520),
Madonna of the Goldfinch,
c. 1507
Oil on wood, 107 × 77 cm

Towards the end of his time in Florence, Raphael still shows the clear influence of the art of Leonardo and Michelangelo in this painting. The group of the Madonna with the infant Christ and Baptist are placed against a landscape background in muted colors. Mary has interrupted her reading and turns to the children with great gentleness. Despite its idyllic charm, the painting is imbued with a mysterious melancholy. The goldfinch in the hands of John is a symbol of Christ's Passion.

Titian (c. 1488–1576),
Reclining Venus, 1538
Oil on canvas, 119 × 165 cm

Of all the Venetian works in the Uffizi, Titian's *Reclining Venus* is justly the best known. Painted in 1538 for Duke Guidobaldo II of Urbino, it is a masterpiece of the Venetian painter's middle period. Titian uses a warm color harmony of deep red and dark green, supplemented by broken white, to create an incomparable atmosphere. The ambiance embraces a Venus who lies in the foreground of a secular, everyday environment, devoid of pose, devoid of contrived attitude, and with natural grace. The soft outline and gold tone of her skin lend her a sensual luster that is in complete contrast to Botticelli's Venus. This is due not just to the 50 years that separates the dates when they were painted but also to the difference between Florentine and Venetian painting. Even the most outstanding Florentine painters were unable to achieve such warmth and painterly sensuality.

Caravaggio (1571–1610),
***Bacchus,* 1589–1596**
Oil on canvas, 95 × 85 cm

The *Bacchus*, from around the year 1593, is the earliest painting undisputedly by Michelangelo Merisi da Caravaggio, who was born in Caravaggio near Bergamo. He was 20 at the time of its execution. It displays the basic features of the artist's novel style, of which it was said that he had abandoned "the idea of beauty for the sake of realism," thus triggering a revolution in art.

The still-life objects that are artfully positioned in the youth's hair or on the table immediately attract attention: wilting autumnal foliage, pomegranate pieces and moldy fruit. Were they intended as a *memento mori* or as a sign of decadence?

The god sits here like a careless youth from a Roman suburb, propping himself up on his bed with lascivious sensuality. The diagonal fall of light flatters his skin. He holds his full glass with an affected gesture. He seems to be in fancy dress, as if he had been posed before the monochrome background.

Caravaggio in fact portrays a studio situation. This "Bacchus" is a model with the tanned face and hands of a worker or peasant. Under the white material, the usual striped mattress peeps out. This "infiltration" of Classical, and later also Christian, subject matter by reality – he always used humble models – reaped for Caravaggio fame and an enthusiastic, international following, but also indignation and disapproval.

S. Croce

With the exception of the Piazza della Signoria, there is no longer another medieval square as large as the Piazza Santa Croce. This is where the great families whose palaces in some cases still line the square organized competitive sports, and where the Franciscans held their fiery public preachings. Vasari reports that in 1285 the cathedral architect Arnolfo di Cambio began a new, larger building to replace a small Franciscan church. The reputation and influence of the Franciscans among the rich families was so high at the time that money poured in, allowing the construction of a church of such size that it aroused disapproval and opposition within the mendicant order. The church was completed in 1385, though the marble façade, campanile, and Dante memorial were added on in the 19th century.

The Interior

In its plainness and enormous breadth (the nave alone is 64 feet – 19.5 meters wide), the cruciform basilica is reminiscent of Early Christian churches in Rome. The grayish–brown stone of the octagonal piers, the pointed arch arcades, and the prominent passage in the nave constitute a high point in Italian Gothic.

Fragments of frescoes in the nave and the paintings of the main apse chapel and adjacent transept chapels by Giotto and his successors bear witness to the grandiose effect of the church in the Trecento. In the 15th century, costly furnishings were added: a pulpit by Benedetto da Maiano, an altar tabernacle, and a wooden crucifix by Donatello, plus Renaissance-period tombs. The greatest change was due to Vasari's intervention: he lowered the raised monastic choir to the level of the nave, and replaced the frescoes of the aisles with altars. Santa Croce is the pantheon of Florence: among those buried here are Galileo, Macchiavelli, Michelangelo, Leonardo Bruni, Rossini, Ghiberti, and others, while other famous men (including Dante) have memorials and cenotaphs.

Donatello (1386–1466),
Annunciation, **c. 1435**
Sandstone (partly gilded),
218 × 168 cm

The Annunciation taber-
nacle in the right aisle of
Santa Croce was once in
the chapel of the Caval-
canti family, and dates
from around 1435. It is
carved from gray *pietra
serena* sandstone, partly
gilded, and is an incomparable combination of classicizing decoration and
spiritual expressiveness.

The Annunciation scene
is set in a niche on solid
consoles under a heavily
molded entablature, which
is flanked by pilasters with
mask capitals. With the
hair and graceful pose of a
Greek goddess, Mary has
jumped up from her seat
in alarm at seeing the
Archangel Gabriel, but at
the same time turns hesi-

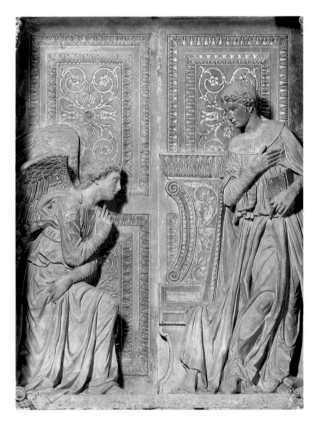

tantly towards him. The two figures are
linked in eye contact. The consequent
divergence in physical posture finds
compensation in the vertical and horizontal structuring of the decoration of the
tabernacle. Putti on the entablature bear
terracotta garlands.

The artist steers the viewer's gaze with
the perspective of the chair. The impression of depth is maintained from the
wholly sculptured heads through the transition to the flatter, delicate relief where
the robes touch the ground.

Giotto (1267–1337),
The Raising of Drusiana, **Cappella Peruzzi,**
c. 1320
Fresco, 280 × 450 cm

The second chapel to the right of the apse chapel was funded by the influential banker Donati di Arnoldo Peruzzi. In 1314, his grandson Giovanni gave Giotto the job of painting it. On the left are important stages in the life story of Florence's patron saint St. John the Baptist, on the right those of St. John the Evangelist – both name saints of the client.

Giotto creates a sense of tension by the disposition and movement of the figures in the scene as the watchers wait for John the Evangelist to arouse a spark of life in the apparently dead woman. At the same time, the emotional charge visibly evident in the watchers and the accuracy of the architecture create a hitherto unknown lifelike quality.

The realistic depiction of Ephesus alludes to the oriental trade connections of the Peruzzi family and at the same time satisfies their need to show off. Giotto's figures made a deep impression on later artists. Masaccio found inspiration here while working in the Brancacci Chapel, and Michelangelo made a pen drawing of Giotto's stooping figure.

Machiavelli – Patriot and Politician

Ruth Strasser

Bust of Niccolò Machiavelli, Palazzo Vecchio, Florence

When 27-year-old Niccolò Machiavelli was appointed head of the Second Chancery and secretary to the Council of Ten in 1498, his native city Florence was in a bad way. The Medici had been driven out of the city four years earlier, and just two months had passed since Savonarola had been burnt at the stake. Factional strife, internal disunity, and unrest ruled the city. The situation was no better in foreign policy. The city was isolated in a loose alliance with France, whose superior power had favored the rule of Savonarola. Like the latter, Machiavelli saw the French campaign in Italy as the beginning of the self-destruction of the whole country. The trouble in Machiavelli's view was that the city states and small republics had failed to close ranks. Only a unified Italy could have held its own against the alien army. The mutual-backscratching diplomacy of Lorenzo the Magnificent's day, based on personal connections, no longer served its purpose and had proved inadequate vis-à-vis the foreign powers. Military force now seemed the appropriate political instrument.

However, to Machiavelli's mind the Italian style of warfare was no longer suitable. He demanded the establishment of a citizen army, because he believed that a state could defend itself only with a standing army. When in 1506 he was commissioned to reorganize the Florentine army, he proposed a citizen militia instead of the usual outside mercenaries. While carrying out his administrative duties, he wrote theoretical studies about military matters, which he later published in his treatise on warfare, the *Libro dell'arte della guerra*. Citizens should henceforth also be soldiers, because only citizens, not mercenaries, made good soldiers. In addition to this, good weapons and good laws were also necessary. What he saw as the deficiencies of a mercenary army is described in his *History of Florence*. The Battle of Anghiari, in which the papal troops, supported by Florence and conscripted mercenaries, defeated the army of the Milanese prince, lasted four hours, during which the battle moved back and forth across a bridge. Only one man died, and this was said to be not the result of sword wounds but because he fell off his horse and was trampled underfoot. The principal booty consisted of horses, standards, and carts. "The fighters were not in danger, they were almost all mounted, armed and sure of their lives as long as they surrendered," writes Machiavelli. "It was not necessary for them to risk their lives. As long as they fought, the armor protected them, and if they could not carry on, they surrendered and so were safe." Battles of this sort were not exceptional in Machiavelli's time. The medieval feudal force or citizen's army had been replaced by hired, paid mercenary troops such as Uccello depicted in his picture of the Battle of San Romano. In the 16th century, people fought for the person who paid them, not solely for patriotic reasons.

Machiavelli was in the employ of the city of Florence until 1512. Most of the time he was traveling in France and Germany as a diplomatic intermediary for the Pope and the Italian dukes. He reported on the political situation and demanded pragmatic responses. When the Medici returned to Florence and the republic

Paolo Uccello, The Battle of San Romano, *c. 1456, tempera on wood, 182 × 323 cm,*
Galleria degli Uffizi, Florence

collapsed in 1512, Machiavelli's political career came virtually to an end. In 1513 he was imprisoned on a charge of conspiracy and banished to his estate in San Casciano under house arrest. There the great works were written: *Il Principe*, the *Discorsi* and the *Storie Fiorentine*.

The Humanists around Pico della Mirandola had already asked themselves how far human willpower and activity (*virtù*) could have any effect on fate (*fortuna*). This aloof and imponderable power seemed to have such supremacy that political action remained without effect, and hope of change was conceivable only in a utopia.

Aware of this crisis, and in sharp contrast to the views of intellectual contemporaries, Machiavelli developed a vision of a united Italian state as the way forward for the future. In a world full of instability and permanent threat, in his view only a powerful prince could unite Italy and preserve peace. In his pragmatically minded writings, he drew up a blueprint for such a political entity. It would be different in its emphasis. In *Il Principe* (The Prince), the solution is the ruler's extraordinary authority, unscrupulouslessness and efficiency (*virtù*), while in the *Discorsi sopra la prima deca di Tito Livio* (Discourses on Livy) the answer was an appropriate structure at constitutional level.

In the *Storie Fiorentine* (History of Florence), written in 1520 for Cardinal Giulio de' Medici, later Pope Clement VII, he expounded his own practical experiences, and developed a historiographical ability schooled in the Classical authors.

By beginning with the fall of Rome and the consequent conflict between emperor and pope, and taking ancient Roman city patriotism as his framework, he broke with the tradition of his Florentine predecessors. Machiavelli viewed the unending factional conflict as the principal cause of Italy's current plight. He depicted the fall of the government as the inevitable consequence of past historical and political developments.

With one eye on the enthusiasm for antiquity in the art and literature of his day, Machiavelli

Niccolò Machiavelli, Il Principe, frontispiece of the Latin translation, Basle 1580

demanded in the *Discorsi* a return to antiquity in politics as well, comparing the current decline with a past he saw as heroic.

After being reconciled with the Medici, Machiavelli was able to come and go in Florence, and in 1519 offered his services to them, although he was given only a few commercial commissions of little importance. In his last years, he increasingly enjoyed writing literary works, including the story *Belfagor* and the comedy *Mandragola*. Shortly before his death, the Medici were toppled again. Machiavelli's endeavors to gain employment in the revived Republic led to nothing – he was accused of collaborating with the previous regime.

Posterity has treated his writings rather cavalierly in coining the term "machiavellian" to describe unscrupulous power politics that ethically justify evil for reasons of state. The 17th-century English writer Samuel Butler even derived the term Old Nick (the Devil) from Niccolò, such was the popular opinion of Machiavelli. It is a willful underestimation of his ability as a politician and statesman.

As if to compensate for this neglect, a British admirer had the following inscription added to his tomb in Santa Croce on the 300th anniversary of his death: *Tanto nomini nullum par elogium* (The greatness of this name is not gauged by praise).

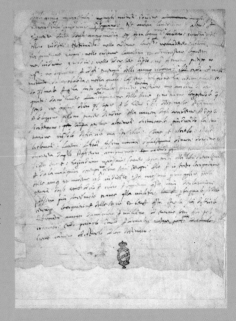

Niccolò Machiavelli, page of manuscript of
I Discorsi, *1519, ink on paper, Biblioteca Nazionale, Florence*

Cappella Pazzi

Around 1430, Andrea dei Pazzi commissioned the architect Filippo Brunelleschi to build a family chapel-cum-monastic chapter house for him. The attic of the portico is carried on six Corinthian pillars, with the center being raised as a triumphal arch. This motif is continued inside in the spacious, barrel-vaulted interior.

A twelve-sided melon dome in the main space links the short barrel-vaulted arms and the small rectangular apse, itself capped by a small dome, to the center. The axes and center intersect in an entirely new manner.

The geometrical clarity of the structure is continued in the interior articulation, the geometrical figures and repeated dimensions. For example, the pilasters of adjoining walls meet in the corner not just to look like load-bearing features but also to preserve the optical balance of the decorative elements. The gray stone emphasizes the load-bearing and parts of the architecture. The colored terracotta reliefs by Andrea della Robbia add sparkle to the overall impression of this "geometry in stone."

Bargello

The Palazzo del Bargello houses the Museo Nazionale, with works by Ghiberti, Donatello, Verrocchio, Michelangelo, and Cellini. As a building, it is one of the principal sights of the city. In 1250, the Florentine government of the *primo popolo* decided to construct its first communal palace. Originally conceived as the seat of the *capitano del popolo*, for whom it was initially named, it was subsequently occupied by the *podestà*, the principal justice official, as a residence and office. From 1574, the communal palace became the seat of the chief of police, the *bargello*.

The massive complex is made up of several individual units. The oldest part is on the south side, and includes the even older 177-foot (54-m) tower. Projecting string courses and Romanesque double-arched windows articulate the stories. Large holes for beams indicate the former presence of a wooden gallery running round. Three Gothic crenellated wings form three sides of the palazzo. The well-proportioned loggia of the interior court dates from 1280 to 1320, when a fourth wing was added. From the early 16th century to the late 18th century, the enclosed court was used for executions. Prominently displayed are two cannons cast by Cosimo Cenni, one with the head of Paul, the other with the Jupiter "moon" discovered by Galileo in 1610.

Michelangelo Buonarroti (1475–1564),
Drunken Bacchus, 1496–1497
Marble, h. 184 cm

This figure – once considered even by experts as an ancient Classical work – was commissioned from the young Michelangelo, presumably in 1496–1497, by Jacopo Galli for his Roman Classical garden.

No other marble sculpture of the whole Quattrocento displays this "soft" outline or almost velvety surface. Unlike ancient Roman sculptors, Michelangelo depicts the divinity as young, unsteady and drunk. The youth raises a bowl up with his right hand. The Classical *contrapposto* technique is treated by Michelangelo with great originality. The slight exaggeration of engaged and disengaged legs enhances the appearance of tipsiness, but Michelangelo so disposes the full body elements as to create a balance within the whole figure.

Donatello (1386–1466),
David, c. 1440
Bronze, h. 158 cm

The first freestanding nude figure since antiquity, this is one of Donatello's most notable achievements, and was presumably intended as a fountain figure. The completely unclothed and androgynous-looking youth places a foot upon the head of Goliath, round which the victor's crown is arranged like a still life. The boy's head is inclined, and gracefully framed by long hair, ribbons, and a hat. The contrast between the bearded head of the giant and the delicate boyish figure is beautifully realized. The feathers on Goliath's helmet graze the boy's inner thigh – the interplay between the contrasting smooth and rough areas is very sensual. David appears here not just as a hero: he also represents youth and beauty defeating age, which was for Florentines a potent symbol of the independent republic.

Dante Alighieri and Italian Literature
Ruth Strasser

Luca Signorelli (1450–1523), portrait of Dante Alighieri, 1485/90, black charcoal pencil on paper, 23.7 × 15.5 cm, Kupferstichkabinett, Berlin

"Nel mezzo del cammin di nostra vita,
Mi ritrovai per una selva oscura,
Chè la diritta via era smarrita."

(In the middle of our life's journey I found myself in a dark wood, because I had lost the right path.)

These opening lines of the *Divine Comedy*, Dante's literary masterpiece, not only mark the beginning of a poetic journey through Hell, Purgatory, and Paradise, but also presumably contain references to a turning point in the poet's real life. According to his own, if coded, information, the journey in the *Divina Commedia* lasts from Good Friday to Easter Sunday 1300, and thus ends at a moment that coincides approximately with the poet's 35th birthday. What happened that Dante appears to say of himself that he had "lost the right path" in the first half of his life, and why does he speak of a "dark wood"?

"I was born and grew up in the great city on the Arno," (*Inferno* XXIII, 94) under the sign of Gemini, i.e., probably at the end of May 1265. Dante Alighieri was the son of a long-established Florentine family that belonged to the Guelph party. Dante never mentions his parents, but he does mention his great-great-grandfather Cacciaguida, whom he meets in Paradise in the Mars heaven and talks with at length about his ancestors. Following a

Classical education, including rhetoric and elegant writing, Dante soon turned to poetry. He studied Virgil, Ovid, the poems of the Provençal troubadours, the Sicilian poets at the court of Frederick II of Hohenstaufen, and then, especially, the leading Florentine poet of the time, Guido Cavalcanti.

"Our poet was of middling stature," writes Boccaccio, "had a long face with an aquiline nose, a prominent lower jaw and strongly projecting lower lip that made him often push out the upper lip, rather round shoulders, brown eyes tending to large rather than small, curly black hair and beard, and was always melancholy and pensive." The encounter with Beatrice was an early turning point in his youth. She was the daughter of the rich merchant Folco Portinari. Both were still children, but Dante idealized Beatrice in a mystic vision to embody absolute, exalted love, and called her his spiritual mentor. After her premature death in 1290, Dante wrote his first work, *La Vita Nuova*, where his soul rises to a new life in the heavenly spheres thanks to his love for the friend of his childhood. From the following decade we have only a few meager details of what was a thoroughly ordinary life: marriage to Gemma Donati, several children (the sources disagree on the number), registry in the "Higher Guild of Doctors and Apothecaries," debts, and

along with all this the study of philosophy and creation of the *Rime*, a collection of love poetry and panegyrics about the ideal woman, in which he moved beyond the medieval courtly

Domenico di Micheline, Dante and the Divine Comedy, *1465, fresco, Duomo (S. Maria del Fiore), Florence*

lyric and, as he notes later in the *Inferno*, developed the *dolce stil novo*, the "sweet new style." With his election in 1300 as prior, one of the highest civic offices, he began to take an active part in politics. Though as a Florentine he was a member of the Guelph party, this had split into two factions at the time. The moderate Whites, who were willing to compromise and were led by Vieri Cerchi, had the majority in the city assembly, and endeavored to establish a balance in the conflict between pope and emperor. The opposite faction of the Blacks was led by Corso Donati, an established conservative family. They maintained a fundamentalist pro-papal policy, attempting to make the whole of Tuscany a fiefdom of the Church. The liberty and independence of the city republic was always a matter close to Dante's heart. (It would later reveal itself prominently in his political treatise *De monarchia*, advocating a clear separation of the power of emperor and pope.) In the following two years he adopted an extreme anti-papal stance directed against Boniface VIII, whom we meet later in the realms of hell in the *Inferno*. When the French king Charles of Valois occupied Florence at the pope's own request in 1301, bringing with him the Blacks, who had in the meantime been banished, sentence was passed on Dante and on his party banishing them for life, with death at the stake if they returned. Thus began the restless wandering in the real life of Dante the poet and politician. His journey took him from princely court to princely court, in various cities and lands of central and northern Italy. He was a welcome guest everywhere, but the free Florentine intellectual felt at home nowhere.

Sandro Botticelli, (c. 1445–1510) Dante and Beatrice in the Mercury heaven (Paradiso VI), Illustration to Dante's Divine Comedy, 1482–87, parchment, Kupferstichkabinett, Berlin

In these first years of his exile he wrote the *Divine Comedy*, the action of which he dates to Easter 1300, i.e., Christianity's first Jubilee year, devised by Pope Boniface VIII as an opportunity to sell plenary indulgences en masse. In the narrative of the *Divina Commedia*, Dante is led out of the "dark wood" by the friend from antiquity, the poet Virgil. The newfound path requires exertion, but has its rewards. In close concentric circles the descent into the Inferno spirals down via the "City of Sorrows," where the souls of the damned are banished without any hope of redemption to suffer punishment and the torments of hell, to the abyss inhabited by Satan, whose maw swallows the worst sinners. From there, the path leads upwards to the Mountain of Purification, which he also lays out in concentric rings. The souls in Purgatory can hope, because they have the chance to be purified of their misdeeds step by step, via repentance, physical punishment, meditation, and prayer, according to the severity of the seven deadly sins: pride, covetousness, lust, anger, gluttony, envy, and sloth. Arriving at the top of the mountain, Virgil's mission is ended. As a representative of pagan antiquity, the ascent to the paradise of heaven is blocked to him. Dante is now taken by the hand by Beatrice. The path leads him through the heavenly spheres to the top of the dome of heaven, where he, mortal man, runs out of words and acknowledges the love that moves the sun and other stars – ... *l'amor che muove il sole e l'altre stelle*, as it says in the last verse.

With this work, which is written in tercets and consists of 100 cantos, Dante unfolds not just the history and philosophy of antiquity, the foundations of Christianity, and the medieval outlook as in a monumental film, but also explores for the first time the relationship of the individual to the divine universe and vice versa, the relationship between the static and dynamic order of the cosmos and the soul of the individual, as well as personal biography. "Because it began terribly and ends well," he therefore called the work a "commedia," but also because for the first time it was written in the popular language of Tuscany (the *volgare*) and not in Latin, the language of the clergy and educated. The adjective *divina* was added later by Boccaccio.

Dante died in the night of September 13/14 1321 at the court of prince Guido da Polenta in Ravenna, where he had spent the last two years of his life as secretary and a teacher of poetry and rhetoric. His tomb is found in a small chapel of the church of S. Francesco in Ravenna. The Florentines have established a Dante Museum in memory of their great son, and erected a large cenotaph in S. Croce and various other monuments throughout the city,

Sandro Botticelli, Cone of Hell, *drawing for the* Divine Comedy, *after 1480, Kupferstichkabinett, Berlin*

even though he was exiled from his native city and never set foot there again.

Ponte Vecchio

There was a bridge across the Arno at its narrowest point even in Roman days, as a prolongation of the Via Cassia. Over the years several wooden structures were carried away by floods. The first stone bridge was the Ponte Vecchio, begun in 1345. Even in medieval times, the city derived considerable revenues from renting the shops on the bridge.

The desire of Cosimo I to have a safe link between the Palazzo Vecchio and his new residence over the Arno, the Palazzo Pitti, led to a major disruption of life on the bridge. Vasari constructed a walkway (now known as the "Corridoio Vasariano") through the Uffizi, along the river and over the bridge. The route runs over the houses and is recognizable from the barred windows. According to a decree of 1595 that is still in effect, only goldsmiths can offer their wares on the bridge.

Santa Felicità

The building dates back to the 4th century, making it probably Florence's oldest church. Its portico was incorporated by Vasari into the walkway to the Ponte Vecchio. Its present appearance results largely from 18th-century reconstructions.

Jacopo Pontormo (1494–1557),
***Deposition*, c. 1525**
Oil on wood, 313 × 193 cm

In 1525, Pontormo was commissioned to provide paintings for the central-plan Cappella Capponi created by Brunelleschi. As well as the remarkable *Annunciation* fresco, he also made the *Deposition* altarpiece, which is still in its original position.

The drapery of the figures is painted in bright, light-filled colors. The figures are gathered around the body of Christ displaying a great variety of gestures and physical contortions, and form a compact group that fills almost the entire pictorial surface. In this extraordi- nary and unique artistic masterpiece, Pontormo dispenses with landscape and architectural background features entirely in favour of studies of the human form.

S. Miniato al Monte

High above the south bank of the Arno is San Miniato al Monte. Like the Baptistery, it is a Romanesque building of the Florentine Proto-Renaissance. The site is possibly that of the oldest shrine in the city, since a place of worship is said to have been raised over the tomb of the Early Christian martyr Minias in about 250 B.C.

A church was mentioned here in the time of Charlemagne, and in 1018 it passed to the Cluniac Benedictines. Around this time a crypt was constructed for the tomb of St. Minias, and ushered in a period of building activity, which by 1200 had produced a new church.

The façade overlooking the city is clad in white and green marble, its design reflecting the basilican system inside. The ground story, completed in about 1070, features semicircular arcades on ancient columns. As in the Florentine Baptistery, perfect proportions were obtained through the use of decorative stone facings.

The middle story is more richly decorated with a mosaic of the *Enthroned Christ, the Virgin and Minias* above an aediculated window and sculptural features. The gable displays further decorative facings that are familiar from the interior of the Baptistery. As the guild of cloth merchants had control of the building and financed the works, it is crowned by their heraldic emblem, whicih is an eagle perched on a bale of wool.

The Interior

An unusual feature is the pair of grandiose transverse arches providing stressed accents in an otherwise regular longitudinal rhythm of nave arches, whose capitals largely date from antiquity. The shafts were faced in plaster in the 19th century, imitating the marble decoration of the clerestory walls. The Romanesque apse mosaic was reworked at the same date. The remarkable marble decoration of the floor was laid in about 1207.

The high-quality ciborium over the altar is by Michelozzo (1448). It hides the original view of the coffin of St. Minias in the extensive crypt beneath the choir.

Spinello Aretino (c. 1350–1410),
St. Benedict Revives a Monk from under the
***Rubble**, c. 1387*
Fresco

The fresco cycle of the life of St. Benedict in the sacristy of S. Miniato al Monte is the work of Spinello Aretino, the son of a goldsmith from Arezzo. In this scene, St. Benedict, who founded the first monastic order in the Western world in the 6th century, revives a monk from under rubble apparently caused by an earthquake. The landscape, depiction of contemporary architecture, treatment of nature and the spatial arrangement of the figures clearly show how indebted Spinello was to Giotto's example even 50 years after the latter's death, though his style lacks the conviction of Giotto.

Palazzo Pitti

The Palazzo Pitti is the largest building in the district of Oltrarno on the south bank of the Arno. It was begun in 1457 by Luca Fancelli for the rich merchant Luca Pitti. The design envisaged seven vertical axes on three floors. When Duke Cosimo I de' Medici acquired the building for his wife Eleonora di Toledo in 1549, Bartolommeo Ammanati began work on extending it to the rear to make a three-wing layout. From 1620, architects Giulio and Alfonso Parigi lengthened the façade to its present extent. At the end of the 18th century, two flanking wings were added. The Palazzo Pitti was the residence of the dukes and grand dukes of Tuscany for over 300 years, and subsequently (until 1946) of members of the Savoy royal family.

The style of the façade is notable for its rustication and the round arches of the doors and windows. On the ground floor, the windows are supported by brackets with lions' heads and the ducal crown, and look like recessed aedicules. In the upper stories, the simple windows have no breast and reach down to the band molding. The surrounding stonework is quite flat here. Ammanati's plan for the inner court – a combination of Florentine rustication and Classical orders – is interesting. At the bottom, rustication rings are placed close together on Tuscan columns, while above that the rustication blocks are on Ionic columns, square and set out. On the top story, the rings return, this time on Corinthian columns.

To the rear of the palace is the extensive park of the Boboli Gardens, which are among the finest gardens in Italy.

Palazzo Pitti – Galleria Palatina and Appartamenti Reali
(Piano Nobile)

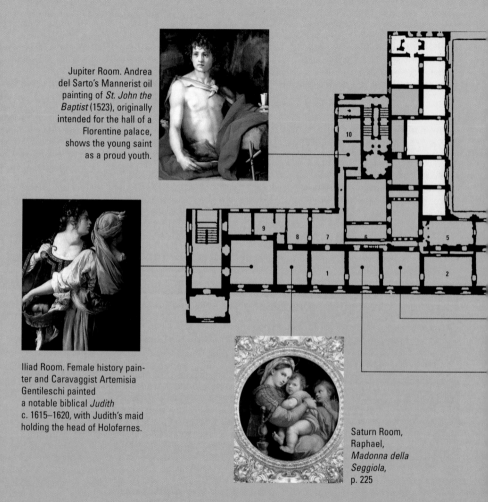

Jupiter Room. Andrea del Sarto's Mannerist oil painting of *St. John the Baptist* (1523), originally intended for the hall of a Florentine palace, shows the young saint as a proud youth.

Iliad Room. Female history painter and Caravaggist Artemisia Gentileschi painted a notable biblical *Judith* c. 1615–1620, with Judith's maid holding the head of Holofernes.

Saturn Room, Raphael, *Madonna della Seggiola*, p. 225

Giardino di Boboli

Appartamenti Reali
(Royal Apartments)

Volterrano Rooms

0   65 ft
20 m

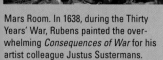

Mars Room. In 1638, during the Thirty Years' War, Rubens painted the overwhelming *Consequences of War* for his artist colleague Justus Sustermans.

Apollo Room. Titian's grand *Portrait of a Gentleman* (c. 1540–1545), the identity of the English sitter being unknown.

Galleria Palatina, Sala di Marte

The extraordinary fame of the art collection in the Palazzo Pitti is largely based on the Renaissance and Baroque paintings in the Galleria Palatina, which was opened to the public by Leopold II in 1828. The master works created by Raphael, Titian, Tintoretto, Rubens, and others, are on display in an environment that still bears the stamp of a princely collection. The pictures are hung above each other according to their content and decorative features, often tying in with the subject matter of the ceiling painting. Thus the ceiling of the Mars Room (Sala di Marte) shows Pietro da Cortona's *Allegories of War* (1646). Matching it is Rubens's great *Allegory of War*, in which the god Mars eludes the embrace of his beloved Venus to follow Discord.

Raphael (1483–1520),
Madonna della Seggiola, c. 1515
Oil on wood, diam. 71 cm

One of the best-known works by Raphael, the tondo is famous for its full, warm colors, its circular composition, and the everyday, populist nature of the picture.

The Mother of God sits on a chair (after which the picture is named) dressed as a Roman woman. She is bending forward to clasp the chubby child in her lap. The baby Jesus cuddles up to his mother in a very natural fashion while the infant John the Baptist approaches from behind. The

figures form almost a complete circle. The viewer's gaze is caught by the bright childish eyes of the boy Jesus, who like his mother looks out of the picture. The impression of great intimacy and human closeness is very unusual.

Raphael painted this work about 1515 in Rome while working there as an architect. Despite the complex composition, his figures possess a natural, dignified beauty.

S. Maria del Carmine

The Baroque church of S. Maria del Carmine with its incomplete façade was built in 1771 after its predecessor burnt down. Of the original Carmelite church, only the sacristy, Cappella Corsini, and famous Brancacci chapel were saved.

Cappella Brancacci, Masaccio (1401–1428), *The Tribute Money*, c. 1427/28
Masaccio and Filippino Lippi (c. 1457–1504), *St. Peter Raising the Son of Theophilus from the Dead*, c. 1425 and 1485,
Frescoes, 255/230 x 598cm

Francesco Brancacci commissioned the paintings for the chapel from Masolino in

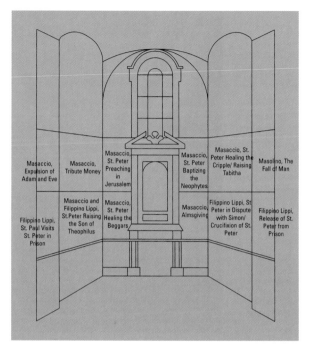

| Masaccio, Expulsion of Adam and Eve | Masaccio, Tribute Money | Masaccio, St. Peter Preaching in Jerusalem | Masaccio, St. Peter Baptizing the Neophytes | Masaccio, St. Peter Healing the Cripple/ Raising Tabitha | Masolino, The Fall of Man |

| Filippino Lippi, St. Paul Visits St. Peter in Prison | Masaccio and Filippino Lippi, St.Peter Raising the Son of Theophilus | Masaccio, St. Peter Healing the Beggars | Masaccio, Almsgiving | Filippino Lippi, St. Peter in Dispute with Simon/ Crucifixion of St. Peter | Filippino Lippi, Release of St. Peter from Prison |

1424, the subject being the life of Peter. In 1426, Masolino brought in Masaccio. Masolino's departure for Rome and Masaccio's sudden death left the works unfinished until 1480–1485 (Filippino Lippi).

Masaccio's frescoes represent a new phase in early Quattrocento painting. He combines the monumentality of Giotto's figures with the self-assured characters of the Early Renaissance. The biblical account becomes a dramatic event in a realistic setting.

Masolino (1383–after 1440),
The Fall **(detail), c. 1427**
Fresco, 214 × 89 cm

Masolino's *Fall* fresco makes an excellent comparison with Masaccio's *Expulsion from Paradise* on the opposite wall. From this it is quite evident how Masolino, as the older man, stuck to a much more traditional – but no less delightful – symbolism-based artistic style.

S. Spirito

The Augustinians settled in Florence in the 13th century. Planning for a brand-new church of S. Spirito started in 1397, but despite economy measures by the monks, it was not until 1434 that the necessary money came together for the costly building, with the help of donations from rich families. A building committee was appointed, and commissioned plans from Brunelleschi. By 1446, the structure was almost ready for the vault when the death of the architect brought work to a halt. Only in 1482 was the church finally completed, though despite the Baroque volutes the façade still looks unfinished. Santo Spirito is consider the "purest" of Brunelleschi's buildings: he was able to plan without reference to an existing structure, and could realize his vision unhampered.

The Interior

The interior is a clear statement of architectural design, with gray stone stripes in the red tiled floor indicating the basic square geometry of the ground plan. The proportions of the nave and aisles and crossing are based on this square. The final constituents are semicircular side chapels. It is the even arrangement of these geometrical elements that produces a sequence directed towards the center of the church, the crossing, which is vaulted with an impressively designed pendentive dome.

Forty-eight slender gray monolith columns with Corinthian capitals mark the intersection points of the basic ground plan squares. This produces the longitudinal rhythm, they and the aisles and chapels being continued all the way round the cruciform plan. The wholly novel approach brought Brunelleschi closer to his ideal of a centrally planned design.

The crossing is now occupied by a Baroque baldacchino that is lavishly decorated with *pietra dura* inlays made of semiprecious stone.

The extensive decoration of the 40 chapels is almost all original. The numerous paintings still occupy their heavy Renaissance frames, their predellas have not been removed, and the usual *paliotti* are still in place on all the altars.

Master of the Johnson Birth, *Madonna del Soccorso*, 1475–1485
Oil on wood

The unusual subject of the Madonna of Succor, here by an unknown master, tended to be an Umbrian specialty. It was very popular among the Augustinians and is based upon an apocryphal legend about the Virgin Mary.

Painted markedly larger than the other figures, Mary thrashes the devil out of a young child, whose mother begs for help on her knees. The design is remarkable for its severe linear floor geometry and alternating tree patterns on the wall, while Mary and the devil are richly decorated.

Tuscan Futurism

Ruth Strasser

"... let's have an end to the portraits, the paintings of interiors, and lakes and mountains, ...the marble jobs, ... the speculative architecture of the reinforced concrete merchants, the decorators, ... the pottery abortions, ... the sloppy illustrators."

On February 11, 1910, one year after the publication of the *Futurist Manifesto* of Filippo Tommaso Marinetti in the Paris newspaper *Le Figaro*, the *Manifesto dei pittori futuristi* (Manifesto of Futurist Painting) was signed by Milanese artists Umberto Boccioni and Carlo Carrà, Roman artist Giacomo Balla, and the Florentine Gino Severini.

From the first day of the Futurist movement, the writer Marinetti and the Milanese signatories had hoped to win the Florentine iconoclasts for Futurism. And they did, though initially not quite as expected. In 1913 three Florentine artists and writers – Ardengo Soffici, Giovanni Papini and Aldo Palazzeschi – had founded a

Advertising card of the Caffè delle Giubbe Rosse

periodical called *Lacerba*, to the horror of the bourgeoisie and great delight of artists and intellectuals in Florence. From that time, the favorite meeting place of these young rebels, known as the *Lacerbiani*, became the Caffè delle Giubbe Rosse in the Piazza Vittorio Emanuele II (now called the Piazza della Repubblica) in Florence, thus named for the red jackets worn by its waiters. In the café, which has been founded by two German brothers, the front area near the door was customarily occupied by German tourists, behind them in the gloom were the young couples, and right at the back was the *bolgia*, the "bedlam," which was open until all hours. In this third room or *Terza Saletta*, in a dense fug of smoke, sat the Florentine avant-garde group arguing in loud voices, with ever more young artists joining in as time passed. "Not my house, I have no house, not the piazza, that's for charlatans and other socialists, not the landscape, not a creature between almond and peach blossom am I, but my corner in the little third room of the Giubbe Rosse, that is my house," is how a regular described the atmosphere of the place. The articles published in *Lacerba* attacking leading

Title page of Lacerba, *issue no. 2*

members of Futurism became ever more outrageous and provocative. One day, Soffici launched one such attack inveighing against Boccioni in another periodical, *La Voce*, saying that his pictures were a mixture of Belgian Impressionism, Segantini-style Divisionism and a kind of second-hand Cubism. In addition, he criticized the Milan Futurists for their banality, lack of ability, and inadequate mastery of artistic techniques. Enough was finally enough. Boccioni, Marinetti and Carrà turned up in Florence spoiling for a confrontation. Verbal and physical clashes ensued between the artists and their critics in the Caffè Giubbe Rosse. Following further strident but no longer violent discussions, the Florentine rabble-rousers, the *Vociani*, were integrated into the Futurist brotherhood – though on condition they could keep their critical attitude and choose their own artistic expression.

There followed the publication of another manifesto, in which the Futurists demanded a break from tradition and the past, academism and imitation, and lauded all kinds of originality, struggle, risk, technology, speed, as well as war, which they expressed in their own specific concepts, formulae and images such as "aggressive motion, feverish sleeplessness, walking at the double, the *salto mortale*, a cuff on the ear and a punch in the face."

Futurist meeting outside the Giubbe Rosse, Christmas 1949 (l. to r.): Pierre Santi, Giacomo Natta, Dino Caponi, Leonetto Leoni, Eugenio Montale, and Arturo Lorta

In his Futurist manifesto of 1913, the Florentine intellectual and artist Gino Severini called for the abolition of "centers of emotion" that "contradict movement," such as the nude, the human body, still lifes, and landscapes. He foresaw the end of the art forms of picture and sculpture, which in his opinion "limit our creative freedom" and carry their destiny – museums and collectors' salons – in them.

He also demanded that "our visual creation live in the open air and be completed in architectural contexts, with which they share active interplay with the external world, whose specific entities they represent."

The outbreak of World War I resulted in a split into, on the one hand, an artistic grouping

Futurist meeting in the Giubbe Rosse (l. to r.): Ugo Capoccini, Leonetto Leoni, Mario Luzi, Eugenio Montale, Alessandro Parronchi and Giuseppe Raimondi

that mainly sought to explore ways of depicting motion in every artistic genre and, on the other, a political group that called for participation in the war and, exalting the "will to power," joined the burgeoning ranks of fascism. Meanwhile the Florentine Futurists rejected the glorification of technology at the expense of aesthetic beauty and harmony, as expressed in the now famous words of Marinetti – "a racing car with an explosive exhaust, a roaring car that rattles like a machine gun, is lovelier than the Victory of Samothrace." In time, their style blended into various other styles.

Gino Severini (1883–1966), Danse macabre, *Collezione d'Arte Religiosa Moderna, Vatican*

Palazzo Rucellai

S. Maria Novella

The palazzo for the Rucellai family, one of the most elegant secular buildings in the city, was designed by Alberti but constructed by Bernardo Rossellino (1446–1461). The rusticated façade is divided into bays of large biforate windows between flat pilasters conforming to the Classical Vitruvian canon of Ionic, Doric, and Corinthian orders. The horizontal axis is formed by continuous projecting band moldings.

The church and monastery of S. Maria Novella lie west of the city center. The Dominicans took over a 10th-century oratory in 1221, and in 1246 began work on a new choir and transept. In 1279, the foundation stone of the nave was laid under the direction of lay brothers Fra Ristorno and Fra Sisto.

The design was on a scale and monumentality hitherto unknown in Florence. By 1300, a basilica design with a transept and flat choir chapels was in place, while the bell tower was extended between 1330 and 1350. Shortly after, the lower part of the façade, with its tall blind arcades and tomb niches, the *avelli* that are continued in the wall of the neighboring cemetery, was faced with decorative patterns. Finally, around 1450 Alberti altered the façade, retaining its lower arcade and center window, which he incorporated into an overall structure which includes an attic story and lofty gable. The ground floor is articulated with engaged columns and a solid entablature. For decorative elements, he largely employed traditional motifs such as the regular marble stripes and rectangular patterning familiar from the Baptistery in Florence. However, the rising volutes are completely novel, as are the billowing sails shown on the entablature frieze, the family crest of the client, Giovanni di Paolo Rucellai.

the harmonious linking of support and vault and the number and elegance of the arches, which despite varying radii looking homogeneous, give a clear rhythm to the interior and direct the eye towards the apparently distant choir.

Vasari had the original Trecento frescoes completely whitewashed over. The Dominican church is richly furnished with tombstones either recessed into the floor or placed on the walls. Renaissance artists such as Brunelleschi, Filippino Lippi and also Ghiberti have left their marks here.

Masaccio (1401–1428), *Trinity*, c. 1427
Fresco, 667 × 317 cm

The Interior

The basilica ground plan with a transept and five chapels was constructed as a spacious interior with groin vaulting, marble-striped pointed arches, and foliated capitals. The lightness of the walls,

Masaccio's fresco counts as one of the most important works of the Early Renaissance. This is the first occasion on which the linear perspective worked out by Brunelleschi was applied in a painting. The famous architect, a friend of the artist, was presumably on hand when the painting was being executed in 1427. The fresco features a unique combination of the three arts of architecture, sculpture, and painting. A Renaissance "chapel" opens up above a painted tomb niche, in front of which the Lenzi donor couple kneel. In the "chapel" is the Cross, with the Virgin and St John to the sides. The dove of the Holy Ghost floats over the head of Christ. The figure of God the Father looms behind the crucifix. The accuracy of Masaccio's architectural perspective is such that it creates a strange tension in its realism.

The meticulous and consistent detail in the way in which Masaccio attains the illusion of a space opening up in the wall on a two-dimensional surface is illustrated in an imaginary cross-section (drawing after Sanpaolesi).

Precise calculation enabled the artist to show all the figures in accordance with their position within a hypothetical architectural space.

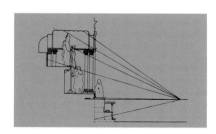

**Cappella Tornabuoni, Domenico Ghirlandaio
(1449–1494),**
Birth of St. John the Baptist, 1485–1490
Fresco

A view opens between ornate painted pilasters into a room in a burgher household.
The new mother is visited by a distinguished lady, with two companions. A
servant rushes in with a bottle of wine and
basket of fruit, the fine material of her
dress billowing coquettishly.

The fresco is a scene from the wonderful
cycles of the life of the Virgin and St. John
the Baptist that Ghirlandaio and his workshop painted between 1486 and 1490 in
the main choir chapel of S. Maria Novella
for the prosperous banker Giovanni
Tornabuoni. The artist's specialism was
painting biblical scenes in contemporary
Florentine guise. The donors were
delighted to see themselves, their loved
ones and wives, friends, and business partners in the pictures.

Cappella di Filippo Strozzi, Filippino Lippi (c. 1457–1504), *Crucifixion of the Apostle Philip and Subduing of a Dragon by the Apostle*, after 1487
Fresco

The banker Filippo Strozzi bought the chapel in S. Maria Novella in 1486 and soon after commissioned Filippino Lippi to paint the walls with frescoes of events in the lives of St. John the Evangelist and his own name saint St. Philip. Strozzi himself was interred in this chapel after his death, his coffin – executed between 1491 and 1493 by Benedetto da Maiano – still lies behind the chapel wall.

The large-format scenes are among the most impressive creations by Filippino, their wide range of imaginative details – which not infrequently paraphrase Classical motifs – showing his extraordinary inventiveness.

S. Lorenzo

The nave of the basilican ground plan of S. Lorenzo differs from the transept in that it is placed on a stepped plinth. The heavy rustication of the façade contrasts with the delicate architectural features of the sides. The various components of the design come together around the choir: the loggia built over the crossing, behind that the huge set-back 17th-century Cappella dei Principi and the 18th-century bell tower, completed by a well-proportioned dome and lantern.

The basilica was consecrated for the first time in 393. A new building begun in 1058 remained virtually unchanged until 1418, when a larger church was planned. The Medici belonged to the parish of S. Lorenzo and, in accordance with their growing influence, they paid for a sacristy – Brunelleschi's Old Sacristy.

The architect's design was so sensationally novel that Giovanni di Bicci de' Medici wanted a new design for the whole church. A year later, in 1421, the foundation stone was laid for the first church of post-medieval architecture in Florence.

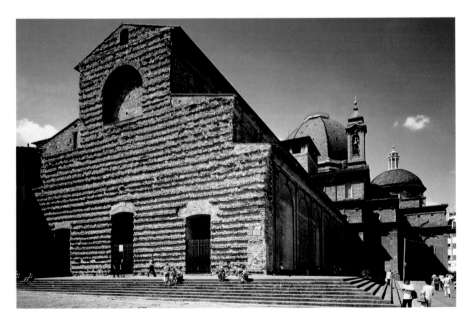

The Interior

The systematic explicit geometry and the harmony of forms and proportions are a statement by the young Brunelleschi of the typical stylistic features of the Renaissance. The semicircles of the nave arcades match the arches of the side chapels and the rhythm of columns and pilasters. The architectural features are linked by a continuous entablature in the nave, aisles, transepts, and choir chapels. The furnishings contain important works by Donatello, Filippo Lippi, Verrocchio, and Desiderio da Settignano.

Rosso Fiorentino (1494–1540), *Marriage of the Virgin Mary*, 1523
Fresco

The mural by Rosso Fiorentino reveals all the characteristics of early-16th century Florentine Mannerism: the subtle drapery motifs and shimmering colors, the masterly depiction of hairstyles, the striking hand gesture of St. Dominic, and the musicians and jesters in the background. Unlike in the usual iconography, Mary is marrying a Joseph who is still very youthful and is elegantly dressed, with blond curls.

de' Medici (Cosimo il Vecchio).

Architectural articulation by pilasters can no longer confine individual scenes – the handsome youths, the Classical-looking scholars and clerics seem like commentators of a biblical event unfolding beneath a frieze of dancing putti without regard to a formal structural frame. Whether the bronze reliefs were indeed intended as a pulpit or constitute part of a tomb for Cosimo de' Medici is a matter of dispute.

Sagrestia Vecchia

The Old Sacristy gave Brunelleschi a further chance to evolve his new architecture. Another commission by the Medici family, it was built between 1419 and 1429 as the first central-plan building of the Renaissance. The sacristy is the family burial chapel. In the center is the sarcophagus of the donor Giovanni di Bicci de' Medici, while on a side wall is the double tomb of two of Cosimo il Vecchio's sons, Giovanni (d. 1463) and Piero Gottoso (d. 1469). Family arms fill the spandrels. Donatello's plaster reliefs show the story of

**Donatello (1386–1466),
Passion pulpit, after 1460**
Bronze, 123 × 292 cm

The most precious articles in the church furnishings are two pulpits by Donatello on the themes of the Passion and the Resurrection. They were done late in the sculptor's life at the behest of Cosimo

St. John the Baptist and thus allude to the donor.

Brunelleschi designed a cube vaulted by a melon dome. The walls were divided up by bold entablatures, above which is the pendentive area beneath the dome. The geometrical shapes of square and circle form the basis of the design, which is reflected in the gray architectural features of wall, pilaster, cornice, and arches. The colored decoration by his friend Donatello must have seemed a contradiction to the architect. Brunelleschi wanted there to be in the dome only a representation of the night sky as it was on July 9, 1422, the day the foundation stone was laid. The walls of the choir chapels are relieved by rounded niches.

Sagrestia Nuova/Cappelle Medicae

As a counterpart to Brunelleschi's Old Sacristy, some 100 years later a New Sacristy or Medici Chapel was built on the north side. In 1520, Pope Leo X commissioned Michelangelo to build a burial chapel for the Medici family, but funerary monuments were completed only for Giuliano, Duke of Nemours and Lorenzo, Duke of Urbino. When Michelangelo finally left Florence in 1534, he left the decoration of the chapel unfinished; it was completed 20 years later by Vasari and Ammanati.

The ground plan, the combination of light wall surfaces with articulatory features in gray *pietra serena* and the basic forms of a hemisphere on top of a cube is still anchored in Brunelleschi mode.

However, Michelangelo created his spatial layout with a looser rhythm and inserted a mezzanine level beneath the dome with an additional cornice.

Michelangelo Buonarroti (1475–1564), Tomb of Giuliano de' Medici, 1526–1531
Marble, h. of Giuliano 180 cm, Night: length of block 200 cm, Day: length of block 211 cm

The tomb architecture on the walls encloses the seated figures of the deceased dukes, to whom the reclining figures are allocated. Presumably they represent times of the day, possibly symbols of "all-consuming time" – Day and Night on the tomb of the Giuliano de' Medici, shown in classical pose and dress, and Dawn and Dusk on the opposite wall with the elegiac, pensive thinker of Lorenzo de' Medici.

As is often the case with Michelangelo, the figures are not worked out completely in all their different parts. They appear to have only just arisen from a "bed" of unhewn stone. Another original figure, the Medici Madonna, replaces a tomb never constructed for Lorenzo il Magnifico and his brother Giuliano, who are interred here in the entrance wall.

Biblioteca Laurenziana

Vestibule

The Biblioteca Laurenziana is one of the most important of Michelangelo's buildings, on which he started work in 1524. The wall of the lofty vestibule or *ricetto* features alternating projecting wall surfaces and recessed columns, a notion that highlights Michelangelo's revolutionary approach: load-bearing elements such as columns are set in niches like decorative statues. The reading room is accessed by a most unusual staircase. Michelangelo only delivered the wooden model for it, which Ammanati implemented at full size, in 1557. The staircase glides from the upper level of the library's reading room down to the floor level in a kind of lava-flow effect that appears to pour into the almost square room. It is the fulfillment of a sculptural view of architecture echoed on the walls, for example in the functionless scrolls on the wall.

Reading Room

The Library was commissioned by the Medici pope Clement VII to house the family's valuable book collection. It included more than 600 manuscripts of Cosimo il Vecchio alone, which are at present stored temporarily in Rome but are due to be returned to Florence.

The particular site and problems connected with the foundations determined the unusual shape and solid walls of the Library. Michelangelo made a virtue of necessity. The pilasters of the side walls thus have a load-bearing rather than a decorative function, carrying the weight of the ceiling beams, which are in turn echoed in the mosaics of the floor. Thus the impression is given of foreshortened rectangular fields that emphasize the spatial depth of the elongated room. The bookshelves likewise are constructed using designs drawn up by Michelangelo. The actual carving of the lecterns was entrusted to leading workshops of the day.

The external design is a rough rusticated ground floor with smoother rustication on the two upper floors. The pronounced band moldings strongly emphasize the horizontals, while the roof is notable for the classicizing, heavily projecting cornice. The rows of fine biforate windows are the main feature of the upper floors, while at ground level, until 1517, great arches opened into a loggia for semi-public ceremonies.

Interior Court

The square interior court is a masterpiece by Michelozzo. It creates a harmonious and light impression, particularly due to the ground-floor arcading. Semicircular arches standing on slender columns with Composite capitals open into a walk that is very reminiscent of a medieval cloister, or of Brunelleschi's loggia at the Foundling

Palazzo Medici-Riccardi

The Palazzo Medici-Riccardi was the first and therefore the tone-setting palace of the Renaissance. It was built in 1444–1469 by Michelozzo for Cosimo (il Vecchio) de' Medici, who had earlier rejected a design by Brunelleschi. Presumably the successful proposal seemed to Cosimo more modest and appropriate. The building remained the residence of the Medici until 1540. In 1659 it was bought by Francesco Riccardi, who had the front extended by seven bays.

Hospital. In the middle floor, the biforate window motif of the exterior façade reappears. The once-open loggia provides an airy surround to the courtyard.

An air of ceremonial splendor is provided by the sgraffiti incised in the plaster, the reliefs in the tondi bearing Medici heraldic devices and mythological scenes. Of the numerous sculptures once installed here, only one remains in place, the *Orpheus* of Baccio Bandinelli.

Cappella dei Magi, Benozzo Gozzoli (1420–1497), *The Journey of Balthasar*, 1459–1461
Fresco

Gozzoli's *Journey of the Magi* (shown here is *Balthasar* on the east wall) is set in a paradisical Tuscan landscape with flowers and animals. Participants of the Council of Florence of 1439 are depicted in idealized portraits, together with the most important older and younger members of the family and leading intellectuals.

S. Marco and the Museo di S. Marco

The Dominican church and monastery of S. Marco stand on one side of the eponymous piazza. The classical stucco façade is late 18th century in style. S. Marco was always closely associated with the Medici family: Cosimo il Vecchio gave the site to the Dominicans of Fiesole and financed the renovation carried out by Michelozzo in 1437–1452. The first prior, St. Antoninus of Florence, opposed the patron when the latter wanted to change the city's constitution. From 1490 Savonarola was prior here, which gave him a pulpit from which to thunder against Lorenzo the Magnificent.

Fra Angelico (c. 1397–1455),
***Deposition*, c. 1430–1440**
Tempera on wood, 185 × 176 cm

Fra Angelico was a monk in S. Marco, and both monastery and museum display numerous examples of his work. One of the most important is the main altarpiece, the predella panels of which are scattered in various museums throughout the world. Another key work by Fra

Angelico, the altarpiece of the *Deposition*, was commissioned by Palla Strozzi for his family chapel. In the middle of the picture, Christ's corpse is being lowered from the Cross. The diagonal of the body and the outstretched arms form the focal point of tension. All the faces are very individual, the flesh tones and gestures varied and the choice of colors for the garments very vivid. On the left is a group of mourning women, and on the right the scourging implements.

Fra Angelico,
Annunciation, c. 1450
Fresco, 230 × 297 cm

The walls of the cells right and left of the dormitory corridor are all painted with frescoes by Fra Angelico, his colleagues, and workshop assistants. Together the frescoes add up to a unique and impressive religious cycle. Mary and the angel of the Annunciation meet in a loggia rather like Michelozzo's cloister for the monastery. Typical of Fra Angelico is the fine linea-

ment of the contours, the very delicate colors – pink, pale violet, a bright blue – and the miniature-like precision of both natural and architectural features. The figures are notable for an innate restraint that admits no violent movement. Fra Angelico dispenses with the angel's usual gesture of blessing, for example, and renders him in the same posture as the Virgin. The resulting portrayal of the encounter is very moving, and emphasizes the modesty with which the Virgin accepts Providence.

Dormitorio di S. Marco

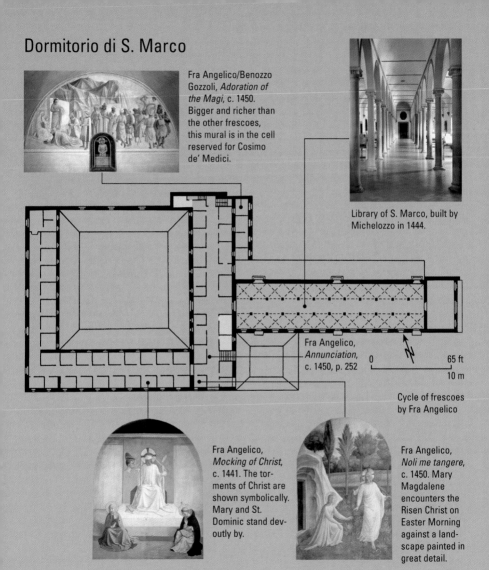

Fra Angelico/Benozzo Gozzoli, *Adoration of the Magi*, c. 1450. Bigger and richer than the other frescoes, this mural is in the cell reserved for Cosimo de' Medici.

Library of S. Marco, built by Michelozzo in 1444.

Fra Angelico, *Annunciation*, c. 1450, p. 252

0   65 ft
      10 m

Cycle of frescoes by Fra Angelico

Fra Angelico, *Mocking of Christ*, c. 1441. The torments of Christ are shown symbolically. Mary and St. Dominic stand devoutly by.

Fra Angelico, *Noli me tangere*, c. 1450. Mary Magdalene encounters the Risen Christ on Easter Morning against a landscape painted in great detail.

Florence's Conscience – Girolamo Savonarola

Ruth Strasser

In the 15th century, Florence was noted for its intellectual and religious tolerance. The emphasis was on communal piety. Vows were thus made for every conceivable purpose, wax images were hung up in churches and generous donations were given. Most popular of all was membership of the two great Florentine fraternities, the *Arciconfraternità della misericordia*, which specialized in the care and burial of the poor, and the *Compagnia di Santa Maria del Bigallo*, which devoted itself mainly to orphans and foundlings. Members of the fraternities came from all social classes. Particularly the wealthy textile manufacturers and bankers delighted – by way of compensating for their everyday profiteering – in acting in the role of anonymous benefactors of the needy. Communal well-being was not to get too raw a deal alongside private well-being. This did of course contain at least a dash of the Christian ideal of *caritas*. Such social commitment has remained a feature of upper and middle-class attitudes in Florence to this day, since it forms part of the essential *fiorentinità*, the quintessential essence of being Florentine. The benefactor is well-to-do both before and afterwards, still has the old family palace, perhaps also the country villa, but such material wealth is kept discreetly hidden. The ideal features such as restraint, modesty, thrift, and a charitable ethos are what you show in public.

Savonarola, however, preached the ideals of poverty and absence of possessions. "If the Church ravages, if it protects harlots, libertines and bandits, and persecutes the meek and destroys Christian life, then it is not Church

Fra Bartolommeo (1472–1517), Portrait of Girolamo Savonarola, *c. 1498, oil on wood,*

power but a devilish power which we not only may but must oppose." Born in 1452, Savonarola came from a landed Ferrarese family. Initially he took up the study of medicine, but abandoned it at 22 – secretly, without his parents' knowledge – to join the mendicant and preaching order of the Dominicans. By then, he was already writing tracts about the decline of the Church and the writings of Aristotle and Thomas Aquinas. As a gifted preacher endowed with lofty missionary zeal, between 1485 and 1489 Savonarola visited numerous Italian cities including Florence, but the Florentines did not take to him.

Nonetheless, from 1490 he was installed at the Dominican monastery of San Marco in Florence, and became its prior in 1491. His sermons now featured the Apocalypse and visions of an imminent end of the world. With his ideals of poverty and lack of possessions, his chastisement of declining morality, degeneration, luxury, waste, and pleasure-seeking in the ranks of the official Church and in Florence, Savonarola exercised great influence on the populace, and was admired by his followers as a prophet. His rhetorical attacks on Lorenzo de' Medici and his son Pietro, and on the Papacy and the Church, became steadily more vitriolic and radical. When the Medici were overthrown in 1494 and Charles VIII of France conquered the kingdom of Naples in 1494–95, his prophecies seemed to be fulfilled, and he made contact with Charles.

Savonarola established in Florence a kind of theocratic democracy in which his ideas were

followed without him taking active part in politics. He remained the éminence grise behind the scene. Alas, the moral zeal of his followers soon turned to surveillance, spying, and denunciation. When on March 18, 1498, in his last sermon before being executed, he demanded the right to resist the Church, Savonarola touched on a sore point. A majority of Florentine society approved of the efforts of a reforming wing among the theologians. They wished to establish a counter-balance to the growing

The Arrest of Savonarola, *wood engraving of 1873*

absolutism of the Pope by means of a conciliar constitution and co-determination in the great, decisive questions of life. These efforts had failed, and the Pope was considered by many as the Antichrist. At the beginning of 1498, Savonarola had published his *Trattato circa il Reggimento di Firenze*

(Tract on the Administration and Government of the City of Florence). This sketches out a form of government based on "justice, peace, and trust among citizens." His earlier prophecies about God's wrath and the imminent apocalypse were transformed into the message that Florence was the chosen republic. The Dominican preacher's idea was that "social relationships ... would be nourished by mutual trust; private dealings of citizens and their intellectual activity ... would be completely free." In his view, this would be possible only if the point of departure and objective were a striving for the communal welfare, the *bene comune*, an ethical principle derived from Aristotle and Tho-mas Aquinas. Yet Savonarola was harshly radical in his views, and demanded the burning of those who yielded to vice and to dissipation, as well as restrictions and the supervision of scholarship, the renunciation of any depictions of the naked body in art. Despite his almost dictatorial sense of mission towards the end of his career, Savonarola referred to the crucified Christ as his model: "I will not preach of myself but Christ... and they will

Medallion commemorating the execution of Savonarola, 1502, bronze, Museo Nazionale del Bargello, Florence

therefore become converted not to my praises but to You..."

When Pope Alexander VI offered him the office of an ecclesiastical dignitary, to wean him from the heedless and outspoken severity of his anticlericalism, Savonarola rejected it: "I desire no cardinal's hat, no miter large or small. I wish for nothing but what You gave Your saints – death... A bloody hat, that is what I desire." This was not his only challenging gesture towards the Church. Earlier he himself had lit a stake and staged a symbolic act of punishment. On February 7, 1497 he arranged a "bonfire of the vanities" in the Piazza della Signoria, when he caused things to be burned which seemed to him symbols of secular vices: musical instruments, pictures, jewelry, playing cards – even the books of Boccaccio and Petrarch because of their "indecent" contents. To prepare for the mom-ent of apocalypse, he argued, people had to reorganise themselves and undergo a political rebirth, radically reforming their government institutions. This was the action that finally prompted Pope

Alexander VI to excommunicate him; but this only spurred him to another, and even more spectacular, bonfire of the vanities the following year in 1498.

On May 23, 1498, after weeks of inhuman torture, Savonarola was condemned, hanged, and his body publicly burned in the Piazza della Signoria as a "representative of heresy, schism, and pernicious innovations." Fearful of relic hunters, the authorities scattered his ashes in the Arno. His tens of thousands of followers, whom he had once gathered about him in Florence Cathedral, had turned into a popular opposition directed against Savonarola himself and finally led to his arrest. Nonetheless, veneration of the austere preacher began soon after his death – his exposition of Psalm 50, the Miserere, which he had written in prison with his hands and feet in chains, was widely disseminated, inc-luding in a printed edition by Luther in 1523. It was only in 1558 that the Church officially acknowledged that his theological ideas coincided with official Church doctrine, and recognized his importance as a charismatic person and visionary.

"A grotesque monster" is how Goethe described him, and 19th-century and 20th-century historians saw Savonarola, the Prior of San Marco, as a grim fanatic who wanted to burn and exterminate the glorious flowerings and fruits of the Renaissance, Humanism and the arts. There is still disagreement about this, with those who see him as a blind religious zealot unreconciled with the notion of a pioneering figure of light.

The influence of Savonarola's preaching was an awareness of the instability of civic life in the absence of adequate political institutions. Floretine intellectuals were increasingly concerend with developing the right polictical constitution.

Unknown artist, The Burning of Savonarola in the Piazza della Signoria *c. 1498, tempera on wood, Museo di S. Marco, Florence*

Galleria dell'Accademia

In the rooms of the former hospital of S. Matteo is the Galleria dell'Accademia. This first academy of art, which was a successor to the St. Luke fraternity of painters, was founded in 1563 by Cosimo de' Medici. In 1784 it was revived by Grand Duke Pietro Leopoldo I.

It was intended to unite teaching and art collecting, academy and gallery functions. The works of Florentine artists from the 13th to the 16th century served as models for students, who were taught the techniques through imitation. In 1873, Michelangelo's *David*, which had over the centuries become an icon for sculptors, was installed in a specially created gallery so as to protect it from the weather.

Michelangelo Buonarroti (1475–1564),
***David*, 1501–1504**
Marble, h. 410 cm

Over 13 feet (4 m) high, Michelangelo's *David* is his best-known work. Made from a tall, narrow block of marble that two other sculptors had already had a go at, it is both colossal and unique. Though the statue was originally intended for the Cathedral, a special commission decided to install it outside the Palazzo Vecchio as a symbol of the independent city republic. Now that the original is in the Gallery, a faithful copy has replaced it in front of the Palazzo. A second copy forms part of the

Michelangelo memorial in the Piazzale Michelangelo, high above the city on the southern bank of the Arno. Michelangelo shows not the victorious David nor the head of the decapitated giant, but resolution and intentness of purpose. The head and right hand, the centers of thought and action, are overlarge compared with the body. Michelangelo breaks with Classical proportions for the sake of truly expressive force.

Michelangelo Buonarroti,
***Waking Slave*, c. 1530–1534**
Marble, h. 267 cm

Other famous Michelangelo works in the Gallery are the much-discussed "Boboli Slaves," named for having been at one time displayed in Buontalenti's grotto in the Boboli Gardens (where they are now replaced by plaster casts). The "Atlas" appears to brace itself against the oppressive burden of the marble block, while the "Waking Slave" laboriously seeks to escape from the stone. In the popular view, the figures are unfinished, but it is precisely their incompleteness, the *nonfinito*, that gives them their expressive force. Their muscular, gigantic bodies are engaged in fruitless revolt. They remain captives in stone, from which only their creator could free them.

S. Annunziata

The Servite church of S. Annunziata, founded in 1250, lies on the north side of a pleasant square surrounded by colonnades. The arch motif, already present in the Foundling Hospital on the east side, was repeated on the Servite fraternity's building on the west, and varied on the church with the tall arcading of the 17th-century portico. Michelozzo, who also designed the forecourt with its arcade and graceful capitals, began rebuilding the church in 1444. The "atrium" is of special note because of the frescoes by Andrea del Sarto, Rosso Fiorentino, and Pontormo.

Andrea del Sarto (1486–1530),
Birth of the Virgin, **1514**
Fresco, 410 × 345 cm

Andrea del Sarto transfers the birth of the Virgin Mary to a splendidly furnished contemporary interior. Dressed in voluminous gowns, court ladies and servants surround the bed of St. Anne, while on the left in front of the fireplace the nurses bustle about the child. The compositional balance with its coloration, spatial disposition, and arrangement of figures suggests why Florentines called del Sarto *Andrea senz'errore* – Unerring Andrea.

Ospedale degli Innocenti

The Foundling Hospital was originally founded by the prosperous silk makers' guild. The terracotta reliefs created by Andrea della Robbia indicate the purpose of the building, which was designed and built by Brunelleschi in 1419. The vestibule sets the tone for the whole square, and lends the orphanage an exalted Classical character. As in a Roman temple, the loggia is opened up to form an arcaded corridor. The Foundling Hospital is often described as the first building in a Renaissance style. The arcade terminates in pilasters that have no static purpose and this innovatory use of pilasters became a standard feature.

Museo Archeologico

The Museo Nazionale Archeologico, one of Italy's most important archaeological museums, has been in the Palazzo della Crocetta since 1880. The palazzo was built in 1620 for the Archduchess of Austria, the wife of Cosimo II. The Etruscan department provides a comprehensive survey of the Etruscans in Tuscany.

François Vase, c. 570–560 B.C.
66 × 57 cm, diam. 181 cm

A notable item in the rich collection of vases is the *François Vase*, found by painter and engraver François in an Etruscan grave near Chiusi in 1845. The Greek

valuable find put on display in the Palazzo Vecchio. An inscription on the right foreleg of the mythical monster indicates it is a votive gift. In Greek mythology, the beast – part lion, part goat, and part snake – lived as a fire-breathing beast on the west coast of Lycia. Both the quality of workmanship and the bronze casting are remarkable.

painter Cleitias and the potter Ergotimus signed it in 570–560 B.C., after which the large Attic scrolled crater, which served to mix water and wine, was exported to Etruria. The painting, done in black on a red ground, shows several strips of hunting, fighting, and sacrificial scenes, which are depicted in an unusually vivid and lively way.

Chimera of Arezzo, end 5th century B.C.
Bronze, 78.5 × 129 cm

This bronze chimera was found in Arezzo during the construction of the city wall in 1553. It was presumably made there in the late 5th century B.C. Cosimo I de' Medici had the tail of the figure restored and the

Accademia della Crusca – Guardian of the Language

Ruth Strasser

The Accademia della Crusca (literally the Bran Academy) was founded in Florence in 1583 under the auspices of Grand Duke Francesco I de' Medici. Its motto is *Il più bel fior ne coglie* (She picks the loveliest flowers), from a poem by Petrarch, and its purpose is to keep the wheat in the Italian language clearly separate from the chaff. The venerable institution still exists, and as a national institution remains based in the region that is the source of the Italian language. Since 1974, it has been accommodated at the Medici villa of Castello on the edge of Florence. Its job is still to preserve the popular language of Tuscany in its pure form together with its folk idiom, and protect it from an overdose of foreign words, anglicisms, and jargon from the computer and media worlds.

During the Middle Ages, Latin predominated as the common language of writing throughout the Mediterranean region, including Italian-speaking countries. Classical Latin itself contained many words borrowed from Greek, and even after the collapse of the Roman Empire, when close contact was maintained with Byzantium and many educated people were fluent in both languages, still more Greek words entered Latin. Alongside this development there were numerous dialects in the individual areas of politically divided Italy that are not known to have been recorded in written form.

The first evidence of a written vernacular is found in the *Placito Capuano*, a 10th-century document concerning contracts regulating the ownership of agricultural land. The first school of Italian poetry arose 200 years later at the court of the Hohenstaufen emperor Frederick II in Sicily, where courtly love songs were composed in a southern Italian dialect. At the same time St. Francis of Assisi wrote his hymns and the *Canticle of the Sun* in the vernacular of central Italy.

With the rise of the city republics and the formation of a burgher class of merchants, bankers, and artisans, records and chronicles began to be written in the vernacular rather than Latin, so as to be comprehensible to all, including the middle and lower classes. However, it was the *tre corone*, the three writers crowned with the laurel wreath, Dante, Petrarch, and Boccaccio, all of them Tuscan-born, who gave the vernacular literary status. With the publication of Dante's *Divina Commedia*, *La Vita Nuova*, his treatise *De vulgari eloquentia* concerning the value of Italian as a literary language, of Petrarch's *Canzoniere,* and of Boccaccio's *Decamerone*, the everyday language of Tuscany, the *volgare*, established itself as a new written language. Its use for literary purposes enhanced its reputation and status, because instead of being associated only with the coarse terms of the spoken language for articles and tasks in domestic and agricultural life, it had now been used to express more refined and elegant concepts, while arcane Latin expressions were updated and given a popular application. The scholarly became popular, the sophisticated simple, abstractions substantial, the general specific. Tuscan turned into Italian.

With the Renaissance, the use of Classical Latin for literary purposes reasserted itself in academic circles, where it had always been the lingua franca. The language of Dante had by then become history, unspoken in Tuscany for over 200 years. As the head of the Florentine Academy, the Humanist Benedetto Varchi pleaded for a new Italian that could also be used for scientific purposes. But because of the lack of standardization and obligatory use, it was only slowly able to oust predominant Latin. In 1612, the Accademia della Crusca published the first dictionary of the Italian language, the *Vocabulario*.

Once this level was reached, discussion in the 17th and 18th centuries centered on the *questione della lingua*, the problem of keeping the language pure. On the one hand, the adoption of French and English words and introduction of special and scientific expressions had altered the character of literary Italian, while on the other hand it was fashionable to write in dialect. The hostile reaction of self-appointed purists was inevitable: "back to Dante" was the demand. Their most prominent member was Alessandro Manzoni (1785–1873), the leading Italian Romantic, whose works are still compulsory reading in Italian schools. Though Manzoni learnt several foreign languages, he preferred to talk in his native Milanese dialect. However, he rewrote his masterpiece, the historical novel *I Promessi Sposi* (The Betrothed), several times until it appeared, "rinsed in the waters of the Arno," in a language based on non-scholarly Florentine usage, thereby establishing for the first time a national form of Italian.

Sala delle pale e delle gerle (lit.: Shovels and Panniers Room; names of Academicians are inscribed on bakers' shovels), Accademia della Crusca, Florence

Fiesole

"Nowhere is nature laid out so subtly and elegantly. The god that created the hills of Florence was an artist," noted Anatole France during his stay in Fiesole. The little town lies above Florence, on a ridge between the Mugello and Arno valleys. In the 19th and early 20th century it attracted numerous writers and painters to this picturesque corner, which is now – as in the 15th century – a villa suburb and destination for outings from Florence.

Fiesole is older than Florence. It was founded in the 7th century B.C. by the Etruscans, and became one of their heartlands. In the 3rd century B.C., the city was allied with the Romans against the invading Gauls, but by 90 B.C. had joined the rebellion against Rome. Fiesole was sacked in revenge, and ten years later degraded to a colony by Sulla. Archaeological finds indicate prosperity had returned 100 years later. The ethnic migrations of the Dark Ages produced devastation, which laid the city low until the 9th–10th century. In contrast to most Tuscan cities, no artisan or mercantile class developed here. Moreover, Florence had a considerable advantage in a navigable river. Thus Fiesole was commercially overshadowed by its near rival, and in 1125 was almost completely destroyed by it.

Today, the site of the ancient forum is the main square, Piazza Mino da Fiesole,

Panorama with the tower of the Palazzo Pretorio

with the town hall, the Palazzo Pretorio, a Trecento structure with later alterations, with double loggias and the arms of the *podestà* (magistrate). In front of it is an equestrian monument of bronze showing the historic encounter between Garibaldi

Etruscan wall

and King Victor Emmanuel II in 1860 on the Teano bridge. The Romanesque cathedral, restored in the 19th century and containing works by the Renaissance artist Mino da Fiesole, occupies a corner of the square. At the highest point, where the Etruscans had their acropolis, are the church and monastery of St. Francis, with a splendid panorama over the plain and towards Florence.

Fiesole

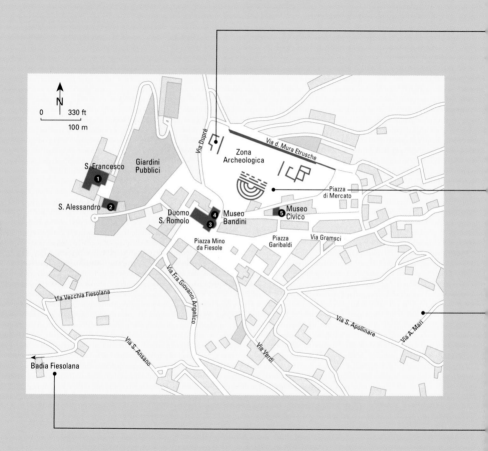

- S. Francesco ①
- Giardini Pubblici
- S. Alessandro ②
- Via Duprè
- Via d. Mura Etrusche
- Zona Archeologica
- Piazza di Mercato
- Duomo S. Romolo ③
- Museo Bandini ④
- Museo Civico ⑤
- Piazza Mino da Fiesole
- Piazza Garibaldi
- Via Gramsci
- Via Fra Giovanni Angelico
- Via Vecchia Fiesolana
- Via S. Apollinare
- Via A. Mari
- Via S. Ansano
- Via Verdi
- Badia Fiesolana

0 330 ft
100 m

N

Tempio Etrusco,
1 Via Portigiani,
p. 270

Teatro
Romano, 1 Via
Portigiani,
p. 271

Mura Etrusca,
p. 267

Other sights of interest
(not covered elsewhere in this book):

1 S. Francesco, Via S. Francesco

2 S. Alessandro, Via S. Francesco

3 Duomo (S. Romolo), Piazza Mino da Fiesole

4 Museo Bandini, 1 Via Duprè

5 Museo Civico, 1 Via Portigiani

Badia Fiesolana,
Via Badia Boccettini,
p. 270

Zona Archeologica

Tempio Etrusco

In the 19th century, the remains of the ancient city were uncovered right in the center of Fiesole. The oldest part is the "Etrusco-Roman" temple, which really means a Roman temple built over the Etruscan one. The smaller one was built in the Etruscan period at the end of the 3rd century B.C. for a goddess of well-being, probably Minerva Medica, and consisted of a rectangular cella with two antae. In the 1st century A.D., the Romans took over the ground plan, enlarged it and built a podium with columns on the south side.

Badia Fiesolana

Halfway between Florence and Fiesole is the former Benedictine abbey of Badia Fiesolana. Rebuilding was funded by Cosimo Vecchio in 1458 and carried out by Bernardo Rossellino to plans by Michelozzo. The harmoniously proportioned interior articulated in white and gray has unusual features: the transept, choir, and nave are barrel-vaulted, and there are no aisles, but deep side chapels instead. The incomplete façade frames a fragment of the 12th-century west front of the earlier building, in Tuscan Proto-Renaissance style.

Teatro Romano

The Teatro Romano was laid out at the beginning of the imperial era (1st century B.C.), and extended by the Emperor Claudius in A.D. 41–54. The theater could hold almost 2,000 spectators, and is set against a hillside in a semicircle. Above the 19 tiers the vomitory – the exit level with its doors – can be made out. Below are the remains of the semicircular orchestra, parts of the proscenium and the *scæna frons*, the structure that faced the audience. On the side are the wings or *versuræ*, leading offstage. Also of early imperial date are the thermal baths, which were greatly expanded in the 2nd century A.D under the Emperor Hadrian.

Withdrawal from the Secular World – Monasteries in the Tuscan Uplands

Ruth Strasser

"Chi ti move, o omo, ad abbandonare le proprie tue abitazioni delle città e lasciare li parenti e amici e andare in lochi campestri per monti e valli, se non la naturale bellezza del mondo?" (What induces you, o Man, to abandon your home in the city, leave behind relatives and friends and go to rural areas, hills, and valleys, unless it be the natural beauty of the world?)

Leonardo da Vinci, *Prophecies*

From the 11th to the 13th century, against a background of religious change and alongside the new clerical devotion to scholasticism, new currents were perceptible also in the monastic world, seeking to realize the ideal of the Christian message and mission in strict asceticism and itinerant preaching. In particular it was young intellectuals not averse to the worldly temptations of the cities, from distinguished, prosperous, and often noble families, who felt the call, either from an inner vocation or following a divine vision. They gave up occupation, wealth, their personal circle of family and friends, and the cultural advantages of urban life to withdraw into the solitude of nature, there to lead a monastic life of contemplation and humility in imitation of the anchorites and hermits.

In secluded places they founded hermitages with strict rules: simple food and clothing, hard

The monastery of Vallombrosa with its two towers

manual and agricultural work, strict fasting periods, night watches, and silent prayer. The Casentino, a region lying to the east of Florence, was considered the ideal place for this kind of life: accessible over the arduous Passo della Consuma, surrounded on three sides by mountains of the Tuscan Apennines, with woods, green hills, and fresh streams – this is how Dante lauded the area, and little has changed since.

Standing at a height of over 3,300 feet (1,014 m), beside a spring and surrounded by centuries-old trees, is one of the largest monastic com-

Ghirlandaio, The Stigmatization of St. Francis near La Verna *(detail), 1483/1485, fresco, Cappella Sassetti, S. Trinità, Florence*

plexes in Italy, the abbey and hermitage of Camaldoli. It was founded in 1012 by Romuald of Ravenna (c. 952–1027, later canonized), who encouraged hermitages within the Benedictine system. Romuald was originally a monk at S. Apollinare in Classe in Ravenna, lived as a hermit near Venice and in the Pyrenees, but then opted for Camaldoli in Tuscany, where other hermits had already installed themselves, as a suitable place for his new reformed community. The monastery was at first only a hermitage and hospice, but it had enormous appeal, and after the Camaldolese Order was recognized it added a monastery which at times accommodated up to 100 monks. In the 15th century it served as a debating venue for Lorenzo il Magnifico's

Neoplatonic academy. Here Alberti, Marsilio Ficino, and other Hum-anists held discussions on the philosophical prob-lems of their day, which were published by Cristoforo Landino in 1480 as *Disputationes Camaldulenses*. The site comprises a monastery with monastic cells, apothecary, church, hostel, and the old pilgrims' hospice.

In 1028, Giovanni Gualberto, a member of the distinguished Florentine Visdomini family, retired with three other hermits to a clearing beside the Pratomagno range of hills, to the west of the Casentino. Having been suddenly inspired not to take revenge for the murder of his brother, he had a vision of the cross of the Florentine church of S. Miniato al Monte inclining towards him.

The original hermitages and chapel, where the four hermits lived for seven years, later developed over time into the powerful abbey of Vallombrosa, whose order (the Vallombrosians) was recognized in 1055 by the pope as an independent Benedictine congregation. It grew very rapidly after the death of Giovanni Gualberto in 1073 and his early canonization (1093). The extensive complex with its two towers and enclosing wall now looks like a castle, but its present appearance is due to the Florentine architects Alfonso Parigi and Gherardo Silvani in the 17th century. Near the monastery, the Paradisino or Little Paradise recalls the saint's original hermitage.

At the southern edge of the Casentino is the monastery of La Verna, at a height of 3,700 feet (1,128 m) on a steep rocky hillside. It is closely associated with the name of St. Francis of Assisi. Surrounded by dense forests of age-old beech and maple woods, it was built on the spot where in summer 1224 Francis withdrew to fast, as was his wont. He had been given the limestone cliff and adjoining forest ten years earlier by Count Orlando Cattani, and he founded a hermitage there.

Cloister of Camaldoli Monastery

In a vision on the day of the Raising of the Cross (September 14), in which a radiant, crucified seraph with six wings appeared, Francis received the impression of the Stigmata, i.e., his body showed the wounds of Christ. The Chiesa delle Stimmate (Church of the Stigmata), founded by Count Simone de Battifolle, commemorates this miracle.

Like many other monastic buildings, it is decorated with glazed terracotta works from the Florentine workshop of Andrea and Luca della Robbia. From a small terrace, you can look down the steep rockface, to which – legend has it – Francis clung in desperation when the Devil sought to plunge him into the abyss.

Antonio Terreni, View of the monastery of S. Miniato al Monte, *Florence, 2nd half of 18th century, etching, Museo Firenze com'era, Florence*

Arezzo

Arezzo

In the 7th century B.C. the Etruscans founded the settlement of *Arretium* on a hill overlooking the river Arno. From the 5th century B.C. on, the metal-working industry turned this new town into an important member of the Etruscan League of Twelve Cities. Having been defeated by Rome at the end of the 3rd century B.C., Arezzo had to supply weapons and tools for the Punic War against the Carthaginians – further evidence of the quality of the Aretine metal industry. Arezzo's partisanship against Sulla during the Roman civil wars led to a temporary decline, from which the town managed to recover during the rule of Augustus, largely thanks to its ceramics industry. The Aretine relief ceramics, which were justly famous throughout Europe, were produced in many workshops. They were fired from fine clay, covered with a red glaze and usually decorated with very fine reliefs.

For many centuries Arezzo declined on account of mass migration, and it was almost wiped from the map. It took until the 12th century for the town to recover – to the extent we can see in the old sector today, where the mendicant orders and a temporary university set up their own centers for literary and artistic activities. Despite falling to Florence in 1289, Arezzo remained an important cultural center and is famous for its gold work to this day.

The town is the birthplace of many famous humanists, most notably the great writer Petrarch. Leonardo Bruni (1369–1444), the chancellor of the Florentine Republic, Giorgio Vasari, the painter, architect and author of "Lives of the Artists," and the poet Pietro Aretino (1492–1556/1557) were also born here. Michelangelo Buonarroti was born in the small town of Caprese in the hills of Arezzo, where his father was mayor. We also have an Aretine monk, Guido d'Arezzo, to thank for inventing musical notation.

Piero della Francesca (c. 1410/1420–1492),
Discovery and Proof of the True Cross
(detail), 1454–1458, fresco, 356 x 747 cm, San Francesco, Arezzo

Aretine vase, start of 1st century B.C., terra sigillata, Museo Archeologico, Arezzo

Arezzo

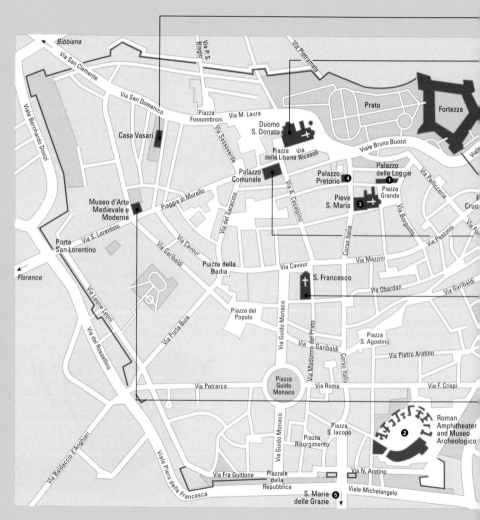

Duomo S. Donato, Piazza del Duomo, p. 294

Casa Vasari, Via XX Settembre 55, p. 302

Palazzo Comunale, Piazza della Libertà, p. 294

S. Francesco, Via Cavour, p. 294

Museo d'Arte Medievale e Moderna, Via San Lorentino 8, p. 302

Other sights of interest

1 Piazza Grande & Palazzo delle Logge, Piazze Grande & Via Giorgio Vasari, pp. 292–293

2 Anfiteatro Romano (Roman Amphitheater) and Museo Archeologico, Via F. Crispi and Via Margeritone 10, p. 304

3 Pieve S. Maria, Corso Italia, p. 286

4 Palazzo Pretorio, Via Pileati, p. 282

5 S. Maria delle Grazie, southern outskirts, p. 305

Via Giacoma Matteotti

Sansovino

Ca Signorelli

Giotto →
Cortona

820 ft
250 m

Palazzo Pretorio

The Palazzo Pretorio was formed from a number of old houses in the 14th century and was comprehensively altered during the Renaissance. From 1404 onwards it was the seat of the supreme judge. The coats of arms of prominent families and companies had to be submitted to the town council in this building, and the three-story façade still displays many of these coats of arms. Over the side entrance on the left is a relief of a horseman from the 13th century. Inside, in addition to sculptures from the Middle Ages and the Renaissance, is the town library, the museum section of which houses valuable incunabula, manuscripts, and miniatures from various periods in Aretine history.

S. Francesco

In 1290 the Franciscans – who were already resident in Arezzo during the lifetime of St. Francis of Assisi – began building the church of S. Francesco, based on a design by the Minorite friar Fra Giovanni da Pistoia. Until 1377 it comprised a single-nave construction with a straight choir end, as of the Lower Church at Assisi. The side chapels to the north were added in the 15th century. The horizontal brick patterns on the façade were designed to reinforce marble facing which was never actually installed.

The Interior

The chief feature of the church's decor is the very famous fresco cycle depicting the story of the True Cross by Piero della Francesca (c. 1410/1420– 1492) on the walls of the choir. The frescoes, which date from 1452 to 1464, are based on the *Legenda aurea* (Golden Legend) by Jacobus de Voragine, one of the most important collections of legends in the Middle Ages. In the Franciscan order's churches, depictions of St. Francis's likeness to Christ were very popular. In his composition, Piero della Francesca combined his own epic interpretation with allusions to contemporary political events: in 1439 the Council between the Eastern and Western church was moved to Florence. Piero borrowed the features of the contemporary Byzantine emperor to portray Constantine the Great.

1 Return of the Cross
2 Prophet
3 Prophet
4 The Death of Adam
5 Discovery and Proof of the True Cross
6 Torture of the Jews
7 The Raising of the Cross
8 Solomon and the Queen of Sheba
9 The Defeat and Execution of Chosroes
10 The Annunciation
11 The Dream of Constantine
12 Constantine's Victory over Maxentius

Piero della Francesca (c. 1410/1420–1492), *The Dream of Constantine*
Fresco, 329 × 190 cm

Piero's painting of the *Dream of Constantine* displays a number of artistic innovations. On the eve of his battle against Maxentius, an angel appears to the sleeping emperor with a cross, saying "by this sign shalt thou conquer." In the dream, Emperor Constantine receives the message, and this moment is portrayed to the viewer as a spectacle of nature. Piero uses moonlight very suggestively in this first "night scene" of the Renaissance: the pale, but powerful light picks out the imperial tent from the indistinct grayness of the encampment. It casts a strange sheen over the scene both within and outside the tent. The servant seems even paler and the weapons of the soldiers gleam with an unreal luster. Solely through his treatment of light, Piero raises sculptural corporeality to another level.

Piero della Francesca (c. 1410/1420-1492), *Discovery and Proof of the True Cross*
Fresco, 356 × 747 cm

The left-hand side of this double scene shows Helena, Constantine's mother, finding the True Cross and the crosses of the two thieves in a ploughed field before the walls of Jerusalem. On the right, in front of a temple to Minerva, the empress and her retinue have gathered round the bier of a corpse, which is brought back to life on being touched by the True Cross. Piero's virtuousity abounds in this, one of his most beautiful compositions. Helena's ladies-in-waiting gather in a semicircle, the youth is dramatically foreshortened, leaning right over to see the Cross, the temple is resplendent in Renaissance style, and the town in the background is unmistakably Arezzo. The solemnity of the gestures is well portrayed through the use of gentle light and the well-thought-out structure of the space. The facial expression of the empress is sensitively observed – tense, concentrating closely on the search, but joyful, her eyes shining on recognizing the True Cross.

Pieve di S. Maria

The parish church dedicated to the Virgin Mary is one of the most beautiful Romanesque buildings in Tuscany. Difficult terrain and the immense scale of the church – which is over 165 feet (50m) long – delayed its completion in the 12th century. At the end of the century, the west façade was complete, but it was immediately altered again as, in the meantime, the city of Lucca had set new standards with its decorative facades and these naturally had to be matched. A second façade was therefore added at Arezzo. Three rows of columns climb upwards over blind arcades on the ground floor. Marble incrustation was renounced in favor of local sandstone. The sumptuousness of the façade comes from the wealth of the columns – in the galleries, the number of these rises from 12 to 24 and then 32 – and also from the great variety of column embellishments and capitals. In contrast with the Luccan churches, there is no final gable. This makes it clear that the façade is a front which is quite independent of the basilica structure of the church. Particularly beautiful is the decoration of the portals: the middle one shows the *Assumption of the Virgin Mary* with depictions of the months, in the arch on the right is a *Baptism of Christ* and on the left, vines and grapes. The campanile, known to locals as the "tower of a hundred holes" was completed in 1330.

The Interior

The irregularity of the ground plan, caused by the unevenness of the site, is also evident inside the church. The three naves of the basilica open out with great clarity, over which there is an open roof truss. The remarkably high columns of the nave and the wide, slightly pointed arches, the big triumphal arch, and the crossing to the vaults give the impression of a Gothic expanse. The arcade gallery in the choir repeats the motif of the columns on the outside. Light enters the nave through 18 double windows and one façade window. On the internal façade are reliefs of the *Birth of Christ* and the *Adoration of the Magi*. The first major restoration took place under Vasari, who converted the main choir chapel, the Capella Vasari, into a family tomb. In so doing he changed the interior completely. The choir screen was removed, a baldachin high altar erected, the walls distempered, the floor covered with bricks, and the windows enlarged. Later Vasari's remains were transported to the *badia* (abbey).

During further restoration in the 19th century, efforts were made to restore the church's former condition and renovations were also carried out on the crypt beneath the raised choir, which contains a reliquary bust of St. Donatus.

Pietro Lorenzetti (c. 1280/1290–c. 1345), polyptych, c. 1320
Tempera on wood, 298 × 309 cm

The most important item in the "Pieve" is the altarpiece of the Virgin and Child with Saints, which Guido Tarlati, the Aretine bishop, commissioned from Pietro Lorenzetti in 1319. It is probably the first dated work of the master, who is the chief representative of the Sienese school in the trecento and who only a few years later painted the famous frescoes in the Lower Church of S. Francesco at Assisi. At the center of the imposing five-panel altarpiece is a picture of the Madonna surrounded by portraits of saints. On gold ground, the patterned white brocade of the Madonna's cloak shines radiantly. Its folds correspond to the austere beauty of the Virgin's expression as she looks lovingly towards her son. The gaze between mother and child reflects an intense affinity, the intimacy of which is increased by the Christ child's firm grasp of his mother's robe. On the left, St. Donatus and St. John the Evangelist are also portrayed, together with St. Matthew and St. John the Baptist on the right, the latter pointing to Christ with his thumb. Here, Lorenzetti has impressively transposed the dramatic expression of Giovanni Pisano's sculpted figures into painting. Over the Virgin, there is also an Annunciation scene: the angel and the Virgin are in different spaces at different heights. They are connected only by the ray of light on the message.

Reliquary bust of St. Donatus, 1346
Silver (gold-plated)

In the crypt underneath the choir is a sumptuous reliquary bust of St. Donatus, the martyred bishop of Arezzo. Two Aretine gold workers, whose names, Pietro and Paolo, have been recorded crafted this dignified portrait of the young bishop in gold-plated silver, bordered with precious stones.

Petrarch – Poet Laureate and Celebrated Humanist

Petrarch (Francesco Petrarca) was born in Arezzo in 1304, but he only spent the first few years of his life in Tuscany. He studied law in Bologna for six years, then went to Avignon, where his family was living in exile. In 1326 he took minor ecclesiastical orders there. After initial uncertainty, he decided in favor of a disciplined life as a humanist scholar. Soon he entered the household of the influential Colonna family, who made him house chaplain and a permanent dinner guest. This connection provided him with access to the most important private libraries in the Netherlands, Germany, and Italy, during his travels from 1333 onwards.

In his lifetime, Petrarch preferred Latin to Italian, but he wrote his most famous works – the love poems and moral poems of the *Canzoniere* and the *Trionfi* – in the Tuscan dialect. In the process he refined the vernacular and, together with Dante and Boccaccio, laid the foundations for a national Italian language. In his literary and historical notes, there are many personal impressions of his travels – from beautiful girls in Cologne to stimulating library visits. In literary terms, Petrarch provided a completely new perspective on the world by regarding it as the subject of individual observance and perception. His

descriptions of experiences in nature, from climbing Mont Ventoux to drinking in the tranquillity of Vaucluse, were also groundbreaking – before this, writers had seldom written about their natural surroundings and especially their subjective impressions thereof.

A similar, revolutionary emphasis on subjective experience, which could be said to place him firmly among the "modern" poets, is also a feature of Petrarch's lyrical poetry. In his

Petrarch, Canzoniere – *Sonnet no. 264, 1414, illuminated manuscript, Bayerische Staatsbibliothek, cod. it. 81, fol. 195r, Munich*

famous series of love poems, the *Canzoniere*, the journal of his love for Laura, he reflects on the shortcomings and frailty of the human subject, and the connection between personal freedom and an increasing isolation. The true historical identity of Petrarch's beloved Laura is disputed: she is often said to have been Laure de Noves, the wife of Hugues de Sade, but there is speculation that she may not actually have existed.

Petrarch in his Study.
Colored drawing from "De viris illustribus," Padua, end of the 14th century, Hessische Landes- und Hochschulbibliothek, Hs. 101, fol. 1v, Darmstadt

Piazza Grande

The trapezoid Piazza Grande stretches out below the Medici fortress. It has been the focal point of public life in Arezzo since ancient times. The traditional equestrian jousts, the *Giostra del Saracino*, dating back to the 16th century, still take place here, as does the famous antique fair. The Piazza's appearance dates largely from the 13th and 14th centuries. Wooden balconies still divide the narrow medieval houses, as they did when they were first built. There are still towers and house-towers dating back to the 13th century – on the east side is that of the Palazzo Lapoli and on the south side is the house-tower of the Cofani family.

The late Romanesque apse of the 12th century Pieve S. Maria dominates the west side of the sloping Piazza Grande. The large-scale blind arcades and galleries were renovated from 1862 on, but they are still in keeping with the west façade which was completed in the 13th century, with the mighty Romanesque campanile towering above it.

Beside the church, the steps of the Baroque Palazzo del Tribunale – the palace of justice – mirror the round form of the choir and even out the level of the piazza. Attached to the late 18th-century five-axis palazzo is the much narrower Palazzo della Fraternità dei Laici, its façade a mix of Gothic and Renaissance elements.

The building was commissioned in 1375 by the lay charitable confraternity of S. Maria della Misericordia, and constructed under the direction of Florentine master builders. In 1434, the builder called Bernardo Rossellino (1409–1464) incorporated a second story with two aedicules for the town patron saints flanking the Virgin with the Cloak. Whilst double pilasters and vase balustrades are typical of the early Renaissance, the Venetian broken arch around the Madonna relief is Gothic. The collared arcade loggia of the façade's upper story was completed in 1460, and since 1552 has been overshadowed by the bell tower wall.

Palazzo della Logge

On the north side, the Palazzo delle Logge was built between 1573 and 1595, to plans drawn up by Giorgio Vasari. The proportions of this late architectural work of Vasari are striking. Like the Uffizi, the building is free of any decorative elements and is similarly monumental. Under the portico, shops and businesses are arranged around a middle passageway and lateral banks of stone. On the piazza in front, the reconstruction is reminiscent of a pillory or *petrone*, as this was once both the town square and the public arena, where criminals were chained up.

Palazzo Comunale

The palazzo with the dovetailed Ghibelline battlements was built for the town council in 1333. The tower also dates back to this time and the clock to 1468. The frescoed town hall on the first floor is reached through a portico-covered inner courtyard and a Renaissance staircase.

Duomo S. Donato

Work on the three-story basilica began in 1277. The avoidance of marble incrustation and the simplicity of the construction, which has no transept, clearly show the influence of the mendicant orders on church architecture.

The cathedral was completed in several stages. Arezzo had been a diocesan town since the 3rd century, but the cathedral and the bishop's palace were situated outside the town. From the 12th century, the town council, the feudal lords and the bishop tried to move inside the town walls, in order to control affairs more easily. As an interim solution, the bishop and clergy moved to the "Pieve." Finally, with the financial assistance of Pope Gregory X, building work began on the new cathedral.

The old cathedral was razed to the ground by the Medici Grand Duke Cosimo I, against the will of the people.

However, building of the two western bays of the new cathedral was delayed for a further 200 years. Work from the 20th century includes the western façade, finished in 1914 in Tuscan new Gothic style, and the 20th-century campanile, which was erected in 1937.

Duomo S. Donato

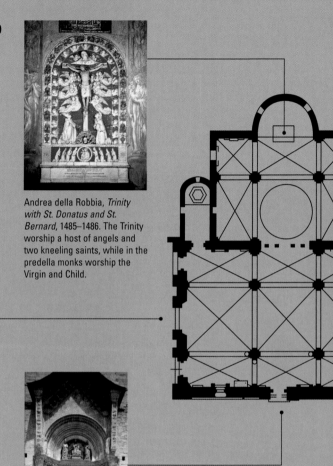

Andrea della Robbia, *Trinity with St. Donatus and St. Bernard*, 1485–1486. The Trinity worship a host of angels and two kneeling saints, while in the predella monks worship the Virgin and Child.

Guillaume de Marcillat, stained glass window (there are more windows by de Marcillat on the right nave wall and in the left choir chapel), p. 301

Side entrance, p. 298

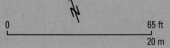

0   65 ft
20 m

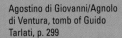
Agostino di Giovanni/Agnolo di Ventura, tomb of Guido Tarlati, p. 299

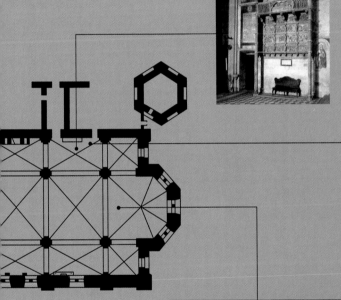

Piero della Francesca, *Mary Magdalene*, p. 300

Main altarpiece with the tomb of St. Donatus, second half of the 14th century. The reliefs on this richly decorated joint work by Florentine and Aretine artists portray the lives of saints and scenes from the life of the Virgin.

Side Entrance of the Cathedral

In front of the southern entrance to the cathedral stand two column stumps made of red porphyry, the remnants of a Roman thermal bath. In medieval building tradition, these are references to the columns of Jachin and Boas at Solomon's ruined Temple at Jerusalem, and also to the power and constancy of God. The lavish effect of the sandstone portal, which dates from 1380, is due largely to the richness of the garments and the reliefs. While antique elements are used in the pilasters, the terracotta group in the tympanum is an example of the "Soft" style of Gothic, around 1400. In a typical robe with many folds, the Virgin holds the Christ child in her arms, with her head bowed. She is flanked by two bishops: Pope Gregory X, who initiated the building of the cathedral, and St. Donatus, the patron saint of the church. The figures are attributed to Spinello Aretino.

**Agostino di Giovanni (1310–c. 1347) and
Agnolo di Ventura, tomb of Guido Tarlati, c. 1330**
Marble

One of the most interesting works of art in the cathedral is the monument to Guido Tarlati, which is dated 1328, shortly after his death. In the Sienese Gothic tradition, Agostino di Giovanni and Agnolo di Ventura made the monumental wall grave out of marble. Under the sarcophagus with the figure of the dead man are 16 images – comparable to a trecento altar painting – portraying the life of the bishop.

Tarlati was appointed bishop of Siena in 1312, and in 1321 the citizens elected him Signore. During his reign the town retained its freedom, captured numerous fortresses, and experienced a brief economic upturn. Battle scenes from Tarlati's life show him as the successful leader of the Ghibellines as well as the imperial curate. This structure was definitely intended as a powerful ruler's tomb. And so it was viewed by contemporaries: when the Tarlati family lost their power in 1341, the head was knocked off the statue. It was not replaced until the end of the 18th century.

The reliefs portray in great detail the life stages of the bishop. As in contemporary painting, the figures are mostly represented in narrow scenes with a landscaped background.

Piero della Francesca (c. 1410/1420–1492),
Mary Magdalene, c. 1468
Fresco, 190 × 180 cm

Parallel to his work on the fresco cycle of the True Cross in S. Francesco, in 1459 Piero della Francesca completed his wall painting of the Magdalen. Reminiscent of a Donatello sculpture, the monumental figure underneath the simple, effective arcade arch is strangely appealing and is one of the artist's most beautiful female portraits.

The plasticity and luminous quality of her radiance, which comes in particular from her austere, slightly flushed face, give Mary Magdalene magnificent presence. The structure is illuminated by natural-seeming light, which gathers in the wonderful oil lamp alight in her hand. The clarity of the large surfaces of color – the green of her dress, the red cape, and its white lining, reinforce the statuesque impression of the whole figure. Apart from the deliberate coloring, Piero also paid attention to details, such as the strands of hair resting on the strong shoulders of the subject. It is typical of the work of Piero della Francesca to bring truly natural appearances – corporeality, perspective, and light – into such calm monumentality, and to raise this to an almost mystical level – here in the reflections of the lighted lantern.

Guillaume de Marcillat (1467–1529),
stained glass window,
The Calling of Matthew the Apostle, **1520**
Stained glass

This cycle of stained-glass windows is an important example of Italian Renaissance glass painting. The artist responsible was Guillaume de Marcillat, originally from Berry in France, who was the first teacher of Giorgio Vasari. He was known in the Vatican through his work for popes Julius II and Leo X.

In the windows of the right-hand or south aisles, Marcillat depicted scenes from the Gospels. The first shows the *Calling of Matthew by Levi.* Then follows the *Baptism of Christ* facing a picture by Piero della Francesco, then *Christ Driving the Money-Changers from the Temple,* the *Adulteress,* the *Raising of Lazarus,* and the *Miracle of Pentecost* on the façade.

The windows are noteworthy for their stunning variety of colors, their harmonious distribution, and the clear, three-dimensional layout of the architectural background. The glassworks of French Gothic required a high degree of proficiency to assemble the colored glass into lead settings. Marcillat combined this technique with Italian Renaissance art and achieved a perfect consistency of figures, space, and architecture.

Marcillat also painted the frescoes in the vaults of the first three nave bays.

Casa Vasari

The Casa Vasari, which today houses a museum and archives, is one of the most interesting artist's houses from the Italian Mannerist period. Giorgio Vasari bought the two-story palace in 1540, while it was still being built, and extensively altered the plans. He decorated the main rooms himself, achieving a remarkable illusionist effect through the use of different techniques, differentiated use of color, and architectural structures. In the drawing room Vasari portrayed the life journey of an artist, guided by the virtues and under the influence of the heavenly bodies. Gods from antiquity, represented as planetary figures, stand to the side. Peace and prosperity are important for the execution of artistic ideas and inventions; thus "Virtue" battles with the fickle "Fortune" and hurls her into the depths.

Museo d'Arte Medievale e Moderna

Luca Signorelli (c. 1441/1450–1523), *Madonna and Child with Saints*, c. 1520
Tempera on wood, 342 × 233 cm

The museum in the graceful Palazzo Bruni-Ciocchi, built in 1445, gives a good overview of the varied art of Arezzo from the 13th to the 16th centuries.

The altarpiece *Madonna and Child with Saints* is by Luca Signorelli, who painted it in about 1520, when he was approximately 70 years old. He painted it for the Confraternity of St. Jerome in Arezzo and it is his last known work. The Madonna sits enthroned, heads of angels above her, attended by the town's patron saints, Donatus and Stephen. At their feet, magnificently clothed, sits the Old Testament King David. St. Jerome and St. Nicholas, who is presenting the donor to the Mother of God, stand on either side of David. God the Father hovers over the entire scene surrounded by angels. With its very simple composition, this type of painting is known as a *sacra conversazione*, and it was very common in Italian Renaissance painting – as a

rule it is not so much a "holy conversation" as in fact a worshipful group. The decorative garments add further contrasts.

Giorgio Vasari ends his chapter on Signorelli in his famous *Lives of the Artists* with the following accolade: "[he was] the man who, by means of the fundamentals of design, especially those of his nudes, and by means of his graceful invention and the composition of his scenes, opened the way to the ultimate perfection of art for the majority of the artisans ..."

Roman Amphitheater

The most significant Roman remains in Arezzo are the ruins of the amphitheater, which was probably built at the start of the 2nd century B.C. during the rule of Hadrian. In the shape of an ellipse, the enormous construction, 338 feet (121 m) long, could hold 10,000 people and was certainly far superior to any other amphitheater in Etruria.

From the Middle Ages to the 18th century, its antique marble was used to construct other buildings – for example, the 14th-century town walls – until 1363 when Bernardo Tolomei, the founder of the Benedictine congregation of Olivetans, purchased the ruins. Towards the end of the 15th century, the monks built a convent in part of the building.

Museo Archeologico Mecenato

In 1936, the archaeological museum moved into the former Benedictine convent. It is named after Gaius Cilnius Maecenas, patron of the Roman poets Horace and Virgil, who has been called the model for all patrons. Maecenas was from an Aretine-Etruscan noble family. Arezzo has this friend and minister of Emperor Augustus to thank for much of its economic progress in ancient times.

Based on private collections of artifacts, the museum displays treasures from prehistoric, Etruscan, and Roman times from Arezzo and its environs. Besides examples of bronze, gold, and glass production, the Aretine vases are particularly worth seeing. These earthenware

S. Maria delle Grazie

S. Maria delle Grazie was built in the mid-15th century, and thus falls into the late Gothic period. It is outside the town center on the site of a shrine with a miraculous spring, which is thought to have been worshiped since Etruscan times and once dedicated to Apollo.

St. Bernardino of Siena added to the shrine, which was still much visited after Christianization, and in 1430 he commissioned Parri Spinelli to paint a *Madonna delle Grazie* for the newly built church there. The harmoniously proportioned two-story arcade hall was added by Benedetto da Maiano at the end of the 15th century. Stylistically, the overall construction and decorative features are early Renaissance.

vessels date from the start of the first century A.D. and were known as "corallini" vases because of their color. Most of them bear a workshop stamp.

Sansepolcro

In the small town of Sansepolcro, on the Tuscan/Umbrian border, access to the main street is via the Porta Fiorentina. This street is the oldest one in town and also the only one with curves, as all the other major roads are dead straight.

According to legend, the town's name of Sansepolcro ("holy sepulcher") came from pilgrims returning from the Holy Land in the 10th century. They brought with them holy soil from Christ's tomb, and in 934 an oratory was founded to house the relic.

Porta Fiorentina

Camaldolite monks looked after the holy place, which became the nucleus of the town. In 1024, an abbey was founded here.

From 1300 until 1451 the commune of Sansepolcro came under the rule of various feudal lords until Pope Eugenius IV sold it to Florence for the sum of 25,000 gold florins. The Florentine lily on the Porta Fiorentina commemorates this change of ownership. The Medici had a fortress built here, and under their rule the birthplace of Piero della Francesca experienced a marked economic upturn. When Piero was buried in Sansepolcro in 1492, the place he had described as a "dump full of mud and clay" had developed into an impressive small town.

Duomo S. Giovanni Evangelista

The abbey church built on this site by the Camaldolites from 1002 and dedicated to St. John the Evangelist became a cathedral in 1513 when Pope Leo X made Sansepolcro a diocesan town. The building was renovated between 1300 and 1350 and many subsequent changes carried out between the late 16th century and the mid-19th century. From 1936 to 1945 efforts were made to restore the original appearance of the interior. Traces of the

Romanesque building can still be seen on the lower story of the campanile and on the façade, the three-part design of which corresponds to a basilica layout. Over the nave is a beautiful rose window that was added later.

Volto Santo, 9th/10th century and c. 1200
Wood, 290 × 271 cm

In the side chapel on the left is the cathedral's most precious treasure – a larger-than-life carved crucifix made of walnut, comparable to the *Volto Santo* in Lucca and of the same, strong, symmetrical type, bearing a Christ figure dressed in a girded, long-sleeved tunic. As in Lucca, this crucifix was worshiped as miraculous and "not created by human hands."

The date of the sculpture is disputed. Some researchers believe that the work belongs to the 10th century and possibly even the 9th, which would make it much older than its counterpart in Lucca. Complete renovation in 1989 uncovered old coloring on the canvas and plaster dating from c. 1200.

Palazzo Comunale – Museo Civico

The town hall, which was built in the trecento and radically altered in the early 16th century, houses the main attraction in Sansepolcro: the Museo Civico. In the collection are works from the 14th to 16th centuries, including paintings by Luca Signorelli and Santi di Tito, who was born here in 1536, and terracottas from the della Robbia workshop. There are also works by Piero della Francesco, whose magnificent town residence is situated right next door. In addition to *The Resurrection*, there is a polyptych painted by Piero between 1445 and 1462 for the Confraternity of S. Maria della Misericordia. In this painting of the "Virgin with the Cloak," the artist has created a most impressive portrait of the Virgin Mary.

Piero della Francesca (c. 1410/1420–1492): *The Resurrection of Christ*, c. 1458
Fresco, 225 × 260 cm

The Resurrection of Christ was painted by Piero della Francesca in about 1458 for the council chamber of the Palazzo Comunale. Here, the artist interprets the subject in a completely unconventional way: the figure of Christ is not floating over the grave, but instead is standing, confident and statue-like, in the center of the picture. Stepping out of the sarcophagus, he has one foot on the edge of the grave and, as ruler of the world, is holding the victory banner firmly in his hand.

In the background, the natural world is divided, with bare trees on one side and a green, flourishing landscape on the other depicting the rebirth of life. The soldiers in front of the sarcophagus are either blinded by the power of the event and have covered their eyes, or are sleeping the sleep of the non-believer. Piero portrays the figures in muted complementary colors and in a natural perspective. Christ, on the other hand, is being transported from this "naturalness" – he dominates the central axis, and his size and prominence accord him a majestic dignity. The pale coloring renders him superhuman and surreal.

Monterchi

For the cemetery chapel of the small town of Monterchi, which has since been renovated, Piero della Francesca painted his world-famous fresco of the Virgin pregnant with her child. It may have been the burial of his own mother in this cemetery in 1459 which inspired him to paint the so-called *Madonna del Parto*. The fresco has been removed and transferred onto canvas, and is now on view at a museum in the town. It is uncertain whether it will ever be returned to the church.

Piero della Francesca (c. 1410/1420–1492):
***Madonna del Parto*, c. 1455**
Fresco, 260 × 203 cm

Like a baldachin, two angels open the brocaded canopy, which is lined with ermine. This lordly magnificence seems unsuited to the austere, rural beauty, who fills up the central space with statuesque composure. She has one hand on her hip and the other sensitively resting on her pregnant body, which is also the central point of the picture and over which her gown is slightly open. The sumptuousness

The cemetery

and the very setting of this scene focus solely on the expected son of God. Through the construction and the coloring of the picture, the Virgin, who is herself completely natural, is portrayed as the "vessel" of God's destiny, witnessed by the completely symmetrical angels, in complementary colors.

The Mysterious People of Etruria

Ruth Strasser

Hardly any other European people has given so much cause for conjecture and legend, or been as shrouded in mystery, as the Etruscans. Even Greek writers such as Hesiod (c. 700 B.C.) and Herodotus (c. 485–425 B.C.) wrote contradictory reports about the migrant princes who were the legendary progenitors of these people, whom the Greeks called "Tyrrhenoi" and whom Roman historians later claimed as Roman ancestors.

After the rediscovery of Etruscan art towards the end of the 18th century, legions of admirers became enthusiastic amateur Etruscologists, and postulated numerous theories about the origin and genesis of these people – often while simultaneously robbing their tombs. Only systematic excavations of utensils and objects of worship from the monumental tombs of the Etruscan necropolises can give the archaeologists information about this extinct race, about their housing, their political and social structures, their trade links, and their religion, art and culture. The items that have been found can be compared to very small pieces of an enormous puzzle, which are continually being reassembled in a different pattern, according to the latest theory on the ancient Etruscans.

The Area

The main area of ancient Etruria in the 8th century B.C. corresponds largely with modern Tuscany: an area bordered by the Tiber in the south, the Arno in the north, the Apennines in the east, and the Tyrrhenian Sea to the west. From the 7th century until the end of the 6th century B.C., the Etruscans traveled northwards across the Apennines as far as Poebene and southwards as far as Campania.

Origins

From the 10th to the 8th century B.C., the Villanova culture dominated in the settlements of the late Etruscans. The Villanovans were an Iron Age group who lived mainly from agriculture and farming, combining wood and mud huts to form village communities, living on isolated mountain tops and plateaus which were easy to protect. At the same time, seafarers from the Aegean had settled on Aithalia, the "soot-blackened" island known today as Elba. They were attracted by the rich supplies of iron ore, which they mined and transported to the mainland, where they also discovered copper, iron, vermilion, and aluminum deposits on the west coast of Tuscany. A further element in the development of the Etruscan people was a group of Greek settlers who came to Campania about 770 B.C. from Euboea (Evvoia) and established trade centers on Ischia and in Cumae. These groups were the ancestors of the people who called themselves either "Rasna" or "Rasenna," and who were called "Etrusci" or "Tusci" by the ancient Romans.

Society and State

The original Etruscan economy, based on a type of pre-monetary exchange in which goods were centrally gathered and later distributed according to need, became much more sophisticated with increasing trade. A strong merchant class developed, as well as a prosperous land-owning class, from which the Etruscan aristocracy was formed in a later period. From the 7th century B.C. onwards the scattered settlements began to take on the appearance of real towns. As in contemporary Greece, Etruria was divided into 12 completely independent city states, a confederacy or league of 12 cities – the *dodekapolis* – governed by a sort of high priest, the so-called *lucumones*, and an elected magistrate chosen from one of the nobility.

Etruscan settlements in ancient times

These cities were united in a loose military confederacy and they convened annually in spring at the shrine of the deity Voltumna in Volsinii (now called Bolsena) for cult games. Later the high priest was replaced by an official who was elected annually.

Trade

At first, the Etruscans exchanged their mining products for luxury goods from foreign, primarily Phoenician, traders in their own country, then from the late 7th century B.C. their trade spread across the entire Mediterranean. Etruscan boats brought iron, ore derivatives, alum, mercury, and also wine and oil in amphorae, as well as bronze and ceramic vessels, to the remotest places and exchanged these for gold, silver, amber, and ivory. It was the rise of the Roman provinces in Africa, Spain, and Gaul that first stemmed the distribution of these popular Etruscan products and limited their sales potential to nearer neighbors.

Writing and Language

Among many other social changes of the 7th century B.C., the Etruscans began to use written characters, borrowing a slightly modified Greek alphabet from the Euboean settlers in southern Italy. At first this served only as an efficient trading tool but, with the founding of the city states, writing soon became accessible to greater numbers of people. Public events, legal agreements, and lists of officials for the administration were all recorded. Although the script is decipherable, it is much more difficult to understand the language itself. Etruscan is not one of the Indo-European languages and indeed has proven not to be directly related to any known language – according to current scholarship it may be the remains of an older submerged Mediterranean proto-language. Decoding this mysterious language is made more difficult by the fact that the main surviving examples comprise some 10,000 tomb inscriptions, mainly epitaphs and dedications, and there are few examples of everyday, less stilted, usage.

Cista Ficoroni from Praeneste (now Palestrina), c. 300 B.C., bronze, h. 53 cm, Museo di Villa Giulia, Rome

Metal Work and Gold Art

In the 8th and 7th centuries B.C. Etruria already boasted significant centers for metal work, namely Vetulonia, Vulci, Tarquinia (Tarquinii), and Cerveteri (Caere), where metal utensils were produced from cold hammered metal riveted at the seams. In the 6th century B.C. new techniques were introduced from Phoenicia and Greece, such as filigree and granulation, as well as improved welding methods. As a result the gold workers of Tuscany reached an artistic and technical level which was never again achieved. They were capable of producing jewelry of extraordinary fineness and delicacy, while new casting techniques also enabled them to create monumental statues such as the *Chimaera* from Arezzo or the *Arringatore* (orator) from Florence.

The Role of Women

The first names and family names of the women commemorated in Etruscan tomb inscriptions are striking. The Etruscan woman played an important role in life as well as death. She was not the demure, stay-at-home, wool-spinning type, like her Roman counterpart, but instead she took part in all of the men's activities: in sporting competitions, tournaments, music and dance, hunting and games. The Greek and Roman writers describe the many freedoms of Etruscan women in appalled and disapproving tones: that they were allowed to recline on sofas to the left of their husbands at the public banquets much loved by the Etruscans and that they would be "there, flirting with other, strange men, drinking plenty and beautiful to look at."

Large fibula from Cerveteri, 7th century B.C., gold, h. 32 cm, Museo Gregoriano Etrusco, The Vatican

Cortona

The home town of artists Luca Signorelli (c. 1441/50–1523), Pietro da Cortona (1596–1669), and of Gino Severini (1883–1966; an early proponent of Italian Futurism), is situated on the Umbrian border, high in the mountains overlooking the Chiana valley, Lake Trasimene and Monte Amiata. Cortona is the former Etruscan city of Curtun. The old city walls, which are about 8,528 feet (2,600 m) long, date back to the 4th century B.C. and are partly preserved in the northern section. Buildings of dark sandstone form a steep, soaring medieval and Renaissance town. At the end of the 8th century B.C., the Etruscans settled in the mountains that separate the Chiana and Tiber valleys – Etruscan grave mounds, called *meloni*, and the grave goods found in them, bear testimony to their presence during this period. Like other Etruscan cities, at the end of the 4th century B.C., Cortona formed an alliance with Rome and became part of the Roman Empire.

In the 5th century the city was destroyed by Goths. The next documentary evidence comes from the 11th century. Cortona, as a "free commune" was quarreling with Perugia and the bishops of Arezzo became involved. In 1325, the city became a bishopric. In the same year, the Casali family seized power and held it until

View of the town

View of the historic old town

1409 when Cortona was sold to the king of Naples. Only two years later, the city was sold for a higher sum to Florence. In 1538, Cortona was integrated into the Grand Duchy of Tuscany. The Medici asserted their power by building a huge fortress on the mound of the ancient acropolis.

Cortona

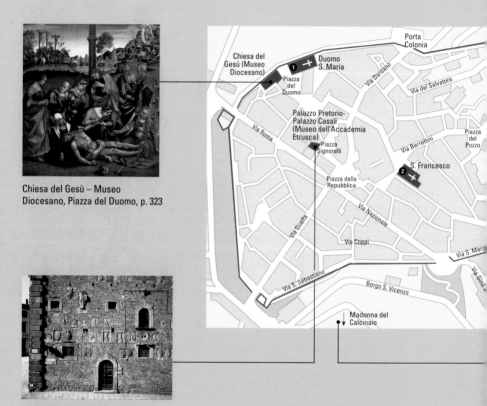

Chiesa del Gesù – Museo
Diocesano, Piazza del Duomo, p. 323

Palazzo Pretorio, Palazzo Casali –
Museo dell'Accademia Etrusca, Piazza
Signorelli, p. 320

Map labels:

Porta Colonia

Chiesa del Gesù (Museo Diocesano)

Duomo S. Maria

Piazza del Duomo

Via Dardano

Via del Salvatore

Palazzo Pretorio-Palazzo Casali (Museo dell'Accademia Etrusca)

Via Roma

Piazza Signorelli

Via Berrettini

Piazza del Pozzo

S. Francesco

Piazza della Repubblica

Via Nazionale

Via Guelfa

Via Coppi

Via S. Mar...

Via S. Sebastiano

Borgo S. Vicenzo

Via Gino...

Madonna del Calcinaio

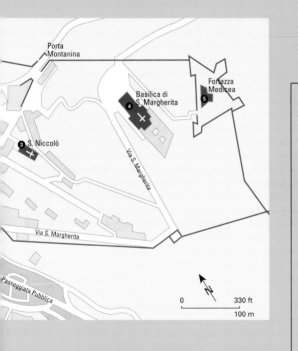

Porta Montanina

Basilica di S. Margherita

Fortezza Medicea

5

4

3 S. Niccolò

Via S. Margherita

Via S. Margherita

Passeggiata Pubblica

N

0   330 ft
           100 m

Madonna del Calcinaio, p. 325

Other sights of interest
(not covered elsewhere in the book):

1 Duomo S. Maria, Piazza del Duomo

2 S. Francesco, Via Berretini

3 S. Niccolò, Via S. Niccolò

4 Basilica di S. Margherita, Piazza S. Margherita

5 Fortezza Medicea (the Medici Fortress)

Palazzo Pretorio / Palazzo Casali / Museo dell'Accademia Etrusca

In the 13th century the Casali family built its family seat at the Piazza Signorelli, which later became the Palazzo Pretorio and the seat of the Florentine governor – the Casali coat of arms adorns the walls to this day. Until the beginning of the 16th century, the artist Luca Signorelli

had his workshop here; 250 years later, it became the home of the renowned "Accademia Etrusca" with members such as Montesquieu and Voltaire. The museum houses outstanding antiquities from the Roman and Etruscan periods.

Etruscan chandelier, 5th century B.C.
Bronze, h. 60 cm

The showpiece of the museum is the unique bronze chandelier from the second half of the 5th century B.C., which

measures 22⁷/₈ in (58 cm) in diameter and weighs almost 132 pounds (60 kg). Around the conical tapering loop in the middle, a large bowl closes around in a ring, linked to 16 small bowls. The hanging light would have been fueled by olive oil, poured into the central ring bowl and feeding the flames of the light bowl. Noteworthy is the concentrically arranged figurative decoration on the underside of the lamp which was made in one piece: in the indented middle serpents coil around a Gorgonian head, which is surrounded by lions, chimeras, and other animals. The end is formed by eight dolphins. The curve contains eight naked satyrs alternately playing syringa or pipes and who are accompanied by sirens in flowing garments. Such winged sirens and satyrs are common elements of Etruscan tomb art, their task being to make music for the dead on their journey.

Over these fabled heads are flame bowls on consoles, decorated with palmettes. Bearded heads of the Greek river god Achelous push up between the bowls and close the outer circle.

Etruscan funerary urn, 2nd century B.C.
Alabaster, h. 46 cm

The figure on the lid of this alabaster urn shows the dead person – unfortunately without a head – in typical reclining pose on a *kline*, which was the usual seating arrangement for banquets, and decorated with *patera* and garlands. The relief shows the Etruscans battling against the Celts.

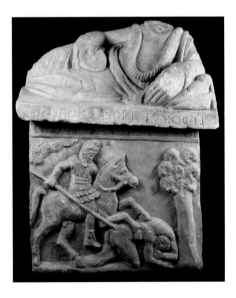

Chiesa del Gesù and Museo Diocesano

The former Chiesa del Gesù is home to the Museo Diocesano, opposite the cathedral in Cortona. In addition to *The Mourning of Christ* by Luca Signorelli, the museum houses some outstanding paintings by artists from Cortona, such as Pietro Lorenzetti and Fra Angelico.

Luca Signorelli (c. 1441/1450–1523), *The Mourning of Christ*, 1502
Tempera on wood, 270 × 240 cm

In his great work *Lives of the Artists*, Giorgio Vasari writes that Signorelli's eldest son and co-worker died of the plague in the summer of 1502, shortly after which another of his sons lost his life in a quarrel. Despite his enormous sorrow over this second great misfortune, the 52-year-old Luca had the body stripped and then, according to Vasari, "with the greatest constancy of heart, without crying or shedding a tear, he drew his portrait so that he could always see whenever he desired, through the work of his own hands, what Nature had given him and inimical Fortune had taken away."

The body of the dead Christ is portrayed in a scarcely outdone realism. The psychological mood of the people grouped around the body is interpreted with great empathy. Their emotions alternate between sorrow and despair, anxious conster-nation and doubtful amazement. The altarpiece made for the church of S. Margherita in Cortona contains narrative details, scenes of the crucifixion and the resurrection, and a beautiful picturesque landscape including a town by a lake in the background.

Fra Angelico (c. 1400–1455), *The Annunciation*, c. 1432–1433
Tempera in gold on wood, 154 × 194 cm
(illustrated overleaf)

The angel is face to face with Mary in an open loggia. Fragile, with a devoted expression, the young woman receives the message from the radiant emissary from heaven. Their dialog is inscribed in gold letters between them. Interestingly, Mary's response is at the top and thus shows the direction of speech.

The blossoming paradise garden which surrounds the loggia gives perspective to the architecture and draws the eye towards the background. There, before a dark night sky, the "expulsion from Paradise" is shown. Fra Angelico thus illustrates the narrative connection between the two events: only through the birth and self-sacrifice of Christ's death can there be deliverance from sin.

On the predella, the most important events from the Virgin's life are portrayed: the *Nativity of the Virgin*, the *Marriage of the Virgin*, the *Visitation*, the *Adoration of the Magi*, the *Presentation of the Virgin* and the *Death of the Virgin*. In the final picture, the

Virgin appears to St. Dominic. The miniature scenes are clear evidence of Fra Angelico's proficiency. Elegantly moving figures occupy all the spaces of the deep, rich landscape and the finely drawn architecture.

Madonna del Calcinaio

The most important church in Cortona is situated on the banks of a river outside the town, where shoemakers once tanned their leather. Early in 1484 a miraculous portrait of the Virgin was noticed on the outside of a container used by a tanner to mix whitewash or *calcinaio* (from which the church derives its name). Today this portrait is housed in the tabernacle above the high altar. The artist Luca Signorelli enlisted his friend, the Sienese architect Francesco di Giorgio Martino, to design the church in 1502. Later followed the vaulting of the cupola (1509) and completion of the main entrance (1543).

The single-nave cupola construction links the central space of the Renaissance with a basilica nave in the form of a Latin cross. The harmonious proportions and restrained, undecorated forms are captivating. The flat pilasters and cornices structure the external appearance. Round windows on the façade in the form of aedicules give lively accents. The brick building is crowned and united by the steep octagonal cupola over a strikingly high drum.

The interior is also solely structured by architectural elements. Lightly plastered wall surfaces contrast with the gray stone of the pilasters, cornices, and gables. The fusion of the cubic shapes with the roundness of the barrel vaults is thus given strong emphasis. The construction of the roof built from lancet arches is striking. With its clear structural design, the church follows the sacred buildings created by Brunelleschi and was one of the models for Antonio da Sangallo's church of S. Biagio in Montepulciano.

Siena

Siena

Siena is a city of brick that has grown over three hills – which accounts for the division into three *terzi* or parts of the city. The tower of the Palazzo Pubblico, the town hall, points upwards like an arrow, rising from the center of the hills with their tangle of brick-colored houses and steeply rising alleyways. In contrast, the cathedral with its black and white marble stripes sits broadly and majestically on the highest point. Several legends surround the origins of the city. For instance, the name is supposed to have come from an Etruscan patrician family called "Seina." According to another version, Senius and Aschius fled their legendary uncle Romulus, the founder of Rome, as he had murdered their father Remus. One rode with a white horse-blanket, the other with a black one – hence the black and white coat of arms of Siena, the *balzana*. The twins settled on two hills and the name "Siena" came from the elder one, Senius. They also brought with them their (and their father's and uncle's) foster-mother, the Roman she-wolf, and made her the symbol of their foundation. In many parts of the city you come across *la lupa*, the she-wolf, on coats of arms.

The hills were certainly settled in Etruscan and Roman times. Since 313 Siena has been a bishopric, but the city did

View of the city with the cathedral

not acquire its Gothic appearance until the height of the Middle Ages. Siena was known as *figlia della strada* (daughter of the road), and on the northern gate, the Porta Camollia, there is the inscription *Cor magis tibi Sena pandit*, "Siena opens its heart to you even wider (than this gate)." Its location on the medieval Via Francigena, which leads through the city, enabled it to become wealthy through the brisk trade between northern Europe and the east which passed along this route, originally a pilgrims' way. Siena expanded and, with the election of consuls in the mid-12th century, it became a "free city."

The financial monopoly was in the hands of influential Sienese families who founded the banking system and subsequently opened branches abroad. Based on this power and the privileges of the Hohenstaufen

Guido da Siena,
Madonna and Child, *1262,
oil on wood, 142 × 100 cm,
Pinacoteca Nazionale*

emperors, the rivalry with Florence grew, as did the struggle for pre-eminence in the surrounding lands. Numerous fortresses were built by both sides. After the death of Emperor Frederick II, there was a famous battle on September 4, 1260 on the hill of Montaperti. Although the army of the Florentine Guelphs was greatly superior in numbers, the Sienese Ghibellines won, supported by their loyal imperial allies Pisa and Cortona and by German knights who had been sent by the son of Frederick II, King Manfred. This victory became a legend: shortly before the start of the battle the Sienese mayor Bonaguida is supposed to have called upon the population to make a procession in honor of the Virgin Mary, and then to have entrusted her in a symbolic gesture with the keys of the city, laying them before her image on the high altar of the cathedral. After the victory the Sienese gave thanks to the Virgin, made her their patron saint and declared the city to be *civitas virginis*, a community under her protection. For this reason, since 1262, the Sienese have had candles burning day and night in the votive chapel of the Madonna in the cathedral. It is this special reverence for the Virgin that is the reason for the many representations of her in Sienese painting and even for the origins of the Palio. The goal of this unique equestrian race, which is held twice a year at festivals of the Virgin Mary, is to obtain the *palio*, a banner bearing her image.

In the mid-14th century the leading merchant families came to power. There were several changes of rulers, until in 1555 Siena, after a devastating siege, was surrendered by the surviving 8,000 inhabitants to Cosimo I de' Medici and the allied troops of Philip II. The city then became part of the Grand Duchy of Tuscany, ruled over by Florence.

Giovanni di Turino, She-wolf, *1429, bronze (gilded), Palazzo Pubblico, Siena*

Catherine of Siena:
Mystic, Politician, and Saint

Only the death of her twin sister at birth in the year 1347 gave any indication that Catherine, the 24th child of the Sienese master dyer Jacopo Benincasa and his wife Lapa, was to become a special person. Her mother, a lively and stern woman, had, so the chroniclers said, only reared this one girl at her own breast and because of this loved her with special tenderness. During the outbreak of plague in 1348 the relatives of her older sister Niccolucia died, and her 11-year-old brother-in-law Tommaso della Fonta was taken into the Benincasa household after the deaths of his parents. Ten years later, Catherine's new "big brother" entered the Dominican order and became her first confessor.

Brought up by her father and mother to be honest and pious, the girl grew up in the same manner as other children of her time. When Catherine was twelve years old, her mother and eldest sister began, after the custom of the time, to prepare her for marriage. She was to make herself pretty, bleach her hair, and take part in social life.

But even several years before, when she was only seven years old, Catherine had given rise to talk for quite different reasons. A vision in which Christ appeared to her above the

Ercole Ferrata, St. Catherine, *c. 1660, marble, cathedral, Cappella Chigi, Siena*

church of S. Domenico and blessed her made Catherine stop in the street as if rooted to the spot. From this moment on, still in a childish awareness of her vocation, her behavior is said to have altered. Not yet fully grown, the girl took a vow of chastity, sought out the loneliness of empty spaces, wanted to leave the city for a life in the wilderness, and drew attention to herself over and over again by her actions. In spite of all warnings and robust repressive measures, Catherine's behavior was so consistent, from quiet prayer and meditation to cutting off her hair, and even to public confession, that her parents finally gave in. In 1362, Catherine joined a congregation of the Dominican order, known as the Sisters of Penitence. This group had married and unmarried women among its members; they lived together as lay sisters and labored in caring for souls and nursing the sick.

The 15-year-old furnished her own cell, which still survives today, and left it only for church services and to pray at the canonical hours. She lived an ascetic life, chastising the body and barely eating, drinking, or sleeping. However, repeated visions did make her return "out into the world." She began to care for the poor and for lepers and devoted herself more and more to preaching.

The charismatic person of the dyer's daughter attracted people in Siena. Soon a *famiglia* was formed, a spiritual family of women and girls of the people, but also of young noblewomen, who joined her. In 1370, at 23 years old, Catherine took the decisive step and finally joined the Dominican order.

The impact made by this woman from Siena was greeted with amazement, but it also

Domenico Beccafumi, The Mystic Marriage of St. Catherine *(detail), c. 1528, oil on wood, 345.5 × 255.5 cm, Collezione Chigi Saracini, Siena*

brought with it envy and suspicion. In 1374 she made her statement in front of the order chapter in Florence. As her fame spread outside the borders of the city, she became involved in discussions with clerics, and became an adviser of popes, a spokeswoman, and an admonitory voice. Hardly able to write herself, she dictated her letters and sermons to clerics who accompanied her and who acted as interpreters in her discussions with the pope, as the latter did not understand Tuscan, and Catherine spoke no Latin.

More and more, her activities exceeded the boundaries of simple pastoral care, conversion, and preaching and moved into the political arena. Her reputation of making sound judgments in matters of faith extended beyond the limits of her home city – she had become the religious conscience of her time. Catherine was pursuing three aims: the return of the pope from Avignon to Rome, the start of a new crusade, and the reform of the church. All three goals, for her, were interconnected. Only through the resumption of the apostolic seat in Rome, the re-conquest of the Christian shrines in the Holy Land, and the renewal of the structures of the church could peace be brought back to Italy.

In her 380 surviving letters, the *Popolana*, the "daughter of the people," addressed friends, her equals in rank, but also the mighty of the world and spoke to them plainly, as if she were standing in front of them. She even admonishes Pope Gregory XI in 1376 in a letter to Avignon: "O how deeply shaming it is to see those, who should be a pattern of voluntary poverty and should be distributing the wealth of the church to the poor, wallowing in the treasures, the pomp and the vanity of the world." She also addressed other conditions for peace: "Your return and the raising of the banner of the cross. Do not hearken to devilish advisers who want to hinder the good and holy work. Do not be fearful, but be a man of courage!" Catherine expressed her criticism of secular government just as openly. She wrote to the vain Queen Joan of Naples: "You wish to pass on the evil which lies in you to your subjects... If you are not prepared to concern yourself with your own salvation, then at least take some trouble over the salvation of those who are given into your hands." Catherine took a serious view of the Christian conviction which said that worldly sovereigns, whose office had been granted to them by the grace of God, had a responsibility to fulfill. This is what she wrote to King Charles V of France: "Have you never considered how much evil you will do if you do not do the good that lies within your power?"

Catherine's thinking was formed by the view that "he who cannot govern himself is not fit to govern others." She was also convinced of the power of love. When she died in Rome at the age of only 33, the pope was back in Italy, but the church and the country were in a state of conflict. As an adviser, a spiritual guide, and an arbitrator, however, she tirelessly tried to rouse people to her cause. Very few of her contemporaries were able to ignore the immediacy of her message. Catherine was buried in the church of S. Maria sopra Minerva in Rome, canonized by Pope Pius II in 1461, declared the patron saint of Rome in 1866, and patron saint of Italy in 1939. In 1970, Pope Paul VI declared her *doctor ecclesiae*.

Il Sodoma (1477–1549), St. Catherine Swooning *(detail), 1526, fresco, Cappella di Santa Caterina, S. Domenico, Siena*

Fonte Branda

The five important fountains of the city are built like fortresses, for in Siena's dry climate water was a precious resource that had to be protected.

The Fonte Branda, lying beneath a steep rocky drop, is one of the oldest and most beautiful in the city. Water was drawn here as early as 1100, but the present building, with its design based on the Gothic forms of the town hall, only dates from the mid-13th century. Three large, pointed arches open up the cren-ellated brick frontage. In the earlier years, dyers, tanners and woolcarders lived in the district around the fountain.

S. Domenico

Rising above the Fonte Branda is the mighty brick structure of S. Domenico, which has been very cleverly adjusted to the rock plateau using several different floor levels. The superb high choir chapel is particularly notable. When, in the mid-13th century, the mendicant orders settled on the slopes around the city center, construction work on the simple basilica church was begun. It attained its present dimensions in the early 14th century. Massive substructures were needed for the new eastern extension with its huge transept – resulting in a broad, extensive, vaulted lower church.

In the Cistercian tradition, the building ends in a straight, simply ornameted chancel. In spite of its simplicity of material and form, the church is nonetheless impressive by virtue of its size.

The Interior

The interior, with its single, unornamented nave, is mounted by an open roof framework, which is visible from within the building. To the east, the chapel ends in a broad, open transept and a square main chancel., each of wich has three side chapels. The colored glass windows are a 20th century donation. Located in the right apsidal chapel are numerous tombs and memorial plates for German university students who died in Siena during the outbreaks of plague in the 16th and 17th centuries. Important paintings dating from the 15th through the 17th centuries by Sienese painters such as Matteo di Guiovanni, the Sienese master builder Francesco di Giorgio Martini (1429–1501), and Rutilio Manetti are hung along the walls of the main body of the church and the apsidal chapels.

The church is closely associated with the life of St. Catherine of Siena. On the front wall of the groin-vaulted Cappella delle Volte, located to the right of the entrance, is the oldest of the portraits of the saint made during her lifetime. The fresco, dating from 1370–1380, which depicts her in the habit of the Third Order of Dominicans and holding a lily, is the work of Catherine's friend, the painter Andrea Vanni (ca. 1322–1413).

Siena

Fonte Gaia, Piazza del Campo,
p. 352

Fonte Branda, Via di Fonte-
branda, p. 352

S. Domenico, Piazza S.
Domenico, p. 336

Piazza del Campo, Piazza del
Campo, p. 346

Battistero, Piazza San
Giovanni, p. 376

Duomo S. Maria Assunta,
Piazza del Duomo, p. 364

Ospedale S. Maria della Scal
Piazza del Duomo, p. 363

AVARITIA · VANAGLORIA

TYRANNIDE

· ARA VS AV ROR

IVSTI

BE I SCA TVI NICOLAI SVSCIPE CVRAM OKTERINA

Cappella di S. Caterina

Il Sodoma (1477–1549),
The Ecstasy of St. Catherine **(detail), 1526**
Fresco

In the center of the church, to the right, the chapel of St. Catherine opens before us, built between 1460 and 1488 on the front wall of the old sacristy in order to receive the relic of the saint's head, secretly removed from Rome to Siena in 1383 by Raimondo di Capua, Catherine's spiritual adviser and confessor. The modern reliquary, with the head, is enclosed in a Renaissance tabernacle of gilded marble.

The walls of the chapel are decorated with scenes from the life of St. Catherine and they form one of Sodoma's major works. On the rear wall are depictions of the *Ecstasy* and *Swooning*, on the left side we see St. Catherine offering comfort to a man condemned to death, one Niccolò di Tuldo. The right wall shows the healing by St. Catherine's intervention of a woman possessed, painted in 1593 by Francesco Vanni. Sodoma also painted the two saints Luke and Jerome in the entrance arch to the chapel.

The balanced and finely nuanced composition of the *Ecstasy of St. Catherine* is impressive due to the pathos in the posture and the sensual features of the portrayed saint. The graceful and yet strong female figures seem quite at ease. The background

displays the influence of Leonardo, including the use of *sfumato*, as well as Roman architectural features in the style of Bramante.

Palazzo Salimbeni

The three-story palace is a typical example of Sienese palazzo architecture of the Trecento and has a closed, defensive appearance. On the ground floor is the Gothic gate, opening under a so-called "Sienese arch." To the side, as on the topmost story, plain rounded-arched windows break up the façade. Only the *piano nobile* is marked out by triforate windows ornamented with tracery. The palazzo has been the seat, since 1472, of the oldest bank in Europe, the *Monte dei Paschi di Siena*, which grew out of a public credit company for citizens in need.

Palazzo Tolomei

The slender, well-proportioned Palazzo Tolomei was built in 1205 by the ancestors of Bernardo Tolomei, who in 1319 founded the Olivetan order. As early as the second half of the 13th century, the palace was renovated. The tall ground floor, with a gateway in the center, has a defensive appearance. The surviving consoles above the side portals (added later) are evidence of the original portico roof. Above the consoles are the symmetrically designed central story, with its five bays, and the uppermost story, which is lower. The lovely, regular biforate windows with their finely structured tracery are especially worthy of note.

Loggia della Mercanzia

Above the Piazza del Campo, in the Middle Ages, the Via Francigena led from the north gate, the Porta Camollia, to the southern gate or Porta Romana, crossing the city's other main road, which led to the cathedral hill to the west. At this point, known as the *Croce del Travaglio*, the city council built the Loggia della Mercanzia, as the seat of the commercial court. The three-arched building was begun in 1417 and finished in 1444; the upper story was added in the 17th century. It was the period of transition from the Gothic to the Renaissance style, and the architects took the Loggia dei Lanzi in Florence as their artistic model.

Images of saints dating from the 15th century, from the workshops of the Sienese painters and sculptors Vecchietta and Antonio Federighi, are placed in shallow niches on the columns. The saints Peter and Paul, Victor and Ansanus are the city's patrons. They are part of an allegorical program of "Good Government," and merchants hoped that a prayer said to the saints "in passing" would gain their support in mercantile dealing. Classical heroes by Antonio Federighi on the marble benches, elegant plasterwork, and frescoes of the cardinal virtues complete the decorative scheme, forming an exhortation to others to do likewise.

Piazza del Campo

"Il Campo" (the field), as the square is known among the Sienese, is one of the most impressive medieval squares of Italy. Set in a hollow in the shell shape of an ancient theater, with its continuation over the market square behind the Palazzo Pubblico leading on to open ground, the square has, since the 13th century, linked the hills of Siena.

The square received its characteristic paving in 1347. The warm red of the brick contrasts with the pale bands of travertine, which divide the square into nine segments in a rayed shape starting from the lowest point by the Palazzo Pubblico, a reminder of the rule of the Sienese guilds, which brought stability from 1287 to 1355. The seat of the "Council of the Nine" was thereby symbolically linked to the square and the city. Since 1297, rigorous building restrictions (though this was not always adhered to in later centuries) have resulted in a unified appearance of the buildings fronting the square. Through eleven roads and alleys, the people could pour into the square when the great bell of the "Mangia" tower sounded and the proclamations of the government were to be heard, or as in 1260 when the victory over Florence was celebrated. Here, in the 15th century, St. Bernard preached against civil war, and here, every year, the traditional celebration of the Palio is held, a reminder of the Middle Ages.

Skill and Splendor – the Palio

Twice a year, at the Palio, probably the most famous of Tuscany's traditional festivals, adults and children of all classes of society fasten the emblems of their *contrada* or city district to their clothing. Little ceramic plaques with the coats of arms and colors of the *contrade* can be seen thoughout the streets and on most of the houses, and these are a signal to visitors, showing them which of the city districts they are in. Today's 17 *contrade* have developed over the centuries from the medieval defense and residential communities that surrounded the towers and palazzi. Even after the end of the free republic, they still fulfilled important functions. The inhabitants had always been bound by a very strong community feeling and a

Table is spread for the district feast on the evening before the Palio

sense of belonging. Their representatives proposed laws, provided the heads of the guilds, built roads and organized life in the district. Even today, every *contrada* has its church, its community hall, a small museum, and its own well. Every two years, a total of forty honorary representatives are elected, with a *capitano* or *priore* at their head. Their duties today are of a social nature, in youth work or in the care of the elderly, or in the organization of city district festivals. However, the most important duties are the preparation and holding of the Palio, the historic horse race, which is held twice a year on festivals in honor of the Virgin Mary.

Palli were also held in Verona, Padua, Ferrara and Bologna during the Middle Ages, but the earliest recorded Pali was held in Siena in 1238, and the traditon continues.

On July 2, in honor of the Madonna di Provenzano, and on August 16, the Feast of the Assumption – on these days sport is played in earnest on the Piazza del Campo. Only victory counts; there are no second or third places. A special feature of the competition rules is that the drawing of

Coats of arms with the animals that give their names to the various contrade *of Siena*

lots decides the participation of a *contrada*, and it also decides the horse available. There are 17 *contrade* (districts) in the city of Siena, but only ten horses may compete for the Palio: the seven who missed out the last time, plus three

Two street scenes at the Palio in Siena

others, decided by a draw. Three days before the race the horses are presented on the square by the breeders and, after a trial race, they are distributed by lot among the *contrade*. Each *contrada* immediately takes the horse it has won to a specially furnished stable, the *casa del cavallo*. The animals are lovingly cared for by colorfully clothed *barbareschi*, grooms who mutter special spells and formulae to keep bad luck from the main actors in the spectacle of the Palio.

After three days of trials and preparations, each *contrada* puts on a sumptuous supper for all the inhabitants of the district. Excitement runs high, the *fantino*, jockey – usually brought in from outside Siena – is sworn in and the *capitano* explains the strategy for the race.

On the morning of the race, each *contrada* takes its horse into its own church, where in a special service the priest blesses both rider and horse. By late afternoon, the Piazza is almost full of people, some of whom are waiting on the very expensive balcony seats for the event. The race itself does not start until early evening. Beforehand, the official representatives of the *contrade* proceed to the Piazza del Campo to attend the procession of the banner bearers and the arrival of the oxcart with the *palio*, the silk banner, which is the true traditional trophy of this event.

Once the race has started, in an atmosphere of mounting excitement, three laps are covered in hardly more than 100 seconds, and any kind of obstruction of the opponent is allowed. Although the race is over quickly, for the losers, the shame lasts longer. If one of the jockeys is thrown, the horse may win the race on its own. The sharp bend past S. Martino is the greatest danger, and although everything is padded with mattresses, the ambulance staff are ready. Frequently a horse falls here and if it breaks a leg has to be put down.

"Each of the fifty thousand spectators screams the name of his *contrada* – like a long slow-burning fuse, which flickers for days across the race track to the final three-minute explosion" – this description in an Italian novel sums up the actual race.

After the race is finished, the winners go back to their *contrade*, and even the horse enters the cathedral with its flag-waving spectators.

Francesco Nenci, The Piazza del Campo with the Procession of the Contrade, *Collezione Monte del Paschi, Siena*

Fonte Gaia

Since 1342, there has been a public fountain at the highest point of the Piazza del Campo. The Fonte Gaia, the "fountain of joy," was consecrated in 1414, amid general rejoicing of the local population. Water was brought to the city center via a pipe 19 miles (30 km) long.

In 1409 Jacopo della Quercia created a basin, richly decorated with sculpted marble panels presenting a symbolic program with the Virgin and Child as central figures, and the Christian and cardinal virtues, scenes from the Creation story, and the legendary origins of Siena arranged around them. The original reliefs have been replaced by copies, and are today to be seen in the Palazzo Pubblico.

Palazzo Pubblico, Torre del Mangia

"It lies like an embrace around the square" is how the Sienese describe their town hall. In 1287 the Sienese city council decide to build itself a permanent seat at this, the lowest point of the "Campo." Ten years later, construction work began on the central part. The façade was magnificently extended in 1310 by the addition of the wings (which were raised by one story in the 17th century), and in 1325 the mighty tower was erected. The building, whose front elevation is slightly concave, set the pattern for Sienese Gothic. The ground floor is built of pale travertine blocks while the reddish bricks of the upper stories produce ever-varying three-dimensional effects in the changing light of the day. The play of light and shadow is particularly impressive due to the shapes of the windows and arches, so characteristic of secular architecture in Siena. The ground floor is opened up with a series of arcades under "Sienese arches," a pointed arch placed in front of a shallow segmented arch. In the upper storys, triforate windows with delicate columns give the broad front of the town hall its

elegance. The city's black and white coat of arms – the *balzana* – underneath every arch intensifies the contrasting effect of light and dark. Since 1425, a great bronze disk with Christ's monogram has been placed here as a reminder of the sermons of St. Bernard. The coat of arms of the Medici family is evidence of Florentine rule of Siena from 1560 onwards.

On the left hand of the Palazzo Pubblico is the bell tower, built in 1325. On its foundation stone, the hope is expressed in Greek, Latin, and Hebrew characters that it may never collapse "either due to lightning or to thunder." Since 1400, it has been known as the Torre del Mangia after the bell ringer, who was nicknamed Mangiaguadagni ("he who eats all his earnings"). The first mechanical clockworks date from 1360, and during the following century they were renewed and later improved several times. The slender brick tower, being 335 feet (102 m) high, has a striking appearance, with its regularly placed air holes, and rises above all the other buildings in the city, despite the low level of its site. With its white tip, it seems lighter and more elegant compared with the Florentine model on the Palazzo Vecchio. The Sienese artist Lippo Memmi devised the wooden model for the travertine top of the tower in 1341. In 1344, the projecting platform and battlemented narrow bell housing were completed. The iron bellframe, dedicated to "Maria assunta" and popularly known as "sunto," has crowned the tower only since the 17th century.

Cappella di Piazza

Four years after the devastating outbreak of plague in 1348, the surviving Sienese built the Cappella di Piazza at the foot of the Torre del Mangia to give thanks for their deliverance. This votive work was so important to the population that in 1352 there was even an exception made from the existing building regulations and the chapel became the sole structure to be allowed to project from the closed front of the square's buildings. The chapel, an open loggia with Gothic vaulting, rises from an almost square ground plan, and its prayer space is separated by richly ornamented marble barriers. The images of the saints in the niches date from the later Trecento, while the Renaissance cladding and the plain roof were added between 1463 and 1468.

Museo Civico

The Museo Civico is housed in what were once the ostentatious rooms of the city administration. In the map room, the *Sala del Mappamondo*, the council once met to discuss important decisions.

Simone Martini (c. 1284–1344),
***Maestà*, c. 1315**
Fresco, 763 × 970 cm

The "Council of Nine" continued the
special tradition of honoring the Virgin
Mary with their commission for a large
Madonna fresco in 1312. Since the victorious battle of Montaperti in 1260, the
Virgin had been the most important
protector and patron of the city. Simone
Martini executed the work *al fresco*, but
used glowing tempera colors, thick
applications of gold leaf, and inset jewels,
glass, and genuine parchment to increase
the sumptuous quality of his work.

Simone Martini opens up a continuous pictorial space, in which the Madonna and Child are enthroned under a broad baldachin. Angels and saints – a total of 32 figures, among them the city's patron saints Ansanus, Savinus, Crescentius, and Victor – form her celestial court. In the medallions are portrayals of Christ, the prophets, and the evangelists and at the bottom, in the center, a double-headed figure symbolizes the old and the new divine law. Here an inscription points out that Mary only "supports the true and the honest, but not the mighty who oppress the weak and cheat the country."

The entire picture, which is one of the most influential works of the *Trecento*, demonstrates the artist's special feeling for a graceful, elegant line, characteristic of the courtly art of the Gothic period, and his particular love of precious fabrics and sumptuous materials.

Simone Martini,
***Guidoriccio da Fogliano,* 1328**
Fresco, 340 × 967 cm

The fresco on the wall opposite the *Maestà* is dated 1328. Although firm evidence is lacking, it is also ascribed to Simone Martini on the basis of stylistic features. In that year, the famed general of Siena, Guidoriccio, had defeated the besieged cities of Montemassi and Sassoforte, in which rebellious Ghibellines had barricaded themselves. The knight Guidoriccio da Fogliano, an impressive figure, is riding across a broad, barren landscape between the besieged castle and the Sienese camp with its black and white banners. He is wearing a richly embroidered mantle of gold brocade, the pattern of which is continued on the caparison of his horse, with the wavy lines of the dark lozenges repeating the curves of the path leading to the fortress of Sassoforte, enclosed in its strong palisade, and of the hills in the background.

Ambrogio Lorenzetti, c. 1293–c. 1348),
Allegory of Good and Bad Government
(details), 1338–1339
Fresco, 296 × 1398 cm (total dimensions)

In the *Sala della Pace*, the government's meeting room, is the representation of "Good and Bad Government," one of the most extensive and important secular fresco cycles dating from the Middle Ages. Commissioned by the "Council of Nine," the Sienese painter Ambrogio Lorenzetti created a symbolic representation of proper political thought, based on the Aristotelian principle

of the care of justice and the common good, which is represented in both metaphorical and concrete terms.

The allegory of "good government" is represented on the northern wall. Seated

on the left is the personification of Justice with the scales. Above her floats the personification of Wisdom and at her feet Concord links two ropes leading down from the scales of justice into a single rope, symbol of agreement, and passes this down to 24 citizens, whose number refers to an earlier government which was the first to allow the people to participate. The rope leads these persons to the figure of an older, bearded man, dressed in a garment in the colors of the city coat of arms, who personifies *buon governo* (good government) and bears the letters CSCV, which stand for *Comune Senarum Civitas Virginis* (Community of the Sienese, City of the Virgin). His throne is surrounded by the counsellors of good government, the cardinal virtues shown together with Magnanimity and the especially beautiful,

white-clad figure of Peace with an olive branch. Above these, the Christian virtues of Faith, Hope, and Charity are floating. At his feet, the Sienese she-wolf is suckling the twins Aschius and Senius. In the service of Justice, knights in armor and soldiers are watching over a group of bound evildoers.

The allegory of "bad government" on the other hand illustrates the dreadful gang of vices – Cruelty, Envy, Greed, and Vanity – that accompany the diabolical tyrant enthroned on the western wall of the *Sala della Pace*. Justice lies bound at his feet. The effects of bad government are all too plain: buildings crumble, robbery and rape are the order of the day, and in the countryside, eternal winter rules.

Ambrogio Lorenzetti,
The Effects of Good Government in the City and in the Country, **1338–1339**
Fresco

The eastern wall shows the effects of "good government" in the city and in the country: the left side shows a view of Siena dating from the 14th century as the example of a flourishing city. It is possible to recognize the palazzi, crowned with the straight-edged merlons that signal the Guelph rule of the time, as well as numerous towers, loggias with shops on many of the ground floors, the gables of churches, and colorful painted façades and terraces.

The hustle and bustle of the inhabitants – merchants in their shops, traders with new supplies for their warehouses, busy masons on the rooftops, and a group of lovely girls dancing – indicate the comfortable prosperity and contentment of the citizens. A shepherd is driving his sheep through the gate, fortified by towers and projecting structures. A carefree company has already ridden out hunting, and people from the country are coming in with heavily laden donkeys to sell their produce in the city. A farmer drives a small pig in front of him, and others are busy working in the fields. In the wide, hilly landscape there are well-tended fields, neatly laid out vineyards, pretty olive groves and orchards, little farms and magnificent castles in the nearby countryside, and forests and rocky slopes in the distance. Above it all, Security, armed with a gallows, is watching over the proper order of things.

Palazzo Sansedoni

The northeast of the "Campo" is bordered by the great Palazzo Sansedoni with its curved, sweeping façade. Agostino di Giovanni, who also had a part in the town hall tower, in 1339 combined three buildings dating from the early 13th century, with their high residential towers, and transformed them into a noble palace of brick. Despite the broad extension across 13 window bays and on four levels, the result was an elegant building. According to the building regulations, the construction material and the elements of the structure conform to those used in the town hall. Triforate windows with delicate

columns of pale travertine columns open up the façade, which is topped by battlements above a frieze of round arches.

Palazzo Chigi-Saracini

The curved façade of the Palazzo Chigi-Saracini follows the bend in the road linking the "Campo" and the cathedral square. Its two-tone pattern attracts the eye: pale travertine has been used for the lower part, red brick for the upper. It is crowned with square-merlon battlements. The elegant triforate windows under pointed arches soften what might otherwise be a monumental and stern appearance. A statue in memory of Pope Julius II, son of Cristoforo Saracini, is in the passage leading to the charming courtyard with its well and decoratively painted portico. The courtyard is closed off by a wall, also topped with battlements.

The palazzo, built in the 14th century, is today the home of a well–known music academy and concert hall.

Ospedale S. Maria della Scala

Domenico di Bartolo (c. 1400–before 1445),
***Treatment and Care of the Sick* (with detail),**
1440–1441
Fresco

According to legend, a cobbler named Sorore is supposed to have founded a hostel for pilgrims here in the 9th century, where the guests also received medical attention. Thanks to donations and legacies, the foundation grew into a wealthy institution: acting at one time as hospital, pilgrims' hostel, poorhouse, and orphanage in one, it also owned large estates in the countryside around Siena. The name is derived from the stairs opposite leading up to the cathedral. Until a few years ago, the building still housed some departments of the hospital; today it is mainly a museum.

The wide room of the *Sala del Pellegrinaio* is not only an important example of medieval hospital architecture of the 14th century, but also it contains a well-preserved fresco cycle, in which Sienese painters have portrayed scenes from everyday life in this charitable institution. Domenico di Bartolo carried out the depiction of the treatment and care of the sick in a roomy hall, separated from the room behind by a skillfully worked screen. Under the watchful eye of the black-clad

rector, the highly respected surgeon Tura Bandini is kneeling down, cleaning the gaping wounds of a young pilgrim. To the right, a monk is depicted hearing the confession of a dying man and giving him the last sacrament.

Duomo S. Maria Assunta

The impressive cathedral, dedicated to the Assumption of the Virgin Mary, stands on the highest point in Siena. The present church, with green and white bands of marble incrustation and its highly decorated façade, is the result of more than 100 years of continuous construction history. On top of what were once twelve steps, intended to symbolize the twelve apostles, the triple-nave structure stretches from northwest to southeast on a cruciform ground plan with a dome and a flat end wall to the choir.

The city government began to commission the earliest plans for this structure in the mid-12th century, at the time of the city's first expansion. A larger church was to replace its predecessor. The late Romanesque basilica, begun in 1210, was already far advanced, and the walls, pillars, and cross-vaulted aisles already completed, when the Cistercians of S. Galgano took over the direction of the work in 1258 and completed the dome and choir. In 1284, the newly appointed cathedral architect Giovanni Pisano began with the design of the façade.

With two large-scale alterations in 1316 and 1369, the cathedral achieved its present size. First of all the choir was lengthened to the east; this required the building of the Baptistery under the church. The transept was also lengthened and widened. Finally, the nave was made taller, as can easily be seen by the change in the incrustation.

The cathedral's west façade was the first in Italy to display the rich treasury of forms and program of figures following the pattern of French Gothic cathedrals. Different colors of marble – white from Carrara, green from Prato, and pink from Siena – increase the richness of the design with their architectural effect.

Giovanni Pisano began work on the broad and very high façade with its three portals in 1284. He designed the ornamentation for the columns, the pointed Gothic pediments, and the pinnacles at the side. Lively sculpted figures (now replaced by copies), related to one another even across considerable distances, display the French influence brought to Italy by the Pisan artist. The portals' sculptural program includes the *Assumption* and the *Glorification* of the Virgin Mary. Prophets, philosophers, and patriarchs point to the Old Testament as the prefiguration of the images of the New Testament.

In 1296 Giovanni Pisano left the city, because of differences with the government. It was not until nearly 100 years later that Giovanni di Cecco completed the three-gabled upper portion of the façade and the rose window above the central portal, taking as his model the cathedral façade in Orvieto, created by the Sienese architect Lorenzo Maitani. The rose window is framed with little tabernacles: 35 busts of prophets and patriarchs are grouped around the Virgin and Child.

Duomo S. Maria Assunta

Piccolomini altar,
Michelangelo
Buonarroti,
St. Paul

Façade, p. 364

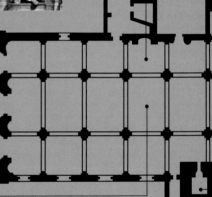

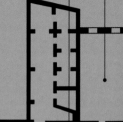

Interior, p.368

Cappella Chigi
(Cappella della
Madonna del
Voto) Gian
Lorenzo Bernini,
St. Catherine,
p. 322

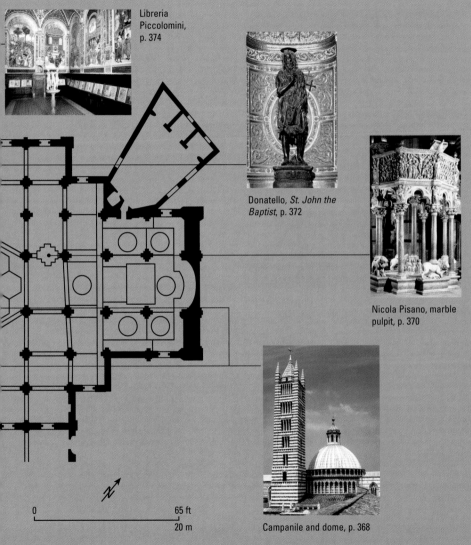

Libreria Piccolomini, p. 374

Donatello, *St. John the Baptist*, p. 372

Nicola Pisano, marble pulpit, p. 370

Campanile and dome, p. 368

0   65 ft

20 m

only the shell of the cupola itself that now rises above the church roof, while the drum has sunk into the interior of the church. The marble incrustation of the wall can be clearly seen behind the dainty columns of the miniature gallery.

The Interior

The view of the interior of the cathedral is overwhelming. Manifold decorations succeed one another and submerge the church interior into a secretive play of light and shadow. The dominant black and white bands of marble are reminiscent of the city's coat of arms. High round arches, supported by slender cluster pillars, divide the basilica-like nave into three aisles. The series of arches dates back to the Romanesque phase of construction. The central nave was raised in the Trecento, and the old vaulting structures end at a slightly projecting cornice which unites the choir, the nave, and the transept. Below it, 172 busts of various popes have been inserted. The gilded figures of the city's patron saints in the richly decorated crossing cupola are of a later date.

An unusual feature is the precious marble inlay pavement, which was started in 1369 and took nearly 200 years to complete. Fifty-six individual fields with philosophers, sibyls, virtues, allegories and biblical scenes provide a picture from Classical history to Christianity and to the founding of the city of Siena.

Campanile and Dome

The tall campanile, rising from the angle between the nave and transept, dominates the eastern side of the cathedral. Its lower stories are so much a part of the wall structure that the tower, with its ever-increasing number of windows towards the top, is no longer really a freestanding campanile. It received its present characteristic appearance, with its regular stripes, in about 1300.

The present crossing cupola, on its hexagonal base and tall drum, was completed in 1264. One hundred years later the nave was heightened, and it is

**Nicola Pisano (c. 1220–before 1284),
marble pulpit, 1265–1268**
Marble, h. 460 cm

One of the most remarkable works of art in the cathedral is the marble pulpit by Nicola Pisano. Apart from the lost original coloring, it is in good condition, despite having been moved and later having steps

and a plinth added. In the contracts commissioning the work the assistants are also mentioned: Giovanni, son of Nicola, still a minor, and Arnolfo di Cambio.

For the structure, Nicola followed his first pulpit in the baptistery in Pisa: nine pillars of granite, porphyry, and green marble support the – here octagonal – pulpit itself. The outer columns are supported alternately by plain plinths and by pacing lions and lionesses. The central column rests on a base with the figures representing the Seven Liberal Arts and Philosophy. Virtues and prophets appear above the capitals and in the spandrels of the trefoil arches. The reliefs of the balustrade, topped by a Classically inspired ledge, portray seven scenes from the New Testament, framed by allegorical corner figures. The theological program of the older pulpit in Pisa, a representation of Christian teaching of the true way to salvation and eternal life, is here taken up once more.

Nicola Pisano, Adoration of the Magi
(Detail of the marble pulpit)

The detailed scenes have been most skillfully chiseled out of the marble: a vast number of figures, almost impossible to count, fill the reliefs. They line up one behind the other, in their richly folded robes, from the smooth background to the occasionally fully three-dimensional heads in the foreground, and they produce a complex play of light and shadow. To the left, the journey of the Three Kings is depicted, while on the right, with great sensitivity and an anecdotal delight in storytelling, the actual core of the events has been sculpted: the oldest king is kneeling before the Christ Child and tenderly kissing the little infant foot. Never before had this scene been portrayed with such unconstrained intimacy.

The events of the Christian gospel are no longer depicted merely for the purpose of making their transcendent content visible, but almost as if they were historical events. The expressive power of Nicola Pisano's figures is enormous, and their realism is probably due to intensive study of the French Gothic cathedral style.

Donatello (1386–1466), *St. John the Baptist*, 1457
Bronze, h. 185 cm

Donatello created the bronze statue of John the Baptist when he was 71 years old. It is one of his greatest works and is evidence of the same dramatic power of expression as his St. Mary Magdalene in the cathedral museum in Florence. It is possible that the artist had previously made a wax model to try out the finely worked tendrils of the goatskin cloak and the hair, which is reminiscent of frayed hemp.

Michelangelo Buonarroti (1475–1564), *St. Paul*, 1503–1504
Marble, h. 124 cm

The young Michelangelo received a commission in around 1500 to create 15 statuettes for the niches in the Piccolomini altar. The artist himself completed only SS. Peter and Paul before leaving Siena; the other figures are presumably made to his designs.

Gian Lorenzo Bernini (1598–1680),
St. Mary Magdalene, **1662–1663**
Marble, h. c. 180 cm

In addition to plans for the extension of the Cappella Chigi, Bernini also provided the niche figures of St. Jerome and St. Mary Magdalene, who seems to be following a vision in a state of blessed ecstasy.

St. Paul looks reserved and thoughtful. The expansive power which Michelangelo put into his later figures still appears to be locked up in the stone. But the stress on their physical bodies, so typical for Michelangelo, can already be felt in the dynamically angled hands, the tense, voluminous folds, and the abrupt movements of the figures.

Libreria Piccolomini

The library was founded in 1495 by Cardinal Francesco Piccolomini (afterwards Pope Pius III) to house the precious books that had belonged to his uncle, Pope Pius II. The sculpture of the *Three Graces* was to be a reminder of the Classical learning of this pope, who was born in 1405 as Enea Silvio (Aenius Silvius) Piccolomini. The mirrored ceiling, decorated with grotesques and virtues, shows, among other things, the coat of arms of the Piccolomini, a cross of half-moons.

Pinturicchio (c. 1452–1513), *The Meeting of Frederick III and Eleanora of Aragon*, 1502–1509

The fresco cycle by Pinturicchio, a painter highly regarded for his decorative work, shows ten stations in the life of the pope. In the meeting of the two protagonists, there are many portraits of members of the imperial and papal families, of cardinals and friends – even of the emperor's interpreter. The ceremony is composed according to the model of the *Marriage of the Virgin*. Pius II, therefore, who is here uniting the pair, still in his office as Archbishop of Siena, is portrayed as above normal height, and in a pose that accords with the iconographical tradition of biblical history.

Battistero di S. Giovanni

The baptistery is beneath the apse of the cathedral and is reached by a steep marble staircase which begins behind the unfinished Duomo Nuovo. After the first few steps a chiseled cross marks the spot where St. Catherine is supposed to have fallen, pushed by the devil.

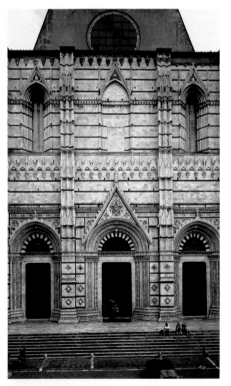

The baptistery was constructed so that it supported the extended cathedral choir. This revolutionary idea, which was chosen in preference to the much more expensive option of constructing a new building from scratch, was pushed through at the beginning of the Trecento by the city council against the views of the cathedral authorities. Also, although the new baptistery was part of the cathedral, at the same time, because of its location, it formed a direct link through the Via dei Pellegrini with the town hall square. The religious and the secular centers were therefore brought closer together.

The baptistery and the substructures for the choir apse were built between 1316 and 1325, and the work was supervised by Camaino di Crescentino. The clearly structured marble façade was not added until 1382 and was never completely finished. Delicate pediments, crockets, niches, and elegant pillars give the late-Gothic frontage a rich and precious character. It has three harmoniously proportioned portals, the central one given emphasis by its richly decorated pediment. The preponderance of decoration in the lower zone of the façade is remarkable, while in the upper story the ornaments are reduced and it is the solid surfaces of the walls which are stressed. There are only three tall, narrow biforate windows to break up the strong character of the upper story; the central one was closed up in the 16th century.

Interior with Font

Powerful pilasters and columns support the broad expanse of the cross-rib vaulting of the rectangular interior, which is divided into three naves. To the west, the apse, built on a polygonal ground plan, opens up. Precious marble and the 15th-century frescoes covering the ceiling, apse, and lunettes mean that the interior radiates a festive atmosphere.

In the vaulting and the arches of the eastern bays there are apostles, prophets, and sibyls depicted by Vecchietta (c. 1412–1480). In the right lunette is the scene *Christ in the House of the Pharisee*, in the one on the left *The Miracle of St. Anthony*. These are by painters from Vecchietta's circle. In the apse are *Scenes from the Life of Jesus*.

In the center there is an especially beautiful font. The design of the marble structure varies the basic form of the hexagon in basin, pillar, and tabernacle. A multitude of marble and bronze figures enliven the fountain. Little putti play music, reliefs tell the story of John the Baptist and female figures personify Christian virtues. Jacopo della Quercia received the first commission to work on the font in 1414. Further artists were brought in for the bronze work, first of all Ghiberti, then two Sienese sculptors, Giovanni di Turino and his son, and finally Donatello. In this way, by 1429, an impressive work of art had been produced, the result of cooperation between Florentine and Sienese artists.

Jacopo della Quercia (c. 1374–1438),
Annunciation to Zacharias, **1428–1429**
Bronze (gilded), 60 × 60 cm

Lorenzo Ghiberti (1378–1455),
The Baptism of Christ, **1427**
Bronze (gilded), 60 × 60 cm

On the lower part of the font there are six gilded bronze reliefs depicting scenes from the life of St. John the Baptist. In the *Annunciation to Zacharias* by Jacopo della Quercia, the architecture of the temple is set at an angle to the background of the picture, so that very slight variations give the effect of great depth. Under a massive arch, the heroic figures of Zacharias and the angel meet. A characteristic of the artist is the heavy effect of the forms: massive architecture alongside powerful figures with chiseled features and classical hooked noses.

The Florentine Lorenzo Ghiberti created two reliefs for the font: *The Arrest of John the Baptist* and *The Baptism of Christ*. Both mark an important stage in the artistic development of the sculptor and demonstrate Ghiberti's stylistic changes. He combines figures mounted on to the background of the relief with *rilievo schiacciato,*

Annunciation to Zacharias	Birth of John the Bap
Jacopo della Quercia 1428–1429	**Giovanni di Turino** 1427

Donatello (1386–1466), *Herod's Feast*, 1427
Bronze (gilded), 60 × 60 cm

The most moving relief on the font is this one by Donatello: it is imbued with great drama, and also gives a remarkable effect of depth.

The Florentine artist used linear perspective in his depiction of the scene, and arranged the architecture parallel to the lower edge of the image. He thus suggested spatial depth with, for instance, the diminishing size of the floor tiles, and also by showing the monstrous action taking place under the arches of rooms set one behind the other: here music is playing for Salome's dance and, right at the back, a henchman is holding the head of the Baptist.

Salome is dancing, surrounded by curious, elegant youths, while the events reach a crisis. The kneeling man in livery offers the hideous plate to Herod, his movement enhancing the almost fully three-dimensional effect of the figures. Among those present, there is growing horror at Salome's cruelty and willfulness, and also at the ease with which her step-father has granted her request.

a technique developed by Donatello which allows for the transition from high relief to the most shallow degrees of modeling. Ghiberti uses this "flattened relief" for the first time in the *Baptism of Christ*, which concerns itself with the central theme of the baptismal font. The three-dimensional effect of the figures decreases ever more from foreground to background. Using this technique, Ghiberti achieves an almost painterly composition, which owes a debt to the curves of the lines in Gothic art.

John the Baptist preaching	Baptism of Christ	Arrest of John the Baptist	Herod's Feast
Giovanni di Turino	**Lorenzo Ghiberti**	**Lorenzo Ghiberti**	**Donatello**
1427	1427	1427	1427

Duomo Nuovo

Only a gigantic skeleton survives of the ambitious "New Cathedral" project. In 1339, the city government of Siena decided to outdo their rivals in Pisa and Florence with a complete new re-building of the cathedral. The existing church was to serve as the transept, to which the new part, consisting of nave and two aisles, and extending over four bays, would be attached on its west side. The Sienese sculptor, goldsmith, and architect Pietro di Lando was entrusted with the direction of the

work. He was specially recalled from Naples, where he was in the service of Robert of Anjou. Work on the new building proceeded rapidly: foundations, walls, and marble decorations arose in swift succession. In the year of the great plague, 1348, building came to a stop. Afterwards, serious flaws became apparent in the foundations, as did irreparable cracks in the walls. As these structural flaws, brought about by over-rapid construction, could not now be corrected, the project had to be abandoned and those parts of the structure in danger of collapse had to be pulled down. According to the historian Jakob Burckhardt, this cathedral would have become the "most beautiful Gothic structure in Italy by a wide margin, and a wonder of the world."

Part of the exterior walls of the nave, the north aisle and the high wall of the façade, the so-called *facciatone*, have remained. Even though it is difficult to imagine what the final shape of this building would have been, what remains nonetheless gives us an image of the "painterly" concept of Sienese architecture of the time. This can be seen in the high interior façade with its double window, extending upwards instead of a rose window. Arches and pilasters give an idea of the design of the structure, while capitals and marble stripes suggest the intended decorative scheme, so that the wall and the enclosed space almost appear as areas of color, and the structural elements as lines and surrounds.

Museo dell'Opera Metropolitana

The Museo dell'Opera Metropolitana, the cathedral museum, has since 1870 been situated in the finished northern nave of the planned new cathedral, behind the walled-up arcades of the first three bays. This was the site, in earlier years, of the marble-workers' workshop, and the place where, for example, Jacopo della Quercia's *Fonte Gaia* was constructed.

Originals of many works made for the cathedral are in the museum, having been removed from their original sites to preserve them from pollution damage. The museum contains not only paintings and sculptures, but also goldsmiths' work, illuminated manuscripts and church textiles. The ground floor contains marble works and sculptures.

Giovanni Pisano (c. 1250–c.1319),
Miriam, Sister of Moses, **1284–1296**
Marble

The cycle of figures sculpted by Giovanni Pisano during his supervision of the building of the cathedral façade consists of ten over life-size statues – prophets, sibyls, ancient philosophers – which have been removed from their original sites to preserve them and replaced by copies.

In a very specific manner, Giovanni Pisano transformed the influences he received from northern European art into his own expressive style. He adopted the curves of the drapery and the way that figures turned around their own axis, but his figures were freestanding and he gave them a broad base. From the base, the individual figures develop in clear forms up to a narrow upper body and an unusually individual expressive face. It becomes clear when looking at Miriam, the sister of Moses, how strongly Giovanni Pisano expresses his vocabulary of forms in the facial features and pose of the body. Miriam's body is turned almost in a spiral, enveloped in the rich folds of her robe. In line with her importance as a prophetess of Judaism, she is depicted with a thoughtful face and a slightly open mouth, listening to the prophesies of Simeon, who is turned towards her. It is this skill in portrayal that allows the sculptor to create the impression of a relationship between the figures even across considerable spatial distances.

Duccio di Buoninsegna (c. 1255–1319),
***Maestà*, 1308–1311**
Tempera and oil on wood, 211 × 426 cm

"O Holy Mother of God, be a source of peace to Siena, give life to Duccio, who has painted You thus," says the inscription of the work for which Duccio di Buoninsegna signed the contract on October 9, 1308. On June 9, 1311 the *Maestà* (Virgin Mary in Majesty) was carried to the cathedral in a ceremonial procession through the street, while the bells rang. It hung there for two centuries as the main altarpiece, replacing the previous votive image to which the citizens of Siena had turned when they put themselves under the protection of the Virgin before the battle of Montaperti. The large scale of this painting has enabled Duccio to give full expression to the local cult of the Virgin.

The altarpiece, as was customary, is painted on both sides. Today the main panels have been separated and can be seen in the cathedral museum. On the front, Mary is seated with the infant Jesus on a wide, decorated marble throne, surrounded by angels and saints. The patron saints of the city are kneeling in the foreground. Size and coloring mark the Madonna out from her companions. She slightly inclines her head to the sturdy boy.

In this painting, Duccio has moved away from the strict Byzantine traditional manner of representing the Madonna. The delicacy of his materials, the fine, decorative lines, and the natural-looking faces were to have a profound influence on the painters who came after him.

Duccio di Buoninsegna,
Christ Crowned with Thorns, **1308–1311**
Tempera and oil on wood, 50 × 53.5 cm

The life of Christ and episodes from the last years of the life of the Virgin were depicted in 53 separate panels, on the predella, top and reverse of the *Maestà*. Duccio here combined inspiration from miniatures in illuminated manuscripts, from enamel and ivory work, and from Eastern mosaics, with a vivid description

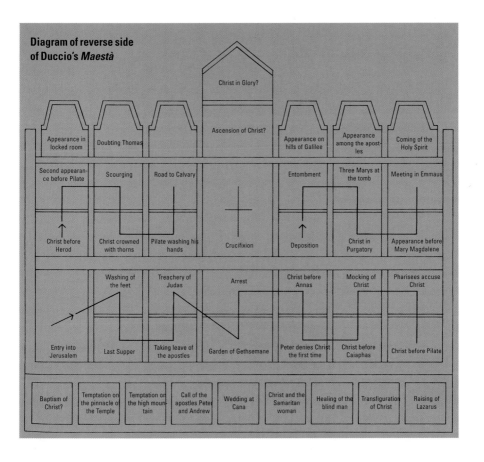

Diagram of reverse side of Duccio's *Maestà*

		Christ in Glory?		
		Ascension of Christ?		
Appearance in locked room	Doubting Thomas		Appearance on hills of Galilee	Appearance among the apostles	Coming of the Holy Spirit
Second appearance before Pilate	Scourging	Road to Calvary		Entombment	Three Marys at the tomb	Meeting in Emmaus
Christ before Herod	Christ crowned with thorns	Pilate washing his hands	Crucifixion	Deposition	Christ in Purgatory	Appearance before Mary Magdalene
	Washing of the feet	Treachery of Judas	Arrest	Christ before Annas	Mocking of Christ	Pharisees accuse Christ
Entry into Jerusalem	Last Supper	Taking leave of the apostles	Garden of Gethsemane	Peter denies Christ the first time	Christ before Caiaphas	Christ before Pilate
Baptism of Christ?	Temptation on the pinnacle of the Temple	Temptation on the high mountain	Call of the apostles Peter and Andrew	Wedding at Cana	Christ and the Samaritan woman	Healing of the blind man	Transfiguration of Christ	Raising of Lazarus

of human emotion in the historical situations presented. Each scene is designed minutely and with a great love of detail, but at the same time as a picture complete in itself. In the *Christ Crowned with Thorns* mocking henchmen surround Christ, whose expression of humble resignation makes him seem almost detached. They wrap him in a brocade mantle, put the crown of thorns on his head (in the presence of Pontius Pilate), and give him a reed for a scepter.

Palazzo Buonsignori – Pinacoteca Nazionale

The battlemented Palazzo Buonsingori, a late-Gothic building adorned with elegant triforate windows, today houses the national gallery of Siena, which with almost 1,000 works contains one of the most important collections of Sienese panel painting.

Guido da Siena (active c. 1262–1270),
***Madonna and Child with Four Saints*, 1270**
Tempera on wood, 96 × 186 cm

This altar piece, *Madonna and Child with Four Saints*, has its origins in the circle of the earliest Sienese painter whom we know by name, Guido da Siena. As the names of other artists are missing, the panel has been assigned to Guido's artistic circle. The work is dated 1270 and is evidence of the mature Byzantine style which spread through Tuscany in the second half of the 13th century and which Giorgio Vasari termed the *maniera greca*, the Greek manner. The panel is incomplete: originally there were six saints.

In the town hall there is a *Madonna in Maestà* signed by Guido da Siena which shows stylistic similarities. This painter had a wide-ranging artistic education; his works were influenced by contemporaries such as the Florentine Coppo di Marcovaldo and the sculptor Nicola Pisano.

Ambrogio Lorenzetti (c.1293–c.1348),
Madonna and Child with Saints, **1319–1348**
Tempera on wood, 87 × 41 cm (left panel), 100.5 ×
55.5 cm (central panel), 87 × 41.5 cm (right panel)

The Child is unrolling a scroll with the
words from St. Luke's Gospel: *beati
pauperes...* ("Blessed are the poor, for theirs
is the Kingdom of Heaven"). This is a
pointer to the possible origin of the three
panels, reconstructed to form a triptych;
the Chiesa degli Umiliati, the Church of
the Lowly. Ambrogio Lorenzetti here
portrays the relationship of mother and

child as very tender and intense. The
infant Jesus is lovingly pressing himself
against his mother's face and his arm is
around her neck.

Mary reciprocates the gesture and
regards the child with a tender gaze. St.
Dorothy on the right and St. Mary
Magdalene on the left are taking part in
this deeply intimate scene. The latter bears
Christ's Passion on her heart and is
holding the vase of ointment with which
she anointed Christ's feet. St. Dorothy
shows the child a posy of roses as a sign of
the martyrdom she has suffered.

Il Sodoma (1477–1549),
Nativity with an Angel and St. John, **c. 1503**
Tempera on wood, diam. 111 cm

When Il Sodoma (Giovanni Antonio Bazzi) came to Siena in 1500 on personal recommendation, he had several years of training as a painter in his home town of Vercelli and in Milan behind him. From Lombardy he brought the fresh, highly detailed naturalism with him, but here he now turned to Pinturicchio and Raphael. He was a master of the *chiaroscuro* technique introduced by Leonardo. All these influences are noticeable in this Nativity, in which the charm of the faces and the idealized grace of the movements are especially attractive.

Francesco di Giorgio Martini (1439–1501),
Coronation of the Virgin, **c. 1472**
Tempera on wood, 227 × 200 cm

In Siena it was the architect Francesco di Giorgio Martini who came closest to that ideal of the Renaissance, the *uomo universale*. Apart from architecture, he devoted himself to painting and sculpture and also distinguished himself as an engineer and as an author of theoretical tracts. His interest in things Classical was most noticeable in his paintings, where he tried to overcome the somewhat unrealistic style of depiction that is characteristic of Sienese painting.

The large altarpiece of the *Coronation of the Virgin* was created around 1472 and is an impressive feast of color. The representation, which is similar to a stage set, is unusual. Christ and the Virgin appear, surrounded by seraphim, on a round platform of dark clouds borne by angels. Prophets are seated in a surrounding plain, and among them there are saints arranged on four levels on both sides. In the uppermost part of the picture, heaven is opening in a circular hole. In a double spiral of air, the figure of God the Father appears, seen from below in fore-

shortened perspective from the soles of his feet to his hair, with hands held out dramatically against the storm, and with flying garments and windblown hair.

Monte Oliveto Maggiore

The abbey of Monte Oliveto Maggiore lies in a harsh landscape of volcanic mounds of gray to pale yellow clay, with steep-sided tufa hills and sharp limestone precipices, in which the roads run along seemingly endless narrow ridges and where only occasional scattered cypresses and single farms act as reminders of human presence – even though human beings have lived here since Paleolithic days. Bernardo Tolomei, later canonized, withdrew in 1313 into this wilderness of so-called *crete*, clay, with his two friends Ambrogio Piccolomini and Patrizio Patrizi. He was 40 years old. He and his friends had left their wealthy families to live in solitude according to the Rule of St. Benedict. In 1319 they were were recognized as Benedictines, and the monastery of Monte Oliveto, the Mount of Olives, was founded. The congregation was confirmed in its rights in 1344 by Pope Clement VI.

From 1387 to 1526 a great monastery was built in red brick. The church, remodeled in the Baroque style, and the late-Gothic campanile can be seen at a distance through the cypresses. The refectory, the library, a pharmacy, the chapter house, and the living and working spaces are grouped around three cloisters.

View of the abbey Monte Oliveto Maggiore

Choir Furnishing (detail), 1503–1505

The single-nave monastery church, renovated in the Baroque style in 1772, is built on the ground plan of a Latin cross. The walls of the nave are taken up with magnificent hand-carved and inlaid choir benches created by the Olivetan monk Giovanni da Verona. Forty-eight of the seats, decorated above and below with tiny arabesques, are decorated with inlay work,

forming a unique series of landscapes, *vedute*, musical instruments, sheet music, birds, and scientific instruments. Especially handsome, too, is the lectern set up in the middle, made by the Olivetan monk Fra Raffaele da Brescia, who created an almost life-size cat sitting under a portico shown in perspective.

Il Sodoma (1477–1549), *Miracle of the Grain Trough*, after 1505
Fresco

In the late-Gothic rib-vaulted great cloister, dating from the 15th century, the most important events in the life of St. Benedict of Nursia, as told by Pope Gregory the Great in the second book of his *Lives*, are portrayed in a series of 36 paintings with rounded tops. The cycle was intended to be a constant model and inspiration for the monks living at Monte Oliveto. In 1495–1498 Luca Signorelli carried out the first frescoes. In 1504–1508, Il Sodoma completed the series with a further 27 paintings, depicting the scenes illusionistically so that they appear to be taking place behind arch-

ways. The *Miracle of the Grain Trough* shows two scenes in succession, telling a story. To the left, we see Benedict's weeping nurse, Cirilla, who loved him as if she were his mother and accompanied him everywhere. While preparing to bake bread, the wooden trough slipped from her hand and broke. It is said that Bernard prayed, and that the pieces of the container fitted themselves back together before him. Behind an ornamental pillar, a group of people (including the wife and daughter of

the artist) are admiring the trough with astonishment – it is now hanging between the acanthus capitals of a church façade. The knightly figure dressed in a richly ornamented cloak is a self-portrait of Il Sodoma. At his feet, he has painted badgers, his favorite animal. He skillfully combines individual narrative scenes with architecture in strict perspective and a bright landscape in the background.

Pienza

Panoramic view of Pienza

The town of Pienza, set on a hill above the Val d'Orcia, was originally the village of Corsignano, and owes its present name to Enea Silvio Piccolomini, later Pope Pius II, who was born here in 1405 to a prominent but impoverished family. The name *Pienza* was chosen, as a good omen, to mean "city of Pius." After a long period of Humanist studies Aeneas, as he called himself in allusion to the mythical forefather of the Roman people, had become well known as a successful diplomat and politician, but also as the author of numerous travel books and love stories. When in 1458, after a short period in office as Archbishop of Siena, he was elected pope, he was dominated by two main ideas: the defeat of the Turkish empire and the securing of his personal fame after death.

In order, as Pope Pius himself wrote in his *Commentarii*, to establish "a lasting sign of his origin," he commissioned the

Florentine architect Bernardo Rossellino to turn Corsignano into a personal monument, a "Pius City," with a group of monumental buildings. Influenced by Leon Battista Alberti's architectural writings, Pius II himself took a hand in the difficult planning stages. The town was inhabited, so it was impossible rebuild it from scratch. There were also economic and topographic constraints, and the project was limited not least by time: when the pope died in 1464, the scheme was doomed to failure.

As the core of the "ideal city," Bernardo Rossellino laid out the central square, the Piazza Pio II, on a trapezoid ground plan and divided the paving into rectangular areas. The effect is of a stage surrounded by important build-ings. The Palazzo Vescovile (episcopal palace) here forms the eastern flank, and the town hall is set to the north of it at an angle. For the Palazzo Vescovile, Pius II was able to convince Cardinal Rodrigo Borgia, later Pope Alexander VI, to build his family palace here. For the tower of the Palazzo Comunale, Rossellino kept to the Florentine model. He gave the façade, facing the central piazza, a light and

open character. On the ground floor, the tall loggia with three arcades of Ionic pillars opens up before us. In the upper stories, *sgraffito* paintings imitate layers of stone and sculptural ornaments. High windows here light up the council hall. The architect also used the same window form in the papal family's palazzo.

This whole site, based on a single plan, was the first attempt at large-scale urban renewal since Classical times.

Palazzo Comunale and Palazzo Vescovile

Pienza

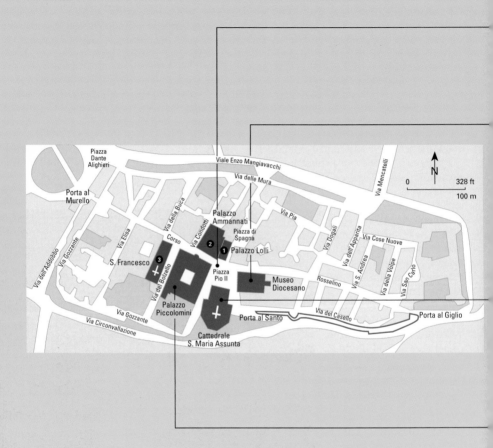

Piazza Dante Alighieri

Porta al Murello

Viale Enzo Mangiavacchi

Via delle Mura

Via Mencatelli

0   328 ft
100 m

Via dell'Addobbo

Via Gozzante

Via Elisa

Via della Buca

Via Condotti

Palazzo Ammannati

Piazza di Spagna

Via Pia

Via Dogali

Via dell'Apparita

Via Cose Nuove

Corso

2

1 Palazzo Lolli

S. Francesco

3

Piazza Pio II

Museo Diocesano

Rosselino

Via S. Andrea

Via della Volpe

Via San Carlo

Via del Balzello

Palazzo Piccolomini

Via del Casello

Via Gozzante

Via Circonvallazione

Porta al Santo

Porta al Giglio

Cattedrale S. Maria Assunta

Palazzo Comunale and Palazzo Vescovile, Corso Rossellino, p. 395

Museo Diocesano, 30 Corso Rossellino, p. 400

Cattedrale S. Maria Assunta, Piazza Pio II, p. 398

Palazzo Piccolomini, 2 Piazza Pio II, p. 398

Other places of interest:
(not covered elsewhere in this book):

1 S. Francesco, Corso Rossellino

2 Palazzo Lolli, Piazza Pio II

3 Palazzo Ammannati, Corso Rossellino

Palazzo Piccolomini and Cattedrale Santa Maria Assunta

Through the arcades of the Palazzo Comunale, we have a view of the Piccolomini palace and the cathedral. For the design of the block-like, three-story papal palace, Rossellino largely copied the Florentine Palazzo Rucellai, which he had completed in 1451 according to Alberti's design. This entirely corresponded to the ideas of his employer, Pope Pius II.

The highly individual cathedral façade is distinguished from the other buildings by the use of pale travertine alone. It is divided up by pillars, columns, and pilasters, and it has a gable with the coat of arms of Rossellino's papal employer. An original feature are the blind arches which rise through two stories. The inserted columns with their Ionic capitals pick up elements of the work of Alberti, the architect favored by Pius.

Interior, View of the Ring of Chapels

The light interior is surprising because of its combination of different styles. Enea Silvio Piccolomini had a good knowledge of northern architecture and was impressed by the division of space in Gothic cathedrals. In his own words, one should feel enclosed "not by a house of stone, but by a house of glass." Rossellini therefore did not build him a basilica, but a three-nave church, with a transept that continues in a ring of chapels. However,

the result was a bright Renaissance space. Ribbed vaults, tracery windows, and clustered columns – all traditional Gothic forms – here seem to have a merely decorative effect. Only the high impost above the capitals has the effect of a constructive link between the two styles.

The decoration also owes a debt to both styles: the sculptural works from Rossellino's workshop bear witness to the Renaissance, but the altar retables are examples of Sienese painting, still Gothic in the 15th century.

Museo Diocesano

Segna di Bonaventura (active 1298–before 1331), crucifix, 1315–1320
Tempera on wood, 221 × 160.5 cm

The diocesan museum, next door to the cathedral, exhibits valuable items of church furnishings which are nowadays kept in the museum for security reasons. For instance, an item from the church of

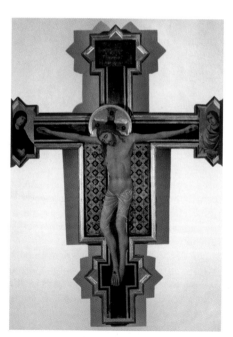

S. Francesco is the impressive crucifix by Segna di Bonaventura, who lived around the turn of the 13th and 14th centuries. He was the nephew of the famous Duccio di Buoninsegna and signed only four works, with "Segna me fecit." The crucifix, painted in tempera, shows the dead Christ on the cross. The suffering and pain of the crucified Christ are emphasized by the half-length figures of the Virgin and St. John the Baptist at the ends of the cross. The representation is marked by an icon-like solemnity, fine but clear contours and strong effects of light and shadow.

Brussels weaving workshop,
Articles of Faith and Mass of St. Gregory, 1495–1515
Wool and silk, 421 × 390 cm

Three tapestries produced at the end of the 15th century in Flemish workshops are of outstanding quality. Pienza acquired them through members of the Piccolomini family. The tapestry pictured here illustrates the mass of St. Gregory. The Man of Sorrows appears to Gregory the Great, who is celebrating mass, in a vision, filling the chalice with his blood. Eight of the total twelve articles of faith of the Creed, the Christian statement of belief, are also depicted. It is possible to recognize representatives of the Catholic church, the community of saints, the forgiveness of sins, the resurrection of the flesh, eternal life, and, right at the top, the Holy Trinity.

Montepulciano

Montepulciano lies on a hill of tufa rock, between the Chiana and Orcia valleys, and according to legend was founded by the Etruscan king Lars Porsenna. After having changed hands several times between Florence and Siena, in 1391 the town voluntarily placed itself under the rule of Florence. It was the birthplace of the Humanist poet Angelo Ambrogini, who called himself Poliziano after the town's Medieval Latin name, Mons Politianus. In the *centro storico* the town presents a different appearance from other Tuscan towns with their medieval buildings; it is completely surrounded by walls, but the style of its buildings ranges from the early Renaissance to the Baroque period. Because the noble families, who had acquired considerable wealth through trade, remained in control for longer than in other places, they had their medieval family palazzi reworked or built anew by famous architects in the latest styles between the 15th and 17th centuries.

These noble families have also given their name to Montepulciano's own well-known wine, called the *vino nobile*.

Palazzo Comunale

The political and religious center of the town has for centuries been the broad, stage-like Piazza Grande, laid out on top of the hill. In the Middle Ages the parish church stood here, until it was replaced by the present cathedral. The square was extended in the early 16th century by wealthy patrician families who built their splendid residential palazzi here, after they had moved their trading center downhill to the Piazza delle Erbe.

The stern-looking block of the three-storied town hall rises on the western side of the square. The medieval building was remodeled, beginning in 1440, by Cosimo il Vecchio de' Medici's most favorite architect, the Florentine Michelozzo, who based his scheme on the Palazzo Pubblico in Florence. The new front façade displays Renaissance elements such as the balanced distribution of windows, the strong accent on the individual stories created by pronounced sills and the central placing of the tower. However, there are also late Gothic influences such as the rusticated blocks on the ground floor and the strongly projecting, battlemented walkway. There is also a beautiful inner courtyard.

Montepulciano

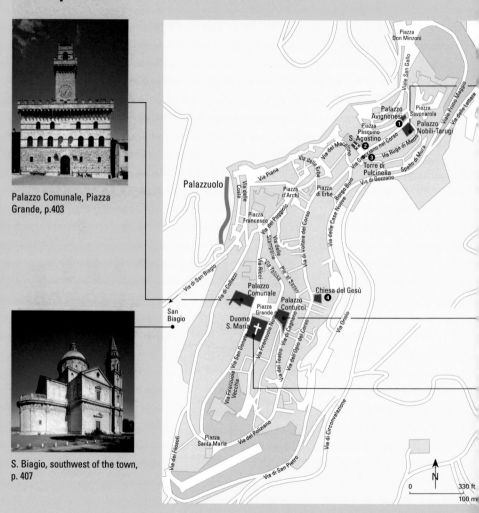

Palazzo Comunale, Piazza Grande, p.403

S. Biagio, southwest of the town, p. 407

Palazzo Avignonesi ①
Piazza Savonarola
Palazzo Nobili-Tarugi
Piazza Don Minzoni
Viale San Gallo
Viale Primo Maggio
Viale delle Lettere
Piazza Pasquino
S. Agostino ②
Via Graciano nel Corso
Via Ruga di Mezzo
Torre di Pulcinella ③
Spetto di Mura
Via di Gozzano
Via del Macellino
Via delle Erbe
Palazzuolo
Via Piana
Via delle Coste
Piazza d'Archi
Piazza di Erbe
Borgo Buio
Via delle Case Nuove
Via di Voltaia del Corso
Piazza Francesco
Via del Poggiolo
Via delle Stampare
Via di San Biagio
Via di Collazzi
Via Ricci
Via Talosa
Pie' al Sasso
Palazzo Comunale
Chiesa del Gesù ④
San Biagio
Piazza Grande
Palazzo Contucci
Via Oriolo
Duomo S. Maria
Via Firenzuola Nuova
Via di Cagnano
Via del Teatro
Via del Ginio del Corso
Via San Donato
Via Firenzuola Vecchia
Via dei Filosofi
Piazza Santa Maria
Via del Poliziano
Via di Circonvallazione
Via di San Pietro

0   330 ft
0   100 m

N

Palazzo Nobili-Tarugi, Piazza
Grande, p. 407

Palazzo Contucci, Piazza Grande,
p. 407

Duomo S. Maria, Piazza Grande,
p. 406

Other sights of interest
(not covered elsewhere in this
book):

1   Palazzo Avignonesi, 37 Via Roma

2   S. Agostino, Via Roma

3   Torre di Pulcinella, Piazza
    Michelozzo

4   Chiesa del Gesù, Via Cavour

Once Montepulciano had been declared a bishopric in 1561, Ippolito Scalza was commissioned to carry out the project. The façade, which has remained incomplete (marble cladding was originally planned for it) rises on a broad foundation of steps and has three portals and three windows. The campanile belonged to the earlier church.

The interior is on the ground plan of a Latin cross, with three aisles and a dome over the crossing. Michelozzo's main work is right at the entrance, and is the tomb of Bartolomeo Aragazzi, man of letters and secretary to Pope Martin V. The monument, which consisted of several parts, was dismantled in the 17th century and it was not until 1815 that seven of the parts were rediscovered and displayed in various places in the cathedral. There is a reclining sculpture of the deceased man, who is surrounded by putti and garlands, personifications of the virtues, Christ giving a blessing, and two bas-reliefs with family scenes. The triptych on the main altar with the Assumption of the Virgin Mary is by Taddeo di Bartolo.

Duomo S. Maria

Built to replace the 12th-century medieval parish church that is already mentioned in records in 714 as a baptistery, the mighty new cathedral structure arose between 1592 and 1630.

Palazzo Nobili-Tarugi

This palazzo, opposite the cathedral, was built in the mid-16th century by the Roman architect Giacomo Barozzi, or da Vignola. The structuring of its three- and five-bay façades emphasizes the horizontal division of the stories that is typical of the Renaissance and at the same time its massive scale is typically Baroque. Here, the ground floor with its open arches and the *piano nobile* are undivided. On high plinths, demicolumns of the Ionic order reach past the middle story to the handsome balustrade of the top floor.

Palazzo Contucci

It was on the eastern side of the Piazza Grande that in 1519 Cardinal Giovanni Maria del Monte – later Pope Julius III – had a palace built by an important architect of the High Renaissance, Antonio da Sangallo il Vecchio. The symmetrical façade shows the clear structuring and language of forms typical of the Renaissance. The row of windows of the *piano nobile*, the main story, with triangular pediments and Ionic columns above voluted consoles, rests on a powerful entablature above the solid base of the ground floor. The Baroque-windowed mezzanine, separated from the travertine façade by the use of red brick, was added by the Contucci family in 1690.

S. Biagio

In the hilly countryside to the south of Montepulciano, the pilgrim church of S. Biagio can be seen from afar, shining in its yellow-gold travertine. Influenced by Bramante's plans for St. Peter's in Rome and modeled on Giuliano da Sangallo's S. Maria delle Carceri in Prato, the impressive central-plan building is on a ground plan shaped like a Greek cross. Antonio Sangallo il Vecchio provided the plans for the church, built between 1518 and 1540. An apse was added to the south, which was a divergence from the norm for central-plan buildings, and although not visible from the inside, it serves as a sacristy. Two northern towers were also planned, of which one was actually built in 1564. As if it were an illustration in an architectural textbook, its structure shows the proper sequence of Doric, Ionic, and Corinthian orders in its stories.

The Interior

The interior opens before us as a regularly proportioned, very three-dimensional space. The crossing, covered by its cupola, determines the size of the barrel-vaulted arms. The structuring, using strong architectural forms in pale travertine, is especially impressive. Pillars, columns and niches form a highly effective wall relief and dominate the interior. Light-catching coffers on the arches of the vault and a heavy, Classically influenced triglyph entablature emphasize the architectural structure. Inside, too, it is clear that Sangallo reduced the structure entirely to geometric forms – square, cylinder, and hemisphere. The only exception to this clear sequence of forms is the later ceiling decoration in the presbytery, which is assumed to have been provided by the Zuccari brothers.

A Memory of Ancient Rome – the Hot Spas of Tuscany

Ruth Strasser

Passare le acque, "to step through the water" – this figure of speech alone expresses what it means to an Italian to take a cure at a thermal spa. It is not only for convalescence after an illness, but also a preventive measure to ensure good health, a pleasant diversion, and a beneficial escape from everyday life. Tuscany, with more than 40 thermal spas, offers a wide range of opportunities.

The largest and most famous of these, Montecatini Terme, owes its existence to Leopold of Habsburg-Lorraine, the son of the Austrian empress Maria Theresa and, in the late 18th century, Grand Duke of Tuscany. The medicinal springs had been known since Roman times of course, but they could not be exploited, due to their unfavorable situation on the edge of a malaria-infested swamp, until improvement schemes were undertaken by the Grand Duke. Classical authors report on laborious attempts at taking the waters, tied up to the neck in sacks and with the head swathed in cloths to foil the bites of the anopheles mosquito. Once the first three thermal baths – the Tettuccio, the Regina and the Leopoldine – had been completed, the place was soon well known in Europe and became a meeting place of high society and its crowned monarchs. New thermal facilities were built, and in the 1920s the site was enlarged and renovated to Art Nouveau taste.

Then as now, three-week courses of treatment were carried out: in the morning, one to two glasses of the water, which contains sulfur and magnesium, are drunk on an empty stomach to regenerate the entire metabolic process, and also to treat complaints of the stomach and intestines and diseases of the bladder, kidneys, liver, and gall bladder. In the meantime, Montecatini has gone on to adopt international standards in hydrotherapy and there are all kinds of additional treat-

Waterfalls with water at a temperature of nearly 100.4°F (38°C) below the spa town of Saturnia

Spa facilities at Montecatini

ments, such as massage, *fango* (mud) pack treatments, medicinal exercise baths, and other hydrotherapy treatments. Montecatini has remained an attraction for the great and the powerful from the world of politics, business, theater, film, and show-business; the international visitors' book is now almost 500 pages thick. Among the most famous vistiors were Giacomo Puccini, who composed the second and third act of *La Bohème* here, and Giuseppe Verdi, who was a keen participant in hydrotherapy and a regular guest for more than 20 years. In the Locanda Maggiore guesthouse he wrote the music for the final act of *Otello*.

Directly in the vicinity, and a little in the shadow of Montecatini, lies the volcanic grotto of Monsummano. This is a limestone cave discovered in 1849 during quarrying work. In order to take the cure, you first remove all your clothing and put on a kind of tunic; then you walk through the so-called vestibule, at temperatures of between 80.6 and 89.6 °F (27–32°C), and then through the caves known, after Dante, as "Paradise," "Purgatory," and

Memmo di Filippuccio (active 1288–1324), Bathers *(detail), c. 1303–1317, fresco, Camera del Podestà, Palazzo del Popolo, San Gimignano*

"Hell," until arriving in the depths at a lake called "Limbo," the steam of which has to be breathed in for just under an hour: an effective treatment for chronic disorders of the respiratory tract.

Only a few miles to the north of Lucca, surrounded by sweet chestnut forests, is the thermal spa of Bagni di Lucca. Its spa buildings were described in 1580 by the French poet Michel de Montaigne as follows: "The baths are covered, vaulted and fairly dark. There is also an outflow of water, a so-called *doccia*; it consists of pipes under which one stands and from which a constant stream of hot water flows on the various parts of the body, but particularly on to the head, treating the part in question thoroughly."

On the lower slopes of the Pisan hills, among the olive groves, lies S. Giuliano Terme with sulfurous water at 105.8°F (41°C), which is used to treat digestive problems. From the beautiful coffee house, which lies half-way up the slope, in the early 19th century Lord Byron and his young friend Shelley, together with their literary followers, used to enjoy the sunsets over the sea.

The warm waters of Casciana Terme, which lies to the south of Pisa in a delightful hilly region, are supposed to have been used as early as the 11th century to treat the Margravine Mathilda of Canossa, much loved by the people of Tuscany, for rheumatism and arthritis.

The largest thermal spa in southern Tuscany is Chianciano Terme, where the treatment specializes in the prevention of liver disorders. The standard of spa equipment and hotels is comparable to Montecatini's. Because of its position in the center of Italy, and not far from the Autostrada del Sole, it is also an important conference center, used by organizations of all kinds, from political parties to charitable bodies.

However, of greater appeal to some visitors are Tuscany's countless springs and natural spas in places far from large hotels and conference centers. One of these is the Cascate del Molino, waterfalls at a temperature of 100.4°F (38°C), outside the spa town of Saturnia. Here you can enjoy free bathing, and at the same time cleanse your skin and also strengthen your circulation.

Another spa where it is possible to avoid the fashionable spa crowds is Bagni di Periolo, to the south of Siena. Here, you stand under a waterfall which comes out of the rock at 105.8°F (41°C), or lie in warm pools in the middle of the Farma river.

Even hotter is the water of Bagno Vignoni, which bursts out of the ground from a depth of some 3,540 feet (1,080 m) at a temperature of 125.6°F (52°C). The village, which lies on a picturesque site above

The hot springs of Bagno Vignoni

the Orcia valley, was already famous in Roman times for its healing waters. A Roman inscription on a travertine stone on the left of the thermal springs site is a reminder of Lucius Trebonius, who built a temple on this spot, dedicated to the nymphs. In the Middle Ages, the baths became famous because of the regular visits by Catherine of Siena and her mother Lapa. The mother, worried about the welfare of her daughter, hoped to use the social diversions of the spa town to distract her from ideas of a career in the church. Later, Lorenzo de' Medici and the famously cultured Renaissance Pope Pius II frequently enjoyed the healing effects of the waters on their gout.

From time to time, the spa also experienced harder times; Montaigne described it as "one single nest of lice" at the end of the 16th century. Even today, its special feature is the position of the large piscina right in the middle

of the village, giving the impression that the center of Bagno Vignoni is covered by water. The site is framed by a small loggia dedicated to St. Catherine and by guest houses. The piazza, which resembles a stage set and is at times empty of people, and the bubbling, steaming springs in their basin filled with yellowish water inspired the Russian film director Andrei Tarkovski to set part of his film *Nostalgia* here.

If you travel through the extensive woodlands of southern Tuscany avoiding the main roads you will come across such treasures for yourself. Warm pools, hot springs, and bubbling mud holes are not unusual. Just like today's Tuscans, their ancestors, the Etruscans and the Romans, valued the thermal springs with their water that cleanses the body, gives it new strength, and invigorates the spirit – which is why *passare le acque* has also acquired the sense of "refined by the waters."

Chiusi

The origins of the mountain town of Chiusi lie in the period around 1000 B.C., when prehistoric settlers of the so-called "Proto-Villanova Culture" left nearby Monte Cetona and settled here. However, the town reached the height of its wealth and culture under the Etrsucans, between the 7th and 5th centuries B.C. The favorable situation of the Etruscan "Clevsins" on a hill of tufa rock above the Chiana valley, together with good transport routes – including the Chiana, navigable at that time – enabled it to rise to become an important member of the Etruscan Confederation of cities. The legendary king Lars Porsenna from Chiusi is even supposed to have conquered Rome as an ally of Tarquinius Superbus. The city was at that time surrounded by an extensive ring of walls built of great stone blocks. There are many Etruscan tombs and cemeteries in the surrounding countryside. In the 4th century B.C. Chiusi came – peacefully – under Roman rule. As a military base, the city received its basic structure, still visible today, in 269 B.C., but lost its former significance.

In the Middle Ages Chiusi was an important Langobard duchy but its status subsequently diminished, especially when the

The Etruscans, almost without exception, cremated their dead and buried the urns in shaft graves. Sarcophagi and partly painted chamber tombs were not used until the 3rd century B.C. The museum therefore has a collection primarily of funerary urns of many different kinds. A specialty in Chiusi were urns with expressive bronze masks fastened to them with wire. From the mid-7th century onwards these were followed by a type of urn known as the Canopic vase, with a lid in the form of a human head, and which bore some resemblance to the human form in that it had hands, arms, and even breasts attached to it. These vases were not portraits, but rather custom-made pieces of work with individualizing tendencies. In the last years of the 6th century there were also stone figures with removable heads and hollow chest cavities for the funerary ashes. From the 3rd century onwards, and probably under the influence of Volterra, a reclining figure sometimes appeared on the urns. Another peculiarity are urns made from a local pale sandstone, the so-called *pietra fetida*, "stinking stone," which are decorated with fine reliefs. The museum also has an extensive collection of Classical vases, bronze items, jewelry, mirrors, cameos, and ivory.

Chiana silted up during the 16th century and the valley turned into unhealthy marshland, greatly increasing the risk of malaria.

Museo Nazionale Etrusco

The Museo Nazionale Etrusco was founded in 1870 and is housed in an elegant, Classical-style palazzo with pillared front. This is one of the most interesting archaeological museums in Tuscany, with important collections of not only Etruscan, but also Greek and Roman art from excavations in the area of Chiusi and from private donations.

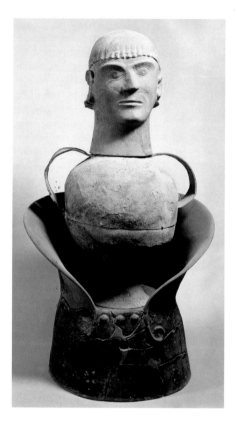

Etruscan Canopic vase, 6th century B.C.
Terracotta, impasto, bronze, h. 61 cm

For the Egyptians, the Canopic jar, or vase, was a funerary container with a portrait head of the deceased which held the internal organs removed from the body during mummification. In this process, liver, lungs, stomach, and abdominal organs were removed and were kept in four clay jars.

The Etruscan Canopic vases from Chiusi, on the other hand, are cremation urns for ashes, with a human head or a form that copies the human body. As part of the veneration of the dead, these urns are often set on a bronze or clay throne and buried individually in large funerary containers. In their features, their hair-styles, and their posture they show a marked portrayal of individual character. However, this is in no way comparable to the later realistic portraiture of the Romans but shows the efforts to create a general facial expressiveness and perhaps also to represent psychological qualities by physical features. In the Canopic vase illustrated here, the head is made from terracotta, the throne is bronze, and the ash container is impasto, a coarse clay slip. Both handles of the container have survived and appear almost like arms. The figure depicted has a narrow face, strongly marked eyebrows, a large but straight nose, and narrow lips, firmly pressed together. The hair surrounds the face like a wreath of tight, separated curls and falls behind the ears down to the nape of the neck. The earnest expression suggests great decisiveness, proud self-confidence, and firmness of will.

Etruscan cippus, 6th/5th century B.C.
Sandstone, h. 55 cm.

A high-quality example of artistic production in Chiusi is this relief on a sandstone *cippus*, a decoratively carved
tombstone. It shows a ritual funeral
procession: music and dancing were
supposed to accompany the dead on their
journey to the next world. The *cippi* were
often set up in front of a tomb chamber.
Above the cube-shaped plinths, there were
usually sculptures – portraits or symbols of
the deceased. In the type of bas-relief
typical of this period in Chiusi, the figures
are portrayed in a lively manner; the
swaying steps and joyous face of the flute
player are particularly impressive, as is the
ecstatic expression of the female dancer.

Etruria was particularly known for its
auleti, a term for which "flute player" is an
insufficient translation. The *aulos* is a reed
instrument formed from one or two cylindrical tubes. The *auleti* often took years to
learn a special breathing technique which
allowed them to store great quantities of
air, and to release it very slowly into
the instrument.

S. Quirico d'Orcia

The parish church of S. Quirico, men-tioned as early as the reign of the Langobard king Luitprand in 712, was part of an early medieval castle site, which later became the seat of a Hohenstaufen governor, securing the territory controlled by the dynasty against Rome. Next to the castle, outside the ring of walls, a settlement grew up. After the surrender of the castle to the Sienese, the latter joined these two settlements together and built a bigger city wall around them.

The newly created town then became an important trade, meeting, and pilgrims' accommodation center, linked to all important cities thanks to the Via Francigena. Under Pope Pius II it was eventually incorporated in the bishopric of Pienza in 1462. The Romanesque hall church, dating from the late 12th century, which received vaulted transepts and Gothic apses as early as 1300, was raised to the status of collegiate church in 1648.

Collegiata di S. Maria Assunta

A broad set of steps leads up to the beautiful western portal. Under a round façade window, the portal is framed by a blind arch. Similar to the portal structures found in Emilia-Romagna, the framing structure rests on knotted columns borne by couching lions. Slender door-jamb columns and multiple stepped archivolts center the structure. On the door lintel there are powerful images of two sirens, symbols of temptation, and ferocious struggling dragons, while in the arch above the lintel the very finely worked, early Romanesque seated figure of the Virgin Mary appears to be emanating radiance. Above the last column on the right there is a human head between palm leaves, and above this again there are two peacocks, symbols of the sun since Classical times.

The structure of the portal on the south side is a repeat of the early west portal, but its design is noticeably later and was perhaps carried out with the help of Giovanni Pisano's workshop. On the double window next to it there is a particularly interesting small supporting figure, heavily borne down by the weight it carries, its face expressing both weeping and laughter.

The campanile is a later feature dating from the period around 1800.

Montalcino

This mountain town, founded by the Etruscans, has served to secure the Ombrone and Asso river valleys since Classical times. In 814, Louis the Pious gave the town to the monastery of S. Antimo. After the battle of Montaperti in 1260, the town, which had been a "free city" since the 12th century, came under the rule of Siena.

The Sienese built the fortress in 1361 to defend their territory to the south. A few hundred refugees withdrew to this *Rocca* when, in 1555, Siena was forced to surrender to Cosimo I de' Medici. Under the rule of Pietro Strozzi, who had been banished from Florence, they declared the "Second Republic of Siena." However, resistance was broken as early as 1559 and the great Medici coat of arms was fixed to the bastions. Montalcino is famous above all for wine: the famous *Brunello*, has been cultivated since the 19th century.

Abbazia di S. Antimo

The Benedictine abbey of S. Antimo, unique in Tuscany and important and wealthy in the Middle Ages, probably dates back to a foundation by Charlemagne in about 800. When imperial power faded from the end of the 13th century onwards, the abbey itself also declined, and it was dissolved in 1462.

The steeply proportioned, triple-aisled basilica was built from 1118 onwards, in regular hewn ashlar blocks. It followed the French model provided by the reformed Benedictine monastery in Cluny in Burgundy, as the surrounding choir demonstrates, with its circle of chapels, unusual in Italy. On the other hand, the isolated bell tower and the lack of varied structural divisions belong to Italian tradition. The small, probably Carolingian or Ottonian chapel with its apse to the south of the choir is constructed of somewhat coarser masonry.

The Interior

Within the 13th-century portal is an architrave with an inscription giving the name of the architect, the monk Azzo from Porcari. The immediate effect of the pillared basilica is one of consistent simplicity: only the capitals are decorated with carvings. The high walls of the nave rise upwards to exposed roof beams. The surface of the walls is broken by mullioned openings, with a gallery behind. French influence is evident in the narrow, cross-rib vaulted aisles and in the ambulatory, the windows of which allow a great deal of light to fall into the sanctuary. In a similar way to the exterior, the structure here too incorporates Lombard elements, such as the absence of a transept and the uninterrupted wall area.

Capitals in the Nave

The marvelous, richly carved capitals are also the result of a combination of elements, from Lombardy and the Auvergne. A local onyx-like alabaster provided the material. The "Daniel capital" stands out among the myriad animal and plant motifs. It is attributed to the Master of Cabestany, an artist who worked in many places in Europe, carrying on the lively sculptural tradition of the southern French monastery of Moissac. His style is marked by extremes of portrayal. The faces, above all, are unforgettable: a short forehead, strongly emphasized eyebrows, protuberant, slanting eyes, pointed noses, receding chins, and jug-handle ears. This sculpture depicts the Old Testament story of the prophet Daniel, thrown into the lions' den and yet remaining unharmed.

Chiusdino

Chiesetta sul Monte Siepi

From Chiusdino, the noble knight Galgano Guidotti is supposed to have traveled, in 1180, the short distance to withdraw into the wilderness on the hill on Monte Siepi where, as he had no crucifix for his devotions, he thrust his sword into the rock. After his death in 1181, a local movement arose up with the aim of honoring him and as early as 1184 had built a chapel over the hermit's grave. On the model of Classical mausoleums and the Church of the Tomb in Jerusalem, a memorial chapel was created, the only Romanesque rotunda in Tuscany. Between the 14th and 18th centuries, the campanile, north chapel, lantern, vestibule, and priest's house were added.

The exterior alone is notable for its use of alternate bands of pale travertine and dark brick. This more economical variation on marble incrustation is common in the country areas of southern Tuscany. The bands of alternate colors are particularly striking, however, when you take a look inside the mortared, ribless cupola.

Exterior view of the chapel

Right: View in the cupola
Below: S. Galgano's sword

Abbazia di S. Galgano

The monumental church of the former Cistercian abbey of S. Galgano, near the memorial church of the holy hermit, is now only a ruin. In 1224, the monks began construction on their only new foundation in Tuscany (in all other cases, they had taken over existing sites) following the model of the mother church in Camari in Latium. Supported by Siena, the abbey developed into a cultural center. Its decline began after it was plundered by the mercenary John Hawkwood in 1364. When the lead from the roofs was sold in the mid-16th century, only six monks were still living here.

The campanile and the vaulting collapsed in the late 18th century, but despite the ruined state of the building, it is possible to recognize a three-aisled church with transept and a choirs without apses, in the typical Cistercian style. The aisle added to the western transept is an innovation. Also unique in central Italy is the interesting structural division of the interior, with projecting structures and engaged columns.

sculptured decoration is to be found on the capitals. Here, the Cistercians were following the rules of Bernard of Clairvaux, who saw decoration on buildings as an unnecessary distraction from worship.

The Interior

While travertine was used for the load-bearing and dividing features and the capitals, the walls and vaulting are of brick. This gives an effect corresponding to the alternating colors of incrustation – one which is not found in any later examples of Tuscan churches.

Also remarkable is the lighting of the interior. Apart from the two western bays of the nave, the walls are divided into four stories with an expanded window zone. Additional light entered the choir and the sanctuary through a large round window. The only

Monteriggioni

So, piercing through the dense and
    darksome air,
More and more near approaching tow'rd
    the verge,
My error fled, and fear came over me;

Because as on its circular parapets
Montereggione crowns itself with towers,
E'en thus the margin which surrounds the
    well

With one half of their bodies turreted
The horrible giants, whom Jove menaces
E'en now from out the heavens when he
    thunders.
    (Dante, *The Divine Comedy*, "Hell," XXXI)

The disputed border territory between
Florence and Siena is easy to monitor from
this hill on the Via Francigena, which was
why the Sienese fortified it in 1203 with a
ring-shaped wall. After their victory in 1260
at Montaperti, they extended the fortifications to cover an area of 570 m² (6135 ft²) and
strengthened the walls with fourteen towers.

In the early 14th century Dante, in his
Divine Comedy, memorably compared the
towers on Monteriggioni's walls to the
giants who surround the deepest pit of
hell. The present-day picturesque village is
still completely contained within its
unique ring of walls, which is reminiscent
of depictions of fortresses in early
European landscape painting.

View of the ring of walls in the evening light

Rivalry in Stone – Dynastic Towers

Ruth Strasser

Today, when we approach the little hill town of San Gimignano, we can see the distinctive features of the "town of fine towers" from quite a distance: a dozen tall towers and a few stumps. These give only a feeble impression of how the 72 mighty tower houses must once have looked. The medieval traveler, journeying on foot or on horseback on the trade and pilgrim roads, would have seen quite a different picture. Whole thickets of towers covered the hilltops and signaled the presence of towns. From a distance, these towers were useful for finding directions. The larger settlements of the plains also presented the traveler with a view of mighty forests of towers. In cities such as Pisa, Lucca, Pistoia, and Florence between 150 and 250 of these stone giants rose up to the skies.

In the 12th century the nobility, moving into the towns, brought the fortified towers of their country castles with them. On a square ground plan, using stone blocks or brick, they built several stories, each consisting of only one room, one above the other, with a fortified entrance on the ground floor and few windows, which were generally mere arrow slits. To get from one room – i.e., one story – to the other, rope ladders were used, which were then pulled up again through openings in the ceiling.

A city regulation of the time asked citizens to take care that the stores and the older people of the household always be kept in the upper stories. This way of life was certainly not comfortable, but it was secure: in case of siege, you could barricade yourself inside the tower. For this reason tower-houses remained popular in the 13th and 14th centuries in Tuscany, when disputes between Guelphs and Ghibellines, and between bishops and the ruling

Ambrogio Lorenzetti(?), City by the Sea, *c. 1340, tempera on wood, 22 × 33 cm, Pinacoteca Nazionale, Siena*

guilds, or perhaps between individual families, frequently ended in fighting. In those times, splendid mansions began to be built next door to the towers, and in many cases, when family groups joined together into *consortieri* (clans), several buildings and towers were linked to make a kind of urban fortress. When danger threatened, people then withdrew to the towers, which had wooden walkways on the second and third floors linking neighboring buildings, so that no one would have to risk the dangers of the streets and alleyways. Even today the narrow openings in the walls can be seen, which supported balconies from which the building could be defended from above, or on which leading families could appear before the crowds at victory celebrations.

It was not only a shortage of space that caused the towers to be built ever higher – as much as 200 or 230 feet (60 or 70 m) high – but also a matter of prestige. The higher the tower, the more powerful the family. If the Guelph party had enjoyed a victory, the towers of all Guelph families were increased in height, and the towers of Ghibellines were razed or at least shortened. If the shoe was on the other foot, buildings were altered again.

It was not until guild governments, elected by the people, came to power that this "tower rivalry" was restrained. The town hall tower was the symbol of the new democratic commonwealth, and as a consequence strict laws to limit the heights of private towers were passed. In Florence, for example, no dynastic tower was allowed to be higher than 98 feet (30 m). In the last years of the 13th century, when almost all the city republics had come

Dynastic towers in San Gimignano

under Florentine control, work began on widening the streets of the towns and on building fine, extensive palazzi for a sophisticated upper-middle class. The fortified towers were demolished and their stones used as building material, or the stumps of the towers were leveled to match the height of the new palazzi. The few towers that still survive are today carefully protected monuments.

S. Gimignano

Fourteen of what were once 72 towers give San Gimignano, the "Manhattan of the Middle Ages," its unusual silhouette. On the ridge of the hill, already settled in Etruscan times, a center for pilgrims and traders developed. From 929 onwards, it was under the rule of the bishops of Volterra. At the end of the 12th century, the town freed itself from its feudal lords by electing its own consuls. The production of cloth and the cultivation of saffron, in demand as a dye for silk, brought wealth, which led to a new ring of walls being constructed in the course of the 13th century.

Neither the *podestà* nor the "Great Council," to which about a quarter of the citizens belonged, could put a stop to all the bitter struggles between the wealthy families. The Guelph leader Ardinghelli and the Ghibelline leader Salvucci built higher and higher towers, for reasons of prestige as well as for the purposes of defense and attack, and after emerging victorious from a struggle, they made certain that

View of the city with dynastic towers visible from afar.

their opponents' towers were razed. When half the population succumbed to the plague in 1348, the town put itself under Florentine authority and fell into a kind of "Sleeping Beauty" trance, which meant that the old buildings in the town were, fortunately, preserved.

The triangular Piazza Cisterna was always the main square, from which the hill town was supplied with water from the well, built in 1346. Medieval palazzi line the piazza, which in part still has the brick paving dating from the 14th century.

Piazza della Cisterna with the Ardinghelli twin towers and the Torre Grossa

S. Gimignano

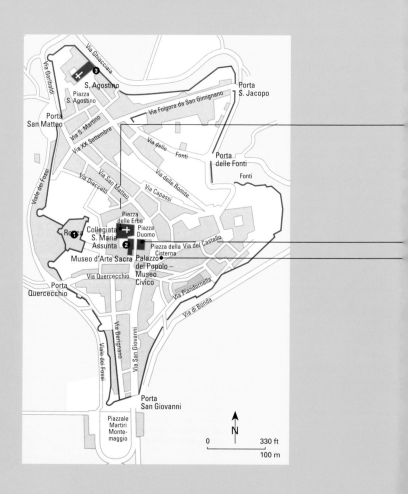

Via Ghiacciaia

Via Garibaldi

S. Agostino ❸

Piazza
S. Agostino

Porta
S. Jacopo

Porta
San Matteo

Via Folgora da San Gimignano

Via S. Martino

Via XX Settembre

Via delle

Fonti

Porta
delle Fonti

Via San Matteo

Via delle Romite

Via Diaccelo

Via Capassi

Fonti

Piazza
delle Erbe

Piazza
Duomo

Rocca ❶

Collegiata
S. Maria
Assunta

❷

Piazza della
Cisterna

Via del Castello

Museo d'Arte Sacra

Palazzo
del Popolo –
Museo
Civico

Via Quercecchio

Via Piandornella

Porta
Quercecchio

Via di Bonda

Viale dei Fossi

Via Bergnano

Via San Giovanni

Viale dei Fossi

Porta
San Giovanni

Piazzale
Martiri
Monte-
maggio

N

0   330 ft

100 m

Collegiata S. Maria Assunta,
Piazza Duomo, p. 438

Palazzo del Popolo – Museo
Civico, Piazza Duomo,
pp. 436, 437

Other sights of interest
(not covered elsewhere in this
book):

1   Rocca

2   Museo d'Arte Sacra (Museo
    Etrusco), 1 Piazza Pecori

3   S. Agostino, Piazza S. Agostino,
    p. 442

Piazza Cisterna, p. 433

Palazzo del Popolo

The Palazzo del Podestà, the house of the commander of the town, and the Palazzo del Popolo are on the present-day Piazza del Duomo, which directly adjoins the Piazza Cisterna. The Palazzo del Popolo was already in use as a town hall before 1288 by the "Great Council," to which 1,200 citizens belonged. In 1300 its tower, the Torre Grossa, was completed and at 177 feet (54 m) it was the tallest tower in the town. According to law, no tower was allowed to be taller than the Torre Grossa or the Torre Rognosa (171 feet/52 m) which, with its unusual bell housing, seems to be growing out of the Palazzo del Podestà. The façade faces the cathedral square. It has three stories and round arched windows, opening under "Sienese arches" situated on the ground floor.

A famous feature is the little balcony from which Dante, as ambassador of the Florentine government, applied his skills in rhetoric on May 8, 1300 to try to persuade the town to join the Guelph League. In the inner courtyard of the town hall, in a roofed vestibule, it is possible to see the place where the law courts met in the Middle Ages. The three surrounding walls are decorated with allegories of law and judgment. The middle wall shows the former Bishop of Modena, St. Gemignanus,

at the side of the supreme judge, the Virgin Mary. The saint is supposed to have saved the inhabitants in the 4th century from an attack by Huns or Goths, and has given his name to the town. In his hand he is holding a model of the town.

Museo Civico

The Palazzo del Popolo contains the Museo Civico, some of whose rooms are decorated with 14th-century frescoes. In the *Camera del Podestà*, the mayor's room, the frescoes show scenes from every-day life, some of which have a rather piquant flavor.

Memmo di Filippuccio (active 1288–1324),
***Scene of Everyday Life*, c. 1320**
Fresco

Memmo di Filippuccio's frescoes, with their profane subjects including a bathing scene, here show a married couple going to bed in their private chamber: we can see an alcove, with a curtain held open by a maid. The curtain still leaves the marriage bed on view. The wife has already fallen asleep in it – the artist shows her with eyes closed and breasts bare.

Collegiata S. Maria Assunta

The collegiate church of S. Maria Assunta is, together with the town hall and the Palazzo del Podestà, the third important building on San Gimignano's Piazza del Duomo: the secular and the spiritual centers of the Middle Ages stood right next to each other. San Gimignano was never the seat of a bishop, but it nevertheless enjoyed important privileges: for instance, its provost had the right to collect tithes.

Since 1362 a large freestanding staircase has led up to the two portals of the church, consecrated in 1148 by Pope Eugene III.

On the plain east façade, which has remained unfinished, a change in the masonry is clearly visible, as the walls of the triple-aisled pillared basilica were increased in height in 1340 to allow for Gothic ribbed vaulting. In 1456, Giuliano da Maiano extended the collegiate church by adding side chapels and a transept.

Nave

Despite later changes, the church's Romanesque structure is still evident in the nave, where the calm succession of columns with their even arches gives an idea of the original appearance of the once flat-ceilinged basilica. The simple squared capitals with stylized leaf decoration are very fine.

The church is famous for its frescoes. In the left aisle, Bartolo di Fredi painted scenes from the Old Testament in 1367. From 1333 to 1341, on the opposite side of the church, a New Testament cycle was created, probably by the brothers Federico and Lippo Memmi, who were both collaborators of Simone Martini. On the interior façade there is the *Martyrdom of St. Sebastian* by Benozzo Gozzoli, dating from 1465, and above it the *Last Judgment* by Taddeo di Bartolo, painted in 1393.

Creation of the world		Creation of Adam		Adam in the Garden of Eden		Creation of Eve		Forbidden fruit of the Tree of Knowledge		
Expulsion from Paradise	Cain killing his brother Abel	Building of Noah's Ark	The animals enter the Ark	Noah leaves the Ark	Drunkenness of Noah	Abraham and Lot leave for Canaan	Lot taking leave of Abraham	Joseph's dream	Joseph in the well	Destroyed
Joseph has his brothers imprisoned	Joseph is recognized by his brothers	Moses and the Brazen Serpent	Pharaoh's army swept away by the Red Sea	The Israelites cross the Red Sea	Moses on Mount Sinai	Temptation of Job	Slaying of Job's servants and cattle	Destruction of the house of Job	Job gives thanks to God	Job's comforters increase his sorrow

Plan of the Old Testament frescoes on the wall of the left-hand aisle.

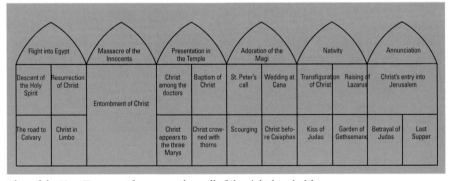

Flight into Egypt		Massacre of the Innocents		Presentation in the Temple		Adoration of the Magi		Nativity		Annunciation	
Descent of the Holy Spirit	Resurrection of Christ	Entombment of Christ		Christ among the doctors	Baptism of Christ	St. Peter's call	Wedding at Cana	Transfiguration of Christ	Raising of Lazarus	Christ's entry into Jerusalem	
The road to Calvary	Christ in Limbo			Christ appears to the three Marys	Christ crowned with thorns	Scourging	Christ before Caiaphas	Kiss of Judas	Garden of Gethsemane	Betrayal of Judas	Last Supper

Plan of the New Testament frescoes on the wall of the right hand aisle.

Bartolo di Fredi (c. 1330–1410),
The Temptation of Job, 1367
Fresco

Domenico Ghirlandaio (1449–1494),
Entombment of St. Fina, 1473–1475
Fresco

The Sienese painter Bartolo di Fredi depicted scenes from the Old Testament with a lively freshness. He added imaginative detail to the biblical topics. For instance, we see Job, who has a particular fancy for musicians and jugglers, surrounded by several musicians, seated with his wife at a royal feast.

In the Cappella di S. Fina, which was added to the church in 1468, the Florentine artist Domenico Ghirlandaio has portrayed the history of the local saint, Fina. While Ghirlandaio was frescoing the walls of the Cappella from 1473 to 1475, at the same time Benedetto di Maiano was carving the sarcophagus of the saint, who died in 1253. Ghirlandaio, after his Florentine beginnings, in executing this fresco found his own style, which was to bring him great success: imaginative architecture, light-filled rooms, views out over the landscape, settings reminiscent of still-life paintings, and portrait-like depictions of contemporaries in the midst of the sacred events.

The young woman's body lies on a bier in front of a gigantic altar niche. Fina, a farmer's daughter, died, worn out by illness and strict asceticism, at the age of 15. The city celebrates its saint every year on March 12 with *fiori di S. Fina*, which are often described as violets, but are actually a type of stock.

The dead girl and her sarcophagus, decorated with a draped cloth, are surrounded by many servers and citizens, while the bishop conducts the funeral service. At the hour of her death, all the bells in San Gimignano are said to have begun ringing. In the background an angel is visible, ringing the bell on the highest tower.

S. Agostino

Between 1280 and 1298, the church of the Augustine canons was built in the north of San Gimignano, near the Porta S. Matteo, in the architectural style that was typical of the mendicant order. The hall church with its exposed timbers and straight-walled chapels has only a slightly protruding transept.

Benozzo Gozzoli (c. 1420–1497),
The School in Tagaste, **1464–1465**
Fresco

In 18 pictures enclosed within Classical-style frames – four of them in the lunettes, plus the four evangelists in the vault – Benozzo Gozzoli presents the life of St. Augustine, based on the autobiographical *Confessiones* and the *Legenda Aurea*, a collection of legends about the lives of the saints which was widely circulated among people in the Middle Ages.

St. Augustine was born on November 13 in the North African town of Tagaste (now Souk-Ahras in Algeria), the son of a pagan landowner and civic official called Patricius and his Christian wife Monica. When he was only a small boy Augustine was taken to the school, where there were also Christian teachers. As he himself later confessed, he did not much like going to school, so his parents are said to have often accompanied him.

Full of delight in telling a story, with strong, bright colors and a highly skilled use of perspective in the architecture, Gozzoli shows the saint being brought to school on the left of the picture. Not without some qualms, father and mother are handing their boy over to the care of the grammar teacher. In a scene taking place simultaneously, little Augustine is standing, his slate in his hands, beside his teacher, who is disciplining a young offender in a not exactly sensitive manner. Both scenes are set in the framework of a single architectural background, which includes buildings that actually existed. In the same way, some of the persons depicted may be assumed to be portraits of important representatives of secular and church life; on the right-hand side of the *Departure for Milan*, there is also a self-portrait of the artist.

The other scenes show moments in the life of this important theologian: the university at Carthage, the journey to Rome, St. Augustine teaching in Rome, the journey to Milan, the meeting with St. Ambrose, the baptism of Augustine, the visit to the monastery on Monte Pisano, the blessing of the faithful of Hippo, Augustine's vision of St. Jerome, and finally the death of the saint. On the way to Monte Pisano St. Augustine meets Christ in the person of a boy who explains to him that it is impossible for the human mind to understand the Trinity, just as it is impossible to empty out the sea with a spoon. It is to this episode that St. Augustine owes his attribute, which is a boy with a spoon.

Ten Days of Tales – Boccaccio and the *Decameron*

The most famous book of early Italian literature – at least the most famous today – is the *Decameron* by Giovanni Boccaccio. It is more popular than Dante Alighieri's *Divine Comedy* or Petrarch's sonnets. It is written in a more popular style, and its topics are more relevant to the situation of the times. Ten young people – seven women and three men – have fled the plague in Florence in 1348 and taken refuge on a country estate. They pass the ten days (hence "Decameron") of quarantine with good food, dancing, and telling stories. This framing plot allows Boccaccio to join together 100 novellas of the most varied kind. There are fables, parables, anecdotes, and scandalous stories, orally transmitted by the people or the court, from oriental or from French manuscripts. This traditional material is re-told in Tuscan. Boccaccio varies the tone according to the temperament of the young people: sometimes it is coarse, sometimes jesting, sometimes gallant. The realistic description of the plague in Florence and its devastating consequences for the city state and its people allows the characters of the protagonists to come across in a particularly radiant, morally faultless manner. This background provides the freedom to tell tales of erotic adventures, female cunning, priestly hypocrisy, and male bigotry in an extremely open and direct manner.

In the introduction to the *Decameron*, Boccaccio says that all troublesome thoughts

Boccaccio, Il Decamerone, *illuminated manuscript, parchment, Bibliothèque Nationale, Paris*

will be banished when reading these tales and he points out, perhaps tongue in cheek, that they are addressed particularly to the ladies, who have fewer opportunities of taking their minds off everyday worries or the pangs of love. They will find "love stories both cheerful and sad, as well as other stirring accounts" which will offer them "both pleasure from the entertaining occurrences they describe, and useful advice on what to avoid and what to strive for."

The 100 stories, written between 1349 and 1351, form an unprejudiced, lively picture of Tuscan life and customs, which already displays distinctive features of the early Renaissance. Using the new form of the novella, a mostly short prose narrative dealing with an unusual, "new" (Italian *novella*) event, and above all written in the richly varied vernacular, *Il Decamerone* is considered by many to be one of the most important master-pieces of early world literature.

Giovanni Boccaccio was born in 1313 as the illegitimate son of a merchant and spent many years in education and study in a circle of literary figures at the court of Naples. The poet, a friend of Petrarch, was later appointed to the chair of Greek in Florence, and died on December 21, 1375 in Certaldo, where he is buried. As a reference to his name, which could be translated as "scandal-mouth," he left a more pleasant version, which has now become a popular Tuscan proverb: *Bocca baciata non perde ventura, anzi rinnova come fa la luna* – "A mouth kissed loses nothing, indeed it renews itself as does the moon" (*Decameron*, II, 7).

Villa Palmieri, view of the lemon grove, San Domenico di Fiesole

Grosseto and Province

Grosseto

Grosseto had its origins in prehistoric times when the Etruscans transformed the swamps at the mouth of the Ombrone river into fertile land, creating several settlements there. From the 3rd century B.c the Etruscan towns from Populonia to Roselle became Roman cities; still later, most of them became diocesan towns. However, Rome's decline and the advent of Saracen attacks depopulated the region after centuries of habitation. Neglect of the irrigation system had an especially crippling effect: low-lying areas reverted to swamps, agriculture was abandoned, and malaria and other diseases became rife. Whoever was able to do so fled from the *mal aria*, the bad air, to cities built on higher ground. Not until the period between the 9th and 13th centuries did Grosseto, under the Aldobrandeschi family, become an important crossroads on the Via Aurelia from Rome to Pisa. The town was subsequently subjugated by the powerful city of Siena.

Remnants of the old city wall dating from the era of Sienese domination in the mid-14th century can still be seen in Grosseto's south gate or Porta Vecchia – until the mid-18th century the only entrance to the city – and in parts of its fortress. When Siena fell in 1554 Grosseto came under Florentine rule, and Cosimo I de' Medici had a new hexagonal wall with corner bulwarks and a fortress built by Baldassare

Le Mura – part of the city's fortifications from the Renaissance era

Piazza Dante with the Palazzo della Provincia

Lanci. This wall was surrounded by a moat connected to a series of canals so that both goods and building materials could be transported by boat. Since the 19th century the walls have been open to the public to allow people to enjoy the stunning view on a walk around the city.

The city was situated by the sea – its present inland location is due to the silting up of the Ombrone delta – and was rich in minerals. Both these factors aroused the jealousy of its neighbors. In 1336 the city fell to Siena, and over 200 years later it finally went to the Grand Duchy of Tuscany. In the 19th century the swamps were systematically drained to combat malaria. From 1830 the city was restored and many new buildings added.

The neo-Gothic palace of the provincial administration, the Palazzo della Provincia, was built on the model of the Siena town hall with Sienese arches, biforate windows, and battlements. It was erected on the remains of the medieval Palazzo Pubblico, or town hall, which was the source of the city fathers' heraldic devices which today adorn the façade of the new building.

Grosseto

Via Oberdan

Siena

Piazza
Tripoli

Baluardo
Garibaldi

Porta
Nuova

Baluardo
della
Rimembranza

Viale Filippo Corridoni

Via Tripoli

Piazza
Popolo

Viale Manetti

Via Mazzini

Via Monte Bello

S. Pietro

Via da Grosseto

Piazza
Baccarini

Piazza
dell'
Indipendenza

S. Francesco

Viale Lorenzo Porciatti

Via Aurelio Saffi

Corso Carducci

Via Ginori

Baluardo
del Molino
a Vento

Via Goldoni

Museo
Archeologico e
d'Arte della
Maremma

Via Garibaldi

Via d'Azeglio

Le Mura
Baluardo
della
Fortezza

Via Manin

Piazza
Duomo

Via Zuavi

Piazza
R. Pacciardi

Via Amiata

Via Gramsci

Via Mazzini

Duomo
S. Lorenzo

Via
Aldobran-
deschi

Piazza Dante
Alighieri

Via G.
Galilei

Via dell' Unione

Viale Vittorio Fossombroni

Viale Ximenes

Via Ricasoli

Via S. Martino

Piazza
Mercato

Via Aurelio Saffi

Baluardo
del Maiano

Viale V. Alfieri

Baluardo
della
Cavallerizza

Porta
vecchia

N

0
330 ft
100 m

Piazza
de Maria

Viale Vittorio Fossombroni

Via Cesare Battisti

S. Francesco, Piazza dell'
Independenza, 2, p. 456

Museo Archeologico e d'Arte della
Maremma, Piazza Baccarini, 3,
p. 454

Le Mura, city wall, p. 448

Duomo S. Lorenzo, Piazza
Duomo, p. 452

Other sights of interest
(not covered elsewhere in this
book):

1 Porta vecchia, Piazza de Maria

2 S. Pietro, Vicolo del Duomo, 3

Duomo S. Lorenzo

After a papal decision transferred the diocesan seat from Rosselle to Grosseto in 1138, the building of a cathedral was planned to replace the older parish church. An inscription on the façade states that construction was begun in 1294, with Sozzo di Rustichino of Siena named as architect. This work came to a standstill after only eight years, however; it commenced again in 1338 under the direction of architects from Siena's cathedral and was finally completed around the middle of the 14th century. Its present appearance is the result of several phases of renovations and repairs. The church was remodeled as early as the 16th century, and a complete restoration then followed between 1840 and 1845 in a historicist and neo-Romanesque style. The original marble cladding was repeated in the exterior with narrow strips of red marble alternating with broad bands of white, probably in imitation of the layout of the old façade. An ascending dwarf gallery separates the lower floor with its three portals from the gable, which is orn-ately decorated with a large rose window.

On the cornice running below the tympanum, the four symbols of the Evangelists stand in front of the buttresses. These are the only surviving decorative elements from the medieval façade.

high buttresses, are neo-Gothic additions by Cesare Maccari from 1897. The interior with its altarpiece by the Sienese artist Matteo di Giovanni from 1474 was also thoroughly restored in the 19th century.

South Portal

As the southern side of the cathedral faces the Piazza Dante it has been given the status of a second façade. This aspect of the building was not greatly affected by restoration work in the 19th century. If the decorations over the portal are discounted, the south side looks very much like it did when first constructed.

Floral and figurative reliefs frame the entrance to the south portal, their alternating colors of red and white adding to the visual appeal. The lintel is particularly attractive and finely worked. Vines enclose the half-length figures of Christ and of the four Evangelists. The Virgin and Child in the tympanum, as well as the figures of the saints to the sides who are standing under tabernacles with

Museo Archeologico e d'Arte della Maremma

The Museo Archeologico e d'Arte della Maremma housed in the former Palazzo del Tribunale is one of Tuscany's most important archaeological museums: its collection includes finds from the prehistoric, Etruscan, and Roman periods. The focus of the collection is the Etruscan city of Roselle, whose structure and patterns of settlement are displayed by means of models, plans, and archaeological artifacts.

With its exhibits of artifacts from the Villanova culture (10th to 8th centuries

B.C.) excavated in Vetulonia, objects from the 7th to 6th centuries B.C. unearthed in Talamone, and treasures from Soana and Pitigliano, the museum spans the entire spectrum of Etruscan culture and displays its most brilliant achievements.

The stone implements exhibited in the museum provide an overview of the stages of development in the progress from the Paleolithic to the Neolithic eras, as well as the different metal-working techniques which evolved during the Copper, Bronze, and Iron ages. Along with roughly worked hand axes, carefully crafted arrowheads and scrapers, as well as metal alloy tools, there are artifacts from all the epochs of prehistory. Ceramics also form a major part of the collection. Vases from the Archaic period in geometric styles are on display, as is other work ranging from the first examples of Bucchero glaze to the black and red figured vase painting of the Archaic and Classical eras. Of special interest are the excavations from the Augustan shrine at Roselle, which feature fragments from 18 over-sized statues depicting various family members of the Emperor Claudius. The archaeological section is complemented by a collection of Christian art with panel paintings, majolica ware and coins from the Middle Ages to the Renaissance.

Etruscan jug with base and lid, c. 730–710 B.C., ceramic, h. 49.5 cm

Sassetta (c. 1392–1450),
Madonna with Child, c. 1450
Oil on wood, 91 × 65 cm

The superb panel painting _Madonna with Child_ – known as _Madonna delle Ciliege_ (the "Cherry Madonna") – is by Sassetta, whose real name was Stefano di Giovanni. The unusual compositions of this innovative artist, much influenced by Gentile da Fabriano, were to have a profound effect on Sienese painting in the first half of the 15th century. His subtle style and markedly rhythmic use of line were indebted to the so-called "International Gothic" movement, but he deepened his depiction of space, opening it up to the new perspectival forms of the Florentine Renaissance.

Mary and the Christ child are depicted with thin, dignified features and the curved lines of their bodies appear to be in perfect harmony with one another. In addition, there is a new sense of an almost intellectual Naturalism. The infant Christ holds onto the finely embroidered garment of his mother with a somewhat dreamy expression, while in his left hand he clutches the stalk of a cherry which is already in his mouth. Mary holds another handful of cherries, only the stalks of which can be seen, while she supports her son's back with her other hand.

Sassetta died on April 1, 1540, from a lung infection which he probably contracted while working on a fresco over the Porta Romana, one of Siena's various city gates.

**Duccio di Buoninsegna
(c. 1255 – c. 1319),
Altar cross, 1280–1283**
Tempera on wood, 286 × 192 cm

The lavish use of decoration and gold leaf on altarpieces found in medieval churches created the impression that they were worked in gold or enamel. From the mid-13th century, however, the growing influence of the mendicant orders with their ascetic principles meant that there were fewer requirements for church ornamentation. Depictions of the Crucifixion and Maestà became simpler. Visitors to the church were to focus their attention on the Passion of Christ and not be distracted by any irrelevant decoration, in accordance with the Lamentations of Jeremiah 1:12: "Is it nothing to you, all ye that pass by? behold, and see if there be any sorrow like unto my sorrow!" The altar cross in San Francesco is attributed to the young Duccio di Buoninsegna from the period when he was still influenced by an older artist, Cimabue. The impression conveyed by the pallid face and the emaciated body is reinforced by the work's dark shadows, while the weight of Christ's sagging head appears to have caused his muscles to contract. His body is realistically depicted.

S. Francesco

In 1220 the Franciscan order took over and rebuilt a church belonging to the Benedictines, who had left Grosseto because of the danger from malaria. The simple building with its eight pointed windows was consecrated in July 1289. Consisting only of a nave, the interior of this hall church is spacious and features an open roof truss. The main decorative work is a fine large cross over the main altar which dates from the late 13th century.

Roselle

Ancient Walls

Where there was once, in antiquity, an open bay at the mouth of the Ombrone there is today the Grosseto plain. At this strategically important site in the 9th century B.C. the maritime and commercial city of "Russelae" was built on a hill to the southeast, and this town later played an important role in the Etruscan League of Twelve Cities. In 294 B.C. Russelae fell to the superior forces of the Romans after a bitter struggle. The Romans rebuilt the town they had destroyed, but the increasing marshiness of the area and attacks by Saracens in the Middle Ages ushered in its decline. Today an impression of the size and extent of both the Roman and Etruscan towns can be gained from the archaeological excavations which revealed an encircling wall over 1³/₄ miles (3 km) long. Public buildings were situated on the Roman forum in a hollow surrounded by hills. The walls of the courts of justice, with their rhomboid decorative pattern, can still be seen while other buildings with complex floor plans were also excavated. Etruscan houses of dried mud were unearthed underneath the Roman ruins.

Religion and the Etruscan Cult of the Dead Ruth Strasser

The Etruscans' holy scriptures, the so-called *disciplina etrusca*, have long since been lost; their teachings and rituals are known only from descriptions by the Roman authors Cicero, Seneca, and Livy. According to the *disciplina*, the vault of heaven was divided into 16 regions: the eastern part housed the gods who favored mankind while in the west dwelled those who were malicious. Originally Etruria's supreme deity was Vertumnus, who was a god of war and vegetation but who could also be a fearful monster. Under the influence of the Greeks the Etruscan pantheon became more Hellenistic: the chief deity, and therefore the one who corresponded to the Greeks' Zeus, was Tinia. It was he who had marked out the Etruscans' land with boundary stones and limited the term of their existence to ten *saecula* or ages. He was supported by the Etruscan Juno, known as Uni, who was the equivalent of the Greek Hera.

Some gods were borrowed directly from the Greeks, some from the Phoenicians, and there

Vetulonia, Entrance to the Tomb of Diavolino, 2nd half 7th century B.C.

Populonia, Tumulus

everything necessary for his journey. The range of tomb types, and the variety of sarcophagi and urns as well as their grave goods, provide us therefore not only with an insight into the Etruscans' religion but also with details about their everyday lives.

The Pozzo Tomb

In the 8th and 9th centuries B.C. the dead were generally cremated and their ashes interred in round urns made of dark-colored clay together with grave offerings. These vessels had a roughly anthropomorphic form with a pot-bellied body, handles like the stumps of arms, and a lid in the form of an inverted pot which resembled a head. These two-part cinerary urns were often placed in a still larger vessel (*ziro*) before being laid in a small grave or *pozzo* lined with stones, $9^3/_4$ to $16^1/_2$ feet (3–5 m) deep. The grave was then covered with a large slab. Vast necropolises grew up which were set apart from the residential areas. Later these areas were generally located outside the Cyclopean city walls. In Chiusi a particular form of urn, the canopic vase, was used: its lid was in the form of a human head with the features of the deceased while the urn itself had a humanoid form with arms, hands, and even breasts. These canopic vases were placed on throne-like chairs and buried in vessels made of clay.

The Fossa Tomb

In the 8th century burial in rectangular burial chambers "fossa) also began to be adopted

were a number of fertility goddesses of local origin. The subdivision of the sky into the four points of the compass was known as the *templum* and was the basis for every conceivable arrangement of secular space such as the symmetrical layouts of towns, or the division of a sheep's liver into 16 parts during a ritual sacrifice in order to divine the will of the gods. Shamans or soothsayers formed their own social elite and even in late antiquity they still had an important function as *augures* (augurs) in the Roman Empire.

The tombs of the Etruscans were furnished with provisions and other items, evidence of a sophisticated concept of the afterlife. Death for the Etruscans meant a journey into the underworld, the next life, and it was undertaken on horseback or in a covered wagon. The tomb therefore represented a new dwelling place and it reflected a concern for the wellbeing of the deceased, who was to be equipped with

alongside cremation. These chambers, between $6^{1}/_{2}$ and 10 feet (2–3 m) in length, were dug into the earth and often lined with stone slabs. Originally, stone circles were built around these tombs to demarcate the area of the dead.

The Tumulus Tomb

With the flourishing of the Etruscan coastal cities, the import of luxury goods from the East and the general spread of a new lifestyle, burial customs began to change as well. The family burial grounds which replaced the burial of an individual urn required the construction of larger buildings. These complexes were to be monumental and permanent, and this led to the first truly funerary architecture developing out of the relatively simple fossa tomb. Vaults were built which were roofed over with masonry or hewn rock and on top of this a "tumulus" was heaped up which was often as large as 164 feet (50 m) in diameter. A straight passageway, the *dromos*, provided entry into the interior of the tomb through a door constructed from massive stone slabs. After passing a series of smaller chambers or niches, a trapezoid door led into the actual domed tomb in the center of which a single, great column reached up to the keystone of the vault; this column symbolized the eternal center of the universe.

The Chamber Tomb

The chamber tombs of central Etruria were constructed in a number of different ways;

some were hewn horizontally into cliffs of tuff, while others were either built from stone or set into the ground (*hypogeum*). The chambers carved out of tuff imitated houses and temples in their use of architectural elements and had, for example, saddle roofs with ridge beams or vaults like the tumuli. Still later they had vestibules with pillars which, in the form of so-called aedicule tombs, came to have ever more ornate façades with niches, columns, pilasters, and friezes. The dead were interred in urns or sarcophagi or placed on biers in niches. The walls contained niches for grave offerings and canopic vases even began to be placed on finely hammered bronze thrones.

Populonia, burial chamber

Tomb Statuary

In front of the tomb complex there was often a *cippus*, a cuboid or cylindrical gravestone with a carved relief. Carved figures which acted as guardians of the dead are also common. Lining the passageways of the tomb were rows of busts mounted on pediments. It is often difficult to tell precisely what purpose a particular statue served in Etruscan tombs. In Vetulonia oversized figures of men and women made from *pietra fetida* (a type of stone so-called because of the unpleasant smell it emits when scratched) surrounded the graves, and in Chiusi female clay figurines were placed on the canopic vases encircling the main tomb. Dozens of bronze votive statues and statuettes depicting both women and warriors have been found; these were originally placed on shelves within the sepulchral chambers.

Skyphos with Sphingen, 7th century B.C., gold, h. 7.9 cm, Museo di Villa Giulia, Rome

The Grave Offerings

Men's graves were equipped with weapons, swords, and lances, and the deceased were also provided with razors, tools and bridles. Women's tombs were furnished with kitchen implements and spindles, and especially with gold and silver jewelry for the afterlife: rings, bangles, earrings, belt buckles, hairpins, clasps for their cloaks, gold foil, and also ornamented mirrors.

Urns and Sarcophagi

Urns and sarcophagi were at first made from porous tuffstone, then terracotta, and later high-quality alabaster. Initially they were made to resemble houses with saddle or hipped roofs, or shrines. Soon, however, these receptacles became decorated with floral or leaf decor, or with figurative depictions such as griffins, dolphins, ostriches, sea creatures, Medusa heads, or Amazons. Later, themes from Greek mythology became increasingly popular. The "Etruscan" tomb scenes are of particular interest; these show the deceased taking leave of his family through the *dextrarum iunctio*, the holding of (right) hands indicating the bond which exists between the living and dead, even from beyond the grave. During his journey on horseback to the underworld the deceased was wrapped in a shroud and accompanied by a servant who carried a bag with provisions on his back.

Soon the demons of the underworld appear: Charun, a monstrous figure with a beard, long sharp ears, and a hooked nose who wields a great hammer, and Lasa who holds a torch to light the way. The lids of the sarcophagi show the deceased reclining on the *kline*, the sofa at which meals were taken. These were not portraits but serial productions which were more or less ornate according to the purchasing power and desires of the patron. Women are generally depicted wearing a girdle and holding a pomegranate, an egg, a fan, or a mirror – attributes intended to symbolize fertility or beauty. Men are shown with a slate as a sign of their education and profession, or they grasp a sacrificial cup with their middle and ring fingers while they spread their other fingers. It is likely that this gesture was meant to ward off evil and keep the demons of the underworld at bay.

Reconstruction of the Inghirami tomb, Museo Archeologico, Florence

Fresco, Tomb of the Baron, 6th century B.C., Tarquinia

Massa Marittima

Once the most impressive city of the Maremma, Massa Marittima lies on a hill that has been occupied since prehistoric times. Here, Etruscans and Romans mined the treasures of the *Colline Metallifere* (the metallic hill), extracting copper, tin, lead, iron, and silver. The history of the medieval city began in 835 when Greek pirates destroyed the diocesan seat of Populonia; the bishop of the time fled into the interior and sought refuge on the hill at Massa. Over the course of several centuries the wealth and power of the bishops in their castle on Monte Regio grew, especially from the duties imposed on metals mined there. In 1228, however, the citizenry of Massa asserted their power and the town became a "free commune." It was at this time that the Upper City, the *Città Nuova*, began to be constructed; most of its buildings date from between the 14th and 18th centuries. Malaria drove many people from the marshlands of the Maremma, and by 1300 the Massa had become an important center of almost 10,000 inhabitants, most of whom lived from mining. In 1310 "Massa Metallorum," as the city was known, passed the first mining laws in Italy. Because of its wealth the town often had to defend itself against larger neighbors, but by 1365 it was no longer able to do so successfully

View of the castle

and Massa finally came under the control of the Republic of Siena. The Sienese she-wolf and coat of arms on the Palazzo Pretorio are evidence of this political change. When Siena was absorbed into the Duchy of Tuscany, Massa Marittima came into the Medici zone of influence. In the meantime, however, malaria had spread into the hills as well; by the end of the 16th century the population had dwindled to 500 and the place finally had to be abandoned. The city and its buildings from this era in history have remained virtually untouched.

View of the city showing cathedral

Massa Marittima

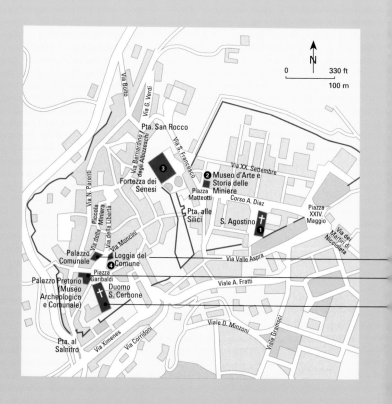

Palazzo Comunale, Piazza Garibaldi, p. 474

Palazzo Pretorio-Museo Archeologico e Comunale, Via Todini, 1, p. 472

Other sights of interest
(not covered elsewhere in this book):

1   S. Agostino, Piazza Socci

2   Museo d'Arte e Storia delle Miniere, Via Corridoni

3   Fortezza dei Senesi, Piazza Matteotti

4   Loggia del Comune, Piazza Garibaldi

Duomo S. Cerbone, Piazza Garibaldi, p. 468

Duomo S. Cerbone

At the center of the city is the Piazza Garibaldi. This square is dominated by the cathedral, Massa Marittima's largest building, which is set atop a stepped podium overlooking the square.

The cathedral was built in two phases between 1228 and 1304. With its nave, two aisles and octagonal dome it was

constructed in the Pisan Romanesque manner although only parts of it were executed in that style's characteristic marble encrustation. Instead, the dominant color is the warm, shimmering golden tone of the smoothly worked travertine stone. The vaulting was a later Baroque addition. Blind arcades surround the upper level of the building, providing the pattern for the exterior. The inlaid lozenges reinforce the affinity with Pisan architectural ornamentation. Round windows and a raised central arch provide the uniform row of arches with a sense of rhythm.

The emphatically vertical nature of the pediment points to a construction date for the façade of around 1300. The pediment's remarkably slim columns, which rest on griffins, animals, and human figures on the upper level, indicate a connection with the studio of Giovanni Pisano. The entire façade is very finely decorated. The lintel of the main portal features a late Romanesque relief which vividly depicts five stations in the life of the saint and bishop Cerbonius, while the blind arches of the lower, and older, façade show carefully worked Corinthian Classical capitals. Overall, antique forms are combined with a medieval delight in images.

Giroldo da Como (active c. 1267–1274), Baptismal font, 1267
Travertine

The font standing opposite the entrance consists of two separate parts. The square lower basin was executed in 1267 by the stonemason Giroldo da Como and features a "deësis" (Christ between Mary and John the Baptist) as well as stories associated with John the Baptist and the saints Cerbonius and Regulus. The temple-like upper section was added in the 15th century.

**Goro di Gregorio (active c. 1300–1334),
Sarcophagus of St. Cerbonius, 1324**
Stone

Situated behind the main altar and in front of a polygonal choir extended in the Gothic period is the most important decorative item in the cathedral, the sarcophagus of St. Cerbonius. This tomb contains the remains of the African bishop of Populonia who died on Elba in 575. A masterpiece of 14th-century Sienese sculptural art, it was created by Goro di Gregorio in 1324.

The lid of the marble sarcophagus features the Madonna and Child surrounded by saints. Goro depicted the Mother of God in a series of medallions as an elegant seated figure. The sides of the sarcophagus are decorated with eight

reliefs depicting the life of the bishop, and these are framed by a wide floral decoration with inscriptions. Cerbonius is shown being thrown to the bears by the Gothic king Totila, and then miraculously rescued. In other scenes the people implore the saint to say Mass; he is charged before the pope with an offence; envoys come to him demanding that he appear before the pope; the saint milks a doe for the thirsty envoys; he appears before the pope accompanied by geese which prove his innocence; and at Mass the pope hears a Gloria being sung by angels. The figures are worked in finely graduated relief and are shown acting against a neutral background. Rocks, trees, and architectural settings provide a context for the various events. The sculptor also adapted elements from contemporary painting.

Duccio di Buoninsegna
(c. 1255–c. 1319),
Madonna delle Grazie, **1316**
Tempera on wood, 168 × 100 cm

In the Cappella della Madonna in the north transept of the cathedral is an altar panel from 1316, the *Madonna delle Grazie*, which shows remarkable affinities with Duccio's *Maestà* in the cathedral museum of Siena. In spite of the stylistic resemblance to this work and its outstanding quality, the *Madonna delle Grazie* has also been attributed to one of Duccio's closest artist colleagues. The front side shows Mary and the Christ child, the rear shows a large crucifixion scene with smaller views of the Passion. This work is remarkable for its relaxed treatment of a Byzantine iconic type, the Hodegetria, which shows the Madonna pointing to her son as the embodiment of the true path. The flowing rhythm of Mary's gold-edged cloak and her delicately bowed head lend a feeling of grace to her body.

Palazzo Pretorio – Museo Archeologico e Comunale

On the southwest corner of the Piazza Garibaldi stands the Palazzo Pretorio. Built in 1230, it is a massive, towerless block of grayish white travertine with an irregular series of biforate windows. The putholes and consoles underneath these openings are evidence that the building once also had wooden walkways and loggias. The municipal crests of both Siena and Massa Marittima are highly visible elements of the façade and are surrounded by emblems which the city commanders and magistrates had added as symbols of their power. Today, the palace houses the Museo Archeologico, which contains artifacts from archaeological digs at Poggio Castiglione and Lago dell'Accesa, majolica from Faenza and Gubbio, as well as numerous Roman coins. It is adjoined by a small collection of pictures owned by the city.

Ambrogio Lorenzetti (c. 1293– c. 1348), *Madonna with Angels and Saints*, **c. 1335**
Tempera on wood, 155 × 206 cm

In 1867 a five-part altarpiece by the Sienese artist called Ambrogio Lorenzetti dating from 1335 was found in the attic of the city's Augustinian monastery. This work depicts the Madonna and Child in an attitude of loving intensity, their faces and bodies pressed against each other in affection. On the steps of the Madonna's throne can be seen personifications of the Christian virtues – faith, hope, and love. Seated on the first step is *Fides* who holds a mirror showing the Trinity.

Spes, dressed in dark green, is seated on the second step with a garland in her hair; on the topmost step, and seen from the front, is *caritas* in a flaming robe holding a heart and arrow in her raised hands. The Madonna is surrounded by members of her heavenly court: prophets and patriarchs under the arcades, and the apostles and female saints in the front row as well as the more recent saints such as St. Cerbonius with his geese. In the foreground, at the foot of the throne, are six angels playing musical instruments, around whom four more angels crowd.

This priceless altarpiece radiates with gold and other luminous colors and in it Lorenzetti describes the path to divine salvation: Faith provides the foundation stone for the spiritual building which is erected by Hope and crowned by Love.

together. These distinct buildings can still be recognized today by their different arrangement of windows and in the joins of their travertine stone. The tower with fewer and narrower windows on the left was the Torre del Bargello; it was built around 1250 as a fortified tower for the Counts of Biserno, who owned the smaller palace to its left. After the Biserno family left Massa Marittima in 1335 the bishop moved into their palace from his residence on the top of the hill while the tower eventually became the core of what is today the town hall. In the years that followed the commune also purchased the house-tower at its far right, which dated from the second half of the 13th century, and the two buildings were joined by means of a central section in 1344. The fine biforate windows continue the pattern of the Biserno tower while the first floor features a bas relief by Urbano da Cortona depicting the she-wolf of Siena.

The battlements and top story with its three windows are historicist additions from the 19th century.

Palazzo Comunale

Like the cathedral, the palaces of the commune authorities are also situated on the Piazza Garibaldi. The mighty four-story Palazzo Comunale is composed of two house-towers from the 13th and 14th centuries which have been joined

Interior (Ceiling)

The interior of the Palazzo Comunale contains the offices of the present municipal administration. The mayoral office, which was once a chapel, is decorated with frescoes from the workshop of the painter Riccio. These depict scenes from the story of Creation.

Riccio was born Bartolommeo Neroni in about 1505, and he served his apprenticeship in the workshop of Giovanni Sodoma, whose daughter he later married. The style of his frescoes shows him to be the successor of his father-in-law but they also demonstrate the artistic influence of Domenico Beccafumi.

Pitigliano

Pitigliano has one of the most fascinating cityscapes in southern Tuscany. Its houses seem to grow directly out of the yellowish red volcanic tuff, and it is difficult for the viewer to distinguish at first between the windows of the houses and the numerous grave chambers carved out of the rock. Pitigliano lies on a plateau cut through with ravines but which only abuts the nearby range of mountains on one side. Because of this inaccessible but strategically fortunate location, Pitigliano had probably already been settled in the pre-Etruscan era. The Etruscans themselves then carved out a vast subterranean labyrinth out of the tuffstone. In the 1930s they were used as boltholes and refuges, but today they have been converted into storage spaces or wine cellars.

In the Middle Ages the castle was owned by the Aldobrandeschi counts, but it passed to the powerful Roman Orsini family in 1293. In 1545 the Orsini built the prominent fortifications situated at the only point of access to the plateau, and even today this tower dominates the city's skyline. In the following years Pitigliano was used as the bishops' residence, although the neighboring town of Sorano, which was ruled by the Roman Colonna family, was the official diocesan town until 1660. By this time, however, Pitigliano had already been a part of the Grand Duchy of Tuscany for 52 years.

Palazzo Orsini

In the Middle Ages much of southern Tuscany belonged to the Aldobrandeschi family. They derived their name from their famous ancestor Ildebrando (Hildebrand) who was born in the neighboring town of Soana in 1020. As Pope Gregory VII, he defended the spiritual supremacy of the Holy See against the imperial claims of Henry IV. Members of his family were appointed imperial curates, and so became rulers over the entire territory. In 1293 the marriage of Anastasia, the last of the Aldo-brandeschi line, meant that all the land she had inherited from her mother, Margherita, went to her husband Romano Orsini of Rome. After deciding to settle in Pitigliano he built a fortified residence with three round towers. The actual Orsini fortress, Pitigliano's most important building, was not in fact built until the 16th century under Niccolo Orsini. He entrusted the design to Antonio da Sangallo the Younger, who was the most highly regarded military engineer of the day. The small building which was originally at its core was integrated into a vast pentagonal complex with a bastion on the northern side. From there stairs provided access to a citadel with barracks. A square with a magazine and an enormous ditch composed of three terraces built on top of each other separated the citadel from the fortress.

The size of the fortified tower still provides an impression of the extent of the complex. Its defensive character has been softened by the addition of characteristics of the typical Renaissance palace, such as loggias and a grand inner courtyard.

Construction of the medieval fortress and the Renaissance city wiped out most of the remnants of the Etruscan settlement. All that remains are sections in the city wall, massive square blocks of stone which were later integrated into the medieval fortifications. In several places throughout the town the visitor still encounters depictions of the bear, the heraldic animal of the Orsini. To the right of the cathedral façade is a small sculpture of a bear, the *progenie ursinea*.

Aqueduct

From 1543 to 1545 Antonio da Sangallo the Younger – a renowned Florentine architect who had worked as Raphael's assistant and later directed the building of St. Peter's in the 1530s – built an aqueduct for Gian Francesco Orsini. Its 15 arches were based on the Roman model and spanned the gorge of the Lente river. This structure provided the city not only with a secure water supply but also with a unique architectural aspect. The aqueduct flowed into the Piazza dell Repubblica where two 18th-century fountains still remain.

Elba and the Emperor in Exile – Napoleon

"The most joyous event by which history could ever have brought fame to Elba has today become reality. Our glorious ruler, the Emperor Napoleon, has arrived among us. Submit freely to the joy which surely overwhelms your souls. Hear the first memorable words he directed to you when he spoke to the officials who will be your representatives: 'I will be a good father to you; be you good sons to me'." It was with these words that the sub-prefect in Portoferraio, the capital of the Tuscan island of Elba, announced the arrival of Napoleon.

Under the terms of the Treaty of Fontainebleau of April 2, 1814 Napoleon's conquerors had given him various options as to where he might spend the rest of his days. In

Arrival of Napoleon on Elba, *19th-century tinted engraving, Bibliothèque Nationale, Paris*

the end he chose Elba over Corfu or his home island of Corsica as his final refuge and place of residence.

Under the terms of the treaty Bonaparte was permitted to retain the title of Emperor and allocated 700 infantrymen and 150 cavalrymen for his court.

Napoleon gave the inhabitants of Elba just 12 hours to prepare for his arrival, but on the afternoon of May 4, 1814, he was fittingly received: church bells were rung and the island's cannons fired a salute. He was even presented with the key to Portoferraio – although the turmoil of his hasty arrival meant that the proper one could not be found and a hastily gold-plated cellar key had to suffice. Nevertheless, it was a symbolic gesture and, in any case, the emperor solemnly handed the key back to the mayor.

Napoleon seriously intended to carry on ruling from the island of Elba, known to the Etruscans and Romans for its mineral wealth, and he therefore needed suitable quarters. The apartments allocated to him in the town hall were too dark, too cold, and, above all, too unsafe. In constant fear of assassins and with a superb sense for location, he had spotted a suitable place on his arrival. The Palazzo dei Mulini offered clear views and could be easily guarded as the property fell away in a steep cliff on the seaward side. The palace was part of a great complex of double fortifications that had been built by Cosimo I de' Medici in 1548. The buildings themselves had not been constructed until the 17th century, when they served as headquarters for the army corps and artillery. Napoleon had them rebuilt as a

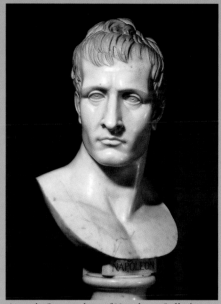

Antonio Canova, bust of Napoleon, Galleria d'Arte Moderna, Florence

residential palace with a central banqueting hall and a fine garden planted with numerous exotic specimens. This garden became one of his favorite places and it may well be that from here he looked out over the sea contemplating, with his characteristic thirst for action, his own future as well as that of his new island kingdom.

One of Napoleon's first tasks was to expand the island's existing tracks into road which were easily passable; he knew there could be no culture, no effective defense, and no flourishing economy without a properly functioning transport system.

Villa Napoleonica di S. Martino, Elba

Napoleon also devoted himself to administration and public health. He worked on sanitation projects, had new wells dug, organized refuse collections, and improved the fighting ability of his troops. The Emperor's younger sister, Paolina Borghese – who had followed him to Elba along with their mother – ensured an entertaining life at court by organizing great banquets and balls, plays, receptions, and concerts. The ducal church was converted into a theater, opening in 1815 under the name *Teatro dei Vigilianti*.

All this, of course, cost money which Napoleon did not have: he allegedly never received the allowance of several million francs which had been promised him by the victorious powers. Taxes therefore had to be collected on Elba and a "duty" was promptly levied on the newly built sewage system. Sometimes taxes were raised by force – the mayor of Capoliveri, for example, was temporarily taken hostage when local residents refused to pay. Still further measures were taken to fill the empty coffers of the state: the tuna-fishing industry, which had flourished under the Medici, was expanded; iron ore was auctioned off and the salt works, too, were exploited. Napoleon also tried to boost the island's agriculture by importing grapevines and mulberry trees with which to breed silkworms.

Napoleon soon found that a single residence was not adequate for his needs, and he cased around for a suitable site for a second one. In a secluded spot in the valley of San Martino, whose beauty and proximity to the city seemed ideal, Napoleon had a modest summer palace built – financed by the sale of several of his sister Paolina's jewels. The German cultural historian Ferdinand Gregorovius sarcastically described this building as the "Versailles of Elba." Later, in 1852, Prince Anatol Demidoff extended it into a pompous villa. Today, the rooms which the Corsican general once occupied can be seen in their original condition as part of a "Napoleon Museum."

Napoleon failed to find peace in either the Palazzo dei Mulini or the Villa of San Martino, however. From time to time he escaped to the hermitage of the Madonna del Monte, a renowned place of pilgrimage from the 16th century which lay 2,066 feet (630 m) above the village of Marciana.

Here, in the isolated wilderness of Monte Giove Napoleon is said to have rested on a bizarrely shaped granite block called "L'aquila" ("the eagle," so named for its shape) and cried out: "Shade and water, what more do you need to be happy?" But he did need more. On September 1, 1814, a young boy and a lady, her face shrouded in a veil, landed in Portoferraio. Napoleon met the pair in secret and led them to the hermitage where he had been living in seclusion for some weeks. His lover, the Polish countess Maria Waleska, and their son Alexander were only able to share the emperor's exile for a few days, however. Alarmed by a rumor that his wife Marie-Louise was about to arrive, and convinced the islanders would not want to counten-ance his extra marital liaison, Napoleon sacrificed his per-sonal happiness to expediency and his supposed popularity. The countess was therefore forced to risk the heavy seas and sail back to the mainland on September 3.

Napoleon's position in the meantime had become in-creasingly difficult. He was surrounded by French spies. The money promised him by the government in Paris never arrived which meant that his soldiers were unpaid and were getting restless. And his father-in-law, Emperor Franz II of Austria, refused to allow his daughter to stay on Elba.

On February 26, 1815, Napoleon took advan-tage of the absence of his English guards to return to the mainland – and to the political battlefield. He landed unannounced in Cannes on March 1, 1815, where he seized power for another 100 days. This intermezzo ended in June 1815 with his final defeat at the Battle of Waterloo and his permanent exile to the island of St. Helena. Elba then became part of the Grand Duchy of Tuscany, and from 1860 it belonged to the united Kingdom of Italy.

Palazzo dei Mulini on Elba, gardens

Livorno

Livorno

Mentioned in documents as early as 1017, the small Tuscan settlement of "Portus Liburni" was reinforced with a fortified harbor in the 12th century. The port of Pisa was becoming blocked with sand, and, as Livorno was located alongside deep water in the mouth of the Arno, Cosimo I de' Medici, the first grand duke of Tuscany, decided to extend it. It was to become the biggest port town in Tuscany, an important trading center and the arsenal for the fleet. The execution of Cosimo's plan did not actually begin until the rule of his sons, Francesco I and Ferdinando I de Medici, in the last quarter of the 16th century. An enlarged and fortified harbor area was constructed, together with the "new" town whose ground plan was a pentagonal fortress. In the interior the streets run at right angles to each other, five in each direction of the four

The 12th-century Torre di Mathilda in the old harbor basin

points of the compass. Ferdinando I also commissioned the conversion of the northeastern part of the fortification into a huge fortress, the Fortezza Nuova, and promulgated the famous Livorno Laws of 1593, the Constituzione livornina, which granted freedom of residence, trade, and religion, irrespective of creed and political persuasion. So it was that it was later described in the travel notes of Charles de Brosses of 1739 as being "a brand new little town, so pretty and handy as to fit into a tobacco box."

Livorno grew very quickly to become the second largest Tuscan town, and in 1838 had 100 Jewish inhabitants (there had indeed been a synagogue since 1603) and 25 English businesses also operated in Livorno. It had even acquired its own English name, Leghorn, which is still used today. After further enlargements to the town in the 19th century and the rebuilding program following the destruction in the Second World War, Livorno is today a major Mediterranean harbour with a large container port, important ferry connections, shipyards, refineries, and the renowned Italian naval academy. Famous natives of Livorno include Pietro Mascagni, the composer of the opera *Cavalleria Rusticana*, and the sculptor and painter Amadeo Modigliani (1884–1920).

In the old harbor there is a monument to the Grand Duke Ferdinando I (1549–1609), with four black slaves chained to its base. Giovanni Bandini had originally been commissioned to make a

Pietro Tacca, Quattro Mori, *Monument for Ferdinando I de' Medici on the Piazza Micheli*

marble statue of the ruler in 1595, but it was not until 12 years later that the Carraran sculptor Pietro Tacca produced wax models of the chained slaves, and it was 1623 before the monument was finally completed.

Livorno

Fortezza Vecchia and Torre di
Matilda, Piazzale dei Marmi, p. 486

Monumento Quattro Mori,
Piazza del Pamiglione, p. 487

Villa Mimbelli – Museo Civico,
Giovanni Fattori, Via S.
Jacopo in Acqua viva, 65,
p. 492

*Mare
Tireno*

Quartiere Pontino, p. 491

Quartiere Venezia Nuova, p. 490

Other sights of interest
(not covered elsewere in this
book):

1 Nuova Sinagoga, Piazza
Benamozegh

2 Duomo S. Francesco, Piazza del
Duomo

3 Chiesa dei Greci Uniti, Via della
Madonna

4 Bottini dell'Olio, Viale Caprera

Quartiere Venezia Nuova

In the 17th century a plan was made to link the old part of the town of Livorno, the Borgo Vecchio, with both of the two fortresses, the Fortezza Nuova and the Fortezza Vecchia, and the sea. An extension to the town on a sandbank between the sea and the two fortresses and an improvement of the transport facilities for traded goods by waterway were also considered. The plan was to connect the navigable canal from Pisa with the three canals from the two fortresses and integrate it into the town. In the first part of the building program 23 blocks of housing were erected, in which the upper floors were to serve as dwellings for an elevated class of international businessmen and merchants, and the ground floor as store rooms for all kinds of goods.

The cellar levels were linked directly to the canal via tunnels. The goods could be transferred from the boats directly onto

the level of the road by means of special ramps. The consolidation of the whole structure and the erection of supporting posts was carried out by specialists brought in from Venice, and indeed the whole area was finally called "Venezia Nuova." This is one of the few places in the otherwise modern city where it is possible to get a taste of Livorno's colorful past and fascinating traditions.

Il Pontino

The crossing point of the biggest canal, the Fosso Reale, was bridged with a large arch, and an extensive square, the Piazza della Republica, laid out here in the 18th century. The square is 237 m long and accessible underground. Even today this old quarter is very picturesque and lively with its boat moorings, harbor facilities, and bridges.

Villa Mimbelli – Museo Civico Giovanni Fattori

In the southern part of Livorno lies the Villa Mimbelli, a beautifully restored villa, eclectic in style and set in the middle of extensive parkland. It was commissioned by the Livorno businessman Francesco Mimbelli and built in 1865 from plans by the architect Giuseppe Micheli. Since being taken over by the town it has housed a cultural center with a theater, library, and exhibition rooms, as well as the municipal picture collections with works from 15th to 19th cent-uries. Pictures by the painter Giovanni Fattori (1825–1908), who came originally from Livorno, form an important part of the exhibition and are shown together with works from other members of the painting school known under the name "Mac-chiaioli," a variation of im-pressionism. Giovanni Fat-tori and his colleagues Telemaco Signorini, Silvestro Lega, Adriano Cecioni and Diego Martelli were enrolled as students of the Florence Academy, but had distanced themselves from the idealizing academic painting style of their contemporaries. They were searching for new, individual forms of expression and began to practice open-air painting with an opaque application of color, a new palette, and strong light–dark contrasts. After the 1861 World Exhibition in Florence, at which they had attracted attention, an article appeared in the Turin

Gazzetta del Popolo in which the expression *Macchiaioli*, then a pejorative term, was used for the first time.

Fattori was the most independent of the group. He had acquired a romantic preference for loneliness from Delacroix ("Loneliness arouses more memories than does the boredom of the town") and spent much time on the coast to the south of Livorno and in the Maremma. In the "Ricordi autobiografici per Ugo Projetti" of 1907 he explained the expression "Macchia" and the associated concepts: the purely optical perception of a human or animal figure, the physiological perception of clear air or other objects, secondly the representation of atmosphere, the patches of sun on the meadow, the gradations of color in the objects and phenomena of nature, and thirdly, the restlessness of his critical realism which shaped him politically. He felt rather like his often represented stone oaks, whipped by the sea wind and firmly rooted in the Tuscan landscape, but stirred up by a power to which one must not submit.

Giovanni Fattori (1825–1908), Sea Landscape at Antignano, *Museo Civico Giovanni Fattori, Livorno*

Tuscan Festivals and Celebrations

Celebratory processions took place annually on saints' days in towns large and small, and were accompanied by great spectacle. Although ostensibly held for religious purposes, the processions provided many occasions for amusement, with performers and panto-mimes, boxing bouts, and football games. In the year 1457 there were 87 feast days in Florence alone, to which would be added the feasts stipulated on an ad hoc basis by the prin-ce's government. The city must have seemed like one long carnival parade, with endless activities and amusements for residents and visitors alike, regardless of social class or station.

Considerable money and time were invested in the preparations. Well-known artists desi-gned the floats, festival architecture, and coats of arms. Even for contemporary carnivals the work on the costumes takes the whole year. The costly clothing of the participants could only be financed with the help of sponsors.

Some of these processions and their asso-ciated games have been maintained in more or less the same form for centuries. Their origins are in the courtly knights' tournaments, in the tradition of church games or in folk customs. In the "Scoppio del Carro" on Easter Sunday in Florence one finds a combination of old heathen folklore and the feast of the sacrificial death and resurrection of Christ. In the event known as "Fuoco di Pasqua," a richly decorated wagon with fire-works is drawn by two oxen through the dense crowds onto the square between the baptistery and the cathedral. The symbol-laden "explosion of the wagon" happens with

The historic "football match" known as the Calcio storico *is just one of the colorful traditional events that still take place in Florence*

The "Explosion of the Wagon," a Florentine ceremony rich with symbolism, in which a cart and its load of fireworks are set alight to produce a spectacular show

the aid of a burning dove made of papier-mâché, which the archbishop then shoots like a rocket along a wire in the direction of the wagon.

If the wagon and the fireworks ignite immediately there is likely to be a good harvest and businessmen can look forward to a prosperous year. Last but not least, the profession of augury, which is thousands of years old, survives as does that of the Etruscan bird seers, who observe and interpret the flight of birds in order to make prophesies.

Whatever the ocassion, whether it be carnival in Viareggio, the *Gioco del Ponte* in Pisa, the *Giostra del Saracino*, the fighting with a lance in Arezzo, or the *Calcio storico*, the historical football game in Florence, enthusiasm for celebrating can best be summed up by quoting a verse by Lorenzo de' Medici: "Oh, how beautiful is youth which evaporates so quickly, therefore let cheerfulness be a virtue today, for who knows who will be alive tomorrow?"

Pisa

Pisa

The world-famous Leaning Tower has made Pisa the best-known city in Tuscany. This static miracle seems appropriate for the home town of two celebrated mathematicians – Leonardo Fibonacci (c. 1180–1250), who introduced Arabic numerals to Europe, and Galileo Galilei (1564–1642), who revolutionized the medieval cosmos with his scientific insights.

A trading settlement of Greek or Etruscan seafarers called Pisa ("estuary") was established beside a lagoon, presumably in the 7th century B.C., in the delta of the Serchio and Arno rivers. In 180 B.C. Pisa became a Roman colony, as is still evident in the grid-like street plan of the city center. During the reign of Augustus Caesar the town became a naval base called Colonia Julia Obsequens. From the end of the 9th century, when the whole Mediterranean area had come under Islamic control, the Pisan fleet embarked on its triumphant series of victories over Moorish pirates. In the following centuries it defended Rome and southern Italy in great naval battles against the Saracens, cruised past Carthage, and reconquered Elba, Corsica, and Sardinia. Participation in the successful First Crusade (1096–1099) enabled the city to establish numerous new trading posts on the coast of Asia

The Piazza del Duomo, with baptistery, cathedral, and campanile

Minor. In 1113, Pisa's fleet comprised 300 ships and 45,000 sailors, extended its control to the Balearics and finally captured Tunis as well.

Economic prosperity was soon followed by political power: at the end of the 11th century, emperor and pope recognized Pisa's constitution, which extended far beyond the immediate city area. In 1091, Pisa became an archiepiscopal seat, and in 1162 Emperor Frederick Barbarossa sanctioned Pisa's right to a strip of coast extending from Liguria to Latium. But as a loyal ally of the Hohenstaufens, Pisa's heyday passed with the end of that imperial dynasty in 1254. In domestic trade there was increasing competition from rivals Lucca and Florence, and the battle for maritime trade was finally lost to Genoa in 1284, when the Pisan fleet was utterly beaten near the Meloria reef. In 1406 the Florentines captured Pisa, thus fulfilling a longstanding desire for a harbor, though the latter became increasingly silted up and was eventually given up in favor of the newly developed port of Leghorn. It was not until the Medici Grand Dukes Cosimo I and Ferdinando I intervened in the 16th century that prosperity returned. They founded the botanic gardens, constructed a canal linking the city with the sea, installed running water and extended the still-famous university.

Pisa

Campo dei Miracoli, p. 502

Palazzo dell'Orologio, Piazza dei Cavalieri, p. 524

Palazzo dei Cavalieri (Scuola Normale Superiore), Piazza dei Cavalieri, p. 526

Other sights of interest

1 S. Maria della Spina, Lungarno Gambacori, p. 526

2 Museo Nazionale di S. Matteo, Lungarno Mediceo, p. 527

3 S. Piero a Grado, 4.5 km SW of Pisa, p. 530

S. Stefano dei Cavalieri, Piazza dei Cavalieri, p. 524

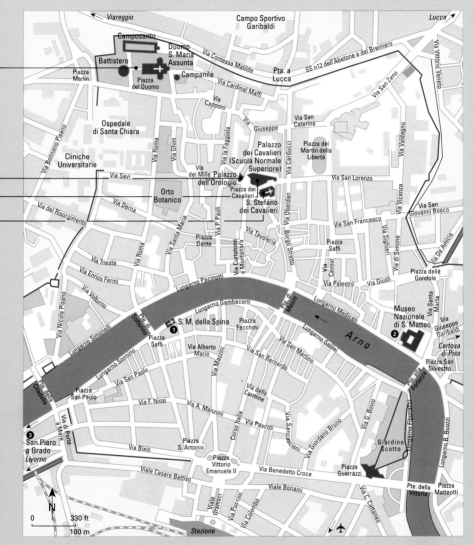

Campo dei Miracoli

The Campo dei Miracoli, the Plain of Miracles, is even today a harmonious whole, a site where the city republic established its cathedral, the baptistery, the famous campanile and Camposanto (cemetery) in its golden age.

Before that, the site was a cemetery outside the city walls, with room for a spacious layout. Planning was based on the model of classical temples and of Early Christian churches in Rome, but combined Lombard forms with eastern motifs. The foundation stone for the cathedral of Santa Maria Assunta was laid in 1063, and building continued for over 300 years. Each phase continued what already existed (particularly the expensive use of marble), merely changing the emphasis with different arch shapes.

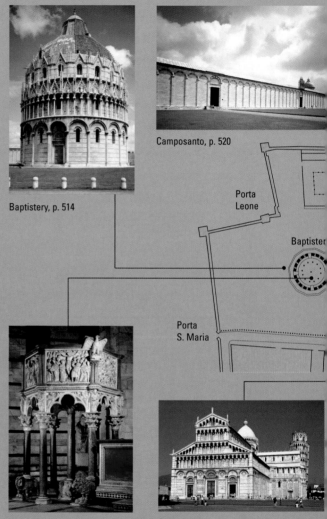

Baptistery, p. 514

Camposanto, p. 520

Porta Leone

Baptister

Porta S. Maria

Nicola Pisano, marble pulpit, p. 510

Cathedral façade, p. 504

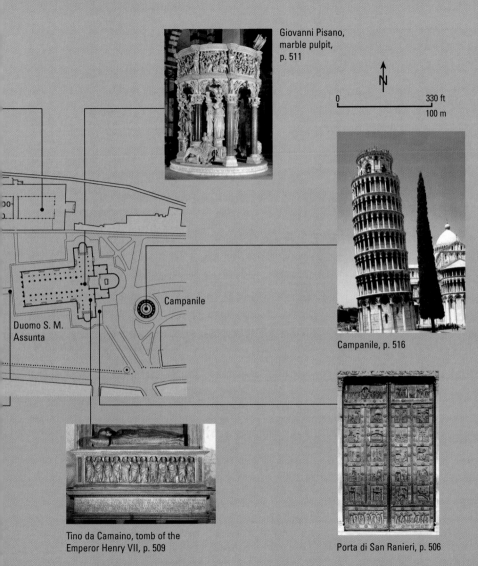

Giovanni Pisano, marble pulpit, p. 511

N

0 ———— 330 ft
———— 100 m

Campanile

Campanile, p. 516

Duomo S. M. Assunta

Tino da Camaino, tomb of the Emperor Henry VII, p. 509

Porta di San Ranieri, p. 506

Duomo S. Maria Assunta

"Six large ships laden with heavy treasures fell into their hands," runs the inscription on the façade, commemorating the victory by the Pisan fleet over the Saracens in Palermo in 1063. The booty brought back provided the funds to build the cathedral. Even the architects are recorded there – Buschetus and Rainaldus.

Buschetus began work on the cathedral immediately. It was a Latin cross with double aisles each side of the nave, single aisles each side in the transept and an oval dome. A few decades after the dedication in 1118, the nave was extended by three bays to the west by the new architect Rainaldus and given a new west front.

Here the ground story is divided up by blind arcading incorporating the three doorways and arches on detached columns with pilasters behind. Above this, the façade wall is set back, leaving room for dwarf galleries. Notable features of these include the close succession of columns, the Classically profiled moldings, and the jewel-like facings of variegated marble. At second-story level, the gallery tapers into the aisle roofs, above which is a double nave gallery crowned by a figure of the Virgin.

The decorative system begins in earnest at ground-floor level, with marble stripes and blind arcades. Buschetus combined eastern architecture with Graeco-Byzantine features, Oriental ornamentation and a Lombard or Ravennan decoration involving blind arcading and lesenes. It was a pioneering style that developed into the distinctive 12th-century Italian Romanesque.

The three original bronze doors by Bonanus melted during a cathedral fire in 1595. The replacement doors, newly cast from the same bronze and featuring scenes from the life of the Virgin, came from the workshop of Florence-based Flemish sculptor Jean de Boulogne (Giambologna, 1529–1608). A Byzantine-style mosaic with the *Assumption* occupies the tympanon of the central doorway.

A dominant motif is the diamond, shaded off towards the middle and emphasized on the outer edge with colored marble. Similarly stressed architecturally are the colored horizontal stripes encircling the whole building. In almost playful contrast are the variegated facings. They employ near-Eastern motifs of late Classical origin, introduced to Italy via Sicily.

Choir Apse

Bonanus Pisanus,
***Porta di San Ranieri*, c. 1180**
Bronze, h. c. 500 cm

The main entrance of Pisa cathedral was formerly the Porta di San Ranieri on the

east side of the south transept, which is closer to the city than the west front.

Of the four doors that Pisan-born sculptor Bonanus created for the cathedral, this is the only one to survive. The panels of the two doors were cast in bronze by the *cire perdu* method around 1180 and then mounted on wood.

The leaves are divided into four large and two small panels, in flat frames decorated with rosettes. The panels are filled with reliefs depicting scenes from the life of Christ and the Virgin, in a sequence that can be read from left to right in the four large and twenty small fields that occupy both doors. The first is the *Annunciation* bottom left, the last the *Death of the Virgin* top right. The top and bottom levels are each occupied by two larger reliefs: at the top the *Christ in Majesty* (left) and *Enthroned Virgin* (right), at the bottom the prophets strolling beneath palms deep in discussion, representing the link between the Old and New Testaments, though the motif is Classical. Both leaves are framed and structured by a surround of rope moldings. Bonanus's door is not only the oldest bronze door in Tuscany and one of the earliest with narrative scenes in Italy, but also the first large-scale relief in Pisan art. It impresses with the clarity of its construction and evocative depiction of the active figures. Bonanus sets the scenes simply and yet with astonishing three-dimensionality on a neu-tral background. The reduction to the essentials is as typical of this artist as the classicizing drapery of the figures and the palms bent by the wind. It must be assumed that Bonanus was familiar with Byzan-tine ivory work. The scenes are enlivened with narra-tive details such as Joseph bowed from the strains of travel in the *Flight into Egypt*. The source for the designs was presumably *cofanetti*, ivory boxes that were used for carrying relics from the Orient.

Christ in Majesty with six adoring seraphim		Enthroned Virgin with four angels	
The Harrowing of Hell	The Three Women at the Tomb of Christ	The Ascension	Death of Mary
Washing the Feet	Last Supper	Arrest of Christ	Crucifixion
Temptation of Christ	Transfiguration	Resurrection of Lazarus	Christ Enters Jerusalem
Presentation in the Temple	Flight into Egypt	Massacre of the Innocents	Baptism of Christ
Annunciation	Visitation	Birth of Christ	Adoration of the Magi / The Fall
Prophets discoursing		Prophets discoursing	

The Interior

The interior of the cathedral is an over-whelming sight, with a mixture of Early Christian, Byzantine, and Islamic motifs. With double aisles in the nave, single aisles in the transepts, galleries, a clerestory, and a crossing dome standing on an octagonal drum, the Duomo is an early monumental structure of medieval Italy. The columns with their granite shafts form a regular rhythm of circular arches, the capitals modeled for the most part on ancient examples, though few ancient capitals were actually re-used.

The style of the marble facing is individual. Dark strips of varying intensity alternate with contrasting white surfaces and ornamental medallions, while evenly spaced alternation is reserved for the gallery piers and arches of the aisles. The mosaic of the apse – a Christ in Majesty with the Virgin and John the Baptist – dates from 1302, and Cimabue's involvement is documented. However, the greatest artistic treasure is the marble pulpit by Giovanni Pisano by the crossing. The gilt coffered ceiling of the body of the church was commissioned by Ferdinando de' Medici after the fire of 1595.

Tino di Camaino (c. 1280–1337), *Tomb of the Emperor Henry VII*, 1315
Marble

Henry VII, who was meant to continue the Italian policy of the Hohenstaufens and carried the entire hopes of the Ghibellines with him, unexpectedly died of malaria in Buonconvento near Siena, on his way to Rome in 1313 for his coronation. The Pisans had the corpse of the young emperor they venerated interred in the cathedral, and commissioned a tomb from Tino da Camaino.

The sculptor had been trained in the workshop of Giovanni Pisano. He designed a sarcophagus that rests on consoles and is fronted by representations of the apostles. The figure of the emperor lies on it surrounded by a round-arched blind niche, which at a later date was painted with angels by Ghirlandaio's workshop.

The Narrative Art of the Pisani   Ruth Strasser

Nicola Pisano, pulpit, 1260, Baptistery, Pisa

Around the mid-13th century a stonemason arrived in Tuscany from southern Italy, probably Apulia. He was called Nicola. Apart from being a real master of his craft, he had two quite decisive advantages over his guild colleagues: first, he worked with a "running" auger, in other words, a tool that could be used with a crank. This was an enormous technical advantage compared with his colleagues' way of working. Second, he used his eyes not just to check his work like all other stonemasons, but to notice things apart from the usual sources of visual inspiration. His models were above all Etruscan and Roman sarcophagi such as those that could be found in and around churches and cathedrals, or displayed in cemeteries because they were often re-used for Christian burials.

Nicola had been commissioned to make a pulpit for the baptistery in Pisa. When it was complete, it was so unusually lovely that he himself was very proud of his work and wrote a Latin inscription below the picture panels: "Nicola Pisano carved this excellent work in

Birth of Christ	Adoration of the Magi	Presentation in the Temple	Crucifixion	Last Judgment

1260 – may so talented a hand be praised as it deserves." He was henceforth called Nicola Pisano (Nicola of Pisa), and was at once summoned to Siena to make a second pulpit of this sort for the cathedral there.

He was helped on the job by his younger son Giovanni, who emulated his father in everything. It was therefore no accident that Giovanni, after he had been appointed site manager for work on the cathedral façade in Siena because of his artistic abilities and had carved many much admired over-lifesize sculptures, also wanted to try his hand at pulpits. Like his father, who had meanwhile died, he did two: the first between 1298 and 1301 for the church of St. Andrea in Pistoia, the second ten years later for Pisa cathedral, so that he too came to be called Giovanni "Pisano."

There are four marble pulpits that differ fundamentally from the type of pulpit hitherto common, because the Pisans made polygons than can stand independently in the church and do not have to be propped against a wall or pier. The pulpit became a massive, sculptural entity you could walk round and look at from all sides. This tallied with new ideas circulating about the reform of church services and the liturgy. As the populace no longer understood the Latin that was used in the sermons and

ceremonies, it was vital for Christian teaching to be directly accessible.

The preferred way to do this was with pictures, whose symbolic content invited reflection and imitation. And what was better suited to this than colorful church windows,

Giovanni Pisano, pulpit, c. 1310, Pisa Cathedral

Annunciation and Stories of John the Baptist	Birth of Christ	Offerings of the Magi	Presentation in the Temple and Flight into Egypt	Massacre of the Innocents	Betrayal and Scourging of Christ	Crucifixion	The Elect	The Damned

Nicola Pisano, pulpit relief with the Birth of Christ, *1260, Baptistery, Pisa*

frescoes on the church walls, and the sculptural program of doorways, pulpits, and altars? The figurative representation on all the pulpits was also completely new. Medieval sculpture involved mainly the art of relief, with sculpture being generally subordinated to the architectural frame. In the Pisan pulpits the sculptures are detached from the background and seem to burst the frame. With their marked three-dimensionality, the figures are charged with a dynamism that almost has them stepping out of the picture.

This strongly sculptural impression is based on a precisely calculated disposition of light and shadow. Work proceeded from right to left, and before tackling the first row of figures from top left down, the depth of the second row of figures had to be worked out for the distribution of shadow.

Common to both sculptors was their approach to antiquity. Following Classical examples, they gave their figures life and dignity – and a degree of realism and individuality – with curly hair and flowing beards. A

Giovanni Pisano, pulpit relief with the Birth of Christ, *c. 1310, Pisa Cathedral*

highly sculptural treatment of drapery conveyed stateliness.

Classical marble reliefs also provided models for poses and gestures the sculptors could take over to convey passions and emotional tension in their figures, and help the viewer to identify with them.

The transition from the written and spoken word to three-dimensional representation appealed directly to believers' hearts, and with their realistic physicality the carved figures awoke a profound response in them.

The lions holding a lamb or ram between their paws symbolically guard the holy place and represent the victory of Christ over the Antichrist.

Baptistery

Begun in 1152 to a design produced by Diotosalvi, the Baptistery stands on the greensward like a monumental reliquary. The Gothic hoods, finials, and rich figurative decoration were added from 1260 under the direction of Nicola and his son Giovanni Pisano. In 1358, the Romanesque dome was replaced by a pumpkin dome. The doorway facing the cathedral is decorated with sculptural tendrils, foliage and some elegant rosettes. The *Labors of the Months* in the relief panels on the left and the energetically discoursing apostles on the right date from the 12th century.

In the architrave relief, angels and apostles jostle around Christ, the Virgin, and St. John in the style of a Byzantine ivory relief. The original of the *Virgin and Child* by Giovanni Pisano in the lunette panel dating from 1295 is in the Camposanto.

The Interior

The interior of the Baptistery opens up as a harmonious, contemplative space with excellent acoustics. The piers and columns alternate rhythmically, and separate the central space from the ambulatory. Conspicuously high arcading draws attention to the gallery level, and thence to the vault, which is not a dome in the real sense. As in the Roman pantheon, until the end of the 14th century the topmost part was open to the sky.

Directly below, the octagonal font with its marble inlays, rosettes, and figured decoration in relief panels occupies the center of the Baptistery. This work, by Guido Begarelli from Como, dates from 1246. Beside it is the older of the two pulpits by Nicola Pisano, completed 1260 and therefore the first freestanding pulpit anywhere.

Campanile (with detail)

As the inscription on the right besides the doorway records, the campanile was the third structure in the cathedral close, started in 1174, i.e., 1173 because in Pisa New Year began on Annunciation Day, 25 March. The architect was originally thought to have been Bonanus, but according to the latest research it may actually have been Gerardo di Gerardo. The first three levels were constructed by 1185 on top of a foundation of wooden planks. Work was then suspended – possibly because the architect was summoned to another job, or because the alluvial soil had already started to subside.

By 1275, the subsidence was already 7 inches (17 cm). Site management was taken over by Giovanni di Simone, who added another level in and attempted to offset the deflection with columns of different height, i.e. the columns on the south side are higher than those on the north. He, too, failed to complete the works, being killed in the disastrous naval defeat of Pisa by Genoa off Meloria in 1284. The next balancing level was added by Tommaso Pisano only in 1350, completing the tower with a belfry. From then on the angle of inclination increased steadily – and Galileo is supposed to have demonstrated the physical law of falling bodies there.

Even without its dramatic tilt, which has probably now been checked, this campanile is something special compared with the usual square Tuscan bell-tower. Its basic structure is a large cylinder with an empty inner core, wrapped in a columnar exterior that is captivatingly light and elegant. Decorated with blind arcading and engaged columns on the ground floor and evenly spaced loggias of columns on the other floors, it bears a visible stylistic relationship with the cathedral and baptistery. The eight floors are separated from each other by a bold band molding. Only the narrower belfry interrupts the regularity of the stories. Its offsetting counter-tilt is quite noticeable only on closer inspection.

La Torre Pendente – the Leaning Tower of Pisa

Ruth Strasser

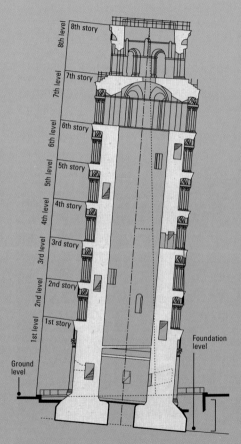

Diagram of the Tower of Pisa

The present-day southward tilt of the tower – part of many Pisans' identity – is 17 feet 1 inch (5.9 m) from vertical, measured at the top of the belfry. Despite many scientific investigations and calculations, it has not yet been established with any certainty whether the tower will actually collapse, either in the near or perhaps distant future.

Whatever the identity of the original architect – Bonanus or, as the latest research suggests, Gerardo di Gerardo – he knew about the sandy, unstable subsoil. Soils in the eastern part of the Piazza dei Miracoli are most stable in the top level of sand and clay. A further soft, yielding layer of sand and minerals follows down to a depth of 130 feet (40 m). In these circumstances, on August 9, 1173, when the ground was totally dry and the water at its lowest, a circular pit was dug about 10 feet (3 m) deep, with a diameter of about 65 feet (20 m). Into this was poured a stone pitching layer about 16 inches (40 cm) thick, and that 2,747 cubic feet (700 cubic meters) of rubble, bricks, and mortar were added up to surface level.

Building began on top of this: first a socle with a few steps and on that the double wall of the inner hollow cylinder. At ground floor level this is still 13 feet (3.9 m) thick, but it narrows to 8 feet (2.4 m) further up. The inside wall is made of randomly coursed mortared rubble from the Pisan hills. The outside is faced with marble slabs about 20 inches (50.8 cm) thick, which are cut smooth and join snugly. The 3 ft 3 inch (99 cm) wide spiral staircase is built into this wall, with 294 steps to the top. Each gallery has 30 columns 3 feet (91.4 cm) from the wall of the inner core. Overall, the eight floors have a total of 207 columns. They are so graceful they look as if they were added merely for decoration, but they nevertheless have an important static function, because their arches and vaulting support the gallery above on each floor.

When building work reached the belfry in 1350, the floor had to be leveled off there. The tilt of nearly 5 feet (1.5 m) was offset by two extra steps on the south side and the belfry was made horizontal as if with a wheel chock. When the structure was finished after 180 years, the overall height was $179^{1}/_{2}$ feet (54.7 m), with an outer diameter at the base of 160 feet (48.6 m) and a weight of about 15,000 tons.

There have been countless proposals for rescue, ranging from dismantling the tower, straightening it and then rebuilding it just as it was, through constructing twin towers with a counter-tilt or building a monumental statue of the Pisan city patron San Ranieri as a support, to the most recent suggestion by a Chinese architect that a layer of rice and dried beans should be pumped under it to shore up the famous structure.

Since 1988 a scientific and technical commission has been attempting to solve the problem. This international body of high-powered architects, structural engineers, and historians first recommended closing the tower to visitors, who by 1990 numbered about 1 million a year. A further measure was to pile up

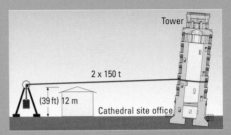

Temporary geotechnical operation at the Leaning Tower.

a counterweight of 600 tons of lead, loaded in concrete troughs, on the north side of the tower. The weight has since been increased to 750 tons. This stopped the steady annual increase in the tilt. After a few hitches – earlier structural reports had been ignored and concrete injections of the 1930s inadvertently sawn through, which led to increased tilting of the tower and endless discussion of who was to blame – measures to solve the problem have resumed. Each floor is being strung round with a steel cable with a special anchoring on the north side.

Despite its tilt, the campanile remained a thing of beauty for centuries. Only now are rescue attempts turning it into what is known as a "cripple with suspenders."

By the summer of 2000, the tower had been moved 12 inches (31 cm) back in the right direction, the overall goal being 16 inches (42 cm) – although the tourist department of the city council might balk at the idea of straightening it altogether!

Camposanto

It is a most unusual complex that encloses the Campo dei Miracoli, situated beside the north wall of the city. There was a cemetery here even in early medieval times. Archbishop Ubaldo dei Lanfranchi is said to have had more than 50 shiploads of earth from Mount Golgotha back to Pisa from his Crusade of 1202 and deposited it on the site. The old cemetery now became a *campo santo* – a sacred field.

Architect Giovanni di Simone, who at the time was also working on the campanile, finally began work on the project in 1278.

He created a cemetery with surrounding covered walks in the form of an elongated cloister and a grassy inner court.

The exterior of the building is plain, with tall regular blind arcades. The entrance is also unspectacular, with only the filigree canopy over it providing some emphasis. This late Gothic architecture contains a figured group with the Virgin and saints and the donor of the mid-14th century tabernacle sculpture, who was called Pietro Galamcorti.

The Interior

Inside, the Camposanto radiates a solemn peace. 413 ft (126 m) long and 164 ft (52 m) wide, it is generously laid out. In the late 14th century the regular arcading of the cloister was filled with tracery. In the 14th and 15th centuries the walls of the cemetery were covered with frescoes showing the *Triumph of Death*, *Last Judgment*, and stories from the Old Testament. Citizens of Pisa were buried in the Camposanto up to the 18th century, as the 600 tombstones in the ground and the re-used Roman sarcophagi confirm (in the Middle Ages, the old coffins were lined up round the cathedral and along the walls here). Even now the Archbishop of Pisa has his final resting place in the Camposanto.

When Pisa was bombed in the summer of 1944, a smoldering fire broke out and irreparably damaged the murals as the roof lead melted and ran down. The *sinopie* (underdrawings) that were uncovered during the restoration have been placed on show in the Museo delle Sinopie opposite the Baptistery.

Buonamico Buffalmacco (active c. 1315–1345),
The Triumph of Death (detail), 1340–1345
Fresco

Recent research suggests that the oldest fresco cycle, the *Triumph of Death*, was executed by Buonamico Buffalmacco. Following the fire, it was removed and now hangs in a room in the north wing.

The various figures' very memorable reactions to death linger in the mind. Worldly idylls and the triumphal march of Death stand side by side in sharp contrast, particularly in the encounter of the knights with the dead. A royal hunting party is brought to a halt by the coffins of three kings, whose corpses are in various stages of decay. The banner with text from the work of St. Macarius draws the moral: "What you are, we were once; what we are, you too will be!" The painter of these frescoes is fond of narrative, lovingly adding details of the royal party's court dress and the heads of individual horses, and shows especially well-known faces from Pisan high society. The falconer, for example, is the ruler of Lucca, Castruccio Castracani, while the bearded figure with the bow is King Louis of the Bavarians, and the knight holding his nose is the ruler of Pisa, Uguccione della Faggiola.

S. Stefano dei Cavalieri

The east side of the square is occupied by the church of Santo Stefano, named for the order of the Knights of St. Stephen and built by Vasari in 1565–69. The early Baroque marble façade goes back to designs by Giovanni de' Medici. The grand ducal arms above the pedimented doorway, combined with the arms of the St. Stephen knights over the windows, recall the special involvement of the Medicis. Worth seeing inside are the carved wooden center ceiling with painted

Palazzo dell' Orologio

The Palazzo dell' Orologio in the Piazza dei Cavalieri, the ancient forum of Roman times and later heart of the medieval republic, was created in 1607 by joining two medieval tower houses across a narrow street. The left tower with its mullion and transom windows is recognizably the Torre delle Sette Vie, the former prison, while the right tower held the republican eagles, as live heraldic devices.

The fate of military commander Count Ugolino della Gherardesca is narrated in Dante's *Divine Comedy*. Accused of treachery, he and his sons and grandsons were locked up in here and starved to death. The palace is also called Palazzo della Gherardesca in their memory.

scenes of the Order, and the beautiful and sumptuous altarpiece.

Palazzo dei Cavalieri

Duke Cosimo I de' Medici selected the former communal palace as the seat of his newly founded order of the Cavalieri di Santo Stefano (Knights of St. Stephen) in 1563. Ostensibly the order was established to protect the coast against Saracen raiders, but in fact it served mainly to control Pisa, as the Grand Master was always the ruling Medici duke (from 1569 grand duke). The architectural conversion was carried out by Vasari, who also designed the lavish sgraffito painting with ornamental grotesques and medallions on the façade. The prominent double steps were only added when Napoleon abolished the order in 1810 and turned the building into the postgraduate university he had founded, the still highly regarded Scuola Normale Superiore. A statue of Cosimo I de' Medici as a Knight of St. Stephen occupies the square in front of the building; the Order's rule of the seas is evoked by his foot resting on a dolphin.

S. Maria della Spina

Profusely decorated with architectural features, the oratory of S. Maria della Spina looks like a precious reliquary. Faced with typical Pisan variegated marble patterns and exuberant late Gothic gables, finials and other tabernacle work, the church was converted between 1323 and 1360 from an older oratory for seamen. Lying right beside the Arno on its southern bank, the building was intended to house a valuable relic that a Pisan had brought back from the Holy Land: a thorn (*spina*) from Christ's crown.

The west front of the aisleless church looks most odd in having only two bays, with a third gable lurking between them on top. The front is divided centrally by a pilaster, above which is a statue of the Virgin and Child with two angels in a baldachin, a work attributed to Giovanni Pisano. The extremely sumptuous figured decoration on the street front and in the tabernacles above the gables with their small rose windows was made in a local workshop of the Giovanni Pisano school.

Originally the church was lower down, right beside the Arno. To protect it from flood damage, in 1871 the church was moved up the bank and rebuilt higher up.

Museo Nazionale di S. Matteo

After the Second World War the former Benedictine monastery of San Matteo, built between the 11th and 13th centuries, was partially converted into a museum to house works of art from various Pisan churches. The museum rooms are arranged round the medieval cloister, with its fine Renaissance doorway. In them are important works of painting and sculpture dating from the 12th to the 15th centuries.

Among the treasures in the collection are the *croci dipinti*, painted crucifixes from the 12th and 13th centuries that hung originally on choir screens or triumph beams in the city's medieval churches. They represent a valuable record of Tuscan panel painting. On show are crosses that represent both the *Christus Triumphans* type (Christ the victor over Death) and the newer *Christus Patiens* type, depicting the suffering Christ. Notable works of sculpture include a wooden angel of the *Annunciation* by Andrea Pisano and the breast-feeding *Madonna del Latte*, a work made of polychrome and gilt marble by his son Nino Pisano.

Simone Martini (c. 1284–1344), *Madonna with Child and Saints* (polyptych), c. 1320

Tempera on wood, center panel 192 × 64 cm, wings 155 × 45 cm each

As Pisa boasted few experienced painters in the trecento, the great altarpieces of the period were ordered from the important art centers of Florence or Siena. An outstanding example in the Museo Nazionale is the polyptych commissioned in 1320 from Sienese painter Simone Martini and his workshop for the monastery of St. Catherine.

The altarpiece consists of seven paintings on a gold ground plus a predella. The Madonna in the center is surrounded by three saints on each side (SS. Dominic, John the Evangelist and Mary Magdalene on the left, SS. Catherine, John the Baptist and Peter Martyr on the right). The St. Catherine figure is a particularly fine example of the art and individual style of Simone Martini. The fine curving lines, precious materials and especially the soft, very tender modulation of the face identify this figure as by his own hand.

Donatello (1386–1466),
S. Rossore **[Roxorus], 1427**
Bronze (gilt), 56 × 60.5 cm

This splendid reliquary bust is one of the principal exhibits of the monastery of San Matteo. The portrait of the canonized knight is of gilt bronze and was made by the Florentine sculptor Donatello between 1422 and 1427. The sash and armor of the figure, like the beard and hairstyle, are in the 15th-century fashion. Donatello presents the Early Christian martyr (whose real name was Luxurius and who was in fact beheaded in Cagliari during Diocletian's reign) as a lifelike and finely modeled contemporary, who is shown in pensive mood. The portrait is remarkable not just for the large eyes beneath a broad forehead, the straight nose and curved lips but also the natural set of the shoulders and the wrap tied across the chest.

The head relic preserved in the bust reached the Florentine monastery of Ognissanti in 1422, and was given to the Order of St. Stephen only when Pope Pius V temporarily abolished the order in 1570. Thus the relics of the saint, who was venerated by the Pisans and has a large national park near the city dedicated to him, finally returned to the city. Their return was of major symbolic importance. In 1406, the Florentines had defeated and robbed Pisa not only of its freedom but also its saints. This at any rate is how the 17th-century chronicler Scipione Amirato saw it.

S. Piero a Grado

West of Pisa, by the original mouth of the Arno, the early Romanesque church of San Piero a Grado stands by itself. It was an important station on the medieval pilgrim route to Rome, and gets its name from the step that St. Peter had to cross when setting foot on Italian soil for the first time.

The present church was built of tuff in the 11th century over Early Christian predecessors. The plain masonry is built of ancient rubble, with narrow lesenes and a continuous frieze of arches beneath the cornices. The east end has three nicely proportioned apses, with circles and rhomboids alternating in their arch moldings.

The Interior

The nave is separated from the aisles by 12 (alluding to the number of apostles) columns sporting ancient capitals. The extensive murals were done by the Lucchese painter Deodato Orlando around 1300. A painted arcade frieze above the red and white checked nave arches displays portraits of popes from St. Peter to Pope John XVII in 1003. In the center zone, the lives of leading apostles are depicted an unusually detailed manner. Twenty panels are devoted to the life of St. Peter, another ten to the life of St. Paul. In the upper part, angels peer out of illusionistically painted wall openings of the Heavenly Jerusalem.

In the western part of the church beneath a ciborium are the remains of the legendary St. Peter altar, brought to light during excavation works.

UBI BEATUS · PETRUS · SEPETUS · FUIT ·

Deodato Orlandi
(c. 1280–pre-1331),
***Burial of St. Peter*, c. 1300**
Fresco

The frescoes in the center part constitute the most detailed surviving life of St. Peter in the Middle Ages, and in their selection and arrangement of events from his life follow the model of the now destroyed frescoes of Old St. Peter's in Rome. Clearly the client, a confidant of Pope Boniface VIII, wished to emphasize the importance of the papacy even to the imperially minded city of Pisa.

Although the slanting faces, almond-shaped eyes and elongated figures are still conceived in the *maniera greca*, the artist's use of grandiose baldachinos and his disposition of the figures within them in an attempt to create a perspective of spatial depth is most unexpected.

The burial of St. Peter takes place in a vaulted, and temple-like building. The shrouded body of the saint is lowered into the coffin by two men, while a bishop administers the sacrament.

Deodato Orlandi,
***Navicella*, c. 1300**
Fresco

While the disciples sit in a boat, St. Peter walks over the water to Christ. According to the account in St. Matthew (14:22–33), Christ extended a hand and said "Oh you of little faith, why did you doubt?"

Of Comets, Heavenly Portents, and Phases of Venus – Galileo's Proofs

"We must measure what can be measured, and make measurable what cannot be measured." A young student was watching the oscillations of the chandelier hanging from the vault of Pisa cathedral. He noticed that the time between the oscillation back and forth – measured by his own heartbeat – remained the same even though the swings got smaller and smaller. In this quite simple way, Galileo Galilei discovered the law of the "isochronism of pendulum motion."

Galileo returned from Florence to the university of his native Pisa in 1581, aged 17, acceding to his father's wish that he study medicine. From his tenth year, he had benefited from a monastic education in Florence, where his family lived (his father was a cloth merchant and a quite important musician), studying literature, music, drawing, and practical mechanics.

Justus Sustermans, Portrait of Galileo Galilei, *1635, oil on canvas, 66 × 56 cm, Galleria degli Uffizi, Florence*

The Classical writings of the philosopher Aristotle and the mathematician Ptolemy constituted the basis of the teaching of science and medicine at the time, and in this, the age of the Counter-Reformation, the Holy

Office of the Inquisition kept a careful check on academic "purity." In 1600, Giordano Bruno was burnt at the stake on a charge of heresy. In the geocentric cosmos propounded by the Church, the Earth as a fixed center was the lowest category in a universe whose stars were peopled by angels, and it was thus meet for the sinful life of Man.

The theoretical basis for calculating the movement of heavenly bodies more simply, published by Nikolaus Copernicus, a canon at the cathedral of Frombork (Frauenburg, Ermland), in the year of his death in 1543, contradicted this concept. His starting point was the movement of the Earth round a central, unmoving Sun. At least officially, however, scholars at the universities and ecclesiastical institutions continued to expound the traditional doctrine.

After four years, Galileo broke off his medical studies and from 1589 made a living as a professor for the "auxiliary" subject of mathematics in Pisa and by giving private lessons. His main preoccupation, however, was his studies of gravity, free fall, and dynamics, the results of which he published in the appendix to his last work, the *Discorsi e dimostrazioni matematiche* (Dis-

courses and Mathematical Proofs). Experiments, measurement, and Euclidean mathematics served him as the foundations for explaining physical processes.

In 1592, he was appointed by the Senate in Venice as a professor in Padua. With a contract for six years, he arrived as a world-famous mathematician at a university where, despite the Counter-Reformation, Protestants were still able to study.

In 1609, Galileo heard of the Dutch invention of the telescope, whereupon he had lenses ground to make a rudimentary telescope. Realizing the potential military uses of the new instrument, he then presented it to the Signoria of Venice.

His wish to return to Florence was realized in July 1610. He became *mathematicus primarius*

Symbolic representation of the breach of the medieval cosmos, 1888, colored woodcut

Galileo Galilei, Compassi di Galilei, *Cod. Galil. 37, fol. 3r, parchment, Biblioteca Nazionale, Florence*

and *philosophus* of Grand Duke Cosimo II of Florence, with an impressive income.

Four months earlier Galileo had sent a still unbound copy of his new book *Sidereus nuncius* ahead to Florence. This astronomical work aroused a storm of enthusiasm among modern scholars and indignation among the conservatives. In it he expounded his discoveries made with the help of his telescope. The work described the surface of the moon with its craters and mountains, the starry nature of the Milky Way, and the moons of Jupiter. There followed the discovery of the phases of Venus and sunspots. No one had ever looked at the sky like this. Copernicus had drawn his conclusions mainly on the basis of mathematical observation. Galileo had applied Copernicus's system to describe the appearance of the heavenly bodies, in other words what we can perceive with our senses, and sought to relate their positions to one other in mathematical terms. "I shall show that it [the Earth] moves and is brighter than the moon, not a cess of dirt and sediment of the world, and I will substantiate it with hundreds of reasons from Nature."

Galileo was still accorded an admiring welcome in Rome, and won over numerous Jesuit converts within the college of cardinals. Denunciation only came in 1616. Galileo was summoned and warned to cease defending the truth of the Copernican theories. The theory itself was condemned as heretical. He himself wrote: "To ban Copernicus now, when his assumption is proving truer every day and his theory more soundly consolidated as a result of many new observations and the activity of numerous scholars – what else would that be than contradict the holy scriptures in a hundred places that teach us that the fame and greatness of the Highest is miraculously revealed in all his works and can be read in a divine way in the open book of the heavens?"

Galileo was convinced that there could be only one truth. As what was contained in the Book of Genesis could not be denied, the holy scriptures would have to be interpreted in a more contemporary manner. In this, Galileo stepped beyond the realm of science, because exegesis of the Bible was the exclusive preserve of theologians at the Holy Office.

When his "old friend" Maffeo Barberini ascended the papal throne in 1623 and Galileo's book *Il Saggiatore* was passed for printing, the astronomer felt more secure. But even the new pope refused to recognize Copernicus's theory.

When Galileo sought a printing permit for the *Dialogo* (the Dialogue on the Two Principal Systems of the World) in 1632, he apparently believed he had worded it in such a way as to conceal his real opinion. Without realizing it, however, he had become caught up in the power struggle between the Dominicans and Jesuits. The pope himself was, unfortunately, no longer on his side.

In 1633 he was tried, and upon the threat of torture was famously forced to recant. The proverbial aside "And yet it does move!" is just legend. Galileo would never have uttered such words in front of the Holy Office. It would have cost him his life.

Sentenced to house arrest, he was nonetheless able to continue his research and keep in touch with colleagues and publishers. His works were banned by the Roman Catholic Church, but were translated from Italian into Latin and printed north of the Alps. When Galileo died, completely blind, in 1642 and was interred in Santa Croce, his insights and the mathematical method of modern natural philosophy could no longer be stopped.

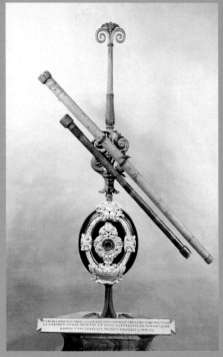

Galileo's original telescope, Museo di Storia della Scienza, Florence

Volterra

Volterra

The historic town of Volterra lies in a relatively isolated spot in a bleak and hilly landscape at an altitude of 1,804 feet (550 m). Between the 7th and 4th centuries B.C. the Etruscan city state of "Velathri" was the agricultural center of Etruria and a member of the League of Twelve Cities. It ruled over a broad coastal strip as well as the islands of Corsica and Elba, trading with Cyprus, Phoenicia, and, most importantly, Greece. From the 5th century B.C. a Cyclopean wall 4.5 miles (7.3 km) long surrounded the city, which then had a population of 25,000, and its necropolis. The only remnants surviving from this period are two Etruscan city gates: the Porta all' Arco and the Porta Diana. The rest of the ancient complex has fallen victim to the so-called "balze," the steep ravines that have opened up to the west of the city as a result of severe soil erosion. In the 3rd century B.C. the town allied itself with Rome and, under the name "Volterrae," was granted the rights of a free city (*municipium*). This status was lost in 79 B.C. when it was on the losing side in the Roman civil war against the patrician ruler Sulla. Later, however, the city regained the rights of citizenship on the recommendation of Cicero.

The town was favored by the Carolingians and Franks for its strategic location and its rich mineral resources. Its heyday came in the Middle Ages when the city took on its present shape. A Volterran native, Linus, had been the first successor to St. Peter as Pope and bishop of Rome, and the town had also become one of the earliest episcopal seats. Its later history was marked by the attempts of its citizenry to form a free commune in opposition to the bishops. The first mayor was elected in 1193 and in 1208 work was begun on Tuscany's first public palace, the Palazzo dei Priori.

Over the years Volterra became embroiled in a number of conflicts with neighboring cities over mining rights for salt. Florence was foremost among these. In the so-called "Alaun War" Volterra was defeated by Lorenzo de' Medici's troops under the Duke of Montefeltro and the prior's palace became the seat of the Florentine general. Wars, sieges, and outbreaks of the plague ushered in a period of economic decline which was not halted until the industrialization of salt mining and the boom in alabaster in the 19th century.

Today, Volterra's 14,400 inhabitants make a living from alabaster and from the tourist industry. There is some industry close to the city such as the "Saline di Volterra" chemical works and a geothermal electricity plant whose subterranean steam supplies the city with power.

Volterra

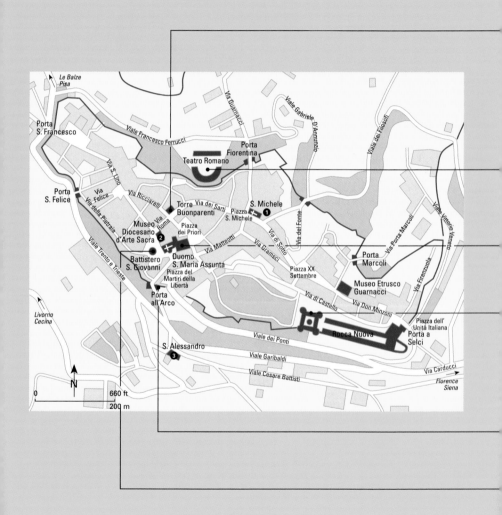

Le Balze
Pisa

Porta
S. Francesco

Viale Francesco Ferrucci

Via Guarnacci

Viale Gabriele D'Annunzio

Viale dei Filosofi

Porta
Fiorentina

Teatro Romano

Via S. Lino

Via Felice

Via Ricciarelli

Via dei Sarti

S. Michele ➊

Piazza
S. Michele

Viale Vittorio Veneto

Porta
S. Felice

Via della Pietraia

Torre
Buonparenti

Via Roma

Museo
Diocesano
d'Arte Sacra ➋

Piazza
dei Priori

Via Matteotti

Via Gransci

Via di Sotto

Via del Fonte

Via Porta Marcoli

Viale Trento e Trieste

Battistero
S. Giovanni

Duomo
S. Maria Assunta

Piazza del
Martiri della
Libertà

Piazza XX
Settembre

Porta
Marcoli

Via Firenzuola

Livorno
Cecina

Porta
all'Arco

Museo Etrusco
Guarnacci

Via di Castello

Via Don Minzoni

Piazza dell'
Unità Italiana

Porta a
Selci

S. Alessandro ➌

Viale dei Ponti

Rocca Nuova

Viale Garibaldi

Viale Cesare Battisti

Via Carducci

Florence
Siena

N

0   660 ft

200 m

Torre Buonparenti, Via
Buonparenti, p. 545

Teatro Romano, Viale Francesco
Ferrucci, p. 546

Duomo S. Maria Assunta, Piazza
S. Giovanni, p. 552

Rocca Nuova, p. 544

Porta all' Arco, Via Porta
all'Arco, p. 557

Battistero
S. Giovanni,
Piazza
S. Giovanni,
p. 556

Other sights of interest
(not covered elsewhere in
book):

1 S. Michele, Piazza S. Michele

2 Museo Diocesano d'Arte Sacra,
   Via Roma 13

3 S. Alessandro, Viale Cesare
   Battisti

Rocca Nuova

A great Renaissance fortress towers over the city from the heights where once the Etruscan acropolis stood. In 1343 the Rocca Antica or Rocca Vecchia (old fortress) with its round tower – known as the *femmina* (woman) – was built in the eastern section. From here the Ghibelline politician, Belforti, headed a regime that exacerbated the existing political tensions in Volterra. In 1361 the Guelph party in the city called for assistance from Florence, an action which eventually resulted in Volterra losing its independence and becoming a free commune in name only. Uprisings against Florentine rule led the Florentines to besiege and capture the town in 1472.

Shortly afterwards, Lorenzo de' Medici built a new, stronger fortress, the Rocca Nuovo, to pacify the city and to serve as a bulwark against Siena. Since the Medici era this vast fortress has been used as a prison.

Torre Buonparenti

Like San Gimignano, Volterra had a large number of torre (house-towers) in the Middle Ages; these were used not only for defense against outside attack but for protection during civil strife and the frequent intra-family feuds that took place within the town. In many cases these houses still have doorways positioned high above the ground; when the main entrance had to be barred in an emergency, access could be gained by means of a ladder which was then drawn up. The house-towers of the Buonparenti family lie on opposite sides of an important crossroads and delimit the main square. They are joined by a brick archway and once had an important strategic function as part of the original city walls. In 1207 the commune passed a law limiting private towers to a height of 30 *braccia* (cubits).

One of Volterra's peculiarities are the so-called "children's windows": small openings set into the wall below the larger windows to enable children to look out without falling.

Although they have long since been bricked up, the outlines of these windows can still be seen on house façades in the town.

Teatro Romano

Excavations in the 1950s between the medieval and ancient city walls revealed the ruins of a temple dedicated to the goddess Bona, as well as a theater and a bathhouse. During the Augustan period at the end of the 1st century B.C. Volterra was presented with a theater by the Caecina, a prominent local Etruscan family. The steeply raked, semi-circular seating was built directly into the hill; the 19 rows of stone benches were reached by radial stairways and a roofed corridor which can still be made out today. At the foot of these benches was the semi-circular "orchestra" where high-ranking spectators would sit, while a trench separated the audience from the raised stage and stage wall (reconstructed today).

The bathhouse which lies directly to the rear was laid out in the first half of the 4th century A.D. from material taken from the then ruined theater. Still visible are the changing room, the *frigidarium* or cold room, the *tepidarium* or steam bath, and the *caldarium* or sauna.

Museo Etrusco Guarnacci

The palace of Monsignore Mario Guarnacci contains one of the greatest assemblages of Etruscan art in Italy. It includes artifacts from the prehistoric era up to Roman times, and its collection of 600 Etruscan cinerary urns is world famous.

The museum began with a donation by Canon Pietro Franceschini in 1732, at the very outset of Etruscan research in Italy. The collector and researcher Mario Guarnacci, who did much to draw the world's attention to the quality and significance of Etruscan art, then bequeathed his own extensive collection to the city in 1761. Since that time the collection has been expanded by the addition of excavated artifacts, gifts and new purchases. The museum's layout has been designed to retain the original collection while providing the visitor with a thematic and chronological journey from the "Villanova" period through the various stages of Etruscan culture to works from the Roman era.

Statuette of a youth, the so-called *Ombra della Sera*, 3rd century B.C.
Bronze, c. 60 cm.

The thin, attenuated bronze figures which were interred in central Etrurian graves seem both fascinating and mysterious to the modern observer.

This 24 inch (60 cm) statuette of a youth has been in the Guarnacci collection since the 18th century and is from Volterra. The poet Gabriele d'Annunzio gave it the apt title of *ombra della sera* or "Evening Shadow." Its proportions do indeed seem like a shadow lengthened by the evening sun and the figure itself is strongly reminiscent of an abstract piece of modern art. Only its head, feet and rudimentary genitals have been modeled as such. Similar figures, thought to represent warriors or priests, were dedicated as requests to the gods or as votive offerings, but it is unclear whether this figure is indicative of a particular cult. The unconventional hairstyle points to the influence of Greek portraiture in the 3rd century B.C.

Urn, *The Death of Actaeon*, 2nd century B.C.

The men and women depicted reclining on the lids of funeral urns are not portraits of the deceased but prefabricated types which were produced in large numbers with only slight variations. The same applies to the images on the urns themselves, which are mostly well-known scenes from Greek or local mythology. They generally record a fatal struggle or a similarly portentous event.

The stone chest shown here depicts a scene popular in funerary sculpture: the hunter Actaeon, who had been taught his skills by the centaurs, is discovered secretly observing the goddess Artemis bathing with her nymphs. The enraged goddess punishes him by transforming him into a stag, and Actaeon is then torn apart by his own dogs who no longer recognize him.

The elegantly attired and heavily jeweled lady on the lid belonged to the Etruscan upper classes. Her hair is skillfully arranged and garlanded, and a fine veil falls to her shoulders. In her right hand she holds a *patera*, the vessel used for catching the blood of a sacrificial animal. Her name is engraved in Etruscan letters on the leading edge of the lid.

Lid of an urn, Urna degli Sposi, 1st century B.C.
Terracotta

This famous urn lid from Volterra shows a married couple reclining in the customary position on the *kline*, or couch. Relaxed and at ease, they are in complete harmony with one another.

The quite disproportionate relationship between the head and body is typical, and the artist has emphasized the life-like expression of their postures. The execution of their convincingly realistic faces and of their clothing is an intriguing aspect of the final phase of Etruscan art at the beginning of the 1st century B.C., and indicates enormous technical virtuosity. These stylistic features are brought out by the use of terracotta, a material that allows for the creation of precise detail through the

application of a modeling stick. The theme – a banqueting couple – symbolizes the value of family ties. The choice of material testifies to the wish of the client to be immortalized in an "antique" form. The Etruscan aristocracy surrounded themselves with such nostalgic recreations of ancient traditions in the wake of Sulla's siege – this was an event that spelled the dissolution of the Etruscan city league and then its imminent integration into the Roman state.

The style of the Etruscan reclining figure exerted enormous influence on the sculpture of succeeding epochs. The forms of Classical Roman tombs, as well as the sculpture of the proto-Renaissance and the Renaissance proper, often display a detailed knowledge and application of Etruscan models.

Piazza dei Priori

The Piazza dei Priori was the focus of political power in medieval Volterra. Lined with both private and public palaces, this square is today one of the finest examples from this era in all of Tuscany.

In their attempts to achieve communal independence at the beginning of the 13th century the citizens of Volterra decided to stop holding council meetings in the cathedral, and in 1208 they began to build the Palazzo dei Priori or prior's palace (left of the picture). The Palazzo is the oldest communal palace in Tuscany and may have served as the model for the Palazzo Vecchio in Florence. Its history can be read in the heraldic devices adorning the façade on the first floor in which the city's leaders, from the priors to the Florentine commanders, left their mark.

This monumental building rises up four stories. Wooden galleries once ran around the building and the putlog holes and consoles for these structures can still clearly be seen. The rounded battlements as well as the tabernacle structure of the tower are 19th-century contributions.

The eastern side of the square is dominated by the Palazzo Pretorio with the Torre del Podestà (to the right in the picture). From 1224 the commune began to acquire the private buildings to the left and right of the tower in order to convert them into the official seat of the *podestà*, the city's chief magistrate.

Duomo S. Maria Assunta

The episcopal church of Santa Maria was consecrated in 1120. It was extended in 1254 and extensively refurbished in the 14th century. In the course of this work the façade was also modified.

The basilica consists of a nave and two aisles. Its plain two-story external wall was probably originally intended to be more richly ornamented. The cathedral architects seem, however, to have reverted to more traditional forms: their adoption of a blind gallery on the pediment as well as the frieze of arches under the pitched roof echo Romanesque forms as they were practiced in Pisa. Nevertheless, the building's round windows and oculi create the impression of a heterogeneous mixture. On the first floor the central axis is emphasized by a beautiful marble portal from 1254. The tympanum features simple but effective encrustation with antique ornaments. The cathedral's 15th-century bell tower has three horizontal rows of double-arched biforate windows.

The Interior

Originally decorated with frescoes, the walls of the interior were painted in the 19th century to resemble strips of marble. In the 16th century the plain Romanesque stone pillars were clad in marbled plaster. The coffered ceiling with its carved wood in paint and gilt is from the same era, as are the majority of the altarpieces in the aisles which mostly feature scenes from the life of the Virgin Mary.

Mariotto Albertinelli (1474–1515), *Annunciation*, c. 1498
Oil on wood

The retable on the second altar in the north wall, on the other hand, is from as early as the 15th century. This depiction of the *Annunciation* is from the studio of the Florentine Renaissance painter Mariotto Albertinelli and was a cooperative effort between Albertinelli and his colleague Fra Bartolomeo della Porta. The painting is fascinating for the Flemish-influenced, enameled coloring of the figures and its precise perspectival composition. Mary is seen reacting to the angel's message with a raised hand and an

expression of questioning bewilderment. The doorway in the center draws the viewer's eye into a beautiful Tuscan landscape in the background.

Albertinelli later abandoned painting to devote himself to "the only true art – cooking," as he put it. He entertained his artistic colleagues in a tavern called *Da Pennello* (The Brush) which he opened in the heart of Florence's old town and which is still there today.

Deposition, 13th century
Wood (partly colored and gilted)

Volterra's cathedral has one of the few remaining large wooden sculptures from the Italian Middle Ages in the form of the *Deposition*, a work by a Pisan artist. In accordance with the tradition concerning triumphal crucifixion groups, Mary and St. John the Evangelist stand on both sides of the cross. Further figures complete the iconography of the deposition scene: Joseph of Arimathea is depicted placing his arm around the body of Christ to support it, and Nicodemus is seen bending down to loosen the nails in Christ's feet with a large pair of pliers.

The figures appear somewhat awkward and their actions unconvincing, though some of these inconsistencies may be due

to an over-enthusiastic application of paint and gilt by later restorers. Generally, however, this artist from the *duecento* seems to oscillate between Romanesque and Gothic influences, as well as between the different requirements of large- and small-scale sculpture.

The cathedral's pulpit is one of a series of great Romanesque pulpits in Tuscany; its rectangular body is supported by four granite columns resting on lions and mythical creatures who are depicted devouring men and other animals.

Pulpit, 12th century
Marble

The square relief panels on the sides show scenes from both the Old and New Testaments: the Annunciation, the Visitation, the Sacrifice of Isaac, and the Last Supper. They are attributed to an artist from the school of the sculptor Guglielmus, who was active in Pisa and who had a great influence on Tuscan Romanesque sculpture from the mid-12th century. The present structure of the pulpit derives from 1584 when, after having been dismantled for a long period, the individual pieces were incorrectly rejoined.

The Last Supper
(Detail from the pulpit)

The depiction of the *Last Supper* shows a table set for the disciples. At the head of the table John, rests his head on the shoulder of his Lord while Judas kneels at the feet; as a mark of his treachery he is shown separated from the other disciples. The devil in the form of a winged, serpentine creature snaps at Judas's heels.

has started and ended within the external walls, giving the building its distinctive appearance. The octagonal, two-story structure is very impressive in its simplicity. The entire building is made from *panchina*, the favorite local stone of the Volterrans. Only the entrance side has been decorated by using uniform strips of white and green – a color scheme that may have been intended for the whole church when it was being renovated in the late 13th century.

The architrave of this fine portal with its splayed embrasure is furnished with a series of sculptures: along with the face of Christ there are the heads of Mary, Salome, and 11 apostles (Judas is missing).

In the interior is a stoup supported on a compound column which in the Middle Ages was made from a "cippo," the stela from an Etruscan tomb. The original font by Andrea Sansovino from 1502 stands on the right of the altar, while the great font in the center dates from the 18th century.

Battistero San Giovanni

This late Romanesque baptistery was provided with its cloister vault in the 16th century. Since that time the arc of the roof

Porta all' Arco

The Porta all' Arco is the sole surviving city gate from the $^1/_4$-mile (7-km) Etruscan wall, a defensive structure that enclosed five times as much land as its medieval equivalent. It was only in the south of the city that later fortifications followed the line of the ancient wall, which is why the Porta all' Arco was integrated into the medieval complex. This imposing monument has been the town's main entrance from the south since it was first built some 2,400 years ago.

The masonry of massive ashlar blocks which has been eroded by the salt-laden sea winds corresponds to that of the Etruscan complex from the 4th century B.C. An impression of its original appearance is provided on an urn in the Guarnacci Museum. The tuffstone arch was built without the use of mortar and was added 100 years after the wall was built, replacing an earlier covering of wood. It is decorated with three heads which are now so severely weathered that they are almost unrecognizable. They may represent Jupiter and the Dioscuri (Castor and Pollux), or the highest gods in the Etruscan pantheon, Tinia, Uni, and Menvra, who equated to the Capitoline gods of Jupiter, Juno, and Minerva, and who were the city's guardians. The barrel vault of the entranceway was built at the same time as the arch. Both of these features have a keystone arch.

Museo Civico in the Palazzo Minucci–Solaini

The elegant Renaissance palace of Minucci–Solaini houses the Museo Civico with its important collection of Tuscan paintings from the 15th and 16th centuries.

Luca Signorelli, (c. 1450–1523)
Annunciation **(and detail), 1491**
Tempera on wood
(282 × 205 cm)

In the *Annunciation* from 1491 by Luca Signorelli, an artist from Cortona, the picture space is divided in two by the perspectival device of a row of columns. Mary is shown shrinking from the sudden appearance of the angel; the position of her body, which is turned half to the side, expresses confusion and something of the fear which first grips her at the sight of the heavenly messenger. The gestures of the two figures, particularly that of the angel, seem almost theatrical. Signorelli's implied shadows and his gentle use of light are reminiscent of Flemish painting and contrast with the luminous purple sky full of brightly colored clouds. This marked sensibility to

the effects of light and lyrical depiction of detail are evidence of the expressiveness and painterly skill of Signorelli's work in the 1490s.

(Illustration following page)
Rosso Fiorentino (1494–1540),
Deposition, **1521**
Tempera on wood
(335 × 198 cm)

The high point of the picture gallery is a major work of Florentine early Mannerism – the *Deposition* painted by the artist Giovanni Battista Rosso. Also known as Rosso Fiorentino, this painter was born in Florence in 1494 and died in Fontainebleau in 1540.

The Cross and a scaffold formed by three ladders can be seen in a flat landscape beneath a glowering sky. The contours and gestures of the helpers and grieving figures complement and relate to one another in a complex circuit of emotion: the figure of Mary Magdalene collapsed at the foot of the cross; the men around Christ with their dramatically extended limbs; and the distressed and disbelieving posture of Mary and, especially, John.

This interlinking of gesture is characteristic of Rosso Fiorentino's Mannerist style. He invests this rather formal compositional

principle with great expressiveness by means of his harsh coloration and his awkward, angular forms. Like their gestures the figures' faces are also steeped in very turbulent emotions: the inner grief and the impotent pain of Mary and of John are brashly contrasted with the distorted, gaping faces of the pointing men on the ladders. The figure clad in red with a blue turban bends violently over the transverse beam of the cross while his counterpart, clad in orange and black, points at Christ and seems to be on the verge of crying out. Fiorentino worked for just one year in Volterra after which he returned once again to Florence. Ten years later he was called to the French court in Fontainebleau, where he was to work until his death.

A Remarkable Stone – Alabaster from Volterra

Ruth Strasser

Looked at from a chemical point of view, alabaster is merely a hydrated calcium sulfate with the formula $CaSO_4$ $2H_2O$. Over a period of millions of years it crystallized out of sea water and was then trapped under other layers of rock. Alabaster's chemical formula says little about this soft, finely crystalline material, however. The Etruscans were familiar with alabaster from the slim, narrow-necked jars of salve imported from Egypt and which were called *alabastron* by the Greeks. By mining alabaster in the region around Volterra the Etruscans began to work the material themselves, and eventually developed a flourishing art in alabaster products. The comparatively soft stone required tools little different from those used to work wood, and with great skill the material was turned into sculptures, urns, vases, and bowls. While cheap and inferior varieties of artificial alabaster are made from compressed dust and cement and are often brightly colored, natural alabaster is found in milky white, green, yellow, reddish-orange, and amber tones. The stone is sometimes veined and has different levels of transparency. The most translucent alabaster was also the purest and most expensive and was preferred for making lamps and the windows of churches and mausoleums.

While marble conveys the impression of icy smoothness and permanence and is therefore preferred for memorials and tombs, the silky

Alabaster workshop

matte shimmer of alabaster gives it a warm, life-giving, sensual radiance. With their lack of hard edges the contours of alabaster objects seem to fade and merge into their surroundings, a characteristic indicated by the common use of metaphors such "alabaster shoulders" and "alabaster skin." Like the human body, alabaster ages and cannot retain a consistent appearance like marble because it weathers to a much greater degree. Exposure to sunlight, water, and extremes of temperature all cause the stone to yellow.

Appendices

Elements of Architectural Form

Religious buildings

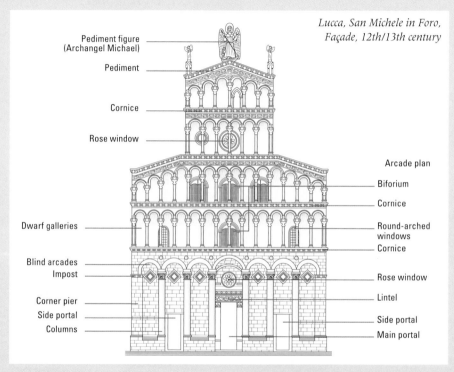

Lucca, San Michele in Foro, Façade, 12th/13th century

Pediment figure (Archangel Michael)

Pediment

Cornice

Rose window

Arcade plan

Biforium

Cornice

Dwarf galleries

Round-arched windows

Cornice

Blind arcades

Impost

Rose window

Corner pier

Lintel

Side portal

Side portal

Columns

Main portal

Loggia façade

Several cathedrals and churches in Pisa, Lucca and Arezzo – such as San Michele in Foro in Lucca – are decorated with magnificent loggia façades featuring horizontally arranged rows of arches. The high walls of the first floor are ornamented with blind arcades on top of which are four covered wall-passages in the form of colonnaded galleries. Ornate decorations on the columns and walls heighten the filigree appearance of this type of architecture which enshrouds the building like a veil.

Encrusted façade

The fragmentary façade of the Badia in Fiesole is an important structure from the Tuscan Proto-Renaissance of the 11th and 12th centuries and an excellent example of therichly patterned encrusted style. The wall is covered with thin slabs of brightly colored Carrara marble and darker serpentine (*Verde di Prato*). The basic geometrical forms of the walls are in harmony with their rigorous arrangment into pillars, round arches and cornices, while the chevrons and finer ornamentation serve to enhance the overall architectural appearance.

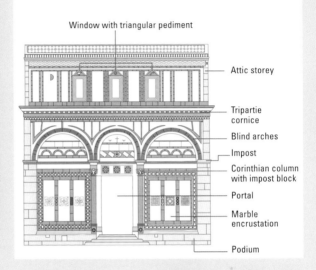

Façade of the Badia Fiesolana, 12th century

Window with triangular pediment

Attic storey

Tripartie cornice

Blind arches

Impost

Corinthian column with impost block

Portal

Marble encrustation

Podium

Elevation

The external walls of the cathedral at Pisa are also densely structured. The blind arcades of the first floor frame the round-arched windows of the aisles, above which slender pillars divide the surface of the wall into both broad and narrow bays. Another blind arcade of pillars and arches appears in the clerestory over the lean-to roof of the aisle.

Pisa, elevation of the south side of the cathedral, 12th century

Exterior of the aisle

Round-arched window

Saddle-back roof

Lean-to-roof over side aisle

Corner pillar

Clerestory with blind arcades

Glazed wall divided by pillars

Round-arched windows

Ground floor with blind arcades

Groundplans

Tuscan churches were often built on the pattern of the early Christian basilica with a nave and two aisles. The nave ended in a semi-circular apse, and occasionally the aisles were also lined with small apses. The elevated walls of the nave rested on a series of pillars or piers which was either vaulted or supported an open roof truss over the clerestory.

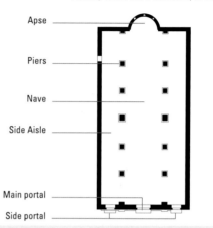

Lucca, San Pietro Somaldi, c. 1200

Apse

Piers

Nave

Side Aisle

Main portal

Side portal

From the 13th century the Dominican and Franciscan orders engaged in a great deal of construction work in the cities of Tuscany. The spacious churches of these mendicant orders could either have a single nave or additional aisles and featured both vaulted roofs and open trusses; these structures generally lacked transepts or a tower. With its rectangular choir chapel ending in a flat wall and smaller transept chapels the Franciscan church in Siena – like other monastery churches in Tuscany – borrowed its design from the Cistercian architecture of France.

Siena, San Francesco, begun 1326

Window

Rectangular choir chapel with flat wall

Chapels

Transept

Window

Nave

Portal

Elevations

The nave wall of a basilica is characterized by a regular series of relatively low arches. The aisle arcades in San Michele in Lucca consist of pillars and semi-circular arches. A cornice running the length of the nave separates the first floor from the clerestory which is pierced by narrow round-headed windows. The roof beams rest on the wall coping.

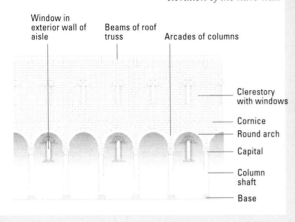

Lucca, San Michele in Foro, elevation of the nave wall

Window in exterior wall of aisle

Beams of roof truss

Arcades of columns

Clerestory with windows

Cornice

Round arch

Capital

Column shaft

Base

In contrast to the traditional basilica, the space of the vaulted Dominican church of Santa Maria Novella in Florence is essentially defined by the tall, broad arches separating the nave from the aisles. The bays of the nave correspond to the width of a pointed arch over which is a low clerestory bay with a small circular window. This peculiarly Tuscan design blurs the boundaries between the nave and the aisles and can also be found in the cathedrals of Florence and Arezzo.

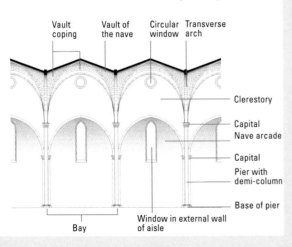

Florence, Santa Maria Novella, begun 1246, elevation of two bays in the nave

Vault coping

Vault of the nave

Circular window

Transverse arch

Clerestory

Capital
Nave arcade

Capital

Pier with demi-column

Base of pier

Bay

Window in external wall of aisle

Secular Buildings

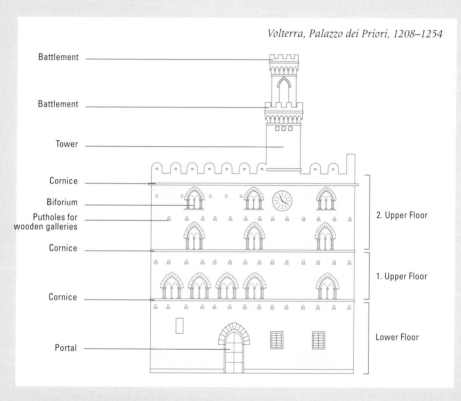

Volterra, Palazzo dei Priori, 1208–1254

Battlement

Battlement

Tower

Cornice

Biforium

Putholes for wooden galleries

Cornice

Cornice

Portal

2. Upper Floor

1. Upper Floor

Lower Floor

Volterra's city hall with its compact structure and battlemented tower served as a model for Florence's Palazzo Vecchio and other Tuscan public halls. Originally the exterior of the building was surrounded by wooden galleries whose putholes can still be seen in the façade. The defensive character of the building was also applied to medieval residences (Siena, Palazzo Tolomei); as late as the 15th century this style was still being used for the Medici villas in Caffaggiolo and Careggi.

Façades

The façades of Tuscan city palaces in the Renaissance were characterized by vertical window axes, the use of cornices to mark clear divisions between the floors, as well as the play of light and shade from the rusticated masonry (Lat. *rusticum*, "rustic, humble"). This kind of masonry can be seen in the lower floor of the Palazzo Gondi in Florence, whose ashlar blocks feature smooth, curved surfaces. The blocks in the 1st upper floor (the *piano nobile*), on the other hand, are

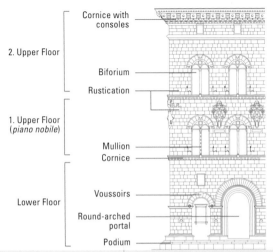

Siena, Palazzo Piccolomini, 1460 – 1495

- Cornice with consoles
- 2. Upper Floor
- Biforium
- Rustication
- 1. Upper Floor (*piano nobile*)
- Mullion
- Cornice
- Voussoirs
- Lower Floor
- Round-arched portal
- Podium

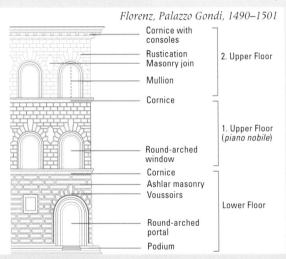

Florenz, Palazzo Gondi, 1490–1501

- Cornice with consoles
- Rustication
- Masonry join
- 2. Upper Floor
- Mullion
- Cornice
- 1. Upper Floor (*piano nobile*)
- Round-arched window
- Cornice
- Ashlar masonry
- Voussoirs
- Lower Floor
- Round-arched portal
- Podium

flat with chamfered edges while the joints of the 2nd upper floor are reduced to fine lines. While the rusticated masonry of the Palazzo Gondi shows considerable variation, the entire exterior of the Palazzo Piccolomini in Siena is covered with a uniform rusticated cladding. Frequently these palaces have a podium bench running around the outside of the building at ground level; a good example of this is the Palazzo Ruccellai in Florence.

Loggias

One of the best-known loggias in Tuscany was built by Filippo Brunelleschi for the Foundlings' Hospital on the Piazza of the Florentine church of Santissima Annunziata. The architect placed a 71-m (233 ft.) long arcade of columns, vaults and round-headed arches over a stepped podium; glazed terracotta *tondi* from the della Robbia workshop were placed between the arches. On the floor above are windows arranged along a short pedestal, their height exaggerated by the use of triangular pediments. The effect the building had within the urban fabric was heightened when another arcade was built on the opposite side of the piazza in the 16th century.

Portals and Windows

Tuscan portals and windows are characterized by a great diversity of form. The most common are portals with a lintel and the wall panel above enclosed by round arches; also frequently found is the so-called Sienese arch with a flattened segmental arch surmounted by a pointed arch. Biforate windows with their two round arches supported by columns and crowned by a further round arch are of medieval origin, but they continued to be popular long after. Biforate windows with a lintel under the arches or with a mullion and transom are evidence of the Renaissance tendency to differentiate between load-bearing and non load-bearing elements in the interests of a strictly tectonic design.

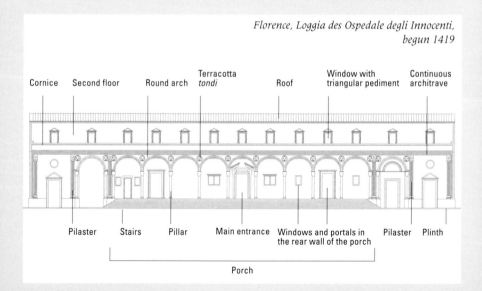

Florence, Loggia des Ospedale degli Innocenti, begun 1419

Cornice · Second floor · Round arch · Terracotta *tondi* · Roof · Window with triangular pediment · Continuous architrave

Pilaster · Stairs · Pillar · Main entrance · Windows and portals in the rear wall of the porch · Pilaster · Plinth

Porch

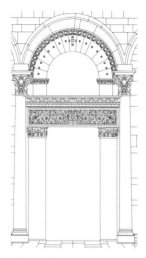

*Pisa, cathedral, portal
12th century*

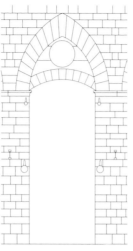

*Siena, Portal of the Palazzo
Grottanelli (Sienese arch),
13th century*

*Florence, Palazzo Vescovile,
Biforate window, 12th century*

*Florence, Palazzo Rucellai,
Biforium with lintel,
1446–1451*

*Florence, Palazzo Vecchio,
Biforiumwith trefoils, after
1299*

*Siena, Palazzo Piccolomini,
Biforium with lintel, transom
and mullion 1459–1462*

Glossary

Acanthus (Lat. *acanthus*; Gk. akantha, "thorn") A type of thistle with large, jagged leaves slightly curled at the ends; a member of the bear's-breech family, it is common throughout the Mediterranean. In stylized form the acanthus has been used as an ornamental motif since antiquity.

Aedicule (Lat. *aediculum* "miniature house"). A niche, window or portal framed by columns, pillars, or pilasters which support an entablature and a triangular or segmental pediment.

Stonework · Sinopia · Preliminary sketch · Painted layer

Al fresco, construction plan of frescoes (detail), Passion Cycle, c. 1330–1340, Protestant church, Waltensburg

Al fresco see Fresco (It. "fresh"). Fresco; a mural painted on fresh plaster as opposed to fresco secco.

Allegory (Gk. *allegoria*, from *allegorein*, "to say something differently"). Pictorial representation of abstract concepts or literary themes. The main techniques are personification; the grouping of figures and objects together in significant scenes; and the use of symbols. Allegory was particularly popular in the 16th and 17th centuries; in the 19th century allegorical pictures were often used both on buildings and on monuments.

Al secco (It. "dry"). A technique for painting murals on dry plaster in contrast to true fresco or *buon affresco*.

Altar (Lat. *alta ara*, "high altar") Sign of the presence of God; refers especially to the place where the sacrament is celebrated. The altarpiece and the antependium provide valuable information on how a specific altar is to be symbolically interpreted. The most common type of altar is the table altar which consists of supports (Lat. *stipes*), a base slab (Lat. *crepido*) and an upper slab (Lat. *mensa*). Three other types also occur: the chest altar has a hollow space below the *mensa* which is accessible from the outside and used to store church relics or items for the altar. The block altar has, as the name suggests, a solid block below the mensa and its front is decorated with tracery or architectural ornament. The sarcophagus altar derives its name from the tomb housed below the altar slab. Altars are either permanent structures or portable, in which case their liturgical function is not confined to one location. The main altar generally stands in front of or in the choir apse, which is oriented to the east. Other altars can often be found in side apses and chapels or in the crypt.

Altarpiece (Lat. *altare*, "sacrificial table") Image which often decorated altars in the Middle Ages. At first made of gold or sculpted, they were later more frequently painted images. The altarpiece consist of a single picture or several panels; they were often placed above and to the rear of the altar or, in the case of the retable, at the back of an altar.

Ambo (Gk. *ambon*, "raised rim") In early Christian and medieval churches a raised podium surrounded by a balustrade from which the Epistles and Gospels were read. Often connected to the choir screen, the ambo developed during the late Middle Ages into a more independent form of the pulpit. Today even simple lecterns are referred to as the ambo, while the place where the scriptures are actually read is indicated by being draped in a cloth in liturgical colors.

Amphitheater (Gk. *amphitheatron* from amphi "on both sides, surrounding" and *theatron* "theater") Roman open-air theater based on an elliptical ground plan and surrounded by tiers of seats; used mainly for gladiatorial contests.

Annunciation In the Gospel according to Luke (1:26–38) the message conveyed by the archangel Gabriel

Architrave, Abbazia S. Antimo

to Mary that she had been chosen to conceive and give birth to Jesus. In the Roman Catholic Church the archangel's greeting became the prayer *Ave Maria*. During the Middle Ages and Renaissance, the depiction of the Annunciation became one of the most widespread themes of European art.

Antependium (Lat. "curtain") Veil or hanging for the lower part of the altar. From the 4th/5th centuries richly woven textiles were used which covered all four sides; in the 9th century it became usual to erect a metal panel on the front of the altar. The themes of the antependium are connected with the religious symbolism represented by the altar.

Antiquity (Fr. *antique* "ancient"; from Lat. *antiquus* "old"), The antique era specifically refers to the ancient Greek and Roman world. It began with the early Greek migrations of the 2nd millennium B.C. and ended in the West in A.D. 476 when the Emperor Romulus Augustus was deposed. In the East the era came to an end when the Platonic Academy was closed by the Emperor Justinian (A.D. 482–565).

Apostles (Gk. *apostolos*, "messenger") The 12 disciples selected by Jesus from the mass of his followers to witness his works and to preach the gospels. After Christ's death they then became highly regarded in the early Christian community. Their main mission was to spread his word and teaching, and it is through the practice of this office that they became Christ's successors.

Apse (Gk. *hapsis*, "arch, volt") Vaulted structure, often with an altar, erected on a semi-circular or polygonal ground plan and roofed over by a half-dome. If constructed at the end of a choir in a church it is also known as an exedra. Smaller apses can often be found in the ambulatory, the transepts, or the aisles.

Aqueduct (Lat. *aquaeductus*, "water channel"; from *aqua*, "water" and *ducere* "to lead") System for carrying water invented by the Romans. Aqueducts generally took the form of arched bridges several stories high, which transported water in channels over long distances by means of gravity.

Arabesque (Fr. *Arabesque*, "Arabic ornamentation"; It. *Arabesco*, "Arabic"), decoration consisting of leaves and vines that is very similar to plant models. It has been known since Hellenistic art and in Classical times was used to decorate pilasters and friezes. It was once more used on a larger scale during the Italian Early Renaissance, thus gaining entrance to later periods in Western art.

Arcade (from Lat. *arcus*, "arch") A series of arches carried on columns or piers at the side of a structure.

Arch Curved structure which in stone buildings provides the only way of spanning larger distances in order to bear a load or transfer thrust to pillars or columns. Distinctions are made between authentic and inauthentic arches depending on type of bond used in the masonry. The highest point of the arch with its keystone is the crown. The "rise" is the name given to the vertical distance between the crown and the line formed by the upper surface of the impost (the course of stonework or brick from which the arch springs). The bottom surface of an arch is called the intrados while the outer face is called the extrados.

Architrave (Gk. *archein*, "to begin, to rule" and Lat. trabs "beam") Main load-bearing beam which rests on upright supports, e.g. columns. Can be divided into fascia, usually as three stepped recesses.

Archivolt (It. *archivolto*, "foremost arch") The decorated or shaped extrados of an arch; common in antiquity and during the Romanesque and Renaissance periods. In Gothic architecture the archivolts of the portals are richly sculpted, often featuring figurative depictions.

Atlas (Lat.; plural *atlantes*) Term derived from the Greek mythological figure of Atlas, son of the Titans, whom Zeus condemned to hold up the pillars of the heavens. In architecture and sculpture atlantes are over-sized male figures that support vaults or entablatures on their heads, shoulders or hands. Various interpretations can be given to atlantes; they often appear as personified giants, prisoners, or blasphemous men but occasionally also as biblical figures. In the Baroque age they were transformed into decorative supporting elements. The Roman term *telamon* is also used for atlantes.

Attic (From Lat. *atticus*) A small story, often covering the roof, positioned over the entablature of an architectural order. In the Baroque era the term meant a half-story divided by windows.

Attribute (Lat. *attributum*, "assigned") Object or characteristic symbol given to a person to identify them; usually connected with an essential element of their lives.

Augustinians Medieval mendicant order, founded in 1256 according to the teachings of St. Augustine (A.D. 354–430), an early Church Father. The order expanded in the 14th and 15th centuries through the unification of churches or congregations. Many supporters of the early Reformation – itself set in motion by the Augustinian monk Martin Luther (1483–1546) – joined the movement under the influence of Renaissance humanism. The Augustinians took on several of the important functions of an education system.

Battisterio S. Giovanni, schematic reconstruction of the first baptismal font of Brunelleschi

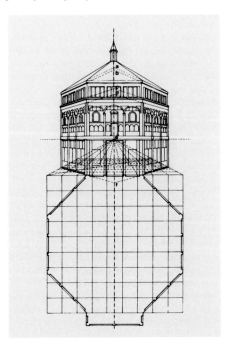

Baldachin (It. *baldacchino*) Textile canopy over a throne or bed; a portable canopy supported by poles and used in processions; in architecture, a richly decorated canopy in wood or stone over a throne, bishop's seat, altar, catafalque, pulpit, or statue. The name comes from the costly silk fabrics worked in gold thread from Baghdad (It. *Baldacco*) which were used to make the first such canopies in Italy.

Baluster (Fr. *balustre*, It. *balaustro*; Med. Lat. *balaustion*) Small, squat pillar of wood or stone supporting a balustrade or banister. The term is derived from the baluster's resemblance to the flowers of the wild pomegranate (Gk. *balaustion*).

Balustrade (It. balaustrata) A railing formed from several balusters. Used especially in the Renaissance and Baroque for banisters, balconies, terraces and the railings of roofs.

Baptistery (Lat.; Gk. *baptisterion*, "bathing-place") A freestanding, generally octagonal and centrally planned structure which was often built on the western side of a diocesan church. Baptisteries were dedicated to St. John the Baptist by virtue of their function as a baptismal church.

Baroque (from Port. *barocco*, "small stone, misshapen") European art movement extending roughly from the end of Mannerism (c. 1590) to the beginning of the Rococo (c. 1725) with a characteristic tendency to the extravagant, elaborate and florid. Along with religious and mythological themes, Baroque art saw the appearance of allegory (the depiction of abstract concepts and themes), genre painting, and landscapes. In painting, a Classical and idealizing strand coexisted with realism; representational techniques were similarly diverse and ranged from the depiction of completely artificial worlds, including the use of optical illusions, through to an exaggerated Naturalism. The term was originally used in the craft of goldsmithing, where a *barocco* was an irregularly shaped pearl.

Base (Gk. "step, walk, foundation," then "walked-on floor; *banein*, "walk"), in architecture the projecting and usually shaped bottom course of a column or pillar which spreads the weight of the column onto a larger surface and forms a point of transition to the plinth; in sculpture, the plinth that a statue or relief stands on.

Basilica (Gk. *basilike stoa*, "royal hall") Term derived from the official building of a Greek magistrate, the Archon Basileus. In antiquity it denoted a roofed building with a double colonnade used for law courts, assemblies and markets. In the Christian era it meant a characteristic type of church building with a high nave and either two or four lower aisles, with a ground plan oriented towards the east. In addition, basilicas had windows on the elevated walls (clerestory) where the roof of the aisle joined the nave wall. The basilican form changed markedly from the 4th century onwards. The complex was enlarged by the addition of transepts, often with terminal apses and later with choirs. In the interior, the walls separating the nave from the aisles were opened up by arcades supported by columns, piers, or an alternating mixture of the two. Galleries could be set over the vaults of the aisles, while between the gallery and the clerestory or between arcade and clerestory there might also be a triforium. In general, the basilica has determined the shape of large churches in the West since the 4th century. In the late Gothic era the basilica was momentarily displaced by the hall church and in the Baroque period by the centrally planned church.

Battlement The breastwork on top of city walls; also the fortified passageways and protective walls of castles. Later, battlements were used purely as a decorative device for crowning walls. Battlements may take several forms: the swallowtailed merlon had a V-shaped gap in the center on which to rest and fire a weapon; the stepped parapet had a stair-like structure and was built on slopes. Battlements with half-rounded merlons in the shape of a shield (round-arched battlement) were older and had already been used by Egyptian architects. The Renaissance saw the construction of battlements whose crenellations consisted of concave-convex arches while in roof battlements the upper section is often pitched.

Benedictines Oldest order of Western monks, founded in Monte Cassino c. A.D. 529 by St. Benedict of Nursia (c. 480–547). The Benedictine rules formed the basis of Western monasticism. The main task of the order was to cultivate liturgy and prayer, and this was supplemented by scholarly, artistic, and physical labor. Prayer and work became fundamental aspects of life, bound together in the expression *ora et labora*. After the destruction of Monte Cassino, the Benedictine order spread from Rome to England and into the Franko-Carolingian empire. Benedict of Aniane (750–821) and the monastery of Cluny, which was founded in 910, reinvigorated the order. The Benedictines' rules fundamentally determined the layout of their monasteries. St. Gall (c. 820) is the first example of fully fledged Benedictine monastic architecture.

Biforate window (Lat. *biforis*, "double-winged") Double window, whose elements are separated by a central column but bound into an optical whole by means of a surmounting double arch.

Bishopric Term used to describe the legal and administrative area over which a bishop exercises sovereign power (synonym: diocese). The establishment, alteration, and dissolution of a Roman Catholic bishopric is a privilege of the Apostolic See. As a general rule, several bishoprics combine to form an ecclesiastical province.

Schematic drawing of the campanile by Giotto di Bondone in Florence

Blind arch A flat arch built into a generally closed wall surface and used as an organizational element in a building's architecture; only rarely do blind arches have a load-bearing function. A regular series of blind arches results in a blind arcade. Arcades which are not completely independent of a wall are called blind galleries, and they too are often used purely for ornamental purposes.

Camaldolites Benedictine order of hermits founded c. 1000 by St. Romuald of Ravenna (c. 952–1027) and named after the hermit colony near Camaldoli in Tuscany.

Campanile (It. *campana*, "bell") The freestanding bell tower of an Italian church. Its isolated position was retained in Renaissance architecture but it rarely appears as a building north of the Alps.

Candelabra (Fr. *candélavre*; from Lat. *candela*, "candle") Extravagant, richly decorated candlestick or lampholder.

Capital (Lat. *capitulum*, "little head") The crowning section of a column or pillar which mediates between the supporting structure and its load. The capital essentially consists of the astragal, the main body, and the square slab of the abacus at the top. In antiquity there were four forms: Doric, Ionic, Corinthian, Composite. During the Middle Ages and the Renaissance there arose various types of capital decorated with foliage, flowers or figurative depictions. The Doric capital was completely unadorned and consisted of a simple cushion (the echinus) crowned by the abacus. The Ionic capital is characterized by the scrolled volutes on both sides and a cushion-like member decorated with egg and dart molding. The Corinthian capital is decorated with carved foliage; a garland of three overlapping acanthus leaves is complemented in the corners by two diagonally projecting volutes. The Roman Composite capital has the volutes and echinus of the Ionic order over the Corinthian capital's basket of acanthus leaves. There is a close relationship between the capitals of the Tuscan and Doric order; the most obvious difference is that the astragal of the Tuscan capital is below the echinus. Over time new forms developed alongside these classical orders. The most important are the cushion, or block, and mushroom capitals; the frustum, trapezoid, and pyramid capitals as well as the basket capital. In the Romanesque period the protomai capital, in which the main body of the capital was adorned with sculpted figures, was in common usage. Gothic architecture is marked by its use of richly ornamented capitals with designs of leaves and other foliage. Later, capitals became reduced to their original goblet shape (bell capital); while in the Renaissance and Baroque eras antique forms were once again resurrected.

Cardinal virtues (L. Lat. *cardinalis* "to stand at the hinge") Four basic virtues which Christian ethics adopted from Plato (427–347 B.C.). They were: *temperamentia* (temperance), *fortitudo* (fortitude), *prudentia* (prudence) and *justitia* (justice). Gregory the Great (A.D. 540–604) added the three divine or theological virtues of *fides* (faith), *caritas* (love) and *spes* (hope). In the late Middle Ages this group of seven formed the basis for a still further expansion of the Christian system of virtue.

Cathedral (Gk. *kathedra*, "chair") Also known as episcopal church or minster, a cathedral is the main church of a diocese and the seat of a bishop. It is known in Italian as a *duomo*.

Cenotaph (Gk. "empty grave") Memorial structure which does not contain the remains of the dead as they have either been lost or are buried elsewhere. It is usually synonymous with a war memorial. Less frequently the word refers to a tomb built while an individual is still alive and which stands empty until their death. Cenotaphs date back to prehistoric times; in ancient Greece and Rome they sometimes took the form of richly decorated stone

Figura serpentinata, Giambologna, Mercury, 1564 – 1580, bronze, h. 180 cm, Museo Nazionale del Bargello, Florence

structures resembling mausoleums. In later epochs cenotaphs were often designed on the lines of earlier models.

Centrally planned building A building which radiates from a single central point. During the Renaissance, such buildings were modeled on examples from antiquity such as the Pantheon in Rome.

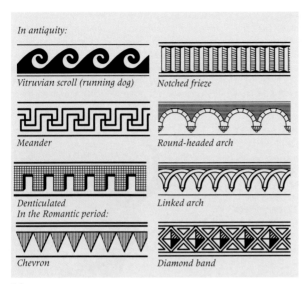

In antiquity:

Vitruvian scroll (running dog)

Notched frieze

Meander

Round-headed arch

Denticulated
In the Romantic period:

Linked arch

Chevron

Diamond band

Friezes

Chancel screen or rood screen, balustrades or walks which separate off the choir which is reserved exclusively for the prayer or singing of the clerics. They often feature pictorial ornamentation.

Chapel (M. Lat. *cap(p)ella*, "small cloak") Small, self-contained ritual area in churches; smaller church lacking parochial rights and used for particular purposes such as a baptismal or mortuary chapel. The term is derived from a small prayer room in the royal palace at Paris in which the cloak of St. Martin of Tours (A.D. 316/7–397) was kept from the 7th century.

Chapterhouse (Lat. *capitulum*, "little head") Assembly room of the chapter (body of clergy) in a monastery, generally situated in the east wing of a cloister. It was used for daily readings from the chapters of the order's rules and for lessons from the Holy Scriptures.

Chevet or apse, the eastern side of a church's choir (reserved for the clerics), which consists of a wall recess and semidome.

Choir (Lat. *chorus*; Gk. *choros*, "round dance, song, and dance group") The area of a church reserved for the use of the clergy or choir; often raised and spatially distinct from the rest of the building. Since the Carolingian era the term has been used to describe that part of the nave which extends beyond the crossing (the intersection of nave and transept), including the terminal point of the apse (an extension of the end wall with a vaulted roof).

Choir screen (Lat. *chorus*; Gk. *choros* "round dance, song and dance group") The balustrades or walls which separate the choir from the rest of the church.

Church masons' guild Organization of all the artisans, artists and specialists involved in the construction of the principal or episcopal church in a city. The guild ensured that all the work on the church was carried out in a unified manner.

Ciborium (Lat.; Gk. *kiborion* "beaker, vessel") Freestanding canopy in the form of a baldachino resting on four columns used to emphasize the position of the altar.

Cinquecento (It. "five hundred") Italian term for the 16th century.

Cistercians (Lat. *Sacer Ordo Cisterciensis*, "Holy Order of Cîteaux") The Cistercian order had its origins in the reformed Benedictine monastery of Cîteaux founded in 1098 by Robert von Molesmes (1027–1111). The new order set out to achieve fully the monastic ideal encapsulated in the rules of the Benedictines; the Cistercians therefore considered themselves a reforming movement within the Benedictine order. The basis for the order's constitution and its organization are contained in the

Charta Caritatis (confirmed by Pope Calixtus II in 1119). The movement then expanded rapidly under the influence of Bernard of Clairvaux (1091–1153). In accordance with the rules of the order, Cistercian architecture is characterized by a lack of pomp, paintings, or costly materials.

Clerestory Area of windows in the upper stage of the nave wall in a basilica.

Cloister A vaulted, occasionally flat-roofed ambulatory or passageway surrounding the courtyard of a monastery or cathedral chapter. Often laid out to the south of the church, it is frequently used as a burial ground. The architectural execution as well as the decoration of the cloister, which is often only of a single story, usually have a high artistic value.

Colonnade Series of columns joined by a continuous entablature rather than arches.

Condottiere (It. "leader") A mercenary in 14th- and 15th-century Italy.

Console (Fr. "corbel, support"; Fr. Lat. *solidus* "solid, firm") A projecting bracket generally with a curved outline or figurative shape which supports arches, shelves, balconies, or figures.

Contrapposto (from Lat. *contrapositus* "set against") Fundamental principle concerning standing figures in sculpture; derived from the Classical Greek tradition, especially the *Doryphoros* by Polyclitus (c. 460–415 B.C.), and supported by a theoretical body of work. Opposing forces in a figure are distributed across a supporting and a relaxed leg to form a harmonious balance. The *contrapposto* technique was taken up again during the Renaissance.

Corbel Also known as a console; a projecting stone which supports a weight.

Cornice Projecting strip of molding running along the top of a building or wall.

Crocket A sculpted ornament in various floral and leaf shapes which appears in a regular series on the ridges of Gothic buildings (e.g., on pinnacles and gablets). Crockets support the visual impression of an ascending movement in the architecture.

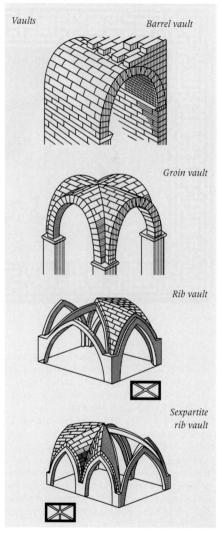

Vaults

Barrel vault

Groin vault

Rib vault

Sexpartite rib vault

Incrustation, cathedral floor, Duomo, Siena

Christian era. The extension of these chambers by a vaulted passageway led to the formation of catacombs. In the ring crypt a path leads around the *confessio*. An increase in the numbers of pilgrims who came to venerate martyrs or the sacred relics of a church resulted in the construction of hall crypts, consisting of longitudinal sections which provided a larger and more unified space. Crypts built outside the plan of the church are known as external crypts. As a rule the crypt forms an essential part of a church complex; due to its location underneath the altar it is a meaningful expression of the central idea of death and resurrection.

Cycle (L. Lat. *cyclus* and Gk. *kyklos* "circle") A term used in the fine arts for a closed series of works related to each other in both form and content, e.g. the depiction of the life of a saint.

Doctors of the Church (Lat. *patres ecclesiae*) Papally sanctioned teachers and leading theologians of the early Christian era whose writings have the force of doctrine for the Church's teachings on faith and morals. The four Latin Doctors of the Church are Ambrose (c. 340–97), Augustine (c. 354–430), Jerome (340/47–420), and Gregory the Great (c. 540–604). Since the 8th century they have been related to the four Evangelists and their symbols. The four Greek Doctors of the Church are Athanasius, Basil, Gregory, and John Chrysostom.

Dome A simple, spherical vault which spans a circular, square, or polygonal space. The elevation of a dome can take several forms, e.g., saucer dome, calotte, domical vault, onion dome. The height of the dome can be increased by the addition of a drum, a cylindrical sup-

Cross-in-square church A church built on a cross-shaped ground plan and crowned by a central dome. The arms of the cross may also be surmounted by domes of the same size or smaller (e.g., San Marco, Venice) or feature barrel vaults; developed in Byzantine architecture, where this type was widespread.

Crossing The area marked by the intersection of the nave and transepts in a church; the area is often clearly distinguished through the use of design elements to emphasize its position within the church.

Crypt (Lat. *crypta*, Gk. *krypte* "covered way, vault") Area underneath the choir of a church. The crypt's precursor was the grave of a saint or martyr (known as *confessio*), which was constructed underneath the altar in the early

porting structure. Erecting a dome on a square base results in one of four options: 1. In the sail vault the base of the dome is a notional circle whose diameter is the diagonal of the square on which it is to be built. The segments of the dome which extend beyond the square then appear to be cut off in the vertical axis; 2. With the Bohemian dome the area which is to be vaulted over is smaller than the ground plan of the square base; 3. The pendentive dome is a notional sail dome truncated horizontally with the resulting circular area spanned by a hemisphere. The spherical triangles at the corners of the truncated dome are called pendentives; 4. In the dome-on-squinch the diameter of the dome is the length of one side of the square. The corners of the square base are built up in a series of arches of increasing radius so that the interior of the base appears as an octagon with alternate short and long sides; the short sides at the corners are known as squinches and they form a transitional zone between base and dome. Both pendentives and squinches are located at the point where two walls meet but because squinches result in an octagon and pendentives in a circle these two types are put to different uses. The squinch is used for octagonal crossing towers and cloister vaults while the pendentive is used for true domes.

Dominicans (Lat. *Ordo Fratrum Praedicatorum*, "Order of Preachers", "Order of Friars Preachers") Mendicant order established in 1216 by St. Dominic (1170–1221) in Toulouse, and dedicated to the dissemination and defense of the faith through education and preaching. The Dominicans were especially involved in combating the unsanctioned, "heretical" movements which operated outside the ambit of the Church during the Middle Ages. For this reason in 1232 the Dominicans were permanently charged by the Holy See with leading the Inquisition, the ecclesiastical courts which tried those accused of apostasy.

Doric column A vertical architectural element without a base that is part of the Doric order of columns (Greek architectural system), with sharp arris stonework, a fluted shaft and a capital (undecorated) consisting of an annuali (ring moulding), echinus (cushion-like torus) and square abacus (top slab).

Drum Cylindrical or polygonal structure between a building and a dome, sometimes provided with windows.

Duecento (It. "two hundred") Italian term for the 13th century.

Dwarf gallery A wall-passage on the outside of a building and generally just below the intersection of the roof and external wall. It is named for the small columns (dwarf columns) supporting arches (arcades) or, less frequently, an architrave. The dwarf gallery appeared at the end of the 11th century in the Upper Rhine (Speyer from 1080), as well as in Upper Italy (Lucca, Pisa, Parma). The dwarf gallery disappeared with the advent of Gothic architecture; the most recent examples are from the Central and Lower Rhine (c. 1230).

Eclecticism (Gk. *eklegein* "to select") Generally pejorative term used in art and architecture to describe the unoriginal adoption from previous epochs of existing themes, structural forms, and representational techniques and designs.

Embrasure Splayed opening for a window or portal; often richly sculptured or with a stepped pattern.

Encrustation See Incrustation.

Entablature Upper section of an architectural order (a classical architectural system) consisting of an architrave (the main load-bearing beam), frieze (horizontal decorative strip), and cornice (a projected molding below the roof).

Etruscans (Lat. *Etrusci, Tusci*; Gk. *Tyrsenoi, Tyrrhenoi*; Etr. *Rasenna, Rasna*) A historical people whose existence was documented from the 8th century B.C. Their territory was situated between the Tiber, the Apennines, and the Arno. Though the Etruscans played a leading role in Italy until the 4th century B.C., their origins are still shrouded in mystery. It is thought they had linguistic and cultural ties with areas further east, but even the Iron Age Villanova culture of Upper and Central Italy c. 700

B.C. merged seamlessly into that of the Etruscans. Apart from their artworks the most valuable cultural artifacts left behind by the Etruscans are their tombs and grave offerings. The word Tuscany comes from the medieval term *Tuscia* for ancient Etruria.

Evangelists' symbols (Gk. *Euangelistes*; Lat. *evangelista*) The winged creatures (tetramorph) which represent or serve as emblems for the authors of the Gospels: Matthew – angel, Mark – lion, Luke – bull, and John – eagle. They are also symbolic of Christ, who embodies the unity of the Gospels. The symbols are derived from a divine vision received by the Old Testament prophet Ezekiel (1:4 ff.) and the Revelation of John (4:6 ff.).

Exedra (Gk. "external seat") Niche with a bench at the end of a columned passageway; term for the apse or altar niche at the end of the choir. The word is often used to refer to any other semi-circular niche.

Figura serpentinata (It. "snake-like figure") A figure or group of figures depicted in twisted forms so that they spiral upwards. Common in 16th-century sculpture (Mannerism), where it allowed artists to approach the ideal of a three-dimensional work visible from all sides.

Flying buttress An arch or half-arch between the nave wall and an external pier. Its function is to counteract the thrust from the roof and vault.

Foil A tracery form, especially in Gothic architecture, of conjoined arcs (lobes) of equal sizes. The number of foils is indicated by prefix e.g. trefoil, quatrefoil, multifoil, etc. The foil appeared first in windows, and Gothic architecture made extensive use of foils for walls.

Forum (Lat. "marketplace"), the marketplace in a Roman town, where judicial procedures and public affairs were also carried out; usually a long rectangle surrounded by public buildings which were later combined together by colonnades (rows of columns with an architrave).

Franciscans (Lat. *Ordo Fratrum Minorum*, "Order of the Lesser Brothers") Mendicant order founded by Francis of Assisi (1181/82–1226) in 1209 (1223) which took particularly stringent vows of poverty and asceticism. The Franciscans were the most passionate venerators of the Virgin in the Middle Ages and she served as the patron of their order.

Fresco (It. "fresh") Wall painting in which pigments have been applied to wet plaster.

Fresco painting (It. "fresh") Mural technique in which pigment is applied directly to wet plaster. Due to the fast drying time, only that part of the wall can be plastered which the artist intends to paint in a single session – the so-called *giornate*. In contrast to *fresco secco*, which is painted on dry surfaces, true frescoes do not rapidly deteriorate provided climatic conditions are good.

Capitals

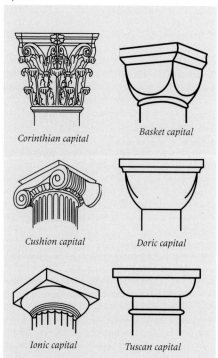

Corinthian capital

Basket capital

Cushion capital

Doric capital

Ionic capital

Tuscan capital

Incrustation (Lat. *incrustare*, "to cover with a skin") Cladding of bare walls and floors with more valuable materials such as colored and polished stone slabs – generally of marble or porphyry – which are laid in patterns to provide a decorative effect. In 11th-century Tuscany an independent technique used to achieve a large-scale ornamental effect on church façades.

Intarsia (It. *intarsiare*, "to produce inlaid work"; Arab. *tarsi* "to inlay") Inlay of wood but also of ivory, mother of pearl, tortoiseshell, or metal. The patterns are created either by hollowing out the wood and replacing it with other materials, or by joining many smaller pieces together and gluing them to a surface.

Jesuits (Lat. *Societas Jesu*, "Society of Jesus") Roman Catholic order founded 1534/39 by Ignatius of Loyola (1491–1556) to combat the heresies of established Catholic orders, and to counter the efforts of the Protestant Reformation. Through its writings and academic work, as well as its missionary work and teaching, the order had a great influence on the education system.

Land Art Also known as Earth Art, a type of art which appeared in the mid-1960s and which took as its object the natural or urban–industrial landscape. These artistic interventions focused on themes concerning the particular characteristics of the landscape, the problematic character of technological progress in images of landscapes, and the esthetic perceptions and responses of the artist. The intellectual roots of Land Art lie in the landscape paintings of the 18th and 19th centuries.

Lantern (Lat. *la(n)terna* and Gk. *lamptera* "lamp") Round or polygonal turret surrounded with windows and situated over the opening to a dome or vault.

Latin Cross, a cross with a lower shaft which is longer than the other three shafts. It is the preferred type of groundplan for medieval Western sacred buildings.

Lesene (Fr. *lisière* "edge, seam") Slightly projecting vertical panel which serves to divide up a wall surface and is often surmounted by blind arches (arches set into the wall) or friezes with round arches.

Duccio di Buoninsegna (1250/1260–1318/1319, Maestà, (Madonna Ruccellai), 1285, Tempera on wood, 450 × 290 cm, Galleria degli Uffizi, Florence

Loggia (It.) Open passageway framed by arches supported on columns or pillars and generally placed at the front of a building; in Tuscany a self-contained structure as seen in the Loggia dei Lanzi (begun 1376) in Florence.

Lunette Lunette arch (Fr. *lunette*, "little moon"). Semicircular opening or area over doorways, niches or windows. Lunettes are generally decorated.

Mosaic, Banquet of Herod (detail), c. 1225, Battistero San Giovanni, Florence

Maestà (It. "majesty, enthroned in glory") Term for a depiction of the Madonna and Child enthroned and surrounded by saints and angels. Found predominantly in Italian painting of the 13th and 14th centuries.

Majolica Italian term for tin-glazed, painted ceramics (fired clay); the Italian term is derived from the island of Majorca, which was once the center of trade in majolica. The French term is *faïence* (from Faenza, the most important production site in Italy).

Maniera greca (It. "Greek manner") Term characterizing certain stylistic elements in Italian painting of the 13th and 14th centuries which was influenced by Byzantine models. The concept appeared for the first time in the writings of Lorenzo Ghiberti (1378–1455), who used it to describe an entire epoch. Later, Giorgio Vasari (1511–74) used the expression to refer to a flat style of painting which emphasized contours and which had a somber and stiff quality. Byzantine influence is especially apparent in painted crucifixes and images of the Madonna. The *maniera greca* was particularly important in Tuscany, where it formed the basis for leading works by Ciambue, Duccio, and Giotto. The style declined in importance towards the end of the 13th century and was slowly replaced by other tendencies which came to be known as the proto-Renaissance or Early Renaissance.

Mannerism (Fr. *manière* "manner"; from Lat. *manuarius* "of the hands") Epoch in art history from around 1520 to 1600, i.e. between the Renaissance and Baroque eras. Mannerism did away with the idealized forms, proportions, and compositions developed during the Renaissance. Painting during this period was characterized by highly energetic scenes; the elongation of the human body and its depiction in anatomically unrealistic positions; an emphasis on compositional complexity; and an irrational, theatrical use of light.

Medallion (Fr. *médaillon*, "large medal") Picture or relief (raised sculpted depiction on a flat surface) in a round or elliptical frame.

Memento mori (Lat. "remember you must die") This is an admonishing reminder of the inevitability of death and the transience of all earthly things. Refers therefore especially to the Christian concept of moral conduct in this world as well as the fact that a life not lived in righteousness and fear of God faces the Last Judgment and the torments of damnation. The memento mori was employed for the first time in the 13th century.

Mendicant order (Lat. *mendicare* "to beg") Monastic orders with a centralized constitution. They were pledged to an ascetic lifestyle and to take a vow of poverty. The mendicant orders arose at the end of the 13th century as a counter-movement to the secularization of the church and their members lived by working or begging. They were particularly devoted to pastoral care, teaching, and mission work. The Franciscans, Dominicans, Capuchins, Augustinians, and Carmelites are all mendicant orders.

Mezzanine (It. *mezzano*; Lat. *medianus*, "central") A low story or half floor between two higher ones and which generally contains the less important rooms in the building. Mezzanine floors are situated over the first floor or main floor, or below the level of the cornice. If located above the level of the cornice such a floor is known as an attic. The addition of mezzanine floors means that the interior of a building may be more esthetically proportioned, and for this reason the mezzanine became a popular design tool in Baroque and neo-Classical palace architecture.

Minorite (Lat. *Ordo Fratrum Minorum*, "Order of the Lesser Brothers") Branch of the Franciscan order which became independent in 1517 and developed out of Franciscan debates on poverty.

Mosaic (from Lat. *musaicum, musivum*; from Gk. *mousa*, "muse, art, artistic work") Two-dimensional decorative or figurative work constructed from colored, polished pieces of stone or glass. In antiquity, mosaics were used mainly to decorate floor surfaces; the technique was perfected in the 5th and 6th centuries in Italy (Rome, Ravenna) with the introduction of glass mosaic and it took on the functions which hadtraditionally belonged to murals.

Nave Long section of a church between the façade and the transept or choir. The nave may be single-spaced or have aisles, as in the basilica and hall church, and it serves as the liturgical space for the lay congregation as well as the location for side altars. From the 4th century the elevation of the nave underwent an increasing number of changes. The most remarkable of these occurred in the basilican form where galleries, triforia, and clerestories developed over the aisles and arcades. These elements served to structure and decorate the wall surfaces, and they can also be found in the transepts and the choir.

Necropolis (Gk. *nekros* "deceased" and *polis* "city", Sp. necrópolis) Ancient or Early Christian cemetery located outside the walls of a city.

Non finito (It. "unfinished") Term used for a sculpture deliberately left incomplete; originally used to describe several pieces by Michelangelo (1475–1564) including the *Pietà Rondanini* (Milan, Castello Sforzesco). The technique was often used to heighten the expressiveness of a sculpture.

Octagon (from Gk. *okto* "eight" and *gonia* "corner") An ancient sign symbolizing the perfection of the cosmos; in architecture it signified a centrally planned structure built on an octagonal ground plan.

Non finito, Michelangelo Buonarroti (1475–1564), Matthew, c. 1503-1505, marble, h 271 cm. Galleria dell'Accademia, Florence

Olivetans A monastic order established in 1313 by Bernardo Tolomei (1272–1348) and two other citizens from Siena (Ambrogio Piccolomini and Patrizio Patrizi). Based on the Benedictine rule, the order was confirmed by the pope in 1344. The Olivetans had their beginnings in Accona and were named after Monte Oliveto (the Mount of Olives). The Olivetan order differs from the Benedictines in its frequent change of location (and, therefore, of its monasteries) and the limited period for which its officials are appointed. Both of these measures provide for a greater degree of movement within the order; the latter measure was intended to prevent the abuse of official positions.

Oratory (M. Lat.; from Lat. *orare*, "to pray, speak") Small private chapel for prayer and religious services. Initially reserved for the clergy or royalty but in some cases accessible to the public from the 16th century.

Orders of architecture Ancient system of architecture in which columns, capitals, architraves, and cornices are harmonized with one another. In Greek architecture the distinction is made between the Doric, Ionic, and Corinthian orders. These orders were more or less adopted by Roman architecture but with variations such as the Tuscan order, which featured Doric elements, and the Composite order, which had elements from the Ionic and Corinthian orders.

Pillars

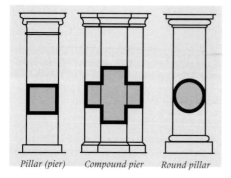

Pillar (pier)   *Compound pier*   *Round pillar*

Palazzo (It. "palace") Initially a royal residence, later a large and richly decorated residence for the nobility and other wealthy patrons which was intended to represent their social standing.

Panel painting Picture painted on wood or, in smaller formats, on copper. Panel painting appeared in the 12th century and was later superseded by the use of canvas for paintings.

Parnassus (Gk. *Parnassos*, a mountain near Delphi in Greece) Seat of the god Apollo and the nine Muses, goddesses of the arts. Later Parnassus came to represent the realm of poetry; and it was depicted from the Renaissance onwards – particularly in the Baroque era – in scenes showing Apollo enthroned and surrounded by the Muses.

Patriarch (Gk. from *pater* "father" and *archein* "to be the first, to rule") Term used in the Old Testament for the head of a family or tribe; later used for the tribal fathers of Israel (particularly for Abraham, Isaac, and Jacob). Since the 5th century the head of an autocephalous church has been known as a patriarch. The word is also used as an honorary title for bishops; even today the pope as well as the bishops of Venice, Lisbon, and Jerusalem are known as patriarchs. The term has a similar significance in Judaism and for the Orthodox churches.

Patron Person who commissions artists and who promotes the arts. An alternative term is Maecenas, a word derived from the Roman nobleman Gaius Cilnius Maecenas (c. 70–8 B.C.) who was an active supporter of the poets Horace (65–8 B.C.) and Virgil (70–19 B.C.).

Pediment, the classical flat triangular or segmental arch pediments were imitated during the Renaissance, Baroque and Neoclassical periods and, as in the originals, can be broken or have a cornice running through it; in other words the central part can be missing or projecting to a greater or lesser extent. The tympanum (area within the pediment) can be decorated.

Pendentive (Fr. "hanging arch") A concave, spherical triangle or spandrel and one of the techniques for supporting a dome on a square or polygonal base.

Perspective (M. Lat. *perspectiva (ars)*, "transparent (art)") The realistic depiction of three-dimensional objects on a two-dimensional surface. In the Italian Renaissance the mathematically exact construction of perspective was discovered by Filippo Brunelleschi. The laws of linear or centralized perspective were worked out by Leonardo da Vinci. In these, the point at which all the lines of perspective meet in the distance of the picture (the vanishing point) is at the center (linear perspective). The height of the pictorial horizon is defined by the height of the vanishing point. Perspective is also frequently located according to the point of view of the observer: depending on the location of the observing eye the perspective may be either a bird's eye view or a worm's eye view. Parallel perspective is the opposite of centralized perspective.

Piano nobile (It.) The main floor of a building with reception rooms which is generally located over the first floor.

Pietà (It. "mercy, pity" from Lat. *pietas* "piety") Also known as a *Vesperbild* (Ger. "evening picture"). Depiction of the grieving Virgin holding the body of Christ in her arms.

Pilaster (It. *pilastro*; from Lat. *pila* "pillar") Rectangular pier built into a wall and projecting only slightly from it with a base, shaft, and capital. Often fluted, i.e., with closely spaced parallel grooves on the shaft.

Pillar (from Lat. *pila*) Supporting structure of square, rectangular, or polygonal cross-section, which can be divided into base, shaft and capital. Depending on their location and shape, distinctions are made between e.g. freestanding pillars, wall pillars, corner pillars, and buttresses (exterior pillars which transmit the horizontal thrusts from the vault and roof).

Pinnacle (Lat. "wing, point") Decorative element in Gothic architecture; a small turret with a high pointed roof, either square or octagonal, and often used to crown the pediments of windows, as well as portals and buttresses (exterior pillars which transmit the horizontal thrust from the vault or load from the roof).

Polyptych (from Gk. *polyptychos*, "many folded") Altarpiece (painted or sculpted altar ornament) made of more than two parts; particularly well suited for depicting large, thematically complex programs.

Ponderation (from Lat. *ponderare*, "weigh up") Equal distribution of the weight of the body over a supporting and a relaxed leg, and the consequent harmonious arrangement of the rest of the body.

Portico (Lat. *porticus*, "hall of columns") Open structure surrounded by columns in front of the main entrance to a building and often surmounted by a pediment.

Predella (It. "*podium*, altar-step") Plinth-like structure for altars, sometimes used to store relics (venerated objects or fragments from the remains of a saint). The predella is often decorated with paintings.

Presbyterium (Gk. *presbyterion*, "council of the elders") Also known as the choir, the main area of the church altar originally reserved for the bishop and presbyters.

Proto-Renaissance Also called the pre-Renaissance; stylistic concept coined by Jacob Burkhardt for the various ways in which antique art was absorbed into the art of the Middle Ages before the beginning of the Renaissance proper. It is especially evident in the adoption of antique forms and motifs in Italian architecture from the end of the 11th century in Tuscany (e.g. San Miniato al Monte and baptistery, Florence, both 11th/12th centuries). Strong classicizing tendencies were evident in southern Italian sculpture under Friedrich (Frederick) II. (triumphal arch in Capua) in which there was a conscious attempt to emulate the power of imperial Rome. The proto-Renaissance is also connected with architecture in Provence (the Provençal school of architecture) and the art of the sculptor Nicola Pisano (c. 1220–bef. 1284), which was influenced by Roman sarcophagi.

Putto (It. "boy"; fr. Lat. *putus*) Depiction of a small, naked boy with or without wings. An invention of the Italian early Renaissance, images of putti borrowed from the infant angels of Gothic art which were in turn influenced by the Eros figures of antiquity.

Relief, Lorenzo Ghiberti (1378–1455), Moses, 1425–1452, Bronze, 80 × 80 cm, Gates of Paradise (detail), Battistero San Giovanni, Florence

Quattrocento (It. "four hundred") Italian word for the 15th century.

Refectory (M. Lat. *refectorium* from Lat. *reficere* "to restore") A dining room reserved for monks in a monastery; often divided into winter and summer refectories.

Relic (from Lat. *reliquiae* "left over, left behind") Part of the remains of a saint, or an object formerly in his or her possession which is highly venerated.

Relief (Fr.; from Lat. *relevare* "to raise") Composition chiseled into or modeled on a flat surface so that it projects from that surface. Distinctions are made between high, low, and *mezzo rilievo* depending on the degree to which the design projects from its base.

Reliquary (from Lat. reliquiae "left over, left behind") An ornately designed receptacle for relics.

Renaissance (Fr.; It. *rinascimento*, "rebirth") Art historical period in the 15th and 16th centuries which spread throughout Europe from Italy; the late phase from around 1530–1600 is also known as the Mannerist period. The term can be traced back to Giorgio Vasari (1511–1574), who coined the term *rinascimento* (rebirth), intending it to mean only the passing of medieval art. Humanism had promoted the development of a new image of man and the universe based on ancient Classical models and this led to the notion of the *uomo universale*, the man who is equally gifted in all intellectual and physical endeavors. The fine arts therefore ceased to be thought of as a trade and joined the ranks of the liberal arts, while artists themselves began to enjoy a higher social status and sense of self-confidence. Art and science were mutually related as in the discovery of mathematically verifiable rules for perspective or in anatomical knowledge. Architecture drew on the theories of Vitruvius (c. 84 B.C.) and was characterized by the adoption of Classical architectural elements and the development of an architecture suited to palaces and castles. The centrally planned structure, a building which radiates from a single point, developed into the building which typified Renaissance architecture.

Retable (Fr. retable; Lat. retabulum, "rear wall") or altarpiece, sculptural or painted altar decoration ususlly mounted behind the altar or over its rear wall. It can consist of a single work of art or several panels.

Reticulated vault, late Gothic vault form in which the ribs (weight bearing sections of the roof) form a network disguising the division of the bays.

Rib girder-like projecting moulding, frequently shaped, designed to strengthen the groin of a vault. Between the ribs are the cells, which are not load-bearing.

Rib vault the intersection of two barrel vaults (semi-circular and segmental arch roofs) of equal size at right angles. The intersections are called ribs.

Rilievo schiacciato (It. "flattened relief") A technique developed by Donatello (1386–1466) for working the surface of a relief into minute gradations; this was aimed at achieving the effects of a painting or drawing as well as the illusion of depth.

Rococo (from Fr. *rocaille*, "scree, grotto shells"), European period of art from 1720/30 to 1770/80, characterized by a decorational style which favours lightness, playfulness and small scales. In painting, this is underlined by a brightening of the colour palette.

Romanesque (from Lat. *romanus* "Roman") Concept introduced in France in the first third of the 19th century to describe the repertoire of forms from Roman architecture (round arches, piers, columns, vaults) which was used in European building in the early Middle Ages. The term covers the period from around 1000 (in France; later elsewhere) until the mid-13th century. The Romanesque began to give way to the Gothic from as early as the mid-12th century in central France, and there were various different national inflections of style and approach. Romanesque architecture flourished particularly in Burgundy, Normandy, Upper Italy. and in Tuscany. Its chief glory was in church architecture. Characteristic of Romanesque architecture is its practice of structuring the whole through the addition of individual, plastically composed elements as well as the interplay of cylindrical and cuboid forms.

Rosette (Fr. "little rose, rose-shaped ribbon") A round leaf or flower ornament which radiates from the center.

Rotunda (It. *rotonda*) A round, centrally planned building erected on a circular ground plan; may also mean a round room situated within a building.

Rustication (Lat. *rustica*; from *rusticus*, "rural, rustic") Masonry consisting of massive blocks of stone (ashlar) with roughly worked faces. Rusticated stonework is frequently found in the Tuscan buildings of the Early Renaissance.

Sacristy (M. Lat. *sacristia*; from *sacer*, "holy, consecrated") Side room of a church in which priests robe and prepare themselves for services; also used for the storage of sacred vessels and vestments.

Sarcophagus (Gk. *sarcophagos*, "flesh eater") Ornately decorated coffin of wood, metal, baked clay, or stone.

Scholasticism (from Lat. *scholasticus*, "of a school")

Rustication, Palazzo Strozzi, begun 1489, Florence

The philosophy and science of the Middle Ages which were based on classical philosophy, the exegesis of the Bible and the teachings of the church.

Segmental arch Arch described by a segment of a circle whose center is located well below the springing line (the line of the last voussoir of the arch on top of the impost). The arc of a segmental arch is therefore smaller and flatter than that of the semi-circular round arch.

Seicento (It. "six hundred") Italian name for the 17th century.

Seneca, Lucius, Annaeus (c. 4 B.C.–5 A. D.) Roman politician, Stoic philosopher and poet; born in Córdoba.

Servites (Lat. *Ordo Servorum Mariae*, "Order of the Servants of Mary") A monastic order founded in 1233 after a vision of the Virgin received by seven respected citizens of Florence. The rules of the Augustinians form the basis of the Servite order. In addition to confessions of faith and the practice of pastoral care, the Servites devote themselves to education as well as teaching at the papal theological faculty, the *Marianum* in Rome.

Sgraffito (It. from *(s)graffiare*, "to scratch") Technique for decorating façades in which a fresh layer of plaster is applied to an existing plaster wall consisting of other differently colored layers; while still wet this outer layer is scraped away to form decorative elements and patterns and reveal the various colors of the layers below. The use of sgraffito dates back to the 14th century, especially in Tuscany; the first and most influential example north of the Alps is the palace in Dresden. In contrast with fresco painting, sgraffito is particularly hard-wearing, even when exposed to the open air. The technique enjoyed widespread popularity and was even used for the façades of prosperous middle-class houses. In pottery, the term sgraffito is also used to refer to an ornamental technique in which the desired pattern is scratched from one layer to reveal other layers of contrasting color.

Sibyl (Gk. *sibylla* "prophetess") Ancient prophetess who predicted the birth, Passion, and Resurrection of Christ. There was originally just one sibyl, but the number later grew to ten. In the early Christian church the number was extended to 12, in an analogy to the 12 prophets of the Old Testament.

Signory From the late Middle Ages the governing body of Italian cities. The leading positions were generally held by a single family.

Single-spaced hall church Church with a single, central space and without aisles.

Soft style Also known as the International Style; tendency in European art between 1380 and 1430 and part of the late Gothic era/early Renaissance. The Soft style conceptualized the painted or sculpted figure in a new way; figures became more slender and less solid with the folds of the drapery more finely modeled. These developments can be seen in the so-called *Beautiful Madonnas* and they lent sculpture and painting a new intensity of color and light in order to emphasize the immaterial and incorporeal (Master Theoderich, Master Bertram, Jean de Brugel). Patrons of this style were mostly drawn from the patrician class and royal courts, and early centers were the courts of Paris, Burgundy and Prague as well as the central Rhine region and archbishopric of Cologne.

Spandrel Triangular wall surface whose sides are described by the curve of an arch, a horizontal drawn from its apex and a vertical line taken to its lowest point (springer). Pendentives are a type of spandrel and are the spherical triangles formed by the transition from the square base of a dome to the curve of its vault.

Spolia (from Lat. *spolium* "spoil, booty"; from *spoliare* "to rob, plunder") Weapons as the booty of war; elements of a building or artwork which have been plundered and later re-used.

Squinch A partial vault in the shape of a hollow half cone with an opening

Sacristy, S. Spirito, 1488–1492, Florence

pointing downwards and situated at the corners of two walls meeting at right angles. Four squinches built into the corners of a tower allow a dome to be erected over a square plan such as that of a church crossing. Generally executed in brick or masonry, the squinch was developed in Roman and in Islamic vaulted architecture; an example from the early 5th century is San Lorenzo in Milan.

Stone inlay cladding of walls and floors with colorful, polished stone slabs, usually of marble or porphyry, which are arranged in patterns thus structuring the surfaces and bringing them to life in a decorative fashion.

Stucco (It. of Germ. origin "rind") A quick-drying mixture of gypsum, lime, sand, and water. Depending on the ingredients, which may include lime or marble chips, a variety of effects may be achieved such as that of scagliola (*stucco lustro*) which imitates marble. Stucco is a malleable material which may be modeled on site, and it is used for ornamentation on ceilings and interior walls. Often used for freely applied decorations; for producing profiled structures by means of molds; or for polished wall plaster.

Synagogue (Gk. *synagoge*, "place of gathering"; from *synagein*, "bring together"), place of worship, Jewish temple.

Tabernacle (Lat. *tabernaculum* "small tent, small hut") In architecture a recess with columns and a pointed canopy often used to house statues e.g. on Gothic buttresses; an ornamental receptacle for the consecrated host.

Tempera (from Lat. *temperare*, "to mix correctly, to moderate") Painting technique in which the pigments are mixed with a binding agent of whole eggs or egg yolk, glue or casein (a protein derived from milk). Tempera pigments dry faster than oils so that wet-on-wet painting is not possible. Fine effects of shading and transition can be achieved, however, by building up a number of layers from parallel strokes. Color contrasts between wet and dry tempera make it difficult to achieve the same color tone when applying new paint. From the 15th century tempera gradually gave way to the more popular oil painting, but the technique was taken up again at the end of the 19th century.

Andrea Orcagna Tabernacle (1358/1359), Marble, Or San Michele, Florence

Terracotta (It. *terracotta*; from Lat. *terra* "earth" and *cotta* "burnt") Fired, unglazed clay used in antiquity for building and architectural sculpture; the term also refers to reliefs, small sculptures, and other implements from the same material. The glazed terracotta reliefs of Luca and Andrea della Robbia were peculiar to Florence and the skill of their execution secured them a monopoly in the 15th and 16th centuries.

Thermae (Gk. *thermos*, "warm, hot"), public baths in the Roman Empire; the central parts of the baths were the *frigidarium* and *piscina* (cold swimming pool), the lukewarm *tepidarium* and the hot *caldarium*, which were heated by hypocausts (spaces or channels beneath the floors). Adjacent to them were dressing and massage rooms, saunas and leisure rooms, even libraries.

Titus (39 – 81) Roman emperor (79 – 81).

Filippo Lippo (c. 1406–1469), Madonna with Child, c. 1450, Tondo, Tempera on wood, diameter 135 cm, Galeria Palatina, Palazzo Pitti, Florence

Tomb Magnificently decorated, often self-contained structure such as a mortuary chapel or mausoleum. More common are the ornately designed sepulchers found e.g. in churches and cloisters.

Tondo (It. "sphere, plate"; from Lat. *rotundus* "round") Circular painting or relief.

Torso Originally an incomplete sculpture or ancient statue missing its limbs. Since the 16th century the torso has also come to mean a sculptor's draft in which the head and arms are deliberately not executed. The term has since been conceptually expanded so that today, for example, one may speak of a building's torso.

Tracery Geometrically constructed architectural ornament of the Gothic period based on the circle and used in the upper part of a window; later used to decorate pediments, walls, and other surfaces.

Transept Transverse arms of a church running at right angles to the nave which in early Christian basilicas formed the end of the church. A church may have a second transept arm in the west, and an addition is also possible at the eastern end.

Travertine (It. *travertino*, from Lat. *Tiburtinus lapis*, "Tiburtine stone") A porous calcareous stone mined in Italy near the modern city of Tivoli. It appears in narrow layers, the colors showing considerable variation through the strata from white, to light brown-yellow, brownish, or green tones; in older buildings the stone can even take on a bright yellow-gold or brown hue. Travertine was used in ancient Greek times; it was the preferred building material in Classical Rome and was used to clad the Colisseum (from A.D. 70). Travertine is used only rarely for sculpture.

Trecento (It. "three hundred") Italian word for the 14th century.

Trefoil Decorative motif in Gothic art formed from three circles of the same size arranged in a cloverleaf pattern.

Triclinium (Lat.), 1. dining room in Roman houses, 2. dining hall for pilgrims in a monastery.

Triforium (Lat. "three openings") A wall-passage between the arcade and clerestory of a nave; generally seen in basilican complexes where it is situated above the roofs of the aisles between the arcade and/or gallery below and the clerestory above. Distinctions are made between the row triforium and the group triforium. The former runs in a more or less continuous line along the wall while in the latter blind arches bracket discontinuous series of arches into twin or triple arcades. If there are only blind arches and no wall-passage then the term used is blind triforium. The triforium may appear in the nave, the transept, and the choir; its use mainly dates from the period between 1100 and 1260 and it is primarily seen in France and in the region around Cologne and Basel.

Triptych (Gk. *triptychos*, "in three parts"), a picture made up of three panels, in particular a mediaeval winged alter-piece, consisting of a fixed center and two moveable side panels.

Triumphal arch (Lat. *triumphus*, "victory procession"), since the 2nd century B.C. a free-standing gateway with several openings in honor of a general or emperor.

Tympanum (Gk. "drum") The flat field of a pediment or the area above a portal; often decorated with sculpture, it forms part of the overall figurative program in Gothic cathedrals.

Vault Arched ceiling or roof generally constructed from wedge-shaped stones resting on walls or pillars which bear the downward thrust; like the arch itself, the joints between the stones radiate from a single, central point.

Venus Roman goddess of Spring and gardens, closely connected with the concept of grace and charm; later equated with the Greek goddess of love, Aphrodite.

Vestibule (Lat. *vestibulum*, "forecourt, entry"; Fr. *vestibule*, "entry hall, forecourt"), entry room of a house.

Volto Santo (It. from Lat. *voltus sanctus*, "holy countenance") Name of an over-sized wooden crucifix in the cathedral at Lucca which shows the crucified Christ

Ciborium, 8th/9th century, S. Maria, Sovana

attired in a long-sleeved, belted tunic. This crucifix from the late 13th century replaced an even older one which, according to legend, had been carved by Nicodemus, one of the figures mentioned in the New Testament. Angels are said to have carved the face of Christ, hence the name Volto Santo. The crucifix has been venerated since the 11th century for its miraculous powers. North of the Alps, this type of carving became so widespread from the late Middle Ages that it began to be mistaken for the so-called Wilgefortis, the Virgin of Troubles, who is often shown as a crowned and bearded woman on the cross clad in a long robe.

Volute (Lat. *voluta* "snail, scrolled") Spiral, scrolled ornament originally appearing on Ionic capitals; also used in pediments and as a mediating element between the vertical and horizontal parts of a building.

Votive picture (Lat. *votivus* "worshipped, consecrated") An image offered out of gratitude for an averted disaster or to support a petition, and which is proof of mercy having been shown to the donor.

Biographies

Alberti, **Leone Battista** (1404 Genoa or Venice–1472 Rome). Battista personified the concept of the *uomo universale*, the universally talented humanist scholar. He lived from 1432 to 1434 in Rome and afterwards in Bologna, Mantua and Ferrara. From 1443 he was mainly resident in Rome. Alberti acted as adviser to the wealthy princely houses of Italy; he was the architect of the Palazzo Rucellai and the façade of Santa Maria Novella in Florence, as well as of San Andrea in Mantua. The best known of his writings are his *Ten Books on Architecture*, which established his reputation as the most important aesthetic theorist of the 15th century.

Ammanati, **Bartolomeo** (1511 Settignano, near Florence–1592 Florence) Ammanati trained as a sculptor with Baccio Bandinelli in Florence and Jacopo Sansovino in Venice. He then returned to Florence where he lived until his death, apart from brief sojourns in Venice, Padua, Rome, Pisa, and Naples. A Mannerist sculptor in the style of Michelangelo, he worked mainly on fountains and tombs. Ammanati was one of the most important of the early Baroque architects in Italy. He established his reputation with his work on the façade of the Collegio Romano in Rome, as well as the Ponte Trinità and the garden frontage of the Palazzo Pitti in Florence (begun by Brunelleschi).

Andrea del Sarto (1486 Florence–1530 Florence) Real name Andrea d'Agnolo di Francesco. The name del Sarto derived from the profession of his father, a tailor (It. *sarto*). According to Vasari, del Sarto was first apprenticed to a goldsmith before continuing his training with Piero di Cosimo. From 1508 he is recorded as having belonged to the Guild of *medici e speziali* to which painters then also belonged. From 1511 he worked in the same studio as Jacopo Sansovino and, probably, Franciabigio. In 1518 he was invited by the French king, Francis I, to the palace at Fontainebleau but returned a year later to his home town. Andrea del Sarto executed a number of important commissions for frescoes and

Anonymous artist, Portrait of Leon Battista Alberti, *17th century, oil on canvas, 63 × 45 cm. Galleria degli Uffizi, Florence*

altarpieces; along with Fra Bartolommeo he is considered the greatest master of the Florentine High Renaissance and one of the forerunners of Mannerism.

Arnolfo di Cambio (c. 1245 Colle Val d'Elsa–c. 1305 Florence) Di Cambio trained in the 1260s in the workshop of Nicola Pisano in Pisa and Siena. From 1276 he lived in Rome, where his projects included the tombs for Cardinal Annibaldi in San Giovanni in Laterano and for Pope Hadrian V in San Francesco at Viterbo. In 1281 Arnolfo worked in Perugia, in 1282 in Orvieto, and afterwards again in Rome. In 1296 he returned to Florence, where he held various positions including that of sculptor and architect for the new cathedral.

Bandinelli, Baccio (1488 Gaiole, Chianti–1560 Florence) Real name Bartolommeo Brandini. He received his training from the sculptor Giovanni Francesco Rustici. As a loyal follower of the powerful Medici family he received numerous commissions, especially from the Medici popes Leo X and Clement VII and, later on, from Grand Duke Cosimo I. His major work – the monumental marble group of *Hercules and Cacus* on the Piazza della Signoria in Florence – was created in competition with Michelangelo. Bandinelli, a leading representative of Mannerism, produced a number of fine small bronzes.

Barbarossa see Frederick I, Emperor

Barozzi, Giacomo (1507 Vignola/Modena–1573 Rome) Known also as Vignola, Barozzi trained as a painter in Bologna before turning to architecture. He first arrived in Rome in around 1530 and finally settled there to work for the Farnese family in 1546 after brief periods in France and Bologna. It was in Florence that he created major, influential works such as the Mannerist Villa Giulia on which he collaborated with Vasari and Ammanati. In 1546 he was appointed head architect of St. Peter's.

di Bartolo, Fredi (c. 1330–1410 Siena) This artist was first recorded in official documents in 1353 when he opened a workshop together with Andrea Vanni. One of the greatest Sienese painters from the second half of the 14th century, he worked mainly in his home town as well as in San Gimignano and Montalcino; his son, Andrea di Bartolo, also worked in his studio. Fredi di Bartolo, who also exercised various political offices, was influenced by the style of some of his illustrious predecessors such as Simone Martini and his school.

Berlinghieri, Berlinghiero (c. 1175/80–before 1236) Father of the painters Barone, Bonaventura, and Marco Berlinghieri, the only official record of his life is in a list of citizens from Lucca who swore an oath of peace with Pisa in 1228. His work has been reconstructed on the basis of a signed altar cross in the Museo Nazionale di Villa Guinigi. His paintings show the Byzantine influences that characterized 13th-century Italian painting.

Berlinghieri, Bonaventura (c. 1207–after 1274) Active in Lucca from 1228 where he worked in a studio with his father, Berlinghiero, and six brothers of whom Barone Berlinghieri, a painter, and Marco Berlinghieri, a book illuminator, are known. The high-quality work of the Berlinghieri family had an impact far beyond the boundaries of Lucca. Although it is almost impossible to make stylistic distinctions between their work, the altarpiece of St. Francis with scenes from the saint's life has been attributed to Bonaventura on the basis of a signature. Still strongly influenced by Byzantine art, its simple narrative form is a fine example of 13th-century Italian painting.

Bernini, Giovanni Lorenzo (1598 Naples–1680 Rome) Studied under his father, who was a sculptor and painter and with whom he traveled to Rome in 1605. Bernini at first enjoyed the patronage of the Borghese family, but later worked as a sculptor and architect for popes Urban VIII – his main patron – Innocent X, Alexander VIII and Clement IX. His broad sculptural oeuvre includes all the relevant genres such as portraits, festival decorations, fountains, mythological figures, saints, and tombs. Bernini had an enormous influence on the Baroque city of Rome, not only as the architect of St. Peter's but also through many churches and fountains he designed.

Boccaccio, Giovanni (1313 Florence–1375 Certaldo) After serving an apprenticeship with a merchant, Boccaccio studied law in Naples. From 1348 he made his living as a poet and scholar in Florence. His final years were spent in isolation on his estate in Certaldo. In 1374 he traveled for the last time to Florence to hold the first public lectures on Dante's *Divine Comedy*. Boccaccio's epic poetry reached its peak in his *Decameron* and along with Petrarch he is considered one of the first great humanist scholars. His theoretical work encompasses several epoch-making volumes on antiquity.

Bologna, Giovanni see Giambologna

Botticelli, Sandro (1445 Florence–1510 Florence) Real name Alessandro di Mariano Filipepi. Botticelli was

Giovanni Lorenzo Bernini (1598–1680), Self-portrait as a Youth, *c. 1623, oil on canvas, 39 × 31 cm, Galleria Borghese, Rome*

active mainly in Florence. After an apprenticeship as a goldsmith he became a pupil of Filippo Lippi in the 1460s. He was inspired by Pollaiuolo and del Verrocchio, later by Ghirlandaio and Perugino, and received stimulus from the humanist circles around Lorenzo de' Medici (1469–92). Botticelli developed an Classicizing form of mythological imagery characterized by striking fantasy figures. Around 1482 he received a commission for three large frescoes in the Sistine Chapel of the Vatican.

Bronzino, Agnolo (1503 Monticelli near Florence–1572 Florence) Real name Agnolo di Cosimo di Maiano, also Agnolo Tori; one of the greatest practitioners of Florentine Mannerism. Bronzino was a pupil of Raffellino del Garbo and Pontormo. He responded enthusiastically to

the work of Michelangelo, which he encountered on a trip to Rome in 1546/47. From 1530 to 1533 he painted for the Duke of Umbria in Pesaro. After returning to Florence he became one of the city's most sought-after artists and the court painter to the Medici. Initially an imitator of Pontormo, Bronzino turned increasingly to rigorous and objective rules of design. His individualistic use of color allowed him to endow his paintings with a cool quality and his pictures are marked by their plasticity and physicality. In addition to his work on religious and allegorical themes Bronzino was a noted portrait painter.

Brunelleschi, Filippo (1377 Florence–1446 Florence) Trained first as a goldsmith in his home city of Florence before turning to sculpture; later, at the end of the 1420s, he began a career as an architect. On his travels to Rome, Brunelleschi studied works from antiquity and their influence can be seen in his clearly proportioned spaces and rigorous geometrical proportions.

His work is concentrated mainly in Florence and he is considered not only the founder of Renaissance

Sandro Botticelli(c. 1445–1510) Self-portrait (detail from: Adoration of the Magi*), c. 1475, tempera on wood, Galleria degli Uffizi, Florence*

architecture but also the inventor of centralized perspective.

Buffalmacco, Buonamico (active 1315–1345) Trained in Florence in the early years of the 14th century, probably under Andrea de Rico (alias Tafo). The sculptor Ghiberti and the writers Giovanni Boccaccio and Franco Sacchetti have furnished important details on the artist's life and they described him as having an intelligent and witty personality. His work is in the tradition of Giotto, his most representative pieces being the frescoes in the cathedral in Arezzo and in the Camposanto in Pisa.

Caravaggio (1571 Milan (?)–1610 Porto d'Ercole) Real name Michelangelo Merisi. Caravaggio trained in Milan from 1584 to 1588 under Simone Peterzano and later worked in Bergamo. In about 1592 he went to Rome where he found favor at the court of the pope. He was imprisoned several times in 1604 and spent his remaining years on the run. His work is characterized by realism, dramatic chiaroscuro, and a strong sense of detail. Rejected by many of his contemporaries, Caravaggio later had a great influence on many artists in both northern and southern Europe.

Cellini, Benvenuto (1500 Florence–1571 Florence) Cellini's adventurous life is recorded in his famous autobiography from 1559; his writings on sculpture and the art of the goldsmith have also survived. After serving an apprenticeship as a goldsmith in Florence, Siena, Bologna and Rome he worked from 1524 for Popes Clement VII and Paul III as Master of the Mint and as a manufacturer of medallions. After fleeing a murder charge he arrived at the French court where he worked for the king, Francis I In 1545 he returned to Florence where he created one of the most famous of Mannerist sculptures – the bronze *Perseus with the Head of Medusa*.

Cimabue, (probably c. 1240–(?)) Real name Cenno di Pepo. Cimabue probably worked around 1260 in the mosaic workshop of the Florence baptistery. He is recorded as having been in Rome in 1272 and in Pisa in 1301/2. Cimabue began to break with the tradition of Byzantine art by introducing three-dimensionality and a

Florentine School, Portrait of Filippo Brunelleschi (detail), c. 1500-1565, tempera on wood, Musée du Louvre, Paris

greater level of dynamism in his figures. He moved away from medieval traditions, so achieving a less stylized depiction of monumentality and a more intense emotional focus. This new approach made him one of the forerunners of the new style of Italian painting.

Daddi, Bernardo (c. 1290–1348) Daddi began his artistic career around 1320, probably after having trained with Giotto. His specialty was the large-scale studio production of small devotional images, often as portable altars, which were rendered in a lively narrative style and with a fine miniature technique.

Dante (Dante Alighieri; 1265 Florence–1321 Ravenna) Born into a family of the minor Florentine aristocracy, Dante received a solid education and devoted himself to literature and poetry from an early age. He was active in political as well as intellectual life of the city and was appointed to several high public offices. In 1302 he was unjustly banished from Florence and never returned. His chief work, *The Divine Comedy (Divina Commedia)* is a

Florentine School, Portrait of Donatello (detail), c. 1500-1565, tempera on wood, Musée du Louvre, Paris

verse epic in three parts and was written during his years in exile at the courts of various Italian princes.

Donatello (1386 Florence–1466 Florence) Real name Donato di Niccolò di Betto Bardi. Donatello was probably a pupil of Lorenco Ghiberti and Nanni di Banco in Florence. Although mainly active in his home town, he also worked in Siena, Rome, Padua, and other parts of Italy. Donatello is considered the greatest sculptor of the 15th century. The diversity and innovative quality of his extensive body of work were unequalled by any other artist. In his early period he concentrated mainly on making standing figures in marble, but from the 1420s on he concentrated on producing bronzes.

Duccio di Buoninsegna (c.1250–1260 Siena–1318/19 Siena) Duccio was at first a painter of coffered ceilings and furniture, and a book illuminator; his work was first recorded in Siena in 1278. He worked in Florence and probably contributed to the frescoes in the upper church of San Francesco in Assisi. Duccio received his inspiration from the Sienese school and Cimabue. Though he still worked in the shadow of Byzantine art he adopted elements of the new stylistic movements in order to develop a modern pictorial language. His works are characterized by a fine use of line, bright coloration, bold modeling of figures.

Fibonacci, Leonardo (c. 1180 Pisa–c. 1250 Pisa) Also known as Leonardo of Pisa or Leonardo Pisano, he grew up in the Algerian port city of Bejaïa, where his father worked as a customs official. In his youth he traveled widely in the Mediterranean as a merchant before settling in Pisa. His knowledge of Arabic mathematics, which he accumulated on his journeys, was preserved in his book *Liber abaci* (1202 and 1228). Highly esteemed as a mathematician during his lifetime, his writings were widely debated at the court of Frederick II.

Fra Angelico (c. 1397 Vicchio di Mugello near Florence–1455 Rome) Real name Guido di Piero, also Beato Angelico. Fra Angelico was a prominent painter in the period between the late Gothic and early Renaissance. He entered the Dominican monastery in Fiesole as a qualified painter at the age of 20.

In 1436 he moved with the entire monastery to San Marco in Florence, which had been donated to the order by Cosimo de' Medici. In 1447/48 and again in 1452 he worked in Rome, as well as undertaking commissions in Orvieto. In his frescoes and panel paintings he increasingly adopted the new forms of the Renaissance.

Fra Bartolommeo (1472 Soffignano near Florence–1517 Pian'di Mugnone near Florence) Real name Bartolommeo Pagholo del Fattorino, also known as Bartolommeo or Baccio dell Porta. From 1484 he was apprenticed to Cosimo Rosellini and, together with Mariotto Albertinelli, he set himself up as an independent artist in 1490. As a follower of Girolamo Savonarola (1452–98) he entered the Dominican order in 1500, renouncing painting until 1504. Fra Bartolommeo was influenced by Flemish painting as well as the work of Giovanni Bellini and Leonardo, and is considered one of the foremost artists of the High Renaissance. Calm, meaningful gestures of somber effect and a simple compositional structure are characteristic of his work. A number of artists, including Pontormo and Raphael, drew inspiration from his art.

Frederick or **Friedrich I** (c. 1122–1190) Holy Roman Emperor, known as Barbarossa. As Frederick III he became Duke of Swabia in 1147, in 1152 king of Rome and emperor in 1155. In 1156 he married Beatrice of Burgundy. He conducted several campaigns in Italy – to effect his coronation as emperor, to secure his power in the cities of Lombardy and to pacify the schism between Popes Alexander III and Victor IV. In 1184 he had his son Henry VI crowned King of Italy and married him to Constance, the heiress to Sicily. He drowned in the River Saleph in Asia Minor during the Third Crusade.

Gaddi, Taddeo (c. 1300 Florence–1366 Florence) The greatest pupil of Giotto and his close collaborator for many years. He also drew inspiration from the works of Lorenzetti and the sculptor Tino di Camaino. Influenced by these models, Gaddi developed a freer conception of pictorial space achieved by a greater emphasis on diagonal depth and the use of multiple figures in his compositions. His frescoes and panel paintings are also marked by richness of detail and a less monumental approach.

Galilei, Galileo (1564 Pisa–1642 Arcetri, near Florence) Studied mathematics for four years at the University of Pisa, where he later taught before going to the University of Padua. In 1610 he became mathematician at the court of the Grand Duke in Florence. As a follower of the ideas of Copernicus he proposed a heliocentric world view, according to which the earth orbited the sun and therefore could no longer be regarded as the center of the universe. He became involved in a long conflict with the Roman Catholic Church which reached its peak in a controversial trial in 1633 and which led to him spending the last years of his life under house arrest.

Gentileschi, Artemisia (1593 Rome–after 1651 Naples) One of the most famous female artists of her epoch. She was taught first by her father, Orazio Gentileschi, who brought her into contact with the paintings of Caravaggio, and then by Agostino Tasso. In 1614 she went to Florence where she was closely associated with the Academy and where her work enjoyed great success. In around 1620 she returned to Rome before finally settling in Naples in 1628. At the end of the 1630s she worked briefly for the English court. Gentileschi painted powerful, passionate scenes whose psychological elements are dramatically intensified. Her work in Naples, on the other hand, was made under the influence of a profound sense of religiosity and consists almost exclusively of conventional ecclesiastical pictures.

Ghiberti, Lorenzo (1378 Florence–1455 Florence) Ghiberti received his education in the workshop of his stepfather, the goldsmith Bartolo di Michele (Bartoluccio) and he was probably trained as a painter. In 1424/25 he visited Venice and from 1425 to 1430 he lived in Rome. His studio in Florence, in which numerous artists were trained, was one of the greatest bronze foundries of the 15th century. Ghiberti wrote the *Commentarii*, which contain a history of Italian art, as well as his autobiography.

Ghirlandaio, Domenico (1449 Florence–1494 Florence) Real name Domenico di Tommaso Bigordi. Along with Botticelli, Ghirlandaio was the leading fresco painter of the Early Renaissance in Florence. After completing an apprenticeship as a goldsmith, he was trained by Alesso Baldovinetti. His style is marked by a strong sense of

Lorenzo Ghiberti, Self-portrait (detail from the Gates of Paradise), 1452, bronze, Florence baptistery

plasticity and emphatic contours. The crowd scenes in his religious pictures depict important Florentine personalities as participants in biblical events, thus emphasizing the secular world – a technique which anticipated genre painting. Michelangelo was trained in Ghirlandaio's workshop.

Giambologna (1529 Douai–1608 Florence) Real name Giovanni da Bologna, also Jean de Boulogne. Trained in Flanders under the sculptor and architect Dubrœcq. In 1545 he traveled to Rome to study the works of antiquity and those of Michelangelo. His main work was produced in Florence, particularly while he was in the service of the Medici dukes. It was there that he operated an extraordinarily productive and influential workshop. His marble and bronze sculptures – particularly his small bronzes – exhibit the traits of a fully developed Mannerist style with their complex, twisted figures and skillfully interwoven groups.

Giotto di Bondone (c. 1267 (?) Colle di Vespignano near Florence–1337 Florence) Giotto is one of the defining artists of Western culture; he was almost certainly asso-

ciated with Cimabue and may have been his pupil. After 1292 he worked in Assisi, then in Rome, Padua, Naples, Milan, and Florence, where he was appointed cathedral architect in 1334. Giotto broke completely with Byzantine traditions – not least because of the important stimulus he received from his study of French Gothic statuary. He developed an anatomically accurate but monumental view of the human figure, as well as a new formal expression for the portrayal of religious scenes. Giotto depicted his costumed figures acting in realistically rendered landscapes and interiors.

Goes, Hugo van der (c. 1440 Ghent–1482 Roodeclooster near Brussels) One of the most prominent Netherlandish painters of his era. He was granted the title of master in 1467, and a year later worked for Charles the Bold in Bruges. Although he became dean of the Ghent painters' guild in 1474, he then entered the monastery of Roodeclooster as a lay brother. In 1481 he journeyed to Cologne. Influenced by the Old Masters, van der Goes achieved a greater differentiation of physiognomy which heightened the expressiveness of his figures' gestures; his radiant coloration gives all his works an impression of unearthly brilliance. His *Portinari Altar*, painted in Florence in 1483, had a great impact on other Italian artists such Ghirlandaio, Filippino Lippi, and Leonardo.

Gozzoli, Benozzo (1420 Florence–1497 Pistoia) Real name Benozzo di Lese. Gozzoli combined the painting styles of Tuscany and Umbria and in so doing provided a bridge between the Gothic and Renaissance eras. In 1444 he worked with the sculptor Lorenzo Ghiberti in Florence, and in around 1448 he collaborated with Fra Angelico in the Vatican. Thereafter he was active as an independent master in Montefalco, S. Gimignano, Florence, and Pisa. Gozzoli also executed panel paintings as well fresco cycles. His paintings are characterized by a lively narrative style which depicted sequences of events, and a fresh use of color.

Gregory VII Pope, Hildebrand of Soana (1019/1030 Tuscany–1085 Salerno) Brought up in Rome, Gregory went to Cluny as a Benedictine monk where he joined the movement for reform. He was a strong supporter of celibacy and was vehemently opposed to simony.

His bitter conflict with Henry IV concerning investiture reached its peak in 1077 when the excommunicated king was compelled to travel to Canossa as a penitent. In 1083 Henry succeeded in taking Rome and he installed Clement III as a counter-pope. Gregory died in exile.

Hildebrand see Gregory VII, Pope

Leonardo da Vinci (1452 Vinci near Empoli–1519 Cloux near Amboise) Leonardo was a pupil of del Verrocchio from around 1468, and later worked for his teacher from about 1477. He was a member of the Florentine painters' guild from 1472. From 1482/83 until 1499 he worked for Ludovico il Moro in Milan where he returned in 1506 after periods in Mantua, Venice, and Florence. In 1513 he went to Rome and three years later, in 1516, he accepted an invitation from Francis I to go to France. Leonardo worked as a painter, sculptor, architect, and engineer, and undertook scientific as well as artistic studies. Leonardo da Vinci is one of the greatest figures in Western

Christoforo dell'Altissimo, Portrait of Leonardo da Vinci *(detail), 1566–1568, Galleria degli Uffizi,*

art and he embodies the Renaissance ideal of the universally educated artist.

Lippi, Filippino (c. 1457 Prato–1504 Florence) Filippino Lippi was the son and pupil of the painter Fra Filippo Lippi. After the death of his father in 1469 he completed an apprenticeship with Sandro Botticelli in Florence. Along with Botticelli, he is considered the most important Florentine painter during the transition from the early to the High Renaissance and one of the seminal figures in Western art. His most productive period was during the 1490s. He painted large altarpieces, individual allegorical depictions, portraits, and several outstanding frescoes.

Lippi, Fra Filippo (*c.* 1406 Florence–1469 Spoleto) Fra Filippo Lippi was accepted into the Carmelite order in 1421 and he lived in the monastery of Santa Maria del Carmine in Florence until 1432. He was mentioned for the first time in documents as a painter in 1431. After periods in Padua and Venice he was entrusted with commissions by the Medici in Florence from 1437. He was resident in Prato from 1452 where he executed the large

Portrait of Giotto di Bondone *(detail), c. 1500–1565, tempera on wood, Musée du Louvre, Paris*

murals in the main choir of the cathedral with scenes from the life of John the Baptist and St. Stephen. From 1467 he worked on frescoes in the cathedral at Spoleto.

Lorenzetti, Ambrogio (c. 1293 Siena–c. 1348 Siena) One of the great masters of Sienese Gothic. He was probably trained by his brother Pietro, after which he worked in his home town until around 1324.

In 1327 he joined the joined the Guild of Apothecaries and Doctors in Florence. He was active again in Siena from around 1332. Lorenzetti's work represents a fusion of the Sienese painting tradition with elements of Florentine art, and his work continued to deepen intellectually the themes and styles developed by Giotto and Martini. Firm, intelligible forms and a pure, robust coloration are characteristic of his early work, in which he was also able to emancipate objects from pictorial space. His later works display a conception of space which approaches that of a consciously perspectival depiction, and his figures become more individually rendered.

Lorenzetti, Pietro (c. 1280/90 Siena–c. 1345 Siena) Official documents record Pietro Lorenzetti's work between 1320 and c. 1344, and he is numbered amongst the leading artists of the Sienese school from the early 14th century. Influenced by the art of Duccio and Giotto, he also took up the innovations of the sculptor Simone Martini and the expressiveness of the painter Giovanni Pisano. In contrast to his brother Ambrogio, he composed rigorous and symmetrical scenes into which he incorporated figurative groups to great effect. Close observational skills and a sensitivity to changing light conditions are characteristic of his painting style. In his mature creative period he was able to give free rein to his narrative talents.

Machiavelli, Niccolò (1469 Florence–1527 Florence) The son of a lawyer, he received a thorough classical and humanist education. From 1498 he assumed high administrative offices in the Florentine Republic. As an envoy he traveled to the various courts of Italy as well as to the pope, emperor and French king. When the Medici returned to Florence in 1513 he was dismissed from his post and imprisoned. Machiavelli spent the rest of his life on his country estate where he wrote his most famous works such as *Il principe (The Prince)*.

da Maiano, Benedetto (1442 Maiano near Fiesole–1497 Florence) Probably trained with his father who was a wood carver and stonemason. As a young man he also frequently worked with his brother Giuliano. In his own studio in Florence he created numerous altars, tombstones, tabernacles, and pulpit statues as well as busts, mainly for clients in Tuscany; his preferred material was marble. Benedetto da Maiano also worked for the Neapolitan court.

da Maiano, Giuliano (1432 Maiano near Fiesole–1490 Naples) Trained as a joiner and wood carver, his workshop was much in demand and supplied churches, monasteries as well as private homes. He later worked mainly as an architect. In 1474 he began his masterpiece, the cathedral of Faenza; in 1477 he became cathedral architect in Florence and in 1485 he was named court architect to the King of Naples. One of Giuliano da Maiano's greatest services to art was in bringing the style of the Florentine Early Renaissance to Tuscany and southern Italy.

Mantegna, Andrea (1431 Isola di Carturo, near Padua–1506 Mantua) Mantegna began an apprenticeship with Squarcione in Padua in 1441 where he came into contact with the art of antiquity. His most crucial influences, however, were the sculptures of Donatello and the pictures of del Castagno and Jacopo Bellini. He worked independently from 1448 and was called to the court of the Gonzaga dynasty in Mantua in 1460. His work is characterized by anatomically correct figures, a careful eye for detail and a brilliantly constructed use of perspective. These innovations were later to have a major impact on Gentile and Giovanni Bellini.

Martini, Simone (c. 1284 Siena–1344 Avignon) Martini was one of the leading masters of Gothic painting in Siena; he worked both in his home town and for Robert d'Anjou in Naples. In around 1339 he traveled to the papal court in Avignon, where he befriended the poet and scholar Francesco Petrarch. Martini's work was inspired by Duccio, Giotto, and the sculptor Giovanni Pisano, as well as by contemporary developments in

French art. His painting is marked by elegance, sensitivity, and a gentle lyricism; along with Giotto's work it is considered the most outstanding of its day.

Masaccio (1401 S. Giovanni Valdarno, Arezzo–1428 Rome) Real name Tommaso di Ser Giovanni Cassai. Masaccio was one of the most revolutionary artists of his age. In 1422 he entered the Florentine Guild of Apothecaries and Doctors and in 1424 the Guild of St. Luke. During this time he worked closely with Masolino. At the end of 1427, shortly before his death, he traveled to Rome. He was the first to combine a decidedly plastic figurative technique with a thorough use of spatial perspective; he is also noted for his realistic depictions of architecture and landscape.

Masolino (1383 Panicale near Perugia–1440 Florence) Real name Tommaso di Cristofano di Fino. The first documentary evidence for Masolino is in the period from 1403 to 1407 when he was Ghiberti's assistant in Florence. In 1423 he entered the Florentine Guild of *medici e speziali*, to which painters then belonged. In 1424 he executed the frescoes in Santo Stefano in Empoli and in the same year continued his collaboration with Masaccio. From 1425 to 1427 he interrupted this work to travel to Budapest, where he became court painter. After his return to Italy he worked on the frescoes in the Brancacci Chapel of Santa Maria del Carmine in Florence. In 1428 he journeyed with Masaccio to Rome to paint the frescoes in San Clemente for Cardinal Branda Castiglione. Masolino was one of the leading painters of the Early Renaissance; his last commission was for the frescoes in Castiglione d'Olona near Milan.

Medici Florentine patrician dynasty which ruled Florence with brief interruptions from 1434 to 1737, and Tuscany from 1569. One of the most influential members of the family was Lorenzo I, the Magnificent (1449–92), who was an enthusiastic patron of the arts and sciences and who gathered the leading humanists of the day at the Platonic Academy in Florence. His son Giovanni de' Medici (1475–1521) ruled Rome from 1513 to 1521 as Pope Leo X.

Bertoldo di Giovanni, Portrait of Lorenzo de'Medici, *1478, diameter 65.6 mm, Bargello, Florence*

Michelangelo Buonarroti (1475 Caprese, Tuscany–1564 Rome) Real name Michelangelo di Ludovico di Lionardo di Buonarroti Simoni. Michelangelo studied sculpture around 1490 in the workshop of Bertoldo di Giovanni after first being taught painting by Ghirlandaio in Florence. Stimulated by the scholars around Lorenzo de Medici, he studied antique sculpture and philosophy. During a period in Rome from 1496 to 1501 he devoted himself to a study of sculpture. His first paintings were executed after his return to Florence. Michelangelo was employed by the Vatican from 1505 to 1520 and again from 1534; he was appointed head architect, sculptor and painter to the Vatican in 1535. He developed new expressive possibilities in his painting, and created unique spiritualized figures of great plastic intensity.

Michelozzo Michelozzi (1396 Florence–1472 Florence) Michelozzo received his sculpture training from Lorenzo Ghiberti in whose workshop he is recorded as having worked from 1417 to 1424 and 1437 to 1442; he worked

Jacopino del Conte, Portrait of Michelangelo Buonarroti, *c. 1535, oil on wood, Casa Buonarroti, Florence*

the church of Santa Annunziata in Florence.

Orcagna, Andrea (c. 1315/20 Florence–1368 Florence) Real name Andrea di Ciona Arcagnuolo. According to Vasari, he was trained by his brother Nardo. Andrea spent his entire life in Florence working on commissions for frescoes and altarpieces. This versatile artist was also active as a sculptor, architect, and poet. In 1347 his name appeared in a document from Pistoia listing the best artists in Florence; later his skill was praised by Vasari and Ghiberti. Large formats and figures executed in a monumental, statuesque style are characteristic of his work which demonstrates a close understanding of Giotto's art. A lively coloration and a rhythmic, Gothic use of line in the drapery attest to Orcagna's new style which was to become highly influential in Florentine painting.

Peruzzi, Baldassare (1481 Siena– 1536 Rome) Trained in his home town before venturing to Rome in 1503. Like Raphael, Peruzzi worked as both painter and architect. An excellent example of his work is the Villa Farnesina, built for Agostino Chigi from 1506 in Rome and which he and other artists decorated with frescoes. In 1527 he became municipal and military architect in Siena. He was famed for his many stage, theater, and festival decorations; representative of his work is the Roman Palazzo Massimo alle Colonne, a building which marks the threshold between Renaissance and Mannerism.

Piero della Francesca (c. 1420 Borge Sansepolcro, near Arezzo–1492 Borge Sansepolcro) Real name Piero di

with Donatello from 1424 to 1433. Although he was active as a sculptor until the end of his life, his greatest achievements were as an architect; in 1446 he was named Brunelleschi's successor as chief architect for the cathedral in Florence. Between 1430 and 1455 there were hardly any large construction projects in the city in which he did not play an active part. His major works include the Palazzo Medici, the library of San Marco and

Benedetto dei Franceschi. Piero della Francesca was an important Early Renaissance artist and a pioneer in perspective compositions. He lived in Florence from 1439 to 1442 where he worked with Domenico Veneziano. Influenced by Veneziano's art and the innovations of Florentine painters – especially del Castagno – in the areas of coloration and perspective, he developed a weighty pictorial language which was marked by a plastic figurative style and a mathematically precise construction of space. His technique for applying varnish to his pictures was revolutionary and he used it to achieve unprecedented atmospheric effects. Piero della Francesca worked mostly in his hometown but he also completed contracts for clients in Ferrara, Arezzo, Rome, and Urbino.

Pietro da Cortona (1596 Cortona–1669 Rome) Real name Pietro Berrettini. He trained under the Florentine painter Andrea Commodi and worked in the studio of Baccio Ciarpi in Rome from 1613. In around 1620 his services were recommended to the Barberini family by his patron, the Marchese Marcello Sacchetti, and in the years which followed he completed several outstanding commissions. From 1634 to 1638 he was a committee member of the Accademia di San Luca in Rome. Pietro da Cortona was famed not only for his skills as a painter and architect but for his publication of a book on art. He contributed substantially to the development of high Baroque ceiling painting in Italy with his animated, brightly lit, and densely populated frescoes.

Pinturicchio (c. 1454 Perugia–1513 Siena) Real name Bernadino di Betto Biagio Pinturicchio was probably trained in the studio of Fiorenzo di Lorenzo. He was also strongly influenced by Perugino, whom he helped paint the Sistine Chapel from 1481 to 1483. Apart from Perugia and Rome, Pinturicchio also worked in Orvieto, Spoleto, Spello, and Siena where he lived from 1502. He was mainly a painter of frescoes but his legacy also includes religious history paintings and portraits. In his day he was one of the most sought after painters for decorating palaces. He cultivated a graceful, often genre-like narrative style with a decorative effect which was generally free of dynamic or dramatic elements, and he is noted for his intensely luminous coloration. Pinturicchio was one of the first painters in the Italian Renaissance to introduce the grotesque ornamentation of the antique period into his work.

Pisano, Andrea (c. 1290 Pontedera–c. 1349 Orvieto) In around 1330 he came from Pisa to Florence where his work on the south portal of the baptistery was first documented in 1330. After Giotto died in 1337 Andrea Pisano took over as director of construction for the campanile of the cathedral of Santa Maria del Fiore in Florence; in 1340 he is recorded for the first time as being the cathedral architect. From 1343 to 1347 he seems to have managed a workshop in Pisa together with his son Nino, to whom he transferred the duties of *capomaestro* (head of building) in Orvieto in 1349. Andrea Pisano probably died shortly after and, according to Giorgio Vasari, he is buried in the cathedral at Florence.

Pisano, Giovanni (c. 1250 Pisa–c. 1319 Siena) Trained under his father Nicola Pisano, whom he assisted in work on the cathedral in Siena and the fountain in Perugia. His major works include the pictorial decorations in the Siena cathedral (1284–1298), the marble pulpits in the churches of Sant'Andrea in Pistoia (1298–1301), and the cathedral in Pisa (1302–1311). These later pieces, with their lively and dramatic reliefs as well as various Madonna groups, are characterized by the intensity of the relationship between Mother and Child.

Pisano, Nicola (c. 1220 Apulia–before 1284 Tuscany) Probably served his apprenticeship in southern Italy in one of the sculpture schools established by Frederick II. In around 1250 he went to Pisa where his workshop completed the remarkable pulpit in the baptistery in 1260. Between 1264 and 1267 he worked on the tomb of St. Dominic in Bologna, and from 1265 to 1268 the pulpit in the cathedral at Siena. The fountain on Perugia's cathedral square was made in 1278. Nicola Pisano's pioneering sculptural style was influenced by antique models and French Gothic forms.

Pontormo (1494 Pontormo, near Empoli–1557 Florence) Real name Jacopo Carrucci. Arrived in Florence in 1508 where, with the exception of a few brief periods in the surrounding area, he remained for the rest of his life. After his first artistic encounters with Leonardo da Vinci and Piero di Cosimo he probably received his training under Fra Bartolommeo and, from 1512 to 1513, under Andrea del Sarto. In around 1520 his work achieved a new expressiveness which transcended the Classical style of the High Renaissance. Along with Rosso Fiorentino he is considered the main representative of the first phase of Mannerism.

Pozzo, Andrea (1642 Trent–1709 Vienna) Pozzo entered a Jesuit novitiate in Milan as a lay brother in 1665, and from 1676 to 1678 he decorated the Jesuit church of S. Francesco in Mondovi. On the recommendation of Carlo Marattas he was called to Rome by the Jesuit general Padre Oliva at the end of 1681. There, he began work on painting the monumental ceiling of the Jesuit church of S. Ignazio at the start of the 1690s. From 1703 Pozzo worked in Vienna, where he painted the

Raphael (1483–1520), Self-portrait *(detail), oil on canvas, Accademia di San Luca, Rome*

vault of the university church; he also executed the ceiling frescoes in the Liechtenstein palace which feature the deeds of Hercules. He worked as painter, architect, and art theorist; his treatise *Prospettiva de pittori e architetti* appeared in 1693 in Rome.

della Quercia, Jacopo (c. 1374 Siena–1438 Siena) Son of a sculptor and goldsmith, Quercia was the leading Sienese sculptor of the Early Renaissance. He worked mainly in Siena, Bologna, and Lucca. In 1401 he took part in the competition for the bronze doors of the Florentine baptistery. His elegant tomb for Llaria del Carretto in the cathedral at Lucca, which was indebted to Gothic tradi-

tions, marked the beginning of a career which reached its final peak in the highly expressive, dynamic reliefs he made for the main portal of the church of San Petronio in Bologna. Later artists of the High Renaissance such as Michelangelo were to find his work influential.

Raphael (1483 Urbino–1520 Rome) Real name Raphael Santi. Raphael was first taught by his father, the painter and poet Giovanni Santi, before training with Pietro Perugino in Perugia from 1500. In 1504 he went to Florence and in 1508 he was summoned by Pope Julius II to Rome. From 1509 his projects in Rome included the frescoes in the *stanza* of the Vatican. After the death of

Bramante in 1514 he became director of building work at St. Peter's cathedral. In 1515 he was appointed conservator of Roman antiquities. Raphael is regarded as the greatest painter of the high Renaissance.

della Robbia, Andrea (1435 Florence–1525 Florence) Andrea served his apprenticeship in the workshop of his uncle, Luca della Robbia, which he took over in 1470. He continued the family's astonishingly successful production of glazed, colored terracotta statuary, but developed the glazing technique still further so that it could be applied to larger, multi-figured altarpieces. He also made busts and numerous reliefs, most of which depicted the Madonna, for private devotions. The intense coloration of Andrea della Robbia's work blurred the boundary between painting and relief.

della Robbia, Luca (1399/1400 Florence–1482 Florence) Little is known about Lucca della Robbia's artistic origins; he was first mentioned in documents in Florence in 1431. As well as being a sculptor, he developed a technique for producing glazed terracotta sculptures which he mainly used to decorate tondi and lunettes with colored reliefs. Lucca dell Robbia is one of the most outstanding sculptors of the 1400s and, along with Lorenzo Ghiberti and Donatello, he was one of the founders of the Florentine Early Renaissance.

Rossellino, Bernardo (c. 1409 Settignano–1464 Florence) The son of a stonemason, Bernardo Rossellino maintained a large sculptural workshop in Florence in which his brother, Antonio, was also trained. After completion of his tomb for Leonardo Bruni in the Florentine church of Santa Croce, he received further commissions for sepulchral monuments which he executed in collaboration with members of his workshop. From 1451 to 1453 he was an architect in the employ of Pope Nicholas V, and in 1461 he became cathedral architect in Florence. In 1460 Pope Pius II entrusted him with important architectural commissions in Pienza.

Rosso Fiorentino (1494 Florence–1540 Fontainebleau) Real name Giovanni Battista Rosso, he served his apprenticeship in the workshop of Andrea del Sarto. In around 1520 he worked for a year in Volterra, afterwards returning to Florence. Hoping to be awarded commissions by Pope Clement VII, he traveled to Rome in 1524 but was forced to flee in 1527 during the Sack of Rome. He then spent several restless years in Perugia, San Sepolcro, Città di Castello, and Arezzo. In 1530 he was called to the court of the French king Francis I. On the recommendation of his friend Pietro Aretino, he was entrusted with the decoration of Fontainebleau palace, where his greatest work, the design of the gallery of Francis I with frescoes and stucco, was a seminal stylistic influence on the school of Fontainebleau established by both Fiorentino and Primaticcio.

da Sangallo, Antonio the Elder (c. 1460 Florence–1534 Florence) A partner of his brother Giuliano in their studio for 40 years. Always somewhat in the shadow of his older brother, he executed a range of architectural projects in Tuscany and Rome. His chief work is the church of Madonna di San Biagio in Montepulciano.

da Sangallo, Antonio the Younger (1484 Mugello, near Florence–1546 Terni, near Rome) Nephew of Giuliano and Antonio da Sangallo the Elder, he went to Rome in 1503. From 1539 he directed the construction of the church of St. Peter's. His major work is the Palazzo Farnese in Rome which he began in 1534 and which was completed by Michelangelo and Giacomo della Porta.

da Sangallo, Giuliano (c. 1445 Florence–1516 Florence) Probably trained under his father, a carpenter and stonemason. As a 20 year old he went to Rome to study Classical architecture, recording his impressions in several sketchbooks which have survived to the present day. In around 1470 he returned to Florence where he soon came to the attention of Lorenzo de' Medici. Most of his villas, palaces, and churches in the Early Renaissance style as well as the fortresses he later designed were built in and around Florence, though he also carried out some work for Pope Julius II in Rome.

Sassetta (probably 1392 Siena–1450 Siena) Real name Stefano di Giovanni, he was probably trained in the studio of Paolo di Giovanni Fei. He is first recorded in official documents in 1427. Sassetta is considered the most important Sienese painter of the quattrocento. The style

Titian (1488/1490–1576), Self-portrait, c. 1566, oil on canvas, 86 × 9 cm, Museo del Prado, Madrid

of his work marks the transition from the International Gothic to the Early Renaissance and shows the influence of Masaccio and Masolino. Sassetta retained the use of line and development of pictorial depth which Simone Martini had introduced to Sienese painting a century before, and his simple compositions exhibit a unique narrative style.

Savonarola, Girolamo (1452 Ferrara–1498 Florence) At the age of 23 Savonarola broke off his study of philosophy and medicine to enter the Dominican order. He arrived in Florence as a preacher of repentance, becoming leader of the monastery of San Marco. His uncompromising sermons and apocalyptic visions were popular, and after the Medici were expelled in 1494 he and his followers were able to push through political reforms. His open vilification of the pope led to his excommunication in 1497, and in 1498 he was burned at the stake as a heretic.

Signorelli, Luca (c. 1450 Cotona–1523 Cortona) Probably trained in the workshop of Piero della Francesca in Arezzo whose painting style is reflected in Signorelli's own early work. Under the influence of Antonio del Pollaiuolo and Andrea del Verrocchio he discovered in Florence his own energetic formal language in which the figures have geometrically stylized postures and which marks a high point in the painting of the late cinquecento in central Italy. In around 1482 to 1483 Signorelli executed two frescoes in the Sistine Chapel in Rome under the direction of Perugino. He spent the remainder of his life in southern Tuscany and Umbria where he worked in Spoleto, Volterra, Perugia, and Sansepolcro.

Sodoma (c. 1477 Vercelli–1549 Siena) Real name Giovanni Antonio Bazzi. Born in Piedmont, he was apprenticed to a local painter, Giovanni Martino Spanzotti, between 1490 and 1497. In 1500 the Spanocchi banking dynasty used their influence to send the young artist to Siena. In 1508 Sodoma was called to Rome to paint the Stanza della Segnatura in the Vatican, but he was unable to progress beyond the work's early stages. In 1510 Sodoma was recorded as being in Siena for his marriage. In 1512 he designed the famous Alexander fresco in the Villa Farnese for Agostino Chigi. After 1515 he was chiefly active in Siena, though in his later years he also worked in Volterra (1539–1540), Pisa (1540–1543), Lucca (1545), and Piombino.

Titian (1488/90 Pieve di Cadore–1576 Venice) Real name Tiziano Vecellio. Titian was probably trained by Giovanni Bellini in Venice. From 1515 he worked for the d'Este, Gonzaga, Farnese, and Rovere dynasties as well as King Francis I of France. In 1533 he became court painter to Emperor Charles V. and received the Order of the Golden Fleece. In his late period Titian was almost exclusively in the service of Philip II. He is considered the greatest Venetian painter of the 16th century.

Uccello, Paolo (c. 1397 Pratovecchio, near Arezzo–1475 Florence) Uccello received his artistic education in the workshop of Lorenzo Ghiberti in Florence from 1407 to 1412 and he assisted Ghiberti in the execution of the doors for the Florentine baptistery. From 1425 to 1431 he is recorded as working on the mosaics in San Marco in Venice. He then completed two large frescoes with scenes taken from Genesis in the Chiostro Verde, the cloister of Santa Maria Novella, in Florence. Influenced by Masaccio and Donatello, Uccello developed into the greatest artist of his generation in the use of perspective.

Vasari, Giorgio (1511 Arezzo–1574 Florence) At the age of 13 Vasari arrived in Florence, where he received a wide-ranging humanist education. From 1531 he lived variously in Rome and Florence and he studied art from antiquity up to his own day. As a painter he was indebted to Mannerism, and he executed frescoes as well as panel paintings. Among his most important projects as an architect was the Uffizi in Florence. His *"Lives of the Most Excellent Painters, Sculptors and Architects"*

(1550/1568) is the most important source book on Italian art.

del Verrocchio, Andrea (1436 Florence–1488 Venice) Real name Andrea de' Cioni. Verrocchio became the leading master of Florentine sculpture after the death of Donatello. In Florence he mainly produced works in a small format, as well as architectural sculptures. In 1486 he went to Venice where he created the statue of the condottiere Bartolomeo Colleoni, erected in front of the church of Santi Giovanni e Paolo. Of his paintings only the Baptism of Christ, a collaborative project with his pupil Leonardo da Vinci and housed in the Uffizi (c. 1470/80), can be attributed to him with any certainty.

Vignola see Barozzi, Giacomo

Giorgio Vasari, Self-portrait, 1566–1568, oil on canvas, 100.5 × 80 cm, Galleria degli Uffizi, Florence

Further Reading

Ashbrook, William: Puccini's Turandot: *The End of a Great Tradition*. Princetown, Oxford 1991

Bambach, Carmen: *Drawing and Painting in the Italian Renaissance Workshop*. Cambridge 1999
Baskins, Cristelle L.: *Cassone Painting, Humanism and Gender in Early Modern Italy*. Cambridge 1999
Baxandall, Michael: *Painting and Experience in Fifteenth Century Italy: a primer in the social history of pictorial style*. Oxford 1988
Berti, Luciano: *The Uffizi*. London 1993
Boccaccio, Giovanni: *The Life of Dante* (trans. Vincenzo Zin Bolletino. NY, London c.1990
Boccaccio, Giovanni: *The Decameron* (trans. G. H. McWilliam). London 1995
Borst, Arno: *Medieval worlds: Barbarians, Heretics and Artists in the Middle Ages*. (trans. Eric Hansen). Cambridge c. 1981
Bowsky, W.M.: *A Medieval Commune. Siena under the Nine,1287-1355*. London 1981
Brandes, Georg Morris Cohen: *Michelangelo: his Life, his Times, his Era*. Constable 1963
Brucker, Gene Adam: *Florence 1138–1737*. London c. 1984
Burckhardt, Jacob: *The Civilisation of the Renaissance in Italy*. London 1995

Carner, Mosco: *Puccini: A Critical Biography*. London c.1992
Catherine of Siena, Saint: *The Letters of Catherine of Siena* (trans. Suzanne Noffke. Tempe, Ariz. 2000
Cavallini, Giuliana: *Catherine of Siena*. London 1998
Chastel, Andre: *Art of the Italian Renaissance* (trans. Linda and Peter Murray). New York 1988
Cleugh, James: *The Medici: A Tale of Fifteen Generations*. London 1976

Coelho, Voctor: *Music and Science in the Age of Galileo*. Dordrecht 1992
Connell, William: *Florentine Tuscany*. Cambridge 2000
Crichton, G.H.: *Romanesque Sculpture in Italy*. London 1954
Cronin, Vincent: *The Florentine Renaissance*. London 1992

Dante, Alighieri: *The Divine Comedy* (trans. Robert M. Durling). New York, Oxford 1996
de Tolnay, Charles: *The Youth of Michelangelo*. Princetown 1947
de Tolnay, Charles: *The Medici Chapel*. Princetown 1948

Fruttero & Lucentini: *Il Palio delle contrade morte*. Milan 1985

Garin, E.: *Astrology in the Renaissance*. London 1982
Godman, Peter: *From Poliziano to Machiavelli*. New Jersey 1998
Goffen, Rona: *Titian's Venus of Urbino*. New York, Cambridge 1997
Grayson, Cecil (ed.): *The World of Dante*. Oxford 1980

Hager, Serafina (ed.): *Leonardo, Michelangelo, and Raphael in Renaissance Florence from 1500 to 1508*. Washington D.C. c. 1992
Hartt, Frederick: *History of Italian Renaissance Art*. London 1994
Heydenreich, Ludwig H.: *Architecture in Italy 1400–1500*. New Haven, London 1996
Hibbert, Christopher: *Florence: the Biography of a City*. London 1994

Hine Mundy, John: *Europe in the High Middle Ages 1150–1309.* Harlow 1991

Hollander, R.: Dante: *A Life in Works.* New Haven; to be published July 2001

Hollander, Robert: *Boccaccio's Dante and the Shaping Force of Satire.* Michigan c. 1997

Kempers, Bram: *Painting, Power and Patronage: the use of the Professional Artist in Renaissance Italy* (trans. Beverley Jackson). London 1992

Kent, F.W., Simons, Patricia, Eade, J.C.: *Patronage, Art and Society in Renaissance Italy.* Oxford 1987

Lowe, K.J.P.: *Church and Politics in Renaissance Italy.* Cambridge 1993

Machiavalli, Niccolo: *The Prince* (1513) (trans. George Bull). London 1999

Machiavelli, Niccolo: *Florentine Histories* (1532) (trans. Laura F. Banfield And Harvey C. Mansfield Jr.). Princetown, Oxford c.1988

Machiavelli, Niccolo: *Machiavelli and His Friends: Their Personal Correspondence (ed. Atkinson, James B., Sices, David).* Dekalb, IL 1996

Marchetti, Leopoldi and Bevilacqua, Carlo: *Italian Basilicas and Cathedrals.* Novara 1950

Michiavelli, Niccolo: *The Discourses of Machiavelli* (trans. Leslie J. Walker). London 1975

Mormando, Franco: *The Preacher's Demons: Bernardino of Siena and the Social Underworld of Early Renaissance Italy.* Chicago, IL 1999

Origo, Iris: *The Merchant of Prato – Fransesco di Marco Patini.* Hamondsworth 1979

Pallottino, Massimo: *The Etruscans.* Hamondsworth 1978

Petrarch, Francesco: *Canzoniere* (1366) (trans. J.G. Nichols). Manchester 2000

Pocock, J.G.A.: *The Machiavellian Moment.* Princetown 1975

Polecritti, Cynthia L.: *Preaching Peace in Renaissance Italy: Bernardino of Siena and his Audience.* USA 2000

Pope-Henessy, John: Italian Gothic Sculpture. London, 1955

Pope-Henessy, John: *Italian Renaissance Sculpture.* London, 1955

Ricketts, Jill M.: *Visualising Boccaccio: Studies on Illustrations of the Decameron from Giotto to Pasolini.* Cambridge 1997

Santini, E.: *Compagnie e mercanti di Firenze antica.* Florence 1957

Schultz, B.: *Art and Anatomy in Renaissance Italy.* Ann Arbor 1985

Scott , Geoffrey: *The Architecture of Humanism.*

Stych, F.S.: *Boccaccio in English: A Bibliography of Editions, Adaptations and Criticism.* London 1995

Torriti, Piero: *All Siena: the Contrade and the Palio.* Florence 1999

Vasari, Giorgio: *Lives of the Painters, Sculptors and Architects* (trans. Gaston du C. de Vere). London 1996

Weinstein, D.: *Savonarola and Florence. Prophecy and Patriotism in the Renaissance.* Princetown 1970

Weiss, R: *The Renaissance Discovery of Classical Antiquity,* Oxford 1969

Index of People

Credits

Most of the illustrations used in this publication were provided by Scala Group S.p.A. of Florence. The publisher would also like to thank all contributing museums, archives, and photographers for permission to reproduce images, and for their generous support in the production of this book. The publisher has made persistant efforts to trace the remaining copyright holders. Persons and institutions who may not have been contacted are requested to contact the publisher.

© Archiv für Kunst und Geschichte, Berlin (17, 22, 23, 50, 53, 206, 255, 535, 605, 606, 609 bottom) Photo: S. Domingié (256, 273) Photo: Orsi Battaglini (275); A.P.T. Livorno, Photo: © A. Bozzolani (484/485, 486, 490/491, 492); A.P.T., Prato, Photo: A. Moni (129, 137); © Architektur-Bilderservice Kandula, Witten, Photo: Stefan Drechsel (259 left, 516); Associazione culturale Arte continua, San Gimignano, Photo: © Attilio Maranzano (121); © Bayerische Staatsbibliothek, Munich (290); © Achim Bednorz, Cologne (425); © Biblioteca Medicea Laurenziana, Florence (138, 144); © Bibliothèque Nationale, Paris (480); © bildarchiv preußischer kulturbesitz bpk, Berlin, Photo: Jörg P. Anders (212, 214, 215); © Sergio Bettini (117, 119); © Markus Bollen, Bensberg (116/117, 428/429); © A. Bonini, Collodi (PT) (112); Lorenzo Bruni, Florence (118); Cod. Atl. fol. 381, verso-a, Biblioteca Ambrosiana Milan, from: Die Erfindungen von Leonardo da Vinci, Charles Gibbs-Smith 1978, p. 24, ill. top l. (588 Reg. 5 Ill. 1); © G. Dagli Orti, Paris (586 Reg. 1 Ill. 1); Oskar Emmenegger, Zisers, Graubünden (572); Peter Frese, Munich (44/45, 58/59, 90/91, 126/127, 158/159, 160/161, 170/171, 222/223, 268/269, 280/281, 318/319, 340/341, 396/397, 404/405, 434, 450, 466, 488/489, 500/501, 542); © Georg Henke, Bremen (464); Hessische Landes- und Hochschulbibliothek, Darmstadt (291); © Robert Janke, Boslar (8, 36, 37, 38, 47, 48, 49, 63, 64, 70, 72, 73, 85, 92, 94, 98, 101, 102, 104, 106, 110, 128, 136, 150, 152/153, 162, 168, 169, 178, 200, 201, 235, 250, 260, 276/277, 292, 293, 298, 302, 306, 307 left, 307 right, 308, 316, 325, 328/329, 344 bottom, 345, 346/347, 354, 360, 395, 402, 403, 408, 414, 415, 424 left, 426, 427, 431, 432, 436, 449, 470, 476/477, 496/497, 498, 505, 508, 520, 521, 524 bottom, 530, 531, 544, 552, 554 bottom, 555, 556, 557, 562/563); © Ulrich Kerth, Munich (348); © PHOTO 3 di Fabio Lensini & C., Siena (34, 35, 46, 62, 84, 88/89, 93, 103, 305 o., 331, 337, 342, 362/363, 396, 397 top right, 400/401, 406, 438 right, 455, 475, 533, 546); © Look, Photo: Jürgen Richter (4, 10, 326/327, 390/391, 394, 446/447, 538/539), Photo: Jan Greune (14/15), Photo: Max Galli (418); © Museo Teatrale alla Scala, Milan (51); © Werner Neumeister, Munich (350 right); Eduard Noack, Cologne (230); © Opera della Primaziale Pisana, Pisa (517); © Nicolò Orsi Battaglini, Florence (114, 122/123, 158, 161, 172, 231, 232, 266, 420, 431, 438 left, 442, 445, 509, 526, 590); © Mario Pagni, Soprintendenza per i Beni Archeologici della Toscana, Florence (156); © Lothar M. Peter, Berlin (468, 504); © Dirk Reinartz, Buxtehude (115); Rolli Arts, Essen (12/13, 20/21, 24, 25, 40, 74, 130/131, 144, 145 bottom, 165 left, 180/181, 186/187, 227 left, 237 left, 253, 284 left, 296/297, 313, 349, 353, 366/367, 378/379 bottom, 385, 439, 502/503, 507, 510/511 bottom, 518/519, 564/565, 566/567, 568/569, 570/571, 574, 576, 578/579, 582, 594,); © Frank Rother, Bergisch Gladbach (483); © Soprintendenza per i Beni A. A. A. S. di Arezzo, restoration sponsored by B. P. L., Photo: Alessandro Benci (278, 285); © Hubert Stadler, Fürstenfeldbruck (411); Theaterwissenschaftliche Sammlung der Universität zu Köln (52); © VG Bild-Kunst, Photo: Carlo Innocenti (116), Photo: Robert Janke (146); © Klaus Zimmermanns, Munich (458, 548)